Extraordinary times are  y people. Seventeenth cent_____- cal and religious though_____- ment, debate and confli_____ towards the modern wor_____

The reflections of tho_____ what sort of society we l_____ ____ _____ Hatton's timely book on George Fox shows us the life of a man of his age, who not only experienced it and its changes, but through his personal journey and determination left us the Quaker movement.

Fox's upbringing and childhood is woven into the world of intense discussion and rebellion which surrounded him, giving us an insight as to how his beliefs developed and were shaped. The story of emerging Quakerism, which then unfolds, is as much a story of politics as faith, emphasising the close connection between the two, and reinforcing Christ's injunction that believers are to be salt and light in the world. That notable Quakers were just that, particularly in the field of social reform, owes much to the George Fox we see emerge in these fascinating and readable pages.

Alistair Burt MP

George Fox gave birth to the Quakers – a religious group long noted for their opposition to slavery, their commitment to the equality of women, and their advocacy of peace. Although the Quakers are relatively well known, their founder has escaped the attention of the general public and many historians. Jean Hatton has provided the public with an important biography that carefully details the historical development of the young George Fox and illustrates how he tried to free the average person from the tyranny of the organised church in the seventeenth century. Perhaps most importantly, she shows that George Fox and the Quaker movement were committed to a renewal of the Christian Church and placed their hope in the Light that Christ places in each person. Readers will find Jean Hatton's work both refreshing and enlightening.

Robin Baker, President, George Fox University

GEORGE FOX

THE FOUNDER OF **THE QUAKERS**

Jean Hatton

MONARCH
BOOKS

Oxford, UK & Grand Rapids, Michigan, USA

Copyright © Jean Hatton 2007.

The right of Jean Hatton to be identified as author of this work has been asserted by her in accordance with the Copyright, Designs and Patents Act 1988.

All rights reserved. No part of this publication may be reproduced or transmitted in any form or by any means, electronic or mechanical, including photocopy, recording or any information storage and retrieval system, without permission in writing from the publisher.

Cover illustration by Fred Apps.

First published in the UK in 2007 by Monarch Books
(a publishing imprint of Lion Hudson plc),
Wilkinson House, Jordan Hill Road, Oxford OX2 8DR
Tel: +44 (0) 1865 302750   Fax: +44 (0) 1865 302757
Email: monarch@lionhudson.com
www.lionhudson.com

ISBN: 978-1-85424-753-7 (UK)
ISBN: 978-0-8254-6106-4 (USA)

Distributed by:
UK: Marston Book Services Ltd, PO Box 269, Abingdon, Oxon OX14 4YN;
USA: Kregel Publications, PO Box 2607, Grand Rapids, Michigan 49501.

Unless otherwise stated, Scripture quotations are taken from the Holy Bible, New International Version, © 1973, 1978, 1984 by the International Bible Society. Used by permission of Hodder and Stoughton Ltd. All rights reserved.

This book has been printed on paper and board independently certified as having been produced from sustainable forests.

British Library Cataloguing Data
A catalogue record for this book is available from the British Library.

Printed and bound in Wales by Creative Print & Design.

Contents

*This book is dedicated to the memory of Kate Amaral,
artist, writer, comrade and friend.*

Introduction

MY JOURNEY WITH George Fox was not an easy one. I was drawn to him while researching a previous work, on the Quaker prison reformer Elizabeth Fry, and I began on the perhaps somewhat naive assumption that I would both like and admire him, and that his story would travel relatively comfortably from the source material through my mind and onto the page. The reality turned out to be somewhat different. Certainly I admired George Fox. I admired his persistence in the quest for a meaningful understanding of faith, and then his willingness to open himself to experiences that, by his own admission, were sometimes as painful as they were illuminating. I also admired his determination to proclaim his message in the face of opposition, his refusal to be cowed by authority, his consistent fight for justice, and his willingness to suffer for what he believed to be righteousness and truth.

Despite all this, there were often times when George Fox infuriated me, when he left me tense and irritable and seething with anger. Partly this was the result of the arrogance and self-righteousness that is so often evident in his *Journal*. But I think it was also partly the result of something else, an echo of a conflict that was always at work within him. While on the one hand he proclaimed a message of hope, that set people free from fear, on the other there was something destructive about him, that was aimed at those who disagreed with him and those he saw as betraying him.

Somehow, I think that the tensions and anger I felt were also experienced by many individuals who encountered George Fox in his own lifetime. The hostility and violence that so often followed his appearances in churches and elsewhere cannot simply have resulted from denunciations of Calvinism and a declaration of the message of the Inner Light. Nor can the venomous attacks on him by enemies within his own movement have been entirely provoked even by severe differences of opinion. I suspect that much of the hostility was not only about what George Fox said, but about how it was that he said it. Which is an interesting reflection on a man who inspired the foundation of a movement which today often works in the area of conflict resolution.

However, those who work in that area also know that human interaction involves complex issues and the many interwoven layers that go towards making up each individual personality. And George Fox was indeed a complex and many-layered man, as much driven by his past as by the ideas he developed later in life. Therefore, as well as presenting him as a man who inspired a significant religious movement, and who was a major figure in the struggle for religious toleration, I hope that this book goes some way to illustrate that the movers and shakers of our world, even those who inspire movements committed to peace, often combine within their own beings a range of contradictions – contradictions which often fuel the engine that drives them through life.

During the turbulent two years I spent with George Fox, I have been indebted to a number of people. I should like to thank them all for their help, and for the interest they often showed in the subject. Firstly I should like to thank Heather Rowland and her staff at the Library of the Society of Friends (LSF), London, especially Josef Keith, Joanna Clark and Jennifer Milligan. I should also like to thank Laura Stokoe for her comments regarding George Fox's handwriting and for the suggestion of a possible childhood infirmity. I am grateful to Cath Hughes at the Library and Information Centre, Atherstone, for information regarding schools in the area in the seventeenth century, and to Lorna Dirveiks of the Atherstone Heritage Centre for details of the Statutes Fair. I would like to thank Susan Mills, Librarian at the Regent's Park College, Oxford, for providing information regarding "one Pickering, a Baptist". I am also grateful to Nadia Van Maurik for explaining the complex history of the Netherlands, and the lineage and role of William of Orange. I am also indebted to the Cambridge University Press, for their permission to quote extensively from the *Journal of George Fox* (edited by Norman Penney, 1911) and from the *Short Journal*, the *Itinerary Journal* and the *Haistwell Diary* (edited by Norman Penny, 1925), and also to transcribe them into modern English. Finally, I would once again like to thank Susan Howard for her careful reading of my manuscript drafts and for her insights regarding the personality of George Fox and my ambivalent reactions to him. I would also like to thank her for her company, and her car, on our own journey through time from Fenny Drayton to Swarthmoor Hall.

During the process of researching and writing this book it became very clear to me that outside the Quaker movement George Fox is not well known. Since in the seventeenth century his name was recognized all over England, I see it as a loss to history that he should have so disappeared from the country that once knew him so well. I hope that this book will go some small way to rectifying that loss. Far more important, perhaps, is what I believe to be George Fox's relevance to the world of today. Although he never wavered from the view that his truth was "the truth", experience and reflection eventually led him to promote not only the belief that the Light of God is to be found in all people, but also the belief that all people should have the right to respond to that God in liberty of conscience. Experience and reflection also led him to the conviction that human difference cannot be solved by outward wars and fightings. It would perhaps be to the benefit of our troubled world, its people and its leaders, to reflect long and hard on both of these conclusions – the value of toleration and the rejection of violence.

Jean Hatton
Chesham, Buckinghamshire, May 2007

Dating and Calendar

*I*N SEVENTEENTH-CENTURY England the years were reckoned according to the Julian calendar, in which the year began on 25 March and ended twelve months later on 24 March, and which continued in use until 1751. In the rest of western Europe, the Gregorian calendar, in which the year began on 1 January, had been in use since 1582. The Julian calendar was also ten days behind the Gregorian. Thus, in England, the execution of Charles I took place on 30 January 1648, while on the Continent of Europe it took place on 9 February 1649. An added complication for the researcher of the period, if their study involves Quakers, was their practice (also used by some Baptists and other dissenters) of using numbers instead of the pagan names for days and months. Hence, "first day of second month" corresponds to 1 April according to the Julian calendar. However, in some cases, especially if sending letters overseas, numbers relating to the Gregorian dates were used, or sometimes, Julian and Gregorian dates together. When contemporaries spoke of the beginning of the year, they referred to April rather than January. As far as possible in this book, all dates have been shown according to the Gregorian calendar, while other wordings have been changed accordingly – for example, "in the spring of the year" rather than "at the beginning of the year". However, it is possible that in some cases, dates and phrases have been overlooked, and for this I apologize.

CHAPTER ONE

Pure Faith My Joy
Pure foi ma Joye

Purefey Family Monument,
Fenny Drayton Church, Leicestershire

"*T*HAT ALL MAY KNOW the dealings of the Lord with me," he said, "and the various exercises, trials, and troubles through which he led me in order to prepare and fit me for the work unto which he had appointed me... I think fit briefly to mention how it was with me in my youth."

George Fox was born in 1624, in the month of July, the height of the English summer. His home was the Leicestershire village of Fenny Drayton, that in his own time was called Drayton in the Clay. Almost on the Warwickshire border, it lies in the heart of the English Midlands, a land of level horizons, heavy leafed trees, and placid, slow-moving rivers; a land whose fertile soil, a mixture of clay and loam, produces lush pastures, rich crops, and fat cattle. And though in the seventeenth century Drayton was a small community, numbering no more than 20 or 30 homes, together with the nearby small towns of Atherstone and Mancetter it formed part of a busy network of agriculture and trade that stretched back over a thousand years.

Situated in the centre of the land, Drayton had also been close to some of the events that shaped England's long history. In the first Christian century, the Roman invaders cut the great road Watling Street through the Leicestershire earth, and then founded Mancetter to protect their legions and their merchants as they pushed into Britain's wild north-west. In the Dark Ages, Watling Street briefly became a frontier, as Saxons and Danes fought for supremacy over the country that each called their own. Six hundred years later, in 1485, on the battlefield of Bosworth, just a brief few miles from Fenny Drayton, Richard Plantagenet, King Richard III, lost the crown of England to Henry Tudor, the man who became Henry VII and who would go on to found a powerful and influential dynasty.

As well as armies and their battles, and often despite them, many generations of merchants travelled on Watling Street, driving the packhorse trains that carried woollen and dyed fabrics, copper and pewterware, glass and bead jewellery, parchment and pens, and all the many items that make for trade between people, between regions and between nations. From the southeast, the merchants travelled the 120 miles from London, and sometimes the 170 that brought them from Dover and the ships that crossed the English Channel. On reaching Atherstone, they mighty then continue on Watling Street into Staffordshire and Cheshire before climbing the trails that wound into the mountains of Wales. Or else they might head northeast on a road taking them to Leicester, Nottingham and Lincoln, or north towards Derby, or sometimes east towards Peterborough and Cambridge.

While armies fought, and merchants hawked their wares, in Drayton, in the eleventh century, and building on a much earlier foundation, the first grey stones were laid for the parish church of St Michael's and All Angels. It stands there still at the heart of the village, weatherworn and ancient now, shielded from winter storms by ancient yew trees, surrounded by green turf, and watching over the never ceasing rhythm of seeding, blossoming and fading, the births, the marriages and the burials of many generations of Leicestershire's offspring.

It was to St Michael's, in 1624 or 1625, that a Drayton couple, Christopher and Mary Fox, brought their first child to be baptised. As they watched the clergyman mark him with water, and then name him George, and as they listened to the baptismal promises made by those who stood as godparents and by themselves, they no doubt wondered, as all parents do, what the future had in store for such a small and seemingly helpless being.

Later, as the years passed, as Christopher and Mary Fox watched that helpless infant leave babyhood behind, they saw him stagger and tumble, and then finally walk. As they saw him eventually find his way into every part of their home, gazing with solemn eyes and a frown at each new discovery, perhaps they also began to wonder just why their George was so unlike other boys of his own age.

Many eldest children seem to feel a weight of responsibility, as if by virtue of being firstborn it is somehow incumbent on them to take on the burdens of their family, and sometimes of the world. Yet, in the case of the young George Fox, the burden seems to have been unduly heavy. For the image created by his own words is of a child both solemn and serious, not given to laughter or light-hearted games, and who seems beset by some profound inner anxiety. "In my very young years," he said, "I had a gravity and stayedness of mind and spirit, not usual in children."[1]

Such an image is reinforced by what he evidently said much later to his friend, William Penn, a man who by then was taking forward the work that George had begun. "But from a child he appeared of another frame of mind than the rest of his brethren," said Penn, in the account that became the preface to George's own Journal, "being more religious, inward, still, solid, and observing, beyond his years, as the answers he would give, and the questions he would put upon occasion, manifested to the astonishment of those that heard him, especially in divine things."[2]

Not averse to gilding his own reputation, the astonishment was perhaps a reaction embellished by the adult George Fox himself. That he asked searching questions, however, reveals him as an intelligent child, eager to find meaning in the world around him. Such a combination, and especially that his questions concerned divine things, might have been expected to stir a certain pride in his father. For some reason, however, this seems not to have been the case.

"The neighbours called him 'Righteous Christer'," George said of his father. That they did so, at a time when such prefixes indicated status, suggests that Christopher Fox was a man of some standing among the one hundred or so souls who made up the small community of Drayton.[3] "He was by profession a weaver, an honest man," George added.

In the previous century, the craft of the loom had become a means whereby families who had once been peasants could increase their wealth and social standing.[4] By the seventeenth century, it was part of an industry whereby a successful weaver might become an employer in his own right. Whether honest Christopher Fox simply worked his own looms, or whether he also organized the work of others, arranging supplies of raw materials and being part of a chain of distribution and sale, is unknown. But he was obviously something of a self-made man, a craftsman who through hard work and enterprise had become a person of consequence in his community.

It was a consequence doubly reinforced in the 1630s, the years of George's early adolescence, when Christopher served as churchwarden at St Michael's. For the post not only brought its own degree of status, but indicated the confidence he inspired in Robert Mason, Rector since 1606, and in Sir George Purefey, Lord of the Manor, owner of the parish living, and perhaps the man for whom George Fox was named.[5, 6] Both Mason and Sir George were Puritans, individuals for whom faith and morality were intimately linked, and almost certainly the churchwardens they appointed were men who shared their beliefs, and who were also trusted to be part of an ongoing campaign to build holy communities through the promotion of personal godliness. A truly zealous churchwarden, who was also a zealous Puritan, would ensure that his eyes were regularly on the people, on the lookout for thieves, blasphemers and adulterers, as well as those attempting to avoid attendance at church. Almost certainly he also kept them on his own family. And perhaps the "Righteous" of his title was also an indication of how seriously Christopher took and performed his obligations.

That Christopher Fox was a religious man was acknowledged by his son. "There was a Seed of God in him," he said. And that, together with the details of Christopher's trade and reputation, and a few incidents later in life, was all he ever said. He said nothing that might be interpreted as fondness, or even respect, while once he finally left home he seems to have maintained no contact with his father, nor did he visit his deathbed or attend his funeral.[7]

Such a multitude of omissions somehow speak loudly. They speak of a relationship that was uneasy, of expectations unfulfilled, and of misunderstandings and disappointments on both sides. They also speak of consequences, working themselves out in George Fox's thoughts and emotions, on the surface and deep within his unconscious, and which subsequently played a significant role in driving his journey through life.

George's baptismal record is missing from the Drayton parish register, perhaps a prize of some later souvenir hunter. Fortunately for posterity, however, he noted the month and year of his birth in what is referred to as a *Journal*, but which is in fact a record of his life produced in his middle age.

The Drayton register does record, however, that a sister, Dorothy, was baptized in April 1626, almost two years after George's own birth, and a brother, John, in December 1629. The records of another sister, Katherine, like George's own, are missing. However, in George's will there are bequests made to "my sister Katherine" as well as to young George Fox, John's only surviving son.[8]

The home that these four shared with their parents has long returned to the Leicestershire earth. Although a photograph exists, taken in the nineteenth century, of a house which has sometimes been claimed as the much-extended Fox family home, there is no evidence that this is the case. The actual site is considered to be close to the existing Dog Yard Cottages that are themselves just a short walk from St Michael's.[9] Wherever the actual house stood, and whatever its size, it seems that for George at least, it was also a home to tensions.

Righteous Christer, a successful man with a reputation to maintain in his community, but perhaps made uneasy by something in young George, also seems to have been unwilling to provide an education for his clearly bright boy. It was certainly not the case that he had no impressive options to choose from. Two miles distant, at Atherstone, there was a grammar school founded in 1573 by a Royal Charter of Queen Elizabeth; at Nuneaton, three miles away, a similar school had been founded in 1553 by her brother, King Edward VI. An education at either would have brought enormous prestige to the Fox family. Yet, George never referred to any formal education at all. Since later in life he was mocked for his supposed lack of learning, and for the want of refinement in speech and manners that a grammar school might also have supplied, it was not an omission he would have made willingly.

So, did Christopher Fox, successful weaver, have no time for book-learning? Or did his son's intelligent reflective nature unsettle a man who had made his own way with his hands? If Christopher had indeed hauled himself from the ranks of the peasantry, or been the child of such folk, it may also have been the case that neither intellect nor sensitivity had developed alongside his rise in social and economic status. In such instances, signs of intelligence in children, disturbing to deep insecurities, are sometimes stifled, sometimes even reviled. If such an insecure man were also a stalwart Puritan, and one whose zeal was untempered by cultured reflection, then probing questions about faith, together with the often unorthodox insights of childhood, may have alarmed, or even frightened him. Gazing at an offspring so unlike himself as to appear almost alien, then Christopher Fox might, even unconsciously, have attempted to repress any disturbing intellectual proclivities.

Or was there some other reason, or additional reason, that prevented George Fox from attending school? For however he gained it, he obviously did receive a basic education of sorts. Certainly by adolescence he was reading the Bible, while in adulthood, he not only read widely, but read books of considerable complexity. His written material, however, raises some intriguing questions. That much of what he produced later in life was dictated, can be seen as the result of the chronic arthritis that eventually overtook him. Why he should have done so earlier is not so clear. Unless, of course, he always wrote with difficulty. Certainly the pages in his own hand that have survived show handwriting that is clumsy and ill-formed, while even for an age lacking any real standardization, his spelling is more erratic than most.

That those handwritten texts show a clear understanding of phonetics, does indicate early teaching. The clumsiness and the other deficiencies suggest that it might also have been sparse and interrupted. If this was partly, or entirely, the result of infirmity, then it might have been childhood illness that kept George Fox from school.[10] There is no way of knowing, of course, given the lack of evidence, whether George did suffer some childhood complaint. However, the profound depressions he experienced later, together with episodes of extraordinary paralysis, and claims to the loss of hearing and sight, may well have been a condition which already existed to some extent in childhood. If so, then it may also have been an infirmity that dismayed his father.

With no evidence of schooling, but with some evidence of early teaching, it is possible that George learned his letters from his mother. "Accomplished above most of her degree in the place where she lived," was how he described her to William Penn.[11] How Mary Fox came by that accomplishment, George either did not reveal to Penn, or William Penn to the world. What George did reveal, however, very significantly, was that his relationship with his mother was very different to that which he shared with his father. "His mother taking notice of his singular temper," said Penn, "and the gravity, wisdom, and piety that very early shined through him, refusing childish and vain sports and company, when very young, she was tender and indulgent over him, so that from her he met with little difficulty."[12] Although unstated in so many words, the inference reinforces the conclusion that there were most certainly difficulties between George and his father.

However it was that George Fox learned his letters, and whatever were the tensions surrounding him, he passed his early years in an environment guaranteed to stimulate the thoughts and imagination of a child who was both observant and reflective, and whose mind tended towards spiritual things. In his own little village, and in nearby Atherstone and Mancetter, he saw how the unpredictable English weather filled the barns or left them empty, and how that in turn affected the lives of his neighbours. From Rector Robert Mason, from his parents, and from almost everyone else, he learned that behind the weather, behind individual lives, and even behind the destinies of nations, lay the hand of Almighty God. Bountiful harvests, or devastated crops, individual and national success, good fortune or disaster among personal and national enemies, were all indications of God's favour or disapproval. Moreover, such events were also seen as integral parts of God's eternal plan for the cosmos. Indeed, so intimately was he involved with human activity, and human activity with his ultimate design, that everywhere people looked for signs, in order that they might fathom God's will and act accordingly.

From his poorer neighbours, George might also have overheard grumbles, that Robert Mason grew fat on tithes, the ten per cent in money or produce that every family was bound to provide towards the upkeep of the Church of England. He might also have heard that the Purefeys grew fat on the profits garnered from sheep pastured on land that was once the people's commons, but stolen from them over one hundred years of enclosures.[13] Indeed, all over England, some said, the same theft was repeated, depriving the poor of their ancient rights of grazing, hunting and the gathering of firewood, driving them deeper into poverty, and forcing men to tramp the roads seeking work.

From conversations overheard among his more affluent neighbours, among the merchants of Atherstone and Mancetter, and perhaps repeated by Christopher Fox, George may have heard that the real thief was King Charles, who had imposed on gentlemen taxes never sanctioned by Parliament, and which contravened their ancient liberties. He may also have heard it said that the king was a tyrant. Perhaps he also heard, as Robert Mason and Christopher Fox talked over his head, that not only was King Charles a tyrant, but a tyrant who was also a Catholic, and whose true allegiance lay not in England, but in Rome.

Since 1603, when James Stuart, King James VI of Scotland, became James I of England, tensions between monarchy, Parliament and faith had grown ever more pronounced. Their roots lay in the Protestant Reformation of the previous century. During the years of religious upheaval, as the European states chose either to remain loyal to the Roman Catholic Church, or to embrace the Protestantism of the Reformers, those citizens who chose to differ from their rulers were frequently seen not only as religious dissidents, but as traitors to their country. As their worship was made illegal, many were executed; often they were burned alive, while thousands more abandoned their homes and their homelands. In Tudor England, as the Protestantism of Henry VIII and his son, Edward VI, was suppressed in favour of the Catholicism reimposed by Henry's daughter, Queen Mary, thousands of refugees fled to the Protestant states of northern Europe.

Those who spent their exile in Geneva came under the influence of the Reformer John Calvin. Together with his fellow Reformers, Martin Luther and Ulrich Zwingli, Calvin regarded Roman Catholicism as a corruption of the Christian faith, seeing its emphasis on sacraments and ceremony as the superstitious remnants and accretions of paganism. Like Luther, Calvin also maintained that individuals were saved for eternal life by faith in Christ's sacrifice on the cross, and not by the "good works" promoted by the Catholic Church and which, over the years, had become inextricably linked to sacraments, to ceremony, and to the rituals of which they were a part. He also opposed the claim of the Catholic Church that through its ordained priesthood it was the sole and divinely appointed mediator between humankind and God. Basing his views on Scripture, Calvin insisted that God sought a direct and personal relationship with his people. He also emphasized the authority of the Bible over that of the Pope and the Catholic hierarchy of bishops, and while retaining the sacraments of baptism and the Eucharist, he emphasized the preaching ministry over sacraments and ceremony.

Again basing his conclusions on Scripture, Calvin maintained that human beings were irremediably sinful, and estranged from God by their sin. Nevertheless, he said, the all-powerful God called them to overcome their base nature and seek union with him. The means of doing so was through obedience to the moral imperatives of the Old Testament, and also to the compassionate commands of Christ, without whom nothing could be known of God's justice.[14]

Although all human beings were sinful, said Calvin, it was clear from Scripture that God had nevertheless predestined some individuals for salvation, whom Calvin termed the "elect", while others were irrevocably damned. Moreover, it was for this elect, rather than for the whole world, that Christ had died. Calvin also maintained that God spoke to his people through the human conscience, and that a clear conscience was a sign of election. However, since it was never possible to be entirely certain of one's status, election was to be continually tested, in the struggle against personal sin, in the exercise of individual callings, in the building of a better world, and in the safeguarding of Christ's Church.

The belief that individuals could approach God directly, rather than through the mediations of a priest, together with the emphasis on callings and the building of a better world, resonated powerfully among emerging groups of professional men: lawyers, bankers, physicians, academics and merchants. For them, Calvin's disciplined and positive version of faith underpinned a growing sense of themselves as responsible for their own destinies.

Although Calvin also insisted that the elect were an aristocracy of God's grace, called to provide an example, those who waged God's battle most fiercely, almost inevitably began to feel that they should move into positions of human leadership and authority. And as the professional men also saw their social and economic success as a sign of God's favour, and as they endeavoured to use their wealth and knowledge not only for their own families but for the benefit of their communities and nations, they also began to demand political self-determination for themselves and a share in local and national government.

In 1558, on the accession of Henry VIII's Protestant daughter, Queen Elizabeth, many of the English exiles returned home. Those arriving from Geneva brought with them the faith of John Calvin. Seeing their zeal as an aid to the establishment of Protestantism in her land, and in ensuring her own survival against foreign Catholic powers, Elizabeth encouraged their appointments in churches, cathedrals and universities. In their turn, they set out to construct in England the "holy community" they had seen in Geneva.

Regarding any hierarchy of bishops as a remnant of Roman Catholicism, Calvinist church order was constructed on a Presbyterian model, a system of church government by representative assemblies termed "presbyteries", and in which, in Geneva, the ministers and elders of such presbyteries were also involved in municipal government. Together with the provision of education and ensuring that social justice prevailed, the church also required collective adherence to a Confession of Faith, as well as encouraging the enforcement of a morality that applied to rich and poor alike.

As her throne became increasingly secure, Elizabeth began to regard her zealous Calvinists as a threat to stability in a land divided by years of religious ambiguity and strife. The Act of Supremacy of 1534 had made her father, Henry VIII, "Supreme Head of the Church in England" and had removed England from papal jurisdiction.[15] The break with Rome, however, had not been clear cut. Nor had doctrine been clear cut under Edward, whose more rigorous Protestantism had stressed predestination and salvation by faith, but whose Prayer Book of 1550 simply transformed the ritualistic Catholic Eucharist, or Mass, into Anglican Communion.[16] Subsequently, Mary had attempted to force England back into the Catholic fold. The turmoil, the conflict between Protestant and Catholic, and the persecution on both sides, had torn communities apart and left a wake of profound bitterness.

Determined to ensure national stability, Elizabeth achieved a church settlement through a policy of compromise, by using the apparatus of the state, and by leaving important matters of doctrine deliberately ambiguous. Then she compromised no longer, and against all agitation refused to alter her position on doctrine or ceremony, even when it was exposed as internally contradictory. In the words of her chancellor, Lord Burghley, "The Elizabethan church was peculiarly English: its structure Catholic, its doctrine Calvinist, its liturgy, 'a mingle-mangle.'"[17]

A mingle-mangle, however, was unacceptable to those whose calls for further purification of the English Church led their opponents to label them Puritans. Nor was any hint of a compromise with Rome. For not only did Puritans see Roman Catholicism as the faith of England's Spanish and French enemies, they believed it to be a spiritual enemy determined to corrupt and then overthrow Protestantism. Naming the Catholic Church "Antichrist", they saw its baneful reach and power in all walks of life. In 1580, when, with the blessing of the papacy, the militant Jesuit order established a mission to England with the aim of re-converting the entire nation, then, in the view of Puritans, England's national enemies and Protestantism's spiritual enemies had become most perniciously and dangerously combined. Catholicism was not only the enemy without, but its agents were now working within.

Adamant that Antichrist was an enemy against whom all true Christians must constantly wage war, Puritan vicars and their congregations vociferously opposed what they saw as "popish" beliefs and practices.[18] Seeing Puritans as threatening the precarious stability of her Church, Elizabeth sought finally to suppress them. But by then it was too late; Puritanism had taken a vigorous root. Determined to build God's true Church and oppose the forces of Antichrist, its adherents were prepared to defy all earthly powers.

Nevertheless, in an England at peace, Puritanism was largely confined to London, to East Anglia, and to regions dominated by Puritan overlords. Not until the reign of James I did it begin once again to make itself heard. Scottish James, however, was also a shrewd monarch. While he leaned personally towards Catholicism, and was also convinced that by virtue of divine right a king should control his family and his people, he maintained a diplomatic relationship with those with whom he disagreed. He also maintained a working, if turbulent, relationship with his Parliament.

By the seventeenth century, however, Parliament was increasingly dominated by those professional men so influenced by the doctrines of John Calvin. They were also men for whom Protestantism and Puritanism were uniquely bound up not only with the destiny of England, but with what they saw as English liberties.

In 1625, the year after George Fox was born in Fenny Drayton, following the death of his father, James's son, Charles Stuart, became King of England. Like his father, he leaned towards Catholicism and upheld the doctrine of the divine right of kings. Unlike James, however, who was gregarious and rather crude, Charles was private, fastidious and refined. He could also be impatient and autocratic, and combined inflexibility with a tendency to dissemble in order to gain his own ends. Moreover, unlike the working relationships maintained by his father, an increasingly acrimonious relationship between Charles and his Parliament would eventually end in conflict.

From his very first Parliament, Charles' autocratic manner, his tendency to rely on the advice of favourites and his constant appeals for money in order to further a series of European wars roused suspicion. Fuelling such fears further were the terms of Charles' marriage settlement to the French princess, Henrietta Maria. Though officially aimed at linking French and English power against Spain, and in return for a dowry of enormous proportions, the settlement allowed the princess to practise her religion openly, with the assistance of Catholic priests, and for all children of the marriage to be raised as Catholics. Adding to Protestant anxieties was a separate memorandum agreeing to the relaxation of England's laws against its own Catholic population.

As suspicion of Charles increased, Parliament became ever more reluctant to grant him funds. In retaliation, Charles attempted to raise money by other means. When he began to collect customs duties not sanctioned by Parliament, imposed forced loans on his wealthier subjects and then imprisoned those who refused to pay, suspicion turned rapidly to anger.

Having already dissolved two parliaments, but realizing eventually that his arbitrary methods could not raise sufficient finance for his needs, in March 1628 Charles was forced to summon another. When he called for the immediate granting of taxes, however, Charles' parliamentary opponents, then led by Sir Edward Coke, a former Speaker of the House of Commons, demanded that their grievances be addressed first.[19] Shortly afterwards, the king was presented with the "Petition of Right".

Claiming rights under laws and statutes dating from Magna Carta, the terms of the Petition guaranteed that English men and women would be free from arbitrary arrest, from non-parliamentary taxation, from the free billeting of troops, and from being subject to martial law. Though forced into acceptance by financial necessity, Charles insisted that he did not regard the Petition as binding. His divine right to rule as he saw fit, he said, could not be limited by the Parliament of England.

As Parliament considered how best to respond, many of its members, together with allies all over the country, were linking threats to English liberties with threats to English Protestantism. It was a threat they saw reflected in the increasingly high profile of Catholicism at the royal court, where Henrietta Maria surrounded her religion with elaborate and provocative ceremony, reigned among a circle of prominent British and foreign Catholics, and encouraged conversions to a faith officially proscribed but becoming ever more fashionable. They saw it reflected too in the growing number of Catholic priests, 750 by 1628, many of them Jesuits and many of them English, who now resided openly in England.[20]

They also saw threats to English Protestantism in Charles' promotion of Arminianism, a theology developed by Jacob Arminius, a Dutch academic who argued that rather than the irrevocable divine judgement proposed by John Calvin, predestination was a tendency affected by human freewill.[21] By their conduct, he said, individuals could augment or extinguish an innate inner spark of salvation, thus contributing by good works towards their redemption. As well as broadening the base of those potentially saved, Arminianism also emphasized sacraments, ceremonies, state control over the Church and the divine right of kings.

Puritans, however, saw little to differentiate Arminianism from Catholicism, while those Anglican bishops who subscribed to it seemed no different to their fellows in the hierarchy of Rome. In the Puritans' view, it was a ploy by the Catholic-leaning Charles to overturn Protestantism and to introduce Catholicism to England.

In the same year that Charles spurned the Petition of Right, he elevated William Laud, a former chaplain to King James, and a leading Arminian, to the Bishopric of London. Elsewhere too, the king promoted Arminians to bishoprics. As he did so, what had previously been a long-standing debate among academic theologians became a struggle for power within the English Church. Following advice from his Arminian bishops, Charles subsequently outlawed discussion on contentious issues, including predestination.

Early in 1629, a parliamentary attack on Arminianism, led by Sir John Eliot and the Puritan lawyer, John Pym, was linked to accusations that by continuing to collect certain taxes not sanctioned by Parliament, Charles had contravened the Petition of Right.[22, 23] Regarding the criticisms as an attack on his divine right, Charles prorogued Parliament. When it reassembled in March, a group of MPs issued the Three Resolutions, a protestation attacking Arminianism and urging merchants to withhold their tax. Those who paid, it said, were enemies to the kingdom and betrayers of the liberties of England.

In retaliation, Charles ordered Sir John Finch, Speaker of the House of Commons, to adjourn the current parliamentary session. As he attempted to obey, a group of MPs led by another Puritan lawyer, Denzil Holles, strode forward and held him down in his chair. "God's wounds," shouted Holles, "*you* shall sit till *we* please to rise."[24] Then, with the king's officials hammering on the locked doors of the Commons' chamber, Holles read out the Three Resolutions to roars of support. When he sat down, the Commons voted their own adjournment. Days later, after Holles, Eliot and seven others had been arrested and imprisoned, Charles issued a royal proclamation dissolving Parliament, defending his domestic and religious policies and asserting his right to collect taxes as he thought fit. Henceforward, he said, he would govern England alone, by divine right. His opponents denounced him as a tyrant.

For eleven years, during which time Christopher Fox served as churchwarden in Fenny Drayton, Charles ruled without Parliament. Only from his hand-picked Privy Council, and from his Arminian bishops, did he seek advice. Meanwhile, as he continued to raise money through forced loans, sales of commercial monopolies, and the revival of ancient and often long-forgotten taxes, opposition spread further and grew fiercer. In 1633, when William Laud was appointed Archbishop of Canterbury, the spectre of Catholicism restored to England loomed large in Puritan minds. Almost certainly it loomed large in Fenny Drayton, whose Purefey overlords dated their commitment to Puritanism to the early years of the English Reformation. Moreover, many of the clergymen they appointed to the livings on their estates were men of more than average resolution.

One of the most zealous was Anthony Nutter, Puritan vicar of Fenny Drayon, appointed to the living in 1582 by George Purefey, Puritan great-grandfather of the man who made a churchwarden of Christopher Fox. Soon after his arrival in the village, and eager to be about the Lord's business, Anthony added his name to the Warwick Presbyterian classis, a group of twelve local ministers, including two of England's leading Puritans, Thomas Cartwright and Humphrey Fenn, who combined into a Presbytery to handle matters common to their parishes.[25] Six years later, in 1589, when eighteen leaders of the English Puritan movement were arrested and imprisoned for opposing "popish ritual", Anthony Nutter was proud to be among them.

Though eventually released, between 1593 and 1604 Anthony was several times admonished for refusing to wear a surplice, while in 1594 he was reprimanded for "plucking down the board in the chancel", presumably part of a rood screen. Pressed for further evidence of non-conformity, but obviously sympathetic to their minister, Anthony's churchwardens were cautious. "He does not observe the Book of Common Prayer on all points," they admitted cagily.[26] In March 1604, together with 92 other men of his diocese, Anthony was summoned before his bishop. All were charged with contravening the national conformity to church ritual and the Prayer Book demanded by King James. Anthony, however, was among 30 of the most intransigent, who agreed with the charge and then insisted on presenting their reasons to the king.

In 1605, Anthony was charged once again. "He hath not yet conformed himself neither will conforme himself," said the transcript, "and saith that whatsoever ys the invention of man ys not to be allowed in the service of God."[27] Later that year, convicted of non-conformity, he was deprived of his living. Unrepentant, convinced that he obeyed God's will as revealed in his conscience, he left Fenny Drayton and the people he had served there for many years.

But he also left a village committed to Puritanism, and villagers as resolute as himself. In July 1607, an Episcopal visitation at Leicester discovered that thirteen of them, including both churchwardens, had "not receaved the Communion at Easter last and the reason is because they refuse to take the same kneeling."[28] The same offence, together with contravening the compulsory church attendance on Sundays and holy days required by Queen Elizabeth's 1559 Act of Uniformity, absenting themselves from evening prayer, and other acts contrary to church discipline, were recorded almost yearly.[29] On several occasions, villagers were excommunicated for failing to seek absolution for their religious offences, a punishment which obviously failed to impress since in the Visitation Books and Correction Court Books of the Archdeanery of Leicester the same names reappear time and again.[30] Defiance of such long standing was almost certainly condoned by the rector and by the Purefeys. No doubt it was also seen as inextricably linked to the faith reaffirmed each Sunday at St Michael's, that was summed up in the words displayed on the church walls, inscribed on the Purefey family crest: *Pure foi ma Joye* – "Pure faith my Joy".[31] It was also the Puritan faith into which George Fox was born and brought up.

"Both parents," said William Penn, "endeavoured to bring him up, as they did the rest of their children, in the way and worship of the nation."[32] It was a way that also incorporated the story of Fenny Drayton into the history of England, that maintained that devotion to God and his laws was the supreme goal of life, that conscience was the guide, and that worldly authorities must sometimes be defied no matter what the cost.

Though the memory of Anthony Nutter was certainly an example of that defiance and its cost, not far from Fenny Drayton others had made sacrifices even greater. During the persecutions of Protestants ordered by Queen Mary, Joyce Lewis and Robert Glover, both of nearby Mancetter, were burned alive for their commitment to the Protestant faith.[33] Years later, as their stories were told to young George Fox, he heard them with a mixture of horror and admiration.

From a book that was second in popularity only to the Bible, not only would he have heard many similar accounts, perhaps read aloud to him by his mother, but he would also have seen the sufferings of the martyrs depicted in graphic woodcut illustrations. *Actes and Monuments*, more popularly known as the *Book of Martyrs*, was written by the Marian exile, John Foxe, partly as a condemnation of the executions ordered by Roman Catholic Mary, but also to bolster the Protestantism of Queen Elizabeth. The book also included a version of English history that set out to show that the Christian faith brought to England, in John Foxe's account by Joseph of Aramathea, a wealthy disciple of Jesus, was the true Christian faith of the Apostles.[34]

Furthermore, said John Foxe, who like his fellow Puritans maintained that the true faith had been betrayed by the Roman Catholic Church, it had become the divinely ordained mission of England, often against almost impossible odds, to uphold that true faith against the allies and agents of Antichrist. In the early years of Elizabeth's reign, when England stood alone as the only major Protestant power, Calvinist zeal and John Foxe's *Book of Martyrs* ensured that the

Protestant faith was linked firmly to English nationhood. When that faith was reinforced by seemingly miraculous signs, especially the defeat of the Spanish Armada in 1588, it combined to create a view of England as the "elect nation", chosen by God as his weapon in the war against Antichrist. By the time George Fox was born in Fenny Drayton, few people in England doubted that John Foxe's history was true and that England's historical mission was indeed ordained by God.

From John Foxe's book, George would have learned about John Wyclif. Almost certainly he heard about him from his family and neighbours too, for after being forced from Oxford University in 1381, the rebel priest and academic had made his home at Lutterworth, just twenty miles southeast along Watling Street from Fenny Drayton. It was there, and earlier at Oxford, that Wyclif rejected the sacraments and ceremonies of the Catholic Church, while also promoting the view that God sought a personal relationship with his people. He also maintained that all true Christians were part of God's priesthood, a "priesthood of all believers". At the same time he also called for the Bible to be produced in English, rather than in the Church's Latin, so that people might read for themselves rather than relying on the interpretations of priests. That so much of Wyclif's thought anticipated Luther and Calvin led John Foxe and others to name him the spark that ignited the Reformation, and to incorporate such a view into the theory of the elect nation.

Shortly after Wyclif's death in 1382, his followers, itinerant lay preachers named "Lollards" by their opponents (a name probably taken from a Dutch word meaning "mumbler"), carried his doctrines, and his English Bibles, all over England. Though persecuted for their faith, sometimes martyred when discovered, as the years passed by the Lollards continued to maintain their witness. That nearby Coventry, just ten miles south of Fenny Drayton, had been a Lollard centre for many years, once again told the young George Fox that he lived very close to men and women whose courage and steadfastness had helped to shape not only England's destiny but that of the Christian faith itself.

Moreover, as he listened to the stories of Joyce Lewis and

Robert Glover, and of John Wyclif and the Lollards, and as he learned that his nation had a central role to play in God's great purpose in history, he would also have heard that faith, conscience and principled defiance had very special relevance for him. "Her maiden name was Mary Lago," he said of his mother, "of the family of the Lagos, and of the stock of the martyrs." There are no surviving records of a Lago who died as a Protestant martyr, or as a Lollard, although with virtually no family records relating to the Fox parents, it is impossible to know just what their kindred links might have been. But it was an enduring family tradition, and throughout his life George Fox remembered the pride in his mother's voice as she spoke of the heroes whose blood ran in his veins. He also considered it worthy, and clearly relevant, to be included in the account of his life.

George Fox also remembered, for all his life, every word of the book that was so central to the Protestant and the Puritan faith. "I have heard some of his Friends say," said a reminiscence many years later, "(and those not of the Vulgar size, but Men of Learning and Knowledge) that though the Bible were lost, it might be found in the Mouth of George Fox."[35] George's mother, who, he told William Penn, was especially devoted to his religious education, almost certainly read it to her first child as he lay in his cradle, before perhaps using it later to teach him his letters. Like many other weavers of his day, Christopher Fox may also have read it aloud, propping it before him as he worked at his loom.[36]

Both sounds were steady and rhythmic, beginning early in the morning, often continuing late into the night, and in a small house they were the unavoidable centre of six human lives. The one was the pumping of the treadle, the clatter as the heddles were raised, lifting the warp; the grunt as Christopher threw the shuttle full of yarn, and then a slam as the beater pressed down upon another woven row. The other, keeping time, in the Leicestershire accents of Mary and Christopher Fox, was the rhythm of Scripture, weaving its way into the weft of consciousness and the warp of time. "In the beginning God created the heaven and the earth ... and darkness was upon the face of the deep"; "The people that walked in darkness have seen a great light"; "... my spirit upon all flesh ... your sons and your daughters shall prophesy ... dream dreams ... see visions"; "In him was life ... the light of men ... the light shineth in darkness ..."; "And I saw a new heaven and a new earth ... for the first ... were passed away ... he will dwell with them, and they shall be his people ..."[37]

Yet, although every day he heard the Scriptures, both in St Michael's and in his own home, and though he soon knew by heart every word spoken by God to his prophets, and every parable of Jesus, as George Fox grew older, it seems that somehow it all failed to satisfy. Rather than feeling himself filled, he felt empty; rather than resting in faith, he became increasingly agitated. For the assurance of which others spoke seemed not to be for him. Though he stared at the words on the walls of St Michael's – *Pure foi ma joye* – he sensed no pure faith and experienced no joy.

From George Fox's own brief memory of his early years, and from what he told others, it is possible to discern a child who, as the years slipped away, grew increasingly dismayed at the divergence between what he heard others say and his own experience. Perhaps Righteous Christer, Puritan churchwarden, was indeed a hard taskmaster; constantly exhorting, endlessly expecting, but giving little in the way of encouragement. Perhaps he spoke often of hell and damnation, and of the need for regular examinations of the conscience in order that George might test his election. If George was in fact a sickly child, then perhaps that inner anxiety which appears to have pressed upon him so early, was also the result of guilty feelings, engendered by a failure to be more of the boy his father expected. Or perhaps, as Christopher dismissed his eager questions, he became increasingly reluctant to ask. Indeed, the child who speaks through the man who later recalled his life for posterity, seems to look out from his phrases with a shadow behind the eyes and a frown, self-conscious at being unhappy, and maybe increasingly troubled by one terrible thought. Could it be possible perhaps, that he was not among the elect, and that he was not saved?

CHAPTER TWO

A Glimpse of Sion's Glory

…the Voice that will come of Christ's reigning, is like to begin from those that are the Multitude…

Thomas Goodwin,
A Glimpse of Sions Glory (London, 1641)

"**A**S I GREW UP," George Fox recalled, "my relations thought to have made me a priest." Clearly, the boy who was "more religious, inward, still, solid, and observing, beyond his years", and whose questions "manifested to the astonishment of those that heard him, especially in divine things", had attracted attention. Clearly too, someone, or maybe several people, believed that God had a purpose for him. But not everyone agreed. "Others," George said, "persuaded to the contrary."

Just who saw in him the makings of a Christian minister, and who kept him from a path that would have taken him to school, and then to university either at Oxford or Cambridge, he never revealed. Several times in the account of his life that he produced later he mentioned relations, but sadly he left few details. There was a cousin, referred to simply as Bradford, and an uncle referred to as Pickering. Apart from those two, and his immediate family, nothing else is known. Like so many people whose origins were humble, the details of George Fox's ancestors and of his wider contemporary family, just like the bricks of his Fenny Drayton home, have disappeared into the anonymity of the past.

Perhaps it was Mary Fox, "accomplished above most of her degree in the place where she lived", who suggested the idea. Perhaps it was Christopher Fox, the craftsman weaver, who disagreed. And just as George left few details of his relations, he did not say whether he was disappointed at the decision made on his behalf. Or whether he was angry, or felt cheated. Given his future attitude towards the ordained ministry, however, it seems that he did indeed harbour a resentment. Almost all the clergymen he encountered were Puritans of one form or another, and probably referred to themselves as ministers. By his naming them "priests", George made it clear that he equated them all with the Catholic clergy they themselves so disparaged. More importantly, perhaps, given his subsequent career, the denial of what was clearly regarded as an obvious potential seems to have been another factor in driving George Fox's journey through life.

Nevertheless, regardless of the part he played in his son's lack of education and the rejection of the ordained ministry, when George reached the age of eleven, Christopher Fox took a hand in shaping his future. "I was put to a man," George said, "a shoemaker by trade, and that dealt in wool, and used grazing, and sold cattle." Thus the boy who was not to be a priest would become a craftsman like his father; down-to-earth and respectable, a man who might one day become a churchwarden at St Michael's. Indeed, perhaps this is what Christopher Fox truly wanted for his firstborn son – that he should become a man very like himself. Had George been that sort of a boy, then no doubt both father and son would have looked back on the day when the apprenticeship was agreed and the indentures were signed as the providential beginning of a substantial career. And at first, it did seem that it might be so.

Long tradition, although without firm evidence, suggests that George Gee, a shoemaker of Mancetter, was George Fox's master. Moreover, while he may not have been the master George would have chosen for himself, it was evidently a happy arrangement, where each found something in the other that was beneficial. "A great deal went through my hands," said George, recalling the trust eventually placed in him, that eased some of George Gee's responsibilities, while in turn nurturing George Fox's self-confidence. Later he told William Penn how his master indulged an inclination for husbandry. "He was brought up in country business," said Penn, "and as he took most delight in sheep, so he was very skilful in them; an employment that very well suited his mind in several respects, both for its innocency and solitude, and was a just figure of his after ministry and service."[1]

Yet, despite the apt metaphor, and the satisfaction that George obviously found among the flocks, that a youth of fourteen, fifteen and sixteen should voluntarily spend his days alone in distant fields, also suggests something else. It suggests that the religious anxieties that gave rise to his questions were becoming more intense. If they did indeed concern his election, and thus his eternal salvation, then they were probably also becoming more frightening. At the same time, it also suggests that the youthful George Fox was a young man uneasy in company, a conclusion reinforced by some of his other recollections of those distant days.

"While I was in that service," he said, "I used in my dealings the word Verily, and it was a common saying among people that knew me, 'If George says Verily, there is no altering him.'" Obviously he was scrupulously honest; he was, after all, the son of Puritan parents, while the solidity of his childhood appears to have become a stubbornness that would perhaps become more evident in future years. Yet, contained within those words is a hint of defences erected against a threatening world. Perhaps he had learned them earlier at home, and employed them later against people who were coarse and unpredictable, and who sneered at authority and at its offspring. While most people admired his resolution, he said, there were others, "boys and rude people", who laughed at him. Later in his *Journal* he makes further references to "rude" people, by which he seems to mean the rude multitude – the unlettered and ignorant mass who respond with vulgar sneers, foul language and violence. Clearly, he first encountered them in his youth, in Fenny Drayton and in Mancetter.

There is no reliable image of George Fox, not as a child, nor as a youth. There are, however, images which claim to represent him later in life. In 1858, a painting attributed to Sir Peter Lely was found to have written on the back, "Geo. Fox by Sir Peter Lely." It shows a somewhat plain-featured man, broad of face, who looks from the frame with a benign tranquillity. Yet somehow he does not reflect the restless, abrasive and sometimes abusive author of the *Journal*, nor the fiery condemnations that often flowed from George Fox's pen. Nor is it easy to imagine such a man standing atop a market cross to denounce cheating traders, or going boldly before Oliver Cromwell, or holding the attention of a massive crowd at an open-air rally on a windswept moor. Nor is the writing contemporary with the picture.[2]

Although there are verbal descriptions, these are of George Fox in his later years. "A bulky person," said William Penn.[3] "Pretty tall of stature and a very great boned man," said Ann Docwra, a Cambridgeshire Quaker who met George towards the end of his life.[4] Since tall, great-boned men were once tall, great-boned youths, even if bulk came later, then almost certainly George Fox was a large young man. If his height and bigness were combined with a plain face and a reserved disposition, then he may well have felt awkward and ungainly among the youths of Mancetter. Or before the village girls at Drayton.

Should the uncomfortable combination also include a father who is a stalwart of the Puritan church, constantly exhorting his son to set an example, while at the same time castigating those who prefer to be dissolute, then the results might have been almost unbearable. "When I came to eleven years of age," George said, "I knew pureness and righteousness; for while I was a child I was taught how to walk to be kept pure." In itself it is an intriguing statement. It certainly reinforces the view that the instilling of Puritan morality featured large in the Fox household. Years later, looking back, George clearly considered that such instruction had served him well in life. As a youth already self-conscious about his physical appearance, it was probably a final barrier between himself and friends of his own age.

It certainly caused friction with cousin Bradford, who, early in September 1643, persuaded George to leave his master's business at Atherstone's annual Statutes Fair, and to join him and a friend at one of the town's crowded and noisy alehouses.[5] The day was hot, with the sun blazing from a clear blue sky. Dust raised by the constant movement of sheep, cattle, horses and men hung heavy in the air, together with the pungent scent of apprehensive animals and the rancid aroma of food kept hot for the passing trade. Awake long before dawn, and busy all day, almost certainly the conscientious George was tired, sweaty and thirsty. But, far more alluring than the suggested jug of beer was a promise of a religious discussion. "For I loved any that had a sense of good, or that sought after the Lord," he said.

He describes Bradford and his friend as professors. In the usage of the time it simply meant those who professed a faith, rather than implying any particular qualification. Later in his life, when he used the term "the great professors", George meant those qualified to preach by virtue of their university degrees and their ordination. Like "priest", he intended it to be derogatory.

On that September day, in the company of two professors, he clearly anticipated some rewarding hours. In this, however, he was disappointed. Rather than debate, Bradford and his friend began drinking heavily. Before long, as ale and sunshine went to their heads, conviviality became a drinking contest, with tipsy demands that he who refused to join the party should pay for it. "If it be so, I'll leave you," George said stiffly. Leaving a groat on the table, he walked away.

Perhaps unkind words followed him; rude comments on the insecurities that drove him to solitude and made him appear aloof. Perhaps Bradford or his friend sniggered. Perhaps it had all been a set-up. And maybe, as the drinking continued, George felt deep within his being a familiar shrinking; the unwelcome but inescapable scourge of the vulnerable, that prevents easy friendships and reinforces loneliness.

That same afternoon, the incident provoked a crisis. Given subsequent events, it had evidently been fermenting for some time. Bradford was the catalyst who brought it to birth. By the time George had walked the two miles home to Drayton, the world had grown darker, while the once-familiar Leicestershire landscape appeared confused, as if some giant hand had torn it apart and then reassembled it carelessly, far from its true alignment. Later, as twilight deepened, his sense of the world's disorder, and that he viewed it through a dark medium, grew more intense and more frightening. "I returned home," he said, "but did not go to bed that night, nor could not sleep, but sometimes walked up and down, and sometimes prayed and cried to the Lord."

Finally, in the dark midnight, as George paced the house, bone weary yet wide awake, a voice spoke into his troubled heart. "Thou seest how young people go together into vanity, and old people into the earth," it said, "and thou must forsake all, both young and old, and keep out of all, and be as a stranger unto all."

He left Fenny Drayton on 9 September 1643. He was nine-teen years old, in the grip of acute mental turmoil, and setting off alone into a country that had itself been in turmoil for decades, and at war with itself for nearly twelve months. George Fox, it seems, virtually reflected the state of his country.

When William Laud became Archbishop of Canterbury in 1633, he attempted to eradicate Calvinism from England for ever. Bible preaching was everywhere downgraded, while sacraments and ceremony were made central to church serv-ices. With emphasis placed especially on the Eucharist, all clergy were ordered to wear vestments, to replace simple Communion tables with altars, and to ensure that altars were railed and elaborately covered. St Paul's Cathedral in London, and the Minster at York, were both refurbished, the costs being met by increased and largely resented local taxation. Determined to stamp out the Puritan preaching ministry, Laud issued orders for the forcible closure of the Feoffees for Impropriations, the London-based trust that sponsored Puritan preachers across the land.

In the face of mounting opposition, Laud grew increasingly

intolerant. Using the book-licensing laws, he censored the press, and through the ecclesiastical Court of High Commission he attempted to enforce uniformity. As Bishop of London he had been zealous in persecuting dissidents. In 1632, on his order, an entire London congregation was arrested, tried, and imprisoned.[6] As Archbishop, he aimed his attacks at men far more influential.

In 1637, three leading Puritans – William Prynne, Henry Burton, and John Bastwick – who questioned Laud's authority in a series of illegal publications, were tried before the king's prerogative court of Star Chamber. When they received sentences quite inappropriate for their station – to be pilloried and to have their ears cropped – the resultant fury added fuel to the Puritan cause. Almost certainly the sentence was denounced in Fenny Drayton. Perhaps also reaching Fenny Drayton were some of the handbills that flooded London, denouncing "the Arch-wolf of Canterbury", and accusing him of "persecuting the saints and shedding the blood of the martyrs".[7]

In the next year, further Puritan denunciations followed, especially when a former cloth merchant's apprentice named John Lilburne was condemned by Star Chamber for distributing William Bastwick's pamphlets. During his trial, the young man had added to his reputation as a religious and political radical by keeping his hat on before the judge, an action widely regarded as a symbolic refusal to recognize social superiority and political authority.[8]

The crowds that turned out to support the victims in the pillory, and the men who carried handbills across England, were largely mobilized by a powerful Puritan underground movement, an alliance of several shades of opinion that since Laud's appointment had rapidly gathered strength. By 1637, as George Fox learned the shoemaker's craft at Mancetter, its network covered the country. Those involved included lawyers and country gentlemen (some of whom had also been Members of the Parliament that had been prorogued in 1629), merchants, physicians and huge numbers of Puritan church ministers. As the movement gathered pace, England once more became home to a militant Puritanism, as determined as its Elizabethan predecessor, but with a new confidence born of the years of Parliamentary activity.

In 1640, the year that George Fox turned sixteen, the personal rule of King Charles came to an end. Following his attempts to impose Arminianism on Calvinist Scotland, and to finance it with the sale of lands previously granted to Scottish nobles, after pledging themselves to a National Covenant committed to preserving their nation and its Presbyterian Kirk, a united Scotland threatened England with invasion.

Forced to finance a military campaign in his own land, in the spring of 1640 Charles finally summoned Parliament. Whatever he had hoped for, however, the "eleven year tyranny" had left a bitter legacy. An invasion of England by her Scottish neighbour, the House of Commons informed the king, was far less of a threat than attacks on the liberties of her people. Less than four weeks later, Charles dissolved the Short Parliament.

The Covenanter army immediately swept south. As they did so, a group of English Puritan noblemen collaborated with Presbyterian colleagues in Scotland. At the same time, the Puritan underground mobilized massive demonstrations in London to demand a new Parliament. Others challenged the authority of the Arminian bishops.

Under mounting pressure, Charles finally summoned Parliament. It convened in Westminster Hall at the beginning of November 1640. Years later it would be remembered as the Long Parliament, the assembly whose convulsions echoed those of England, as through the tumultuous years of the English Revolution the nation shook off her medieval past and laid the foundations for the religious and political changes that would carry her into the future.

Masterminded by John Pym, for the very first time an independent Parliamentary leadership began to emerge. Meanwhile, from towns and boroughs across the nation a flood of "grievances" arrived at Westminster, demanding redress for the injustices of the eleven-year tyranny. Meanwhile, backed by their Parliamentary supporters, Puritan ministers sat in conclave to protest at Arminian innovations and the subversive role of bishops. In December, William Laud was impeached for high treason and imprisoned in the Tower.

Early in 1641, Parliament stripped the crown of control over parliamentary sessions. It also stepped up the attack on the bishops. When Charles attempted to make peace with Scotland, demonstrators in London accused him of seeking Scottish aid against the Parliament of England.

In November, news arrived of a Catholic uprising in Ireland. When it was accompanied by wildly exaggerated tales of thousands of Protestants slaughtered, anti-Catholic feeling turned to hysteria. Rumour also said that the pro-Catholic Charles had sanctioned the rebellion.

In the same month, Parliament introduced the "Grand Remonstrance", which listed the offences perpetrated by the king's government in Church and State, while contrasting them with Parliament's demands for reform. It called too for the king's future ministers to be approved by Parliament, as well as for an Assembly of Divines – clergymen nominated by Parliament, to supervise Calvinist reform of the Church. As Parliament debated the issues, individuals found themselves forced to make partisan choices. Were they for king or for Parliament, Royalists or Parliamentarians?

The Grand Remonstrance was passed on 22 November.[9] Had such not been the case, said the Member for Cambridge, a country gentleman named Oliver Cromwell, he would have joined thousands of other Puritans who, since the early 1630s, had crossed the Atlantic to settle their families in the Puritan colony of Massachusetts.

On 23 December, King Charles refused the Remonstrance. During the remaining few days of the month, waves of religious and political fervour swept London. Thousands of citizens signed a petition calling for the removal of bishops from the House of Lords. Others joined the almost continuous demonstrations that surrounded Westminster Hall.

In January 1642, believing that Parliament planned to impeach his Catholic queen, Charles went personally to Westminster to arrest the men he believed to be responsible.[10] Surrounded by armed soldiers, he demanded that William

Lenthall, Speaker of the House, point them out. "May it pleasure your Majesty," came the reply, "I have neither eyes to see nor tongue to speak in this place but as the House is pleased to direct me ... "[11] Days later, together with his family, Charles left London.

In March, the Militia Ordinance gave Parliament control of the county Trained Bands. In April, Parliament took control of the main northern munitions magazine at Hull. In the summer, as George Fox turned eighteen, Charles began recruiting forces in the north of England. Meanwhile, Parliament recruited in the south and the east. In August, after rejecting an ultimatum to surrender almost every royal prerogative, the king raised his royal standard at Nottingham. In October, 30 miles south-east of Fenny Drayton, King and Parliament faced each other at Edgehill in Warwickshire. The outcome, though indecisive, was claimed by Parliament as a victory.

Throughout 1643, as George neared the crisis that drove him from home, news of the unfolding events was carried by word of mouth, by news-book, and by the parliamentary speeches, all of which were printed and circulated.[12] So too was the complete text of the Grand Remonstrance. And as such news and propaganda reached them, many more individuals made partisan decisions. Some based them on political and religious convictions. Others were the product of family connections, or loyalty to masters, landlords, or hereditary nobility. Often they were a complex combination of many interests and loyalties. Supporters of Episcopacy or Catholicism tended to favour the king, while Puritans favoured Parliament. Largely, but not entirely, the upper echelons of the landed classes – peers, baronets, knights and the wealthier gentlemen – were Royalists. Largely, but not entirely, the middling and lesser gentry, the learned professions bar the Church, merchants, master craftsmen, skilled artisans, yeoman freeholders and substantial tenant farmers were for Parliament. All of these decisions were to some extent influenced by geographical factors, with the north and west supporting the king, and London, the south and the east deciding for Parliament.

Such geographical divisions were clearly ones of which George Fox was aware, for the route he took from Fenny Drayton, that led him south-eastwards along Watling Street towards London, ensured that he stayed in a region under Parliamentary control. That he did so was perhaps indicative of his own sympathies. Or, perhaps of his apprehensions, for a son of Fenny Drayton, whose Purefey overlords were already in the field for Parliament, would not want to find himself among Royalist forces. As he drew closer to Northampton, however, the likelihood of such an event lessened with every mile. Zealous for the Parliamentary cause, and a long-time base of radical Protestantism, the town was home to the largest Parliamentary garrison in the south Midlands.

A major manufacturer of footware, Northampton was eager to shoe the army, and with its master cobblers struggling to meet the demand, there were opportunities to be had for a young man skilled in their trade. While he may indeed have taken advantage of them, it seems that, in actual fact, George had little need to do so.

"I had wherewith both to keep myself from being chargeable to others," he said later, "and to administer something to the necessities of those who were in need." Although somewhat reluctantly, the statement was subsequently corroborated by his parents.[13] Neither George nor his parents, however, ever explained where this good fortune had come from. Whether Christopher Fox was far more successful than his son's brief account suggests, whether Mary Lago, who was "accomplished above most of her degree", brought more than education to her marriage, or whether there was some other, more mysterious explanation, is unknown. Over the years, it has led to much speculation, none of which has ever reached a firm conclusion. Indeed, it remains one of several intriguing questions concerning George Fox: the precise nature of his later relationship with the wife and then widow of Judge Thomas Fell, for example, and quite what he was about in the year 1659. In 1643, however, by any standard he was well off, and while he may have feared what lay ahead of him, he knew that he need not face it either homeless or hungry.[14]

In Northampton, whether or not George took the opportunity to supplement his funds, amid the bustle of the town's market, in the churches, and among troops in the streets, he almost certainly heard continuing news of the war. While earlier in the year King Charles had seemed all but invincible, in September the situation was radically reversed when a major Royalist army was defeated at Newbury in Berkshire.[15] Strengthening that reversal was the alliance forged between England's Parliament and Presbyterian Scotland, based on a "Solemn League and Covenant" to which all true Protestants would be invited to add their names. Moreover, the Assembly of Divines proposed earlier, called finally to Westminster in July, would now include Scottish Presbyterians among its numbers. William Laud, meanwhile, was to stand trial for his life.

In June 1644, nine months after leaving home, and having passed through a second Parliamentary garrison at Newport Pagnell in Buckinghamshire, George finally reached Barnet, a small and prosperous town ten miles north of London. As he did so, Archbishop Laud's trial was already under way. In the north, meanwhile, a Scottish army marched south to join forces with Parliament's Yorkshire troops. Marching north to swell their numbers was Parliament's Eastern Association army, whose cavalry commander was Oliver Cromwell. When the armies combined, they would attack the Royalist stronghold at York.

But such events, before which others held their breath, made little difference to George Fox. Indeed, he was barely aware they took place. For though the world had seemed out of alignment since the day he had left Atherstone Fair, at Barnet something occurred that caused it to lurch more violently: "… at Barnet a strong temptation to despair came upon me," he said. It was a remark reminiscent of similar statements made by many contemporaries.[16]

In the religious conflicts of Tudor England, religious melancholy was common. In the seventeenth century, as that conflict resumed, melancholy became ever more prevalent and increasingly acute. Many individuals were obsessed by the question of election; many doubted their salvation and thought only of hell. Suffering agonies of mind, some denied the existence of God, claiming instead that all things came by nature. Others maintained that the Scriptures were a fable, designed to frighten men and women into obedience. Others still said there was no immortal soul; that heaven and hell were no more than states of mind. In the face of the terrors, and the loss of deeply held beliefs, many people were plunged into depression. Not a few were driven to suicide. Like George Fox, they were tempted to despair.

In George's case, religious melancholy seems also to have been compounded by other factors. "When Satan could not effect his designs upon me that way," he said, "then he laid snares for me and baits to draw me to commit some sin, whereby he might take advantage and bring me to despair." Though he said nothing specific, from incidents that took place later in his life, and from his accounts of visions experienced during sickness, almost certainly George Fox's temptations were sexual in nature. They may have been no more than the desires aroused in a young man by the presence or thought of young women. They may have been the relieving of such desires by his own hand. Or, they may have been desires which continue to trouble later generations. But, whatever their precise nature, as a young man who had been "taught how to walk to be kept pure", it seems that for George Fox the whole area of sexuality created anxieties of enormous magnitude.

During the agonizing days at Barnet, and indeed throughout his life, he was also certain that it was "Satan" who orchestrated his temptations. Thus, in the terrifying struggle taking place, that tortured his imagination and troubled his flesh, George saw that what was at stake were not only sexual acts likely to dismay his Puritan parents, but the salvation of which he was already so uncertain.

The resultant conflict, in an intelligent and religious young man, within whom the concept of purity was powerfully instilled, was almost certainly more than his conscious mind could withstand. Thus, the inner conflict became masked by depression. And as he struggled with the melancholy, and against the temptations, the answers he sought were themselves the product of the world of his time.

"I wondered why these things should come to me," he said. Turning the question in every direction, he could only conclude that they were God's judgement upon him. "I was brought to call to mind all the time that I had spent," he said, "and to consider whether I had wronged any." Yet, though he struggled, in order to repent, no trespasses came to him. Instead, the darkness around him, and the conflict within him, grew blacker and ever more desperate. Cutting himself off from all human company, he turned in upon himself. "I kept myself retired in my chamber," he said, "and often walked solitary in the chace, to wait upon the Lord."[17]

Eventually, perhaps forcing himself to do so, he left Barnet and resumed his journey to London. As he did so, he would have learned that at the very beginning of July, Parliament had won a great victory at Marston Moor in Yorkshire, and had then taken York. Earlier on his journey he must also have sought out people he hoped might provide solutions for his uncertainties and answers to his questions. As he neared London, he would certainly have met on the road individuals of many shades of political opinion and Christian faith. If some named themselves Messengers of the Church of Christ, then he would have heard how they travelled the whole country, preaching and baptizing wherever they went. In these latter days, they may have said, days of overturning and of battle, the signs and wonders that were everywhere at hand were a sure mark that Christ's kingdom drew near. Charging him to remember their directions, they urged him to join them at their churches in the city ahead.

George left few details of the weeks, or perhaps months, that he spent in London. But once within the city's eighteen miles of fortifications, he would have found a community in a heightened state of religious and political excitement. At Westminster, English and Scottish divines sat in the Assembly, seeking to lay the foundation for a new religious structure for the whole nation. Although a few were Laudian Episcopalians, the majority were Puritans. Among those, however, while the majority were strict Calvinist Presbyterians, others named themselves Independents. Between the groups there was an increasingly acrimonious conflict.

With the overthrow of Archbishop Laud, another wave of Puritan exiles had returned to England. They were also individuals who regarded a church administered by centralizing presbyteries as no better than one ruled by a hierarchy of bishops. Instead, the Independents, or Congregationalists, favoured a church order that they regarded as "gathered" by Christ, since rather than receiving church membership through baptism as an infant, each member chose his or her allegiance freely as an adult. Subsequently such individuals then took an equal share in church government. By and large Independents also favoured a limited religious toleration, that worship might be as conscience directed. By the time George Fox arrived in London, it was a view shared by many Members of Parliament, who largely, but not always, were those referred to as the political Independents. Opposing them were the Presbyterian Members, who, sharing the views of the more conservative Puritan clergy, sought to transform England into a nation dominated by Calvinist presbyteries.

Had George visited the city's booksellers, clustered around St Paul's Churchyard, then he would have found many volumes detailing Presbyterian and Independent views. He would also have discovered a huge volume of works referring to biblical prophecies, particularly those relating to the Millennium, the coming Kingdom of God promised in the Book of Revelation.

It was a subject which in the past had often attracted religious radicals, particularly those who equated God's Kingdom with a golden age, where the poor would indeed inherit the earth, and where poverty, injustice and inequality would be swept away. Many of those radicals had also seen the injustices of the present age as representing their own understanding of the reign of Antichrist, where both the Roman Catholic Church and that of the Reformers were castigated as apostate. It was also the view of many of those radicals, that the apostasy had begun in the fourth Christian century, when the

Emperor Constantine had transformed a religion of slaves and the poor into the official religion of the Roman Empire. The true church, meanwhile, the pure church of the New Testament Apostles, driven by its deceitful substitutes to the wilderness, waited to be restored to her rightful position. How this would be achieved had been the subject of many interpretations.

In the decades prior to the outbreak of the Civil War, the question of the Millennium had attracted the attention of many reputable scholars. Although many dates were suggested, by the early 1640s a consensus had been reached, that remarkable events in the mid-1650s would herald first the fall of the Antichrist Rome, and then the dawn of the Millennium.[18] Among many English scholars, there was also little doubt that the Millennium would first dawn in the elect nation. In 1641, John Milton, poet and propagandist for the Parliamentary cause, remarked on the "*Precedencie* which GOD gave this *Iland*, to be the first *Restorer* of *buried Truth*."[19]

As Parliament and Puritan ministers alike sought to defeat the king, increasingly they called the common people to their cause. As they did so, they linked that cause both to millennial expectations and to the view of England as the elect nation. They also emphasized the biblical view that it was the poor, rather than the rich and powerful, who had a unique role to play in the ushering in of God's Kingdom: "... you that are of the meaner rank, common People, be not discouraged," said the Puritan clergyman Thomas Goodwin in his 1641 pamphlet, *A Glimpse of Sion's Glory*, "for God intends to make use of the common People in the great Worke of proclaiming the Kingdome of his Sonne ... the Voice that will come of Christ's reigning, is like to begin from those that are the Multitude ... "[20] Thus, the English poor heard themselves exalted as the vanguard of the armies of the Lord. Furthermore, although neither Goodwin nor the colleagues that echoed his sentiments voiced any radical theological conclusions, their words, implying that God's Kingdom was open to all, contradicted their own commitment to predestination.

Many of the common people, however, had already abandoned the national church, both the Anglicanism of

Archbishop Laud, and the Calvinism of the Puritans. Moreover, since the overthrow of Laud and the collapse of censorship, while the Independents had returned from an overseas exile, the dissenters among the common people had emerged from previously secret conventicles. Both they and their beliefs horrified the orthodox.

If George Fox took the opportunity to attend Christ Church, Newgate, and the weekly lectures there of the Presbyterian clergyman, Thomas Edwards, he would have learned all he needed to know about the manifold sects who now proclaimed their beliefs openly. A self-appointed heresy hunter, Edwards had already published two successful books. Largely they opposed religious toleration, which their author regarded as the nursing mother of heresy, the prelude to social anarchy, and a ploy by Antichrist to prevent godly reformation.[21] In 1644 he was in the process of collecting material for a further volume, one which he hoped would expose the practices and the errors of the sects more fully.[22]

The origins of the sects lay largely in the Radical Reformation that had emerged alongside the Magisterial Reformation of Martin Luther, Ulrich Zwingli and John Calvin.[23] Unlike the Magisterial Reformation, however, that spoke to wealthy and powerful men, its Radical counterpart generally expressed the social longings and spiritual needs of the poor, the politically radical, and those individuals who for many reasons found little accommodation within conventional society. And, far more than the Magisterial Reformation, its Radical counterpart was fluid, drawing on diverse strands of religious and political thought, often mixing and mingling them, before emerging transformed to advance in new and sometimes unexpected directions. Such fluidity, plus the Radical tendency to find expression in a spirituality that was immediate and direct, as well as sometimes in revolutionary social action, had horrified the major Reformers. For they saw it as a very potent threat to their own highly structured theories and organizations. But, though they denounced its manifestations as heresy, and consistently opposed them, just as the Roman Church had already discovered, heresy had many heads, and the cutting off of one generally led to the emergence of many more.

Thomas Edwards himself was particularly devoted to the theology of John Calvin, and regarded his own opposition to heresy as a furtherance of the great man's work. However, despite his regular denunciations, the sects continued to proliferate and grow. Among the worst, in his view, were those he called "dippers", but who referred to themselves as the Churches of Christ. Later generations would know them as Baptists. Their origins lay in the sixteenth century, among small congregations who felt unable for many reasons to conform to the Church of England. Unlike men such as Anthony Nutter, who attempted to transform the church from within, other dissenting individuals had constituted themselves as Separatist, and therefore illegal, churches. In the early seventeenth century, two such Separatist congregations, from Nottinghamshire and Lincolnshire, fled to Holland. There they moved among Dutch Anabaptists, absorbing doctrines developed earlier by Menno Simons, a former Catholic priest converted to Protestantism, who after concluding that Christ's sacrifice had been for all people – a "general atonement" – subsequently rejected predestination. Returning with their new faith to England, the refugees laid the basis for an Arminian, or General, Baptist movement. Like the Mennonites, as Menno's followers came to be called, the General Baptists maintained that God's Kingdom was open to anyone who took hold of the free grace offered to all humankind. They also rejected the baptism of infants in favour of an informed acceptance of grace by adults. The means of signifying such acceptance, and acknowledging entry to God's Kingdom, was through a believer's baptism.

With the collapse of censorship, not only had the Baptists emerged into the light, but their "messengers" had embarked on a hugely successful campaign to win converts across the country, and most especially in the Parliamentary army. That most of those messengers, indeed most of the men who led the General Baptist congregations, were of the common people, "Shoemakers, Coblers, Weavers, or Sopeboylers, and the like", was equally offensive to their opponents as their Arminian beliefs.[24] Furthermore, as Thomas Edwards made clear, such men had no respect for godly ministers, rudely keeping their hats on before them in church, and interrupting them during their sermons. At Ravensdowne in Bedfordshire, he said, one of them "got up into the Pulpit, against the will of the minister", and in spite of his objections preached to the congregation, "for Universall Grace, against Paedobaptism, against Tythes ... "[25]

Castigated with equal fervour by Thomas Edwards was the Family of Love, a movement which, like Mennonite Anabaptism, had also emerged in the sixteenth-century Netherlands. Known in England as Familism, it flourished strongly in East Anglia and in Yorkshire, both areas where Lollardy had once been strong. Indeed, as the years had passed by, and as Lollardy had found increasing support among skilled working folk – weavers, shoemakers, carpenters and ploughmen – Wyclif's priesthood of all believers had found expression in lay church leadership and a fierce anti-clericalism. His criticisms of the Roman Catholic Mass, meanwhile, had become a rejection of all sacraments.

Like Lollards, Familists also rejected the ordained ministry and sacraments, while often they also held their property in common. Maintaining that it was the indwelling Holy Spirit that enabled believers to fully understand Scripture, they also regarded the Bible as an eternal allegory. Claiming that heaven and hell were found in this world, Familists held that men and women might recapture on earth the state of innocence that existed before the Fall. For those who achieved such a condition, they said, neither the laws given to Moses, nor those devised by men, were valid.[26]

Equally pernicious, if not far worse, Thomas believed, were women who dared preach as if they were men. "In Lincolnshire," he said, "there is a woman preacher who preaches, (its certain) and 'tis reported also she baptizeth, but that's not so certain. In the Isle of Ely ... is a woman preacher also: in Hartfordshire also ... "[27] Citing where the many heresies might finally lead, he often referred to the events which took place in 1534 in the Westphalian city of Münster, where after gaining control of the city council, German and Dutch Anabaptists had established a theocratic regime. Under the leadership of John of Leyden, a former tailor, collective ownership of property was established, as was polygamy. Governed by a ferocious legal code based on the Old Testament, order was eventually maintained through a reign of terror. After holding out for many months, Münster was finally overcome by forces controlled by the region's bishop in a siege which became a massacre. "This land is become in many places a Chaos, a Babel", Thomas Edwards warned; "... yea, worse; we are beyond that, and in the highway to Münster."[28]

Of all the Baptist churches castigated by Thomas Edwards, most hostility was directed against the congregation at London's Bell Alley. Led by Thomas Lambe, a man described as a soap-boiler, it lay among many other conventicles in the city ward of Coleman Street. It was also the church where the missionary campaigns of the General Baptists were planned, and where the congregation often heard reports from the travelling messengers. One of those messengers was Henry Denne, a Cambridge-educated clergyman who had rejected his ordination to become an itinerant Baptist missionary. Believing that Christ's Kingdom drew near, he assured every new Baptist that the light of Christ's coming would shortly push back the Antichristian darkness that covered England. And included in that darkness was the persecution of the saints by the forces of Antichrist, Episcopalian and Presbyterian alike. "O Lord Christ," he was reputed to pray, "if thou wert now upon the earth, and didst reveal the Gospel to men, they would call thee Anabaptist, Antinomian, Independent, who now call us so."[29]

Writing later of the time spent in London in 1644, George recalled that he made contact with his uncle, "one Pickering, a Baptist". Although he said no more about him, in the records of Star Chamber and High Commission, a certain William Pickering is named as one of those involved in the mass-arrest in 1632 ordered by William Laud. The congregation is known to history by the surnames of the three men who were its leaders over a period of years, as the Jacob–Lathrop–Jessey (JLJ) congregation. Although it split several times, it was also a congregation that encompassed not only Independents, but also Calvinist, or Particular, Baptists, a group which emerged somewhat later than their General colleagues. Thus, if this Pickering were the uncle in question, then his arrest in 1632 raises the intriguing possibility that when George referred to "the stock of the martyrs", he referred to those persecuted by Laud, rather than those burned by Mary Tudor.[30]

In September 1644, during a debate in the House of Commons, the political Independents and their allies upheld the right to refuse the Presbyterian "Solemn League and Covenant". Foremost among the speakers, and making it clear that "the liberty of tender consciences" included Independents, Separatists and Baptists alike, was Oliver Cromwell. Earlier in the year, he had chastised a subordinate officer, Major-General Crawford, who had arrested and then disciplined two Baptists under his command for religious offences.[31] "Sir," Cromwell told him, "the State, in choosing men to serve them, takes no notice of their opinions, if they be willing faithfully to serve them, that satisfies."[32] Thus, not only was religious toleration on England's national agenda, so too was the view that "heresy" was not necessarily to be considered politically subversive. Later in the year, Parliament issued an "Order of Accommodation", an attempt to resolve differences within the Assembly, which accepted a limited degree of liberty of conscience to those within the Protestant fold.[33]

In January 1645, William Laud was beheaded on Tower Hill. For those who had been persecuted by him, who had mobilized against him and fought him, his execution marked the end of a long and bitter campaign. But between his downfall and his death, the struggle that had begun in a desire to overthrow Episcopacy and its perceived links to Rome, had become much broader. Increasingly, England's religious dissenters asked why they should not be free to worship God openly, and freely, and in the manner which their consciences directed.

Among London's dissenting community, George Fox evidently made some impression. "Some tender people would have had me stay," he said. But, though they pressed him, it was in vain. "I could not impart my mind to him," he said of his uncle. "[N]or join with them," he said of everyone else. Later, he recalled that London had seemed to him a dark place, "under the chain of darkness". That he thought it of a city at the centre of such momentous events, suggests that his depression remained heavy upon him. Nor, it seems, had the deep insecurities eased, which set up such a barrier between himself and others of his own age. "I…was under great misery and trouble there," he said. At some point, towards the end of 1644, or early in 1645, he turned his back on the city and set off on the long road home to Leicestershire.

CHAPTER THREE

The Light

For the Measure is within, and the Light of God is within, and the Pearl is within you, which is hid; and the Word of God is within you, and ye are the Temples of God...

George Fox, Epistle 19 (1652)

SATURDAY, 14TH JUNE 1645 dawned chilly and wet in Northamptonshire. Overnight, rain had fallen relentlessly. Nevertheless, under cover of darkness, and on two wide apart grassy ridges close to the village of Naseby, two armies had moved their men and their horses into position. As the morning lightened, and the rain finally eased, the 9,000 Royalist soldiers assembled on one ridge gazed towards 13,500 troops of Parliament's New Model Army on the other. Hours later, although at first it had seemed that victory would go to the king, the New Model Army had inflicted on him a defeat from which he would never recover.

The New Model Army, brought into being earlier in the year, was a revolutionary concept; where for the first time in England's history men might rise through the ranks by virtue of ability rather than birth. It was a revolutionary concept, producing high motivation, and enabling the army's commanders, Sir Thomas Fairfax and Oliver Cromwell, to mold it swiftly into an efficient and disciplined fighting force. "I had rather have a plain, russet-coated captain that knows what he fights for, and loves what he knows, than that which you call a gentleman and is nothing else," Cromwell famously said.[1] For the troops, the motivation produced by equality of opportunity was also underlined by the knowledge that the army was destined for a great purpose. "We were not a mere mercenary army, hired to serve any arbitrary power of a state," they declared later, "but called forth and conjured by the several declarations of Parliament to the defence of our own and the People's just rights and Liberties ... "[2]

Cromwell himself had been the architect of the victory, leading his cavalry into the attack and scattering the Royalist army. Nevertheless, as he made clear in a letter to the Speaker of the House of Commons, he believed the opportunity had been divinely inspired. "Sir," he said, "this is none other but the hand of God, and to him alone belongs the glory."[3]

News of the Parliamentary victory at Naseby swept through the surrounding countryside, reaching Atherstone and Mancetter, just 25 miles away, within hours. Whether the inhabitants rejoiced or were saddened, the consequences of the victory would be enormous. With Parliament supreme, England would advance into a new political landscape, one with few precedents, and where voices rarely heard before would demand a share in shaping their nation's destiny.

Meanwhile, in Fenny Drayton, the parents of George Fox were concerned with the more immediate future of their son. Perhaps it was time he married. A sensible girl, Leicestershire bred, would surely soothe his troubled spirit and curb any tendency to roam. Whether they had someone in mind, who had perhaps already taken a fancy to the serious young man, George never revealed. Besides, marriage was not for him. "I told them I was but a lad, and I must get wisdom," he said.

Christopher and Mary saw it somewhat differently. Rather than a seeker after wisdom, they saw a discontented young man adrift in troubled times. Why not enlist with the local militia, they suggested. Under the superior command of another Puritan Purefey, this time William Purefoy of nearby Caldecote, Leicestershire men had recently taken part in the storming and capture of Compton Wynyates House near Banbury.[4] Now Fenny Drayton's own George Purefey oversaw the occupation there. Perhaps it was he who made the suggestion, assuring the Fox parents that under his watchful eye their restless boy could indulge his yearning for adventure. But, like matrimony, George spurned it. He did not want to be a soldier. Moreover, all their suggestions simply underlined how little his parents understood him. "I was grieved that they proffered such things to me," he said.

Instead, once again, he set off alone. Watching him go, his anxious parents imagined a host of calamities. From the very beginning of the war, the region around Fenny Drayton had been a buffer-zone between the Royalist garrison at Ashby-de-la-Zouch in the north, and Parliamentary strongholds at Leicester to the south-east, and at Warwick to the south. In such a territory, sudden violence was commonplace, as "flying armies" appeared as if from nowhere, fighting bloody skirmishes over precious fields, before disappearing as swiftly as they had come. Meanwhile, as old enemies used the war to settle ancient scores, and as allegiances shifted to suit changing circumstances, rumour and allegation were rife. A young man wandering the countryside alone could well find himself the target of unwelcome speculations, even of accusations and threats.

To George, however, such fears were irrelevant. Mere physical survival did not concern him. He only feared for his immortal soul. For, though London's Baptists had assured him that Calvin's irrevocable decree was not God's plan for humanity, their words brought him no relief, neither lifting his depression, nor relieving his tormented flesh, nor convincing him that God's Kingdom was truly open to all. Until he experienced God's grace for himself, and knew his election was sure, he could not believe himself saved. All he could do, as he tramped the perilous roads of his homeland, was to hope that somewhere in England he would find someone able to help him.

On reaching Coventry, and taking lodgings at the home of a professor, he allowed himself tentatively to hope. Possibly his landlord was a Puritan minister, for like Northampton, the city was a centre for the Parliamentary cause. It was a cause encouraged by William Purefoy, who was Member of Parliament for the town in 1628, the year of the Petition of Right, and who in his youth had spent time in Geneva and embraced Calvinism there. From then on, he promoted the faith wherever he could. In 1641, as MP for Warwick, it was he who led the demand that the Grand Remonstrance be printed and circulated.[5] As he also ensured that Coventry was a haven for Puritan clergymen fleeing Royalist persecution, by 1645, there were almost 30 such refugees in the town. The most respected was Richard Baxter of Kidderminster, who preached on weekdays to the Parliamentary garrison, and on Sundays at Coventry's St Michael's Church.[6]

Shortly after Naseby, Baxter had visited the battlefield. What he discovered there shocked him. "And when the court news-book told the world of the swarms of Anabaptists in our armies, we thought it had been a mere lie ... " he said.[7] His encounter with the troops not only proved it no lie, but convinced him that the "hot-headed sectaries" planned to "subvert both Church and State".[8] From that moment on, he became their relentless opponent. Ministers longer in Coventry than Richard Baxter were far less surprised. The city had been home to Baptists for many years, indeed they themselves traced their origins there almost to the beginning of the century.[9]

Perhaps it was descendants of those early Baptists who first became aware that a new voice had joined their debate. Yet, although the big, ungainly youth spoke forcefully, he clearly found difficulty in expressing exactly what he meant. His country accent too, added to his hearers' confusion. "The side of his understanding which lay next to the world," William Penn said later, "and especially the expression of it, might sound uncouth and unfashionable to nice ears." Nevertheless, as the young man continued, "abruptly and brokenly as sometimes his sentences would fall from him, about divine things," it became obvious that a genuine seeker after God had come among them.[10] Seeing a potential convert, like their colleagues in London, they urged him to stay. But, though "people began to be acquainted with me," George recalled, it was not enough, and once again, he retraced his steps to Fenny Drayton.

Back home, as Christopher Fox no doubt complained of the wasted apprenticeship, perhaps Mary listened uneasily to her son's restless footsteps pacing the floor, and to the lifting of the latch as he let himself out into the dark.[11] "In great sorrows and troubles," he said, "I walked many nights by myself."

As he struggled with his depression, as he pored over his Bible, and as he reflected on the many different voices raised now in England, he asked himself where the real truth of Christianity was to be found. Almost inevitably, it brought him into contact with Nathaniel Stephens, the man who had succeeded Robert Mason as vicar of Fenny Drayton.

Arriving in the parish in the late 1620s, after leaving Oxford with an MA, Nathaniel took sole charge after Mason's departure in 1638.[12] Well read and intelligent, he was also a Puritan in the tradition of Anthony Nutter, committed and determined never to compromise. It was a determination that in 1642 led him to seek refuge in Coventry, where with Richard Baxter, he preached regularly at St Michael's. At the end of 1643, defying the Royalist Colonel Henry Hastings of Loughborough, who threatened to hang any clergyman daring to do so, both men had put their names to the Solemn League and Covenant.[13]

Nathaniel returned to Fenny Drayton late in 1645, and had possibly encountered his young parishioner earlier in Coventry. If so, then perhaps he had also seen him mixing in dangerous company. Like Richard Baxter, Nathaniel viewed the sects with alarm, and was equally determined to oppose them. Back in Fenny Drayton, and perhaps with that as his intention, he evidently devoted considerable time to young George Fox. "Then the priest of Drayton ... whose name was Nathaniel Stephens, came often to me," George said, "and I went often to him, and another priest sometimes came with him."

Clearly they shared substantial discussions, which produced a recognition on the part of the older men that George's search for spiritual insight was indeed a serious quest. Nevertheless, there were also occasions when they felt bound to issue warnings. For like many others throughout the land, George Fox was clearly intrigued by the Book of Revelation. "I had also great openings concerning the things written in the Revelations," he said, "and when I spoke of them, the priests and professors would say that was a sealed-up book." Nathaniel Stephens may also have added that he was something of an expert on the subject, and was already at work on a volume aimed at refuting fanciful speculation.[14] "I told them Christ could open the seals," George said, resentful of the inference that it took a university degree to understand the Bible.

On another occasion, they discussed the crucifixion, with Nathaniel asking George why he thought Jesus cried out as he had on the cross. "I told him at that time the sins of all mankind were upon him," George recalled, "...and so, in that he died for all men...he was an offering for the sins of the whole world." Much later, in his *Journal*, George claimed that Nathaniel was impressed. But that could not have been entirely the case. For, in George's answer, the Presbyterian cler-gyman must have seen the Baptist doctrine of general atone-ment. Furthermore, he evidently took it to task in his Sunday sermons. George, however, chose to remember that as Nathaniel somehow stealing his insights and claiming them as his own. By then, however, George Fox's spiritual journey had taken him further than either he or Nathaniel Stephens could have imagined, while what had perhaps been an uneasy rela-tionship between a young man and his minister, had become an irrevocable division between two different views of faith.

Meanwhile, as Nathaniel nursed his concerns in Fenny Drayton, George went in search of other ministers nearby, with whom to discuss his faith and the state of mind he now referred to as his "condition". Possibly, some of them were recom-mended by Nathaniel himself, hoping that someone else might fare better than he with his difficult parishioner. Perhaps George also reflected, as he tramped the Leicestershire high-ways, that had his relations seen fit, he could have been Nathaniel Stephens' equal, highly educated, amply qualified, and welcoming parishioners of his own into a book-lined study where he too worked on a volume for publication.

What is the ground of despair and temptation? he asked Richard Abel, an elderly minister at Mancetter. To his disgust, Abel recommended tobacco and the chanting of psalms. "Tobacco was a thing I did not love, and psalms I was not in an estate to sing," George said scornfully. Far worse, however, was Abel's subsequent gossiping. "And he told my troubles, sorrows and griefs to his servants," George said, "so that it got among the milk-lasses." Years later, the memory of the giggling girls still caused him to flush with shame. "I saw they were all miserable comforters," he said, "and this brought my troubles more upon me."

Yet, he could see no alternative. Surely, somewhere in England there was someone – Presbyterian, Independent or Baptist – who could help him. How could it not be so? Thus, in time, he walked seven miles north-west to Tamworth. But all he found was "an empty hollow cask" of a man, far less gifted, in his opinion, than those who had recommended him.

Another recommendation directed him back to Coventry, to a certain Dr Cradock.[15] "I asked him the ground of temptations and despair," George said, "and how troubles came to be wrought in man." It was another disappointment. "Now, as we were walking together in his garden," he said, "... I chanced, in turning, to set my foot on the side of a bed." Cradock's reaction shocked him: "... a rage as if his house had been on fire." How could a Christian minister regard a few broken flowers as more important than the great questions of life, death and eternity? "I thought them miserable comforters," George said again, "and I saw they were all as nothing to me, for they could not reach my condition."

Yet, stubbornly, he persisted. Eighteen miles north-west of Drayton lay Lichfield, where John Machen, Prebendary of the city's cathedral, also had a reputation for medicine. Bleeding was the solution, Machen advised confidently, to calm the young man's over-stimulated emotions, relieve his depression, and restore his system to balance. "[B]ut they could not get one drop of blood from me," said George, "either in arms or head, though they endeavoured it, my body being as it were, dried up with sorrows, grief and troubles."

By now, and probably earlier, George's emotional state was manifesting physical symptoms. As thoughts of damnation obsessed him, as he failed to overcome the troubles of his flesh, and as his anxiety mounted, it seems that compounding his condition was the Puritan upbringing that led him to see evil wherever he looked. "I could have wished I had never been born," he said, "or ... born blind, that I might never have seen wickedness nor vanity, and deaf, that I might never have heard vain and wicked words ... "

His condition caused him to shun Christmas. Though banned by the Puritan authorities in 1644, its pagan revelries considered superfluous to Christian belief, the ordinance was so widely ignored that probably not even Nathaniel Stephens could stop Fenny Drayton making merry in the traditional way.[16] George, however, viewed such levity with unease. Rather than feasting, he said, "I would have gone and looked out poor widows ... and have given them some money." Perhaps village festivities of all kinds were a trial, rousing the same awkwardness that in 1643 drove him from Atherstone Fair. "When I was invited to marriages," he continued, "... I would go to none at all." Nevertheless, once again, he was eager to be generous. "[N]ext day, or soon after," he said, "I would go and visit them, and if they were poor, I gave them some money." But, as Drayton's newlyweds expressed their gratitude, perhaps the more perceptive might also have wondered if, behind the generosity, lay a great need, an insecurity and loneliness that yearned for acceptance and friendship.

As they wondered about his loneliness, so too might Fenny Drayton's villagers have observed other troubling aspects of George Fox's behaviour. In London and other large communities, the Sunday church attendance which remained officially compulsory, unchanged from Queen Elizabeth's days, could be safely ignored.[17] In a small and staunchly Puritan village, however, even the briefest absence was all too obvious. Yet, George did not go. "I would get into the orchard or the fields," he said, "with my Bible by myself."

It was during those lonesome hours, and on his journeys in search of answers, that he first experienced what he later referred to as "openings". The first came to him at Coventry, one morning in 1646. All Christians – Papist and Protestant alike – claimed to be true believers, but what was the reality of it? "[T]he Lord opened to me," he said, "... that none were true believers but ... they were all born of God, and passed from death to life." Shortly afterwards, another opening came.

"[B]eing bred at Oxford or Cambridge," said an inner voice, "was not enough to fit and qualify men to be ministers of Christ." "At another time," George said, "it was opened in me that God, who made the world, did not dwell in temples made with hands ... but in people's hearts ... "

In themselves, George's openings were neither original nor unique. His Bible told him that Christians "have passed from death into life".[18] It also told him that "the most High dwelleth not in temples made with hands", but in the hearts of his people.[19] He must also have known that many General Baptist preachers had no formal education.

The significance, however, is that over a period of time, the Scriptures, his encounters earlier with radical believers, and his own questions, reflections and experiences, became fused together into an overwhelmingly meaningful assurance. They were also the catalyst for his liberation from bonds established in childhood, that would eventually lead him to develop an interpretation of faith that would speak powerfully not only to men and women of his own generation, but to others throughout the following centuries.

"And I saw that being bred at Oxford and Cambridge did not qualify or fit a man to be a minister of Christ; and what then should I follow such for?" George asked. Tentatively, he framed an answer; then he allowed it to sink down within him into a place of certainty. As the days and the weeks then passed by, the answer pushed open a door, wide enough for a man who thirsted after God, who knew his Bible as well as any minister, but whose own path to the ministry was blocked by those "others" who "persuaded to the contrary". Moreover, unlike ministers, who gained their knowledge from books, hadn't he, George Fox, received his openings directly from God? And were they not confirmed whenever he opened the Bible he knew so well?

"But the anointing which ye have received of him abideth in you, and ye need not that any man teach you," he quoted to his family.[20] But the verse from the First Epistle of John did not reassure them. For adding to their concerns were the visits of Nathaniel Stephens, voicing his fears that the quest for answers was leading George dangerously astray. But, as he heard Nathaniel's warnings repeated to him, George revelled in the victory he had so recently gained. "I smiled in myself," he said, "knowing what the Lord had opened in me concerning him and his brethren."

Moreover, George Fox was no longer a youth always seeking answers. As the inner assurance began a work of transformation, he sometimes spoke with certainty and interpreted the Scriptures with authority. "I met with a sort of people that held women have no souls," he said, "adding in light manner, no more than a goose." Unhesitatingly, he corrected them. "Mary said," he told them, "'My soul doth magnify the Lord, and my spirit hath rejoiced in God my Saviour.'" [21]

Nevertheless, speaking convincingly to others was far easier than seeing his own way clearly. "[W]hen it was day I wished for night," he said, "and when it was night, I wished for day." Yet, in his Bible he found the reassurance that his revelations were truly from God. "When I had openings they answered one another," he said, "and answered the Scriptures, for I had great openings of the Scriptures."

Increasingly, he also asked himself if behind the openings there was not some divine purpose. Moreover, could it be that it was somehow connected to that mysterious book that closes the Bible? "[T]he Epistles were written to the saints that lived in former ages," he said, "but the Revelations were written of things to come." Like hundreds of his fellow-countrymen, from many highly educated clergymen to humble troopers in the New Model Army, he was convinced that the Millennium drew near.

In the spring of 1647, now almost 23 years old, once again George left Fenny Drayton. "I was moved of the Lord to go into Derbyshire," he said, "where I met with some friendly people, and had many discourses with them." It also seems that he did not walk blindly, but that he was following information already received regarding people who might greet him sympathetically.

Almost certainly some of those friendly people were Baptists converted earlier by itinerant lay preachers, perhaps evangelists sent out from Coventry. When he eventually reached them, however, he found far more than sympathy. For at last, the young man who so often walked alone, found fellowship among a friendly people. Being with them, and talking to them, although he clearly remained a seeker still, for the first time, it seems, he experienced the comradeship of a shared understanding.

Later, he left the hill country behind and headed south-east into Nottinghamshire. At Mansfield, he took lodgings and followed leads among the surrounding Baptist communities. Eventually, one day, he walked into the village of Skegby. Oliver Hooton, then a Skegby villager, recalled later how it was when George first arrived. A group of villagers had been converted earlier by Baptist messengers, he said, but without leadership, most had fallen away. None returned to their parish church, however, and being friends, they continued to meet each Sunday. One half, abandoning any pretence at religion, met solely "to play at shovel-board and to be merry". The other, more spiritually hungry, met as a Separatist congregation. Yet, though they sat in silence before God, prayed and debated, they yearned for inspiration and direction.

Both came to them in the person of George Fox. "The mighty power of the Lord was manifest," said Oliver, "that startled their former Separatist meetings, and some came no more: but most that were convinced of the truth stood, of whom my mother was one and embraced it."[22] Oliver's mother, a middle-aged farmer's wife named Elizabeth, was perhaps the woman Thomas Edwards referred to in *Gangraena*, the book he finally published in 1646, as the female preacher of Lincolnshire. Whether or not that was the case, Elizabeth Hooton was certainly a woman of profound faith and religious vision. She was also a woman whose commitment and courage not only drove her to put faith into action, but would one day lead her very far from her Nottinghamshire home. She also saw the potential in George Fox, and was the first of his following that he mentioned in his *Journal* by name. Henceforward, she had assured him, her heart and her home were open to him, ready to be a hub of what she knew would be a great enterprise.

The affirmation was surely reassuring. For though he sensed

that a purpose was slowly becoming revealed to him, his depression, his disorder of mind and the torments of his flesh kept him from tranquillity and from rest. "I was a man of sorrows in the times of the first workings of the Lord in me," he said.

As the year wore on, and summer faded into autumn, and autumn became winter, he lingered among the Nottinghamshire Baptists. Sometimes he spoke at their meetings, sometimes he simply listened, and sometimes, driven by his melancholy, he tramped the countryside alone. As he did so, elsewhere in England, civil war was turning to revolution.

After Naseby, and the resultant supremacy of Parliament, the question of the political and religious settlement of England began to assume dramatic proportions. Very few individuals doubted that it would include the king. The king was also determined to secure the best possible terms for himself. In May 1646, he handed himself over to the Scottish army. In July, the English Parliament, dominated by its Presbyterian majority, opened negotiations with him: the Army would remain under Parliamentary control, king and subjects alike would sign the Solemn League and Covenant, Episcopacy would be abolished, and religion would be reorganized on the Presbyterian model.[23]

In February 1647, having withdrawn across the border, the Scottish army handed King Charles to the English Parliament. As they did so, Parliament's Presbyterians, anxious to be rid of the New Model Army, which they regarded as irredeemably contaminated by the sects and as a tool of the Independents, repeated an earlier demand that it be disbanded.[24]

The Army chose to disagree. In the brief years of its existence, it had tasted solidarity, victory and pride, and had been hailed as the instrument of the Lord. Its common troopers, moreover, had also heard that "the voice that will come of Christ's reigning, is like to begin from those that are the multitude."[25] Thus, in no way were they prepared to relinquish their divinely ordained role of seeing God's Kingdom of equity and justice established in England. Besides, their pay was months in arrears, and no proper indemnity had been issued for acts committed in wartime. In March, as troops gathered at

Saffron Walden in Essex, ostensibly to begin the disbandment, the New Model Army began to make its voice heard.

Urging that voice on were two groups. The first, the Agitators, were men drawn from the ranks to lobby Parliament to prevent the disbandment.[26] The second, a civilian political group that had emerged earlier in London, were named "Levellers" by their enemies, who accused them of favouring the abolition of property rights and the equalization of wealth. Among their chief spokesmen was John Lilburne, the man pilloried and imprisoned in 1638 for distributing illegal Puritan pamphlets.

The army, supported by many leading Independents, demanded its pay and indemnity. The rank and file also demanded fair treatment for soldiers' widows and orphans. In the House of Commons, Denzil Holles led the Presbyterian Members in carrying a resolution that all mutinous soldiers be declared enemies of the State.

As the army saw its honour impugned, at a packed meeting at Saffron Walden Church, 200 officers refused disbandment and demanded that no further attacks be made on them by Parliament. Meanwhile, the Parliamentary Presbyterians opened negotiations with colleagues in Scotland. An Anglo-Scottish Presbyterian alliance, aided by English Royalists, having restored Charles Stuart to his throne, could then enforce Presbyterian church reform in England. At the same time, the troublesome New Model Army could be disbanded.

Early in June, the Army marched to a general rendezvous at Newmarket in Suffolk. King Charles, meanwhile, agreed to the implementation of Presbyterianism.[27] Shortly afterwards, the Army took Charles into its own custody.

As the Presbyterians accused the Independents of abducting the king, the Army accused the Presbyterians of stirring up war. Shortly after a series of massive prayer meetings at Newmarket, an Army Council was established, consisting of senior and junior officers, plus delegates from each regiment. While denying that it intended to overthrow Presbyterianism, the Army demanded liberty of conscience for all.

Charles then opened negotiations with the Army. Meanwhile,

the Army moved closer to London. On 14 June, in the "Declaration of the Army", the soldiers claimed the right to speak for the people of England.[28] The Army also accused the Presbyterian Members of treason. Next day, to the chant of "Justice, Justice", the Army marched to St Albans. In London, leading Presbyterians began recruiting a rival military organization. When the Independents offered Charles a measure of Catholic toleration, the Presbyterian negotiators sought Scottish military aid.

In July, the Agitators called on the Army to occupy London. As Oliver Cromwell urged caution, his son-in-law, Henry Ireton, and John Lambert, a young officer from Yorkshire, drew up an outline for a constitutional settlement. The document, "The Heads of the Army Proposals", called for biennial Parliaments, a better distribution of parliamentary seats, free elections, and the right to dissent with the monarch. Additionally, a Council of State would oversee the armed forces and foreign affairs; Episcopacy, and legal compulsion regarding religion would both be abolished; while disabilities on Catholics would be eased. The king and his family would be restored to a condition of honour and freedom.

At the end of the month, during a struggle for control of London, Presbyterian demonstrators occupied the chamber of the House of Commons. Speaker Lenthall and 60 Independent MPs fled to Hounslow, where the Army was now camped less than five miles from London. As the Presbyterians prepared to defend the capital, and Charles rejected the *Heads of the Proposals*, supporters in London opened the city's gates to the Army.

On 5 August 1647, accompanied by shouts of "Lords and Commons and a free Parliament," 18,000 men of the New Model Army entered London. Many of them wore sea-green ribbons, proclaiming their support for the Levellers. At Hyde Park they were welcomed by the Lord Mayor, at Charing Cross by the City's Common Council. By the end of the day, the Speaker and the Independent Members were restored to Westminster. Denzil Holles and other leading Presbyterians fled for their lives.

With a threat from Scotland looming, uncommitted MPs increasingly aligned themselves with the Independents and the Army. But, as Agitators and Levellers saw the Army leadership then open negotiations with the king, fears mounted that their own aspirations would be betrayed.

At the end of October, the New Model Army took over the parish church of St Mary the Virgin at Putney. There, they sought to lay the foundation of an England that would reflect everything they believed they had fought for. Under the presidency of Oliver Cromwell, the debate centred on a proposal drawn up by the Levellers, "The Agreement of the People". Stating that sovereign power should reside in the entire people of England, rather than with king or with Parliament as currently constituted, the Agreement called for proportional representation, for biennial Parliaments, and that a single House should be the supreme authority in the land. Together with complete religious toleration, it called for all people to be subject to the law on an equal basis, and for all laws to be made for the common good.[29]

But, when demands were then made for the abolition of the monarchy, the Army Council brought the debate to an abrupt end. Nevertheless, weeks later, during a meeting of the Army's Council of Officers, Colonel Thomas Harrison called Charles Stuart a "man of blood" and urged that he be prosecuted for his crimes. For a moment, there was confusion, with the king slipping seemingly unaccountably from his confinement, and then being taken once more into custody.[30] In November, however, preconditions for a settlement were put to Parliament that would essentially remove all authority and power from the monarchy, and transfer it into the hands of Parliament. In mid-December, King Charles signed the Engagement, an agreement with Scotland whereby a Scottish army, quartered in England, would enforce a Presbyterian settlement. Under its terms, not only Baptists and other Separatists would be suppressed, but also Independents.[31] Days later, the Army Council suggested that Charles Stuart, "a criminal person", should be tried for his life.[32]

Far away in Nottinghamshire, as George Fox continued to wrestle with his anxieties, just as he had abandoned the Puritanism of his childhood, so he abandoned the Baptists: "... for I saw there was none among them all that could speak to my condition," he said. Though he knew he shared much in common with the friendly people of Derbyshire and Nottinghamshire, still there was something lacking.

Yet, sometimes, especially when he fasted for days on end, something happened – as if a storm that rumbled on some inner horizon suddenly erupted: "... such a heavenly joy," he said, "that I thought I had been in Abraham's bosom."

But, again, it was not enough. He was now 23 years old, and as he looked back it seemed that his whole life had been one long, and ultimately fruitless quest. The thought obsessed him, driving him ever deeper into sorrow.

Finally, alone in the midnight streets of a Nottinghamshire town, conscious only of his own echoing footsteps, and the weight of his burden, he knew he had reached a finality. Suddenly, it was all very clear to him, that he would be for ever a stranger – alone and friendless, unknown by God or by humankind. Suddenly, he realized that no one could help him, that all hope in men was gone.

Overcome by the misery of it, he admitted his utter inadequacy. "Then, Oh then," he said, "I heard a voice which said, 'There is one, even Christ Jesus, that can speak to thy condition.' ... and when I heard it my heart did leap for joy."

It was the crisis of his life; the moment when what he had struggled for years to grasp with his natural mind, became imbued with a certainty that left no room for doubt. "This I knew experientially," he said later. And looking back after many years, and attempting to give form to what is essentially beyond words, it still lived in his memory with a supernatural vividness. "I saw the great love of God," he said simply. And, having seen it, it inspired him to go on. "My desires after the Lord grew stronger, and zeal in the pure knowledge of God and of Christ alone."

With that desire increasing, it was as if a fortress in his mind began to crumble. When finally it collapsed, pathways once hidden were suddenly revealed, leading down into depths previously denied, and inward towards layers of possibility.

Similar pathways had also been trodden by many others, by mystics and visionaries throughout the preceding centuries. It was the 1640s, however, that saw the first English translations of works by the German mystic, Jakob Boehme, a man who rejected the institutional church, and emphasized the indwelling Spirit above the Scriptures.[33] Like the Familists, Boehme insisted that heaven and hell might be found in this world, and that the innocency that preceded the Fall might be recovered. He also maintained that it was God's ultimate purpose to restore humanity to that state, and that by the utilization of freewill, God's creatures were an essential part of the restorative process. By the time George Fox wrote his *Journal*, and probably long before, he had almost certainly encountered Boehme's works. How much he was influenced by them at an early stage in his life is debatable. However, if he had read them at this point, they almost certainly confirmed the validity of his own vision.

"I was taken up in the love of God," he said, "... and while I was in that condition ... I therein saw clearly ... " And what he saw came by revelations more powerful than those first early openings in Leicestershire. "For though I read the Scriptures that spoke of Christ and of God," he said, "yet I knew him not but by revelation ... and then the Lord did gently lead me along, and did let me see his love, which was endless and eternal, and surpasseth all the knowledge that men have in the natural state, or can get by history or books."

It was at those times of dazzling insight that George saw what he believed to be the root of his own mental turmoil. "And I saw professors, priests, and people were whole and at ease in that condition which was my misery," he said, "and they loved that which I would have been rid of." Seeing them revealed in their fleshly corruption, and subject to all worldly vicissitudes, it suddenly became very apparent just why such individuals were unable to help him. How different was the encounter with the divine, "the unchangeable truth in the inward parts, the light of Jesus Christ ... who ... did preserve me by his spirit and power."

Though conscious of that divine protection, he discovered nevertheless that the inner way was as hazardous as the roads of the world. For as he sought to know God, he also came face to face with himself. "But oh," he said, "then did I see my troubles, trials, and temptations more than I had ever done!"

He also seemed to recognize that in order to truly overcome such troubles and temptations, a purging was required. "Then ... there did a pure fire appear in me," he said, "then I saw how he sat as a refiner's fire and as the fuller's soap."[34] And, with the purging, came insight: "... and then the spiritual discerning came into me, by which I did discern my own thoughts, groans and sighs, and what it was that did veil me, and what it was that did open me."

Moreover, he also caught a glimpse of something profound: "... the Lord shewed me," he said, "that the natures of those things that were hurtful without were within ... the natures of dogs, swine, vipers, of Sodom and Egypt ... " But, as he recoiled in horror, he could not accept that some of those natures might also be part of his own being. "Why should I be thus," he asked, "seeing I was never addicted to commit those evils."

Since these recollections appear in the *Journal*, clearly they are tempered by hindsight. Nevertheless, the account is compelling, and it is easy to believe that this is similar to the process that took place, a succession of mystical experiences accompanied by powerful flashes of insight. However, though he came to understand a great deal about himself, clearly there was a point beyond which George could not go. At the last moment, he shied away. It could not be himself that he saw, it had to be others, for whom he was to take responsibility. Thus, and certainly by the time he wrote his *Journal*, he found a satisfactory, and largely effective, explanation for the temptations that so painfully obsessed his thoughts and troubled his flesh: "That it was needful I should have a sense of all conditions, how else should I speak to all conditions?"

As he confronted himself, and the prospect of speaking to all conditions, he also became convinced that he would not want for strength. "Christ who had enlightened me," he said, "gave me his light to believe in … and gave me his spirit … which I found sufficient in the deeps and in weakness." With this certainty, and equally convinced that he now possessed "the spiritual discerning", he gazed with new eyes at the world. "As the Light appeared, all appeared that is out of the Light … all was manifest and seen in the Light." He saw too, how the world had come to its current perilous condition. "And by this true spirit … I discerned all the false hearing, and the false seeing, and the false smelling which was atop, above the Spirit, quenching and grieving it; and that all they that were there were in confusion and deceit."

Thus he concluded that it was not through the words of others that God spoke to his people, words either written or spoken, but by the indwelling Light. And like many other mystics, he did not make fine distinctions. To him, the Light that was experienced so directly, was at once Father, Son, and Holy Spirit. That it was indeed the light of Christ, he saw confirmed in Scripture: "John … did bear witness to the light, which Christ the great heavenly prophet hath enlightened every man that cometh into the world withal, that they might … become the children of light … "[35]

To become a child of light, and to have life! This, George Fox had experienced for himself. He had also seen it confirmed in his Bible. Who then should speak of it to others? Looking back, he gazed on his solitary childhood, his friendless youth, the years of unhappy searching, and then, the encounter with the certainty of the indwelling Spirit.

But, though it seems that at this point he truly began to believe that it was for him to open to others that which he had received in himself, he remained unsure. Even before a huge Baptist rally in Leicestershire, when he drew the attention of the whole crowd, somehow it was as if he remained in the days of his searching. For though he had been brought to the Light, his depression and his temptations continued to beset him. Yet, many who heard him were moved, and as they spoke of him, his name and his message were carried through the Midlands. "For in that day the Lord's power began to spring," he said.

"There was one Brown," he said, "who had great prophecies and sights upon his death-bed of me." As they were repeated through the countryside, they became the subject of much speculation. Hearing that George Fox would also attend, a huge crowd was drawn to Brown's funeral. As it gathered at the graveside, and as the coffin was lowered into the earth, before that great crowd, George collapsed. "A great work of the Lord fell upon me," he said.

When he was then carried to a bed, some bystanders pronounced him dead. Others observed that he still breathed. Others still, as time passed, remarked that he was changed. "I was very much altered in countenance and person," he said. Later, he claimed that the entire episode had lasted for fourteen days, and that while in the grip of the strange paralysis, he was taken in the spirit into the heavenly realms. "And I saw into that which was without end," he said, "and things which cannot be uttered."

When he returned to himself, he attempted to give the experience form. "For I had been brought through the very ocean of darkness and death," he said. And, spread over that ocean, he had seen another: "the greatness and the infiniteness of the love of God which cannot be expressed in words." It was, he continued, as if he had indeed been dead. "Then I could say," he said, "I had been in spiritual Babylon ... and the grave, but by the eternal power of God I was ... brought over it ... into the power of Christ." Thus was the transformation sealed. "[M]y sorrows and troubles began to wear off," he said, "... so that I could have wept night and day with tears of joy to the Lord."

Not for the first time, George Fox had mirrored in his flesh the condition of his mind. His collapse, so significantly at a funeral, was indeed a death, the demise of the youth born in Fenny Drayton. Now as he rose from his deathbed, his flesh confirmed what had already taken place deep within his psyche. Like Lazarus, he was called out of the grave, and with his grave-clothes removed, he was set free to go on his way.

CHAPTER FOUR

The Prophet of the Lord

...the Word of the Lord went through him as a Lamp that burneth...

Robert Jones' Testimony concerning George Fox,
20th day of the 5th month, 1691

"NOW WAS I COME UP in spirit through the flaming sword into the paradise of God. All things were new, and all the creation gave another smell unto me than before, beyond what words can utter. I knew nothing but pureness, and innocency, and righteousness, being renewed up into the image of God by Christ Jesus, to the state of Adam, which he was in before he fell."

Thus, the weaver's son from Leicestershire, the boy who was taught how to walk to be kept pure, regained the innocence of humanity's birth.[1] He also saw it as a gain that might be achieved by others. "Now the Lord God opened to me," he said, "...how that every man was enlightened by the divine light of Christ...and that they that believed in it came out of condemnation to the light of life..."

Certainly George Fox absorbed his ideas from other sources. That God's grace was offered to all was held by the General Baptists. A view that in the earthly life humanity could recapture a state of perfection perhaps came from Familists and from Boehme. Nevertheless, they clearly resonated with his own profound personal experience. So much so, that he could only conclude that rather than relying on anything secondary – the opinions of learned men, or the words of a Holy Book – it was to the direct experience of God within that all people should turn. "For I saw in that Light and Spirit," he said, "which was before the Scripture was given forth … that all must come to that Spirit, if they would know God, or Christ, or the Scriptures aright … "

Like those of many other dissidents, his convictions challenged the Calvinist doctrines of predestination and of irredeemable sin. His belief in the primacy of the indwelling Spirit challenged the ultimate authority of the Bible. Together, as well as challenging Protestant orthodoxy, they also threatened the power and dominance of the clergy.

Equally alarming was the challenge that George Fox ultimately levelled at every other church, orthodox and dissenters alike. For, as further revelations came to him, and as he weighed them against all he had ever learned, and the expectations of the times in which he lived, he saw a vision that perhaps at first overwhelmed him. It was a vision that had been seen before: the true Christian Church, overcome by the Apostasy, driven to the wilderness, but longing for restoration. In revolutionary England, home to the elect nation, and alive with millennial expectation, surely the time was at hand.

Could it be possible, George evidently asked, that the Light that spoke so clearly within was the voice of Christ himself, come to restore his true Church to his people? As the answer took shape, so too did an awesome realization. Just as the Word of the Lord had once come to Isaiah, to Jeremiah and to Joel, so it came now to the weaver's son from Leicestershire: "… with and by this divine power and spirit of God, and the light of Jesus, I was to bring people off from all their own ways, to Christ, the new and living way, and from their churches, which men had made and gathered, to the Church of God, the general assembly written in heaven which Christ is the head of … "

Dwelling on the divine command, George saw a battle ahead. For if he was to bring people to the true church, then he must speak out everywhere against the false church that deceived them. That part of that false church was the Puritan church of his childhood, whose emphasis on election and sin had caused him so much suffering, was surely no coincidence.

"Thus travelled I on," he said at the beginning of 1648, "in the Lord's service, as the Lord led me." Unusually tall and broad, that which perhaps once caused distress, now served him well. For it is advantageous for a prophet to be imposing. Moreover, the miles already walked, through sun and through wind, had not only toughened him, but perhaps also moulded a once-plain face into the features of resolution. At the same time, the fire that purged him looked out through his eyes, while his voice – a large man's voice – proclaimed his message uncompromisingly.[2]

With a sure touch for the dramatic, George added to the striking effect. His hair he wore long. Though not uncommon among nobles and gentlemen, it was not usual among men of his own social background. Since Thomas Edwards frequently disparaged the long hair adopted by sectaries ("they wear strange long hair," he said), it seems that it was a deliberate flouting of social convention.[3]

He also discarded the coat and breeches of pale cloth he seems to have worn previously, replacing them with a suit of leather. Durable and resistant to hard weather and rough country, it was also distinctive enough to be memorable. Perhaps it also carried another message too. For the New Model Army's cavalry wore leather coats into battle, when they bellowed their battle-cry, "God and our strength", and lifted their swords for the attack. Now, clad in his own armour of God, and armed with the sword of the Spirit, George Fox signified that he too did battle for the Lord.[4]

"Let the youth speak," insisted Captain Amor Stoddard, at a religious gathering in Nottinghamshire. "Hear the youth speak!" Like Elizabeth Hooton, the Parliamentary officer felt his heart quicken at George Fox's words, and he was determined that the young man should not be interrupted.

Far more often, however, it seemed that it was George who was intent on interruption. "Dost thou call this steeple-house a church?" he demanded of a minister in Leicestershire. The derisive term, used also by Baptists, was designed to make it clear that it was people, not buildings, that constituted a church. Since George was also determined to challenge all manifestations of the Apostasy, his visits to steeple-houses were generally confrontational and aggressive.

The particular steeple-house in question was full, a public lecture having attracted a vast crowd. At the challenging voice, many looked around, including the woman whose question had provoked it. Anxious to understand a verse from the First Epistle of Peter ("Being born again, not of corruptible seed, but of incorruptible"), she had requested clarification.[5] "I permit not a woman to speak in the church," the minister retorted. "[T]hough," George recalled, "he had before given liberty for *any* to speak."

Incensed at the injustice, and "wrapped up, as in a rapture", he defended the spurned woman. Then he declared the nature of a true church: "... the pillar and ground of Truth, made up of living stones ... a spiritual household which Christ was the head of." In such a church, he concluded, "a woman might prophesy and speak."[6] Later, after the woman and her family sought him out, they joined themselves to his following.

Whatever the reasons that brought individuals to that following, each heard in George's message something relevant to themselves. For some it was the assurance that God's Kingdom was open to all. Others, having failed to find meaning in the sermons of Puritanism, found it instead in the experience of the Inner Light. Others still found it in the proclamation that a woman might speak and prophesy. In an age of confusion, for those who heard it and believed it, it was nothing more than the Truth. Filled with the same passion that inspired George himself, many of the newly convinced followed his example.

"Many were moved by the Lord to go to steeple-houses," he said, "to the priests and to the people, to declare the everlasting Truth unto them." As they did so, it was a sign that yet another sect had entered the battle for the soul of Christian England.

Throughout the Midlands, Presbyterian ministers watched with alarm. Earlier, and under pressure from Presbyterian MPs, Parliament had agreed the structure of a Presbyterian England. But, though the final ordinance was passed in August

1648, Independent opposition ensured that nothing was fully implemented. Nor had the Calvinist "Confession of Faith", produced by the Westminster Assembly, been fully ratified, while even Puritan parishes showed little inclination to purchase the *Directory of Public Worship*, designed to replace the Anglican *Book of Common Prayer*.[7]

Feeling themselves threatened, the Presbyterian clergy had no intention of giving way before George Fox. Moreover, as they insisted that the Light of which he spoke was that of conscience only, in that Light they not only saw Arminianism writ large, but behind it the hand of Rome. Some even asked if the belligerent young man were not a Jesuit in disguise, part of the order's plan for the re-conversion of England.[8]

Considering how best to oppose him, some wondered if a solution might lie in the Blasphemy Ordinance which in May 1648, after a two-year battle in Parliament, was finally passed into law.[9] Since one of its penalties was indefinite imprisonment for opponents of infant baptism, and since George Fox, with his belief that Christ had now come, rejected all sacraments, it seemed likely that he would be caught in the Ordinance's net. If not, perhaps the threat of it would cause him to lower his voice.

That, however, George had no intention of doing. Besides, he had something to say not only to ministers, but to all the great Puritan professions, all of them tainted by the Apostasy. "[T]he Lord opened to me three things relating to those three great professions in the world," he said, "physic, divinity (so called), and law." Physicians "were out of the wisdom of God..."; ministers were "out of the true faith ... "; while lawyers "were out of the equity, and out of the true justice, and out of the law of God."

He also spoke at a time of millennial expectations, and his view of the Apostasy and of the restoration of the church was clearly bound up with them. Quite what he expected in the 1640s and early 1650s, however, he never made entirely clear. Caught up in a time of upheaval and civil war, it was enough to know that God's Kingdom drew near. The details would presumably resolve themselves in due course. Until then, people must be called to godliness, while dishonesty and corruption were to be confronted and exposed. The Day of the Lord, a term used by the Old Testament prophets, was enough to encompass many meanings.

"[F]orewarning them of the great and terrible day of the Lord," and in the enthusiasm of his new calling, he issued warnings to anyone he saw as contravening God's commandments. Shopkeepers and merchants were admonished against dishonesty, alehouse keepers for allowing drunkenness, while entertainers of all kinds were accused of stirring the people to vanity. The common people, meanwhile, were criticized for dishonouring Sunday with their sports and games.

Such censure was also a rebuke to the Puritan authorities, who in George's view had signally failed to produce the godly society they claimed to represent. Though theatres were closed in 1642, Christmas celebrations banned in 1644, and many other traditional pursuits and pastimes forbidden, the regulations were widely ignored. "The days they had set forth for holy-days were usually the times when they [the people] most dishonoured God," he said.[10] That, however, as George Fox would in time discover, was not for lack of exhortation. For in the view of many of his countrymen, Maypoles and Morris dancing on Mayday were as English as football games on Sundays, and cockfighting with a surfeit of gambling in Whitweek. So too was drinking far more ale than was good for you if you chose to do so.

Thus, for every person who welcomed George Fox's message of the Light, others received his moral condemnations with anger. The "rude multitude" especially, with whom his relationship clearly remained fraught, seemed particularly resentful at attacks which appeared beggarly and mean.

Some people, who feared or welcomed political radicalism, saw George Fox as a Leveller. "Moreover when the Lord sent me forth ... " he said, "he forbade me to put off my hat to any, high or low; and I was required to Thee and Thou all men and women, without any respect to rich or poor, great or small." Such actions, as John Lilburne and the Baptist invaders of churches knew very well, were guaranteed to cause grave offence. For they challenged the basis of a society where, despite all reference to liberties, social distinctions remained rigid. Dress, deportment and demeanour all indicated a status that was reinforced by modes of speech, terms of address, the doffing of caps and ceding the right of way. Use of the personal singular, *thee*, to a social superior, just as the wearing of a hat before them, was considered a gross insult.

To those offended by such breaches of etiquette, it did indeed appear that political and religious revolutionaries were determined to plunge the land into anarchy. Such a conviction, especially with regard to George Fox, was reinforced even more by his youth. He was, after all, only 24 years old. Nor were many of his followers much older: a large percentage were in their early to mid-20s, while some were even younger.[11] The combination of youth and aggressive self-confidence was enough to fill conservatively minded elders with fear.

To his young supporters, however, George's claim that social distinctions were a mark of the Apostasy was both exhilarating and awesome. It increased their conviction that they were God's soldiers; that they fought to subdue that "proud flesh" which sought hat-honour, "an honour invented by men in the Fall," rather than "honour which came from God only". Indeed, said George, "the Lord showed me" that hat-honour, and all it implied, "was an honour below, which he would lay in the dust and stain." To be part of such a work seemed a very worthy ambition for the young people increasingly known as the Children of Light.[12] And as the Children of Light challenged the Apostasy, and others saw them as another step on the highway to Münster, the drama of England moved forward.

Early in 1648, as King Charles continued to prevaricate, Parliament saw hopes of any settlement vanishing. At the same time, further Puritan bans on traditional sports, plus the taxation that supported the Army, provoked pro-Royalist and anti-Army demonstrations. North of the border, where plans continued to restore Charles to his throne by force, pro-Royalist Scottish nobles mustered an army of invasion. In May, following a two-day prayer meeting, the Army Council resolved that King Charles should be brought to account.

With the king's eldest son, Charles, Prince of Wales,

declaring his support, the Scottish army crossed the border in July. In August, they were confronted in Lancashire by Oliver Cromwell and defeated by him at the battle of Preston. Anxious to retain Scottish and English Presbyterian support, the defeated Prince of Wales agreed to accept Presbyterianism.

In September, when the Levellers called for the adoption of the "Agreement of the People", the Army rank and file declared their support. Meanwhile, as Presbyterians called for negotiations with the king to continue, and Independents became increasingly suspicious that he sought aid from Irish Catholics, Independent supporters nationwide demanded that Charles Stuart be tried for stirring up war.[13] In November, this was echoed in the "Remonstrance of the Army", a document which also called for the purging of Parliament.

At the beginning of December, Colonel Thomas Pride, backed by armed troops, refused admission to the Westminster chamber to some 150 Members regarded as antagonistic both to the Independents and to the Army.[14] Later, following "Pride's Purge", what remained of the Long Parliament, popularly labelled "the Rump", declared itself the supreme power in the land. At the beginning of January 1649, it set up a special court to try the king. Under the presidency of Chief Justice John Bradshaw, Charles Stuart was condemned as a traitor to his people.[15] On 30 January he was beheaded at Whitehall.

Many people saw the elimination of the earthly monarchy as opening the door for the Kingdom of Christ.[16] On the day after the execution, the Independent divine, John Owen, preached before the House of Commons. "The holy, harmless Reconciler of heaven and earth bids us expect the sword to attend his undertakings for … making peace," he assured them, "as the days approach for … the establishement of that kingdom … the great expectation of the saints of the most high … so tumults, troubles … must certainly grow."[17]

In February, as the Prince of Wales was proclaimed Charles II in Edinburgh, the Rump resolved to abolish the monarchy and the House of Lords, to declare England a free Commonwealth and to appoint a Council of State to direct domestic and foreign policy and ensure national security.[18] In the same month, in "England's New Chaines Discovered", the Council, and the growing power of the army leadership, were attacked by John Lilburne. Days later, Lilburne and other Leveller leaders were arrested.

As a petition signed by 80,000 people demanded his release, a far more radical version of the "Agreement of the People" was issued. Together with the original demands, it called for the abolition of tithes, conscription and the death penalty except for murder. It also called for the adoption of trial by jury and full religious toleration.[19]

Meanwhile, in the Army the Agreement was received eagerly. In Salisbury, the rank and file of a regiment heading to Ireland refused to leave England until their arrears of pay and the liberties of the nation were secured. In Oxfordshire, troops mutinied in support of the Agreement and John Lilburne.

In May, as England was declared a free Commonwealth, John Bradshaw became the first President of the new Council of State. In a move to discourage Leveller influence in the Army, the Council of Officers forbade soldiers from presenting petitions except through their officers.

On 13 May, the day when a new Treason Act made it a crime for civilians to stir up mutiny in the Army, Oliver Cromwell led an attack on the Oxfordshire troops. On the 17th, three soldiers, denounced as Leveller mutineers, were shot by firing squad in the village of Burford.[20]

As tensions lay heavy on the land, the troublesome George Fox was arrested. Indeed, when he provocatively challenged the preacher in Nottingham's Church of St Mary, he knew very well that he courted it. For although all were allowed to speak after a sermon, an Act of Mary Tudor prohibited malicious disturbance during its progress.[21]

"... the Scriptures," the Reverend Nicholas Folkingham told his people, "were the touchstone and judge and were to try all doctrines ... and to end all controversies ... "[22] "Oh, no, it is not the Scriptures!" bellowed George Fox. It was "the Holy Spirit, by which the holy men of God gave forth the Scriptures, whereby opinions, religions, and judgements were to be tried."

Warned by Folkingham to be silent, George ignored him.

Then, to the open-mouthed congregation he proclaimed his own message and dismissed their church as a sham. Meanwhile, someone slipped out to fetch the constables. "As I spoke thus amongst them," George said, "the officers came and took me away, and put me into prison ... a nasty stinking place." When he was brought before Nottingham's mayor, sheriffs and aldermen, however, he quickly began to see his arrest as providential. Dishevelled and unrepentant, he proclaimed the message of the Light. Moreover, he said, he was in Nottingham at God's command.

John Reckless, one of the sheriffs, was intrigued, and later brought George to his own home. When he spoke there to Reckless and his wife, "all their family were wrought upon by the power of the Lord," he said.[23]

"Wrought on" was a phrase used often by George and the Children of Light, who saw in the physical trembling, sometimes a collapse, evidence that God was at work.[24] That the Reckless family were thus wrought on, surely reassured him that it was indeed God's will that had brought him to Nottingham. So too did other responses in the town. One young man offered himself as a prisoner in George Fox's place. Two other individuals brought to him a desperately sick friend.

"[S]he had been possessed two and thirty years," he said.[25] That she was brought to him, also seems to indicate a prior reputation for healing, a gift that he no doubt expected to possess. Had not Jesus commanded his disciples to heal the sick, and to cast out demons?[26] Moreover, with the Apostasy nearing its end, then the signs and wonders so evident in the early Christian Church, the gifts of healing and prophecy described in the Book of Acts, would surely rest on the man called to restore that church to the world.[27]

Released from prison early in the summer, George arranged for the sick woman to be taken to Elizabeth Hooton's Skegby home. But though the Skegby Children gathered to assist with her healing, her bizarre behaviour terrified them. "The poor woman would make such a noise in roaring," said George, "and sometimes lying upon her belly upon the ground ... that it would set all Friends in a heat and sweat." He, however, was undaunted, and as "the Life rose in Friends", he saw the healing take place. "She rose up," he said, "and her countenance changed and became white; and before it was wan and earthly ... "[28, 29]

George referred to the sick woman as distracted, a term he also used on other similar occasions. Although impossible to be certain, it was perhaps the condition that a later age knew as hysteria. If so, then in a century which saw much sickness as having a spiritual root, the ministry of a man of insight and charisma, convinced that he did God's will, was no doubt a powerful catalyst for healing.

Since the account was composed later, George also used words that he probably did not use at the time; while he may have said "friends", he may not have said "Friends". It was not until later that the term "Friends" was used, while the name, the Society of Friends, was not used in George Fox's lifetime.

Whatever took place at Skegby, unsettling rumours surrounded it. "At that time," George said, "our meetings were disturbed by wild people, and both they and the professors and priests said that we were false prophets and deceivers, and that there was witchcraft amongst us."[30] Like allusions to Jesuits, allegations of witchcraft were guaranteed to inflame. And so it proved at Mansfield-Woodhouse, five miles from Skegby, when George spoke there in the church. "The people," he said, "with their fists, books, and without compassion or mercy, beat me down in the steeplehouse ... " Later, they "set me in the stocks ... and threw stones at me ... " Eventually set free, he staggered back to his companions. "I was so bruised," he said, "that I could not turn me in my bed." But, just as he saw others healed, so was he convinced that similar restorations took place in himself. "The power of the Lord went through me and healed me," he said.[31]

Towards the end of 1649, George was in Coventry, visiting "a people that were in prison ... for religion." Later, he claimed not to have known beforehand just exactly what they were. "After I had reproved them for their blasphemous expressions, I went away," he said, "for I perceived they were Ranters, and I had met with none before."

By the time he came to recall his life for posterity, however, George Fox was very anxious to eradicate any suggestion of a link between the Children of Light and the anarchic, flamboyant Ranters. But, in 1649, even if he had not encountered them, which is unlikely, he certainly knew all about them. Indeed, it was probably a word hurled at him from pulpits and by those "rude people" who attacked him. For while there were differences between his beliefs and those of the Ranters, the enemies of both were rarely inclined to look hard for them. Moreover, in a period when people drifted from one sect to another, seeking answers in troubled times, while some Ranters probably moved among the Children, equally some Children moved among them.

Like George Fox, Ranters proclaimed the indwelling Spirit. They were also castigated as "Antinomians", the word used by Henry Denne in his prayer, and deriving from Antinomianism, the belief that Christians in receipt of God's grace were liberated from obedience to any moral law dictated by church or state. In one respect, seventeenth-century Antinomianism was a reaction to the despair wrought by predestination. In the heady atmosphere of revolution, however, it found extravagant expression – in smoking tobacco, in excessive consumption of alcohol, and in inordinate sexual activity.[32] But, while some Ranters regarded such indulgences as aids towards a heightened spiritual vision, for others they were a demonstration that "to the pure all things were pure."[33, 34] To all of them it was also a comment on Calvinism: if the elect were saved and the reprobate damned, then why not eat, drink and be merry today?

Many Ranters, including Abiezer Coppe, widely regarded as a leader among them, also saw their activities as a rebuke to a society which the Civil War had signally failed to change. Despite a devastating harvest in 1648, which caused widespread hunger among the poor, the rich continued to enclose the land, and the church to gather its tithes. Moreover, the Agreement of the People, seen by many of the common people as the foundation of a just and godly society, seemed to have died with the Leveller martyrs at Burford.

"For this honour, nobility, gentility, propriety, superfluity," said Coppe, in his *Fiery Flying Rolls*, published in 1649, "… [is] the cause of all the blood that ever hath been shed – from the blood of the righteous Abel to the blood of the last Levellers that were shot to death." But, he warned, speaking to the rich and powerful, and in words that sounded very similar indeed to George Fox's comments on proud flesh, justice would be done. "For lo I come (saith the Lord) with a vengeance to level also Honour, Riches &c., to stain the pride of all your glory … "[35]

In 1650, as Ranters and their fellow travellers were increasingly seen as a threat to public morality, and to the order of church and state, orthodox opinion demanded that they be restrained. Both the Adultery Act and the Blasphemy Act of that year were aimed directly at them. The Blasphemy Act of 1650, more rigorous than that of 1648, made it an offence for any individual to claim to be very God, to be infinite, almighty or equal with God, or to maintain that God dwelt in the creature and nowhere else. It also became an offence to affirm that acts of gross immorality were indifferent, or even positively religious.[36] Leading Ranters, including Abiezer Coppe, were arrested and brought to trial; copies of his *Fiery Flying Rolls* were publicly burned.

Given the widely perceived links between Ranters and the Children that existed at the time, then possibly George's trip to Coventry was to visit members of his own following swept up in the arrests.[37] And with the country in a heightened state of religious and political unrest, when he himself was arrested in October, during a church service at Derby, and then charged under the Blasphemy Act, no one was very much surprised.[38]

Later, whenever he recalled the arrest, in his mind George heard the echo of a church bell. "It struck at my life," he said, as if some inward antenna had warned of impending danger. "I spoke to … the people," he said, "of the Truth, and the day of the Lord, and the light within them…"[39] The entirety of the message, however, was almost certainly more provocative than the brief phrases he chose to recount later.

After being seized once again by armed constables and hustled from the church, he was later interrogated.

Was he sanctified? his questioners asked.

"...sanctified; yes," George replied, for he was in "the Paradise of God."

Had he no sin?

"Sin...he hath taken away my sin," he said, "...Christ my saviour...and in him there is no sin."

And how did he know that Christ dwelt in the Children of Light? his questioners continued.

"By his Spirit that he has given us," George replied.

Then, came the crucial question: "They temptingly asked," he said, "if any of us were Christ."

Though he recalled that he denied the accusation – "Nay, we are nothing, Christ is all" – since he subsequently left on record instances where he referred to himself as "the Son of God", even if he did not use that very term in the Derby church, he almost certainly used something similar.[40]

While he could cite biblical justifications for his use of "Son of God", and indeed later did so, George Fox's experience of the divine was clearly different to that of many who opposed him.[41] For him, it was the experience of the Light that was crucial. The experience of orthodox Puritans was otherwise. For them, words were primary, particularly the written words of Scripture. In his most ecstatic moments, when boundaries became blurred, George may well have lost sight of where George Fox ended and Christ began. Those who shared a similar nature would know on a deep level what was meant. Orthodox Puritans heard only blasphemy.

Clearly, in mid-seventeenth-century England, faith and politics remained closely linked, and beliefs that differed from the prevailing orthodoxy continued to be seen as subversive. Though it was also a view being challenged, since so much of a person's faith was bound up in their own individual self-awareness and allegiances, the challenge provoked enormous anxiety.

"...[T]he power of God was thundered among them and they flew like chaff," George said, recalling how powerfully he declared. Nathaniel Barton and Gervase Bennett, however, the magistrates conducting the examination, saw something quite different. In their view, the prisoner was "taken up in raptures". Eventually, after eight hours of questioning, along with John Fretwell, a companion similarly arrested, he was found guilty under the Blasphemy Act and given a six-month sentence at Derby's House of Correction.

The sentence infuriated him. That he who had brought God's message to Derby should be flung into gaol seemed an outrage. It was an anger fuelled even further when he learned that Derby's Presbyterians were using his conviction to reaffirm publicly that there was no ultimate freedom from sin in the earthly life. Even more was it fuelled when, in order to secure his own release, John Fretwell claimed that George Fox had bewitched him, and after paying heed to John's claims, many local Children then deserted the movement. Rather than driving George to despair, however, his anger became the catalyst for a furious campaign.

"O Friends ... if you had received the gospel freely," he told Derby's clerics, contrasting their tithes with the command of Jesus, "you would minister it freely without money and without price." Moreover, he continued, "you have a form of godliness, but you deny the power ... you stand in the steps of them that crucified my Saviour ... they loved to be called Rabbi, and so do you."[42, 43, 44]

"[D]oth not justice stand afar off?" he asked Derby's magistrates. "O consider what ye do ... take heed whom you imprison ... "[45]

"Think upon Lazarus and Dives ... " he advised Gervase Bennett. "... See if thou be not Dives ... "[46]

Even the bell-ringers of a nearby church were not immune. "Oh, take heed of pleasures," George warned, "and prize your time now while you have it ... "[47]

As his own time passed, and perhaps as his anger subsided, George evidently found opportunities for reflection, especially on the links between the inner and the outer natures, and on that Spirit that came sometimes as the refiner's fire. Clearly the subject intrigued him, an interest that was perhaps additionally stimulated by his encounter with the roaring woman and others like her.

In Derby's House of Correction he began to write down his thoughts on the subject. "A man might be brought to see his evil thoughts and running mind," he said, but could not himself overcome them. If such persons waited in silence before God, however, opening themselves to the Light, then Christ himself "will discover the root of lusts, and evil thoughts, and vain imaginations, and how they are begotten ... and then ... brought forth." When the inner corruption is then made clear, "submit to the spirit of the Lord, that shows them ... and he that hath discovered them will destroy them."[48]

Such insights did not impress Christopher Fox. Earlier in the year, after some probing from Nathaniel Stephens, he had reluctantly admitted that George had indeed left home with a great deal of money.[49] Now, the shame of seeing a son raised a good Puritan imprisoned for blasphemy, brought him with Mary to Derby. After reaching an agreement with Gervase Bennett, and in Bennett's presence, he informed his errant son that in return for Christopher's surety of one hundred pounds, and a promise of future good behaviour from George, the prisoner would be released to his family. Indignantly, the errant refused. Not only was he innocent, he was in Derby at God's command.

Back in prison, he embarked on another round of missives. "Had you known who sent me to you, ye would have received me; for the Lord sent me to warn you of the woes that are coming upon you."[50] The recipients, Derby's magistrates, remained unmoved. When George then bade them "tremble at the Word of God", Gervase Bennett laughingly called him a "quaker".[51] Like the pejorative "Lollard", it was a name destined to echo down the centuries.

In September 1650, the month before George's arrest, after following the Scottish army into Scotland, Oliver Cromwell and John Lambert finally routed them at Dunbar. But, in January 1651, after taking the Presbyterian covenant, Charles II planned another invasion of England. In Derby, amid rumours of Royalist plots, and as the Commonwealth strengthened its forces, the buildings housing the House of Correction became a billet for the Parliamentary militia.

Recalling that time, George maintained that the troops were so impressed by his refusal to be cowed by authority, and clamoured so loudly for his appointment as their captain, that their officers were forced to agree. Somehow, it seems unlikely that the rank and file should badger their superiors into offering a commission to a man of no military experience, who was not only a convicted trouble-maker, but who might also be a Ranter or a Leveller. Far more likely is it, that in order to pacify the troops, and to neutralize George Fox, the military commissioners were invoking an old custom whereby certain prisoners were offered their freedom in return for joining the armed forces.[52]

They "asked me," said George, "if I would not take up arms for the Commonwealth against the King." But, like Gervase Bennett's offer earlier, it was refused. "I told them I lived in the virtue of that life and power that took away the occasion of all wars," George said, a reply based on the New Testament Epistle of James, which regards outward conflict as the result of an inner lust for power and material gain.[53]

Whether or not he used those actual words, or believed later that he had, unlike many young men, George had served neither in the Parliamentary Army nor in any local militia. Nor, according to his own account, and never contradicted by anyone else, did he ever respond to aggression with physical violence. Instead, not only did he allow himself to be beaten, but sometimes he even appeared to encourage it as part of his witness. Thus, it seems that he always took literally the biblical command against killing, and Jesus' command to turn the other cheek.[54] Perhaps such a deeply held conviction was also a product of childhood. Although never referred to, it would not have been unusual if Christopher Fox – strict, perhaps frustrated, and in an age when children were beaten as a matter of course – was excessive in his use of punishment.[55] Nevertheless, whatever was the precise nature of the offer made, George's spurning of it not only earned him a further six-month sentence, but he was also removed from the House of Correction and flung into Derby's common gaol.

There, in a dark and squalid dungeon, he shared the damp

sleeping straw, and the ravenous vermin, of 30 condemned felons. Yet it was in that black pit that he saw how prisons became schools of crime. "I also writ to the judges," he said, "what a sore thing it was that prisoners should lie so long in gaol, and how that they learned badness one of another." When two of his fellow inmates were hanged for theft, it also brought home to him just how partial and unjust was the law. The rich might enclose with impunity the land that once fed the common people, but should poor men steal to feed their families, they must pay with their lives. "I was under such a burden for their taking away men's lives for such small things," he said, "which was so contrary to the law of God."

In August 1651, after marching south, Charles Stuart's Scottish army occupied Worcester. Marching to meet him were Oliver Cromwell, John Lambert and Cromwell's son-in-law, Charles Fleetwood. When Cromwell's army passed near Derby, George Fox was again asked to serve. When he refused, once again there was a price – a dungeon even blacker than before.

It was in that dark place that he received a visit from a group of his own former followers, Children of Light on their way to join the forces of the Commonwealth. Their leader, a former Baptist by the name of Rice-Jones, made it clear to George that his own belief in the indwelling Spirit led him now to deny the historical Jesus. "Thy faith stands in a man that died at Jerusalem," he taunted, "and there was never any such thing." Like some Familists, and others who saw Scripture as allegory, Rice-Jones went on to insist that "never any of the prophets, nor apostles, nor holy men of God suffered anything outwardly, but all their sufferings were inwardly." It was Rice-Jones and his followers, George claimed later, who were responsible for the charge that the denial of the historical Jesus was a common doctrine of the Children of Light. But, he continued, anxious to show that he had countered such heresy from the beginning, "I brought the power of the Lord over his imaginations and whimsies."

On 3 September 1651, Charles Stuart was brought to battle at Worcester. His defeat was overwhelming, and with his forces scattered, he fled England for France. Though fighting continued in Scotland, in England the Commonwealth appeared secure.

In October, George was released. It is hard not to see a link between that and the lessened threat to social stability and national security. Nevertheless, bar three weeks, he had spent an entire year in prison, much of it in a squalid dungeon. Although his physical strength had no doubt guarded him against ravages that would have overcome less stalwart men, it could not preserve him completely. Emerging into the autumn sunlight, he was weakened through lack of exercise, a poor diet and the depredations of lice.

It also seems, and perhaps not surprisingly, that the effects of his imprisonment also affected his perceptions and judgement. Only weeks after leaving Derby Gaol, he approached the city of Lichfield, where in 1651 only two of the cathedral's three spires still reached into the sky; the other had been smashed to a stump by the fury of war.

"They struck at my life," he said, as the two loomed darkly ahead. Clearly, something called to him, and took him hurrying towards the city. On his way, he burst into a field, surprising a group of shepherds. "I was commanded of the Lord to put off my shoes of a sudden," he said, "… and the word of the Lord was like a fire in me." Pressing his shoes on the frightened men, he promised to pay them on his return.

"As soon as I came within the town," he said, "the word of the Lord came unto me again to cry 'Woe to the bloody city of Lichfield,' so I went up and down the streets crying Woe." Since it was market day in Lichfield, the city was thronged, and when George Fox burst among the stalls and the shoppers, his eyes glittering and his hair tangled, the crowd surged away in fear. Watching in horror, they saw him run first this way and then that, all the time crying "Woe!"

"The fire of the Lord was so in my feet," he said, "and all over me." By the time George came to write his account of the events, England was a very different place to the land he had walked in 1651. As he sought an explanation for something recalled later with embarrassment by his own followers and condemnation by others, he wondered if stories of Christians martyred in Lichfield when Diocletian was emperor in Rome might be an answer. For he had certainly seen blood. "As I went down the town," he said, "there ran like a channel of blood down the streets."[56, 57]

Yet in 1651, perhaps his behaviour was not so remarkable. England had experienced three bloody civil wars, executed an archbishop and a king, abolished its monarchy, and seen the common people brutally put down after daring to present proposals for a system of equitable government. Moreover, as the elect nation awaited those events that would herald the Millennium, the whole country was gripped by religious excitement. Many people believed they were prophets, and many individuals, including Abiezer Coppe, behaved far more extravagantly than George Fox.[58]

Perhaps it was the sight of Lichfield's smashed cathedral, combined with his own imprisonment, and also some inner knowledge that such behaviour was not altogether extraordinary, that tipped him once more into a state where his deep emotions were reflected in his outward being.[59]

Nevertheless, it was behaviour that certainly caused distress in Fenny Drayton. "My relations were offended at me," George said. Doubtless, Christopher Fox had something to say about a son who, having spent a year in prison for blasphemy, then raved like a madman through the streets.

Despite the offence cause by Lichfield, however, Derby Gaol had given George time to reflect on the nature of the Inner Light, had shown him that friends could be fickle, and also how the poor were often punished with their lives for taking the necessities they could not afford to buy. The combination of experiences and insight no doubt ensured that the man who left Derby Gaol was far more mature than the youth who had been flung in earlier. It was also a maturity that would carry him successfully into the future. Moreover, it was not only Christopher Fox and Rice-Jones who had visited George in prison. At least one individual seems to have been sent on purpose from Yorkshire, a visit which together with certain correspondence, was now calling George Fox to the north.

CHAPTER FIVE

A Trumpet in Zion

> Blow ye the trumpet in Zion, and sound an alarm in my holy
> mountain; let all the inhabitants of the land tremble: for the day
> of the Lord cometh, for it is nigh at hand.   Joel 2:1

"*T*HEN PASSING INTO Yorkshire," said
George, "I preached repentance through Doncaster and several
other places, and then after came to Balby." And it was at
Balby that George Fox, prophet of Leicestershire, intended to
meet Yorkshire's Seekers.

Among the many "heretics" castigated by Thomas Edwards
and his Presbyterian colleagues were those they referred to as
"Seekers". They were constantly vilified in Edwards' book
Gangraena. In one instance he mentioned "some meetings
lately in the City, wherein some persons of the severall sects,
some Seekers, some Anabaptists, some Antinomians, some
Brownists, some Independents met, some Presbyterians
also ... "[1] The intention, he said, was that the latter might warm
towards toleration.[2] Though the meetings, no doubt to his
relief, were a failure, that Seekers were mentioned as participating is proof that by 1646, when *Gangraena* was published,
there were people convinced that they knew who Seekers were,
and equally, just what they stood for.

In reality, rather like Ranters, they appear to have been
more amorphous than their contemporaries believed: individuals or groups of like-minded acquaintances rather than a
coherent sect.[3] Moreover, no Seeker confessions of faith have

survived, if indeed they were ever produced, and it is from other written evidences, including those of hostile critics, that Seekers are presented to history. Many seem to have been individuals who grew up in orthodox Puritan churches, but who, like so many others, when they were no longer able to accept strict Calvinism, and were at the same time confronted by religious and political conflict and by millennial anxiety, were driven to seek answers elsewhere. Some sought among Independents and Baptists, some among Ranters and Familists. Some moved restlessly from one group to another. The group that finally claimed them, and sometimes held them, was often those known as Seekers.[4]

Like other religious radicals, Seekers objected to tithes and called for religious toleration. They also rejected predestination and the Puritan emphasis on sin. Like George Fox, many had natures that were essentially contemplative, that were nourished by silence and the journey within. Though they knew their Bibles and respected its principles, they sought after something that did not resonate to words. William Erbury, a former New Model Army chaplain, described anonymously in 1646 as "the champion of the Seekers", was familiar with the mysticism of Jakob Boehme and often quoted his works.[5] Like the Familists, and like George Fox, Erbury was also convinced of the reality of the Apostasy. Like John Saltmarsh, a fellow New Model chaplain described as the "the chief Familist in England", he saw the state church imposed by the Commonwealth as yet another manifestation of that Apostasy.[6] The evidence, Seekers believed, was its lack of charismatic gifts, the signs and wonders so evident in the church of the Apostles.

Seeing the ordinances and rituals of the Protestant churches as invalid, Seekers could only withdraw from them and patiently await a new divine dispensation. True Christians, said Erbury, should "sit still, in submission and silence, waiting for the Lord to come and reveal himself to them."[7] It was the opinion of some contemporaries that Seekers believed the new dispensation would manifest itself first by the coming of the Spirit, as in the days of Pentecost, and then by the establishment of a truly spiritual church, without external ordinances, whose inward grace would be confirmed by outward miracles. Some also said that Seekers awaited new prophets or apostles, whose calling would also be confirmed by the miraculous powers conferred on them by the Holy Spirit.

George Fox had assuredly met Seekers before, perhaps earlier in London, and also in the Midlands. Certainly he appeared to share many of their beliefs. As he moved into Yorkshire, however, this time travelling by horseback, he not only intended to meet Seekers, but was clearly expected, and possibly invited.

While in Derby Gaol, he received a visit from a John Leake of Selby, while it seems he had also corresponded with a certain Richard Farnsworth, a man at the centre of a Seeker group based at Balby, a village south-west of Doncaster.[8] "I sent those letters to thee yt thou desired to have wch was written when thou was in prison in derbie," Richard wrote to him the following year.[9] Now, as he rode northwards, it was Richard Farnsworth and his comrade, Thomas Aldam, whom he intended to meet.

Like George, Richard was brought up a Puritan, and in his adolescence he was zealous, attending sermons and lectures, memorizing long passages of his Bible, and admonishing backsliders. He was also, he said, a committed Roundhead, a term used by opponents to describe the political radicals.[10] In his early 20s, when Puritanism gradually lost its meaning for him, at first he was distraught. But, in time, when he and a group of like-minded individuals began meeting regularly at Balby, to sit in silence before God, he finally found a spiritual pathway that spoke to his needs.

Thomas Aldam, from nearby Warmsworth, told a similar story. Like Richard, he was once a fervent Puritan, but when his faith grew dry, he too found meaning in a silent waiting. When the Spirit finally came upon him, he said, the power shook him, rattling his bones and setting his limbs trembling.[11] He had also become convinced, he told George, that it was the Lord's voice in the heart that taught the children of God, Scripture being but outward testimony to that inward word.

If it was indeed the case that George was invited to Yorkshire by the Balby Seekers, he clearly fulfilled their expectations. For very soon, he was moving towards other groups with whom they were in contact. First, he made his way north-west to Stanley, north of Wakefield, where one such group met at the home of a certain Lieutenant Roper. And there, George Fox, who so resolutely refused to serve in Parliament's armed forces, received a very warm welcome from that very same Army.

It was also an Army that in the north of England was engaged in a military occupation. While some parts of Yorkshire were committed to Parliament, most notably the West Riding around Wakefield, Bradford and Leeds, during the entire course of the Civil Wars the north as a whole remained resolutely Royalist. Despite months of fierce fighting, it was only in 1644, after the Royalist defeat at Marston Moor, and the surrender of York, that the north finally fell. Both defeats, blows to Royalist hopes and northern pride alike, were also interwoven with old memories.

Since the onset of the English Reformation much of the north had resisted southern domination and Protestantism alike. In the 1530s, the popular rising known as the Pilgrimage of Grace had linked the northern barons, dispossessed monks, and the common people against Henry VIII. In 1569, when the north rose again, it was with the intention of freeing Mary Queen of Scots from English captivity, and of forcing England's Queen Elizabeth to restore the Catholic faith. Both rebellions were brutally put down; their leaders and foot-soldiers alike were executed as traitors. When the Pope subsequently issued a Bull deeming Elizabeth guilty of heresy, and absolving her subjects from their allegiance to her, many Puritans became convinced that the north was a haven for Antichrist.

Nor had Puritanism ever established deep roots in the north. Only in parts of Lancashire, in Newcastle, and in the West Riding, had it prospered.[12] Over the region as a whole, Catholicism lingered, while in Yorkshire, where Lollardy had left a tradition of anti-clericalism among the poor, Familism now flourished. Even where the Puritan clergy had been strong, many left during the Civil War to escape Royalist retribution, or to take up lucrative southern livings abandoned by Laudian Episcopalians. Later, the arrival of the Parliamentary Army brought the sectarian preachers, who, as they gathered new congregations, almost certainly tapped into the native tradition of dissent. The whole region, far less developed than the more economically advanced south and east of the country, was regarded from London as a dark corner of the land. In 1650, Parliament established a Commission for Propagating the Gospel in the North, together with a similar one for Wales, whose aims were to impose godly religion on those unenlightened regions.

Moreover, since 1644, when the Parliamentary victories at Marston Moor and York were achieved with the help of the Scots Covenanter Army, relations with Scotland had changed. Now, Royalist- and Catholic-leaning Yorkshire, straddling the main route south to London, represented a threat of huge proportions. The military presence, therefore, had several functions: to guard the route to the capital; to pacify a potentially rebellious countryside; and to oversee the winning of hearts and minds. It was also, presumably, to neutralize the Presbyterian clergy, who, like their colleagues in London, saw an alliance between Charles Stuart and Presbyterian Scotland as an opportunity to impose a strict Calvinism on England.

When George Fox was imprisoned at Derby, it was during a round-up of potential trouble-makers. The Army had subsequently attempted, but failed, to co-opt him into its fighting forces. After Worcester, when the Commonwealth once again felt secure, he was released. Within months of that release, he was travelling freely in a region that the Commonwealth's leaders were determined to pacify and dominate.

In November 1650, a correspondent of the Parliamentary news-book, *Mercurius Politicus*, made an intriguing observation. Preachers in the north, he said, "would do as much good service to the state as a regiment of soldiers in a shire."[13] George Fox certainly never made any mention of any agreement with the Army, the Commonwealth leadership, or even particular factions within them. But, by the time he came to write his life-story, such an admission would have been politically and socially unwise. He might even have expunged it from his memory. Nor, indeed, is there any evidence that any such agreement was made. Nevertheless, in the late months of 1651, as he moved through the occupied north, not only did many of the people he encountered share a common political and religious radicalism, but some of them, men very highly placed, clearly expected him and then made their support for him clear.

One of those men was Lieutenant Roper, George's host at Stanley, a town at the heart of the Parliamentary haven of Yorkshire's West Riding. It was also at Roper's house that George Fox met James Nayler.[14] Unlike George, the 33-year-old James had seen active service, serving in the Scottish campaign of 1650 as a quarter-master under John Lambert. He had also achieved fame among the troops as a preacher. "Such power and reaching energy as I had not till then been witness of," recalled one of Oliver Cromwell's officers later, who heard James preach after Dunbar; "... I was afraid to stay, for I was made a Quaker, being forced to tremble at the sight of myself." Nor was he alone, for "the people there," he said, "in the clear and powerful opening of their states, cried out against themselves, imploring mercy, a thorough change and the whole work of salvation to be effected in them."[15]

When James returned home to West Ardsley, a village just west of Wakefield, it was with every intention of resuming the life of a settled Yorkshire yeoman.[16] But, even as he followed the plough, his gaze often strayed to the distant horizon. Then, one day, everything changed. "I heard a Voice," he said later, "saying unto me, 'Get thee out from thy kindred, and from thy father's house.'"[17] Since then, he had waited in faith to discover where he might be directed.

In many ways George Fox and James Nayler were alike: each came from humble origins, and while lacking formal education, both were intelligent and intuitive, as well as possessing great gifts of oratory. Had they explored their individual histories a little, they might well have discovered something else they had in common.

Twice during the first decades of the seventeenth century, in 1623 and 1633, a certain Anthony Nutter, minister of West Ardsley, was indicted for Puritan offences. Though by then he would have been an elderly man, since Anthony Nutter of Fenny Drayton was reputedly a native of Yorkshire, it may very well have been the same man returned home. Shortly after the death of West Ardsley's Anthony, a strong separatist group in the area founded the first Independent, or Congregational, church in the West Riding.[18] Whether Anthony would have sympathized with their eventual rejection of the Church of England is debatable, but that, like him, the Yorkshire Separatists, as well as George Fox and James Nayler, all insisted that "whatsoever ys the invention of man ys not to be allowed in the service of God", is a tribute to a man whose influence clearly reached down the years.

George left Lieutenant Roper and Stanley in December 1651, and changing direction now, he rode 50 miles north-eastwards to Cranswick in the East Riding. There, he was welcomed by another sympathetic officer, Captain Richard Pursglove, while John Leake, the man who "had been to visit me in Derby prison", lived nearby.[19] Pursglove also personally escorted George to yet another influential individual, Durant Hotham of Winthorpe, a local Justice of the Peace, and a man who awaited the Leicestershire prophet with considerable anticipation.[20]

"After that I had some discourse with him," said George. "He took me into his closet, and said he had known that principle this ten year, and he was glad that the Lord did now publish it abroad to people." Perhaps the closet in question was Durant Hotham's study, where in his spare hours he devoted himself to a biography of Jakob Boehme, and where he might thus discuss with considerable insight the theory and experience of the Inner Light.[21]

On the Sunday that George Fox accompanied Captain Pursglove to morning service at Cranswick's parish church, the sight of the tall, weather-beaten stranger in the broad-brimmed hat and worn leather suit no doubt caused a stir. During the previous week he had been at Beverley Minster, and since then rumour had run through the countryside. When John Pomroy, the Puritan lecturer, finally concluded his sermon, it was said, George Fox's challenge to Calvinism had rung out so loud that the Minster had seemed to shake. Any of the Cranswick congregation anticipating something similar in their own church were perhaps encouraged by the sight of the Captain, who appeared to have quite deliberately eschewed his bands, the starched white collar that was so essential a part of formal Puritan attire.

Nor were they disappointed. "Come down, thou deceiver," bellowed George, "for dost thou bid people come freely and take of the water of life freely, and yet thou takest three hundred pounds off them for preaching the Scriptures to them. Mayst not thou blush for shame?"

The text of the sermon was Isaiah chapter 55: "Ho, every one that thirsteth, come ye to the waters ... " Did not God speak through the prophet, inviting people to buy without money? George demanded. Did not Jesus echo the same when he said, "freely ye have received, freely give"?[22] So why then did ministers live on tithes, he wanted to know, which people had no choice but to pay? Clearly unwilling to be involved in a dispute, and no doubt aware that Pursglove's presence was partly to protect George Fox, and partly to emphasize the backing of the Commonwealth authorities, the minister abandoned his church.

In his absence, and with Pursglove standing alongside him, George preached his own message. "I had as much time as I could desire to speak to the people," he said. Whether Purglove had anything to say to them too is unknown.

Later, after George recounted the day's events, Durant Hotham applauded him. He also insisted that if George were abused anywhere in the region where his writ ran, he should send word of it to Cranswick. If it was within his power, Durant Hotham would ensure that the culprits were brought to justice.

Leaving Cranswick, but promising to return, George rode

due west towards York. The weather, he said, was bitter, with frost lying heavy on the wide-open wolds. There were also few habitations in that empty country, and at night, huddled among scrubby trees, or in empty sheep-pens, he often lay chilled and wakeful beneath the cold moon and a sweep of glittering stars.

In York Minster, it was so cold that the breath of the congregation hung mistily before them, while the fingers and toes of Edward Bowles, the Presbyterian preacher, grew steadily more numb. "Then say on quickly," he said crossly, when George demanded the right to speak. This time, however, the congregation were in no mood for more sermonizing, and nor was there any Parliamentary officer to restrain Presbyterian resentment. When George was hustled to the door, and then heaved down a flight of stone steps, a satisfied Bowles saw at least one of the heretical sectaries receive a bruised head and a bloody nose.

Ignoring his wounds, and setting his face against the north wind and the sleet, George crossed the high moors towards the Yorkshire coast. Among the Cleveland Hills, and obviously once again following a pre-arranged itinerary, he attended many large separatist meetings. Nevertheless, not always did he feel himself welcome. At some of the meetings, he said, "they ... took tobacco and drank ale." To George, such smokers and drinkers were clearly Ranters. But, it was also a term that was used loosely to describe excess of all kinds, and he certainly used it later in relation to those persons whose beliefs and behaviour he regarded as disorderly. Thus it might simply have been the case that he encountered individuals who roused him to awkwardness or anger. Nevertheless, there were clearly many among the meetings who once again expected him, welcomed him and were impressed by him, and who then added their names to the loosely linked network that was gradually consolidating into a coherent movement.

"So the Truth began to spread up and down that country," he said, "and great meetings we had." At this early date there is no indication of how large the various groups were or how sizeable the movement might have been. "Great meetings" could have been 50 people, 500 or 5,000. Clearly, however, in a time of ferment, when it was largely through personal appearances that news and ideas were spread, many people turned out to hear the increasingly well-known George Fox. Clearly too, the numbers of those linking themselves either as individuals or as groups to the Children of Light were growing steadily larger.

In retaliation, Yorkshire's Presbyterian clergy began to organize. For not only was the movement a threat to their spiritual sway, and to their own version of faith, but George Fox's attack on tithes represented a serious threat to their livelihoods.

With that, however, George had no sympathy. One man, he said, the minister of a seaside parish, was so insistent that every penny due to him was paid, that "if the people went a hundred miles off a-fishing, he would make them pay the tithe money, though they catched the fish at such a distance and carried the fish to Yarmouth to sell."

But, just as messages were sent among Yorkshire's friendly Seeker groups, informing their comrades of George Fox's movements, so too were similar letters sent among the Presbyterian clergy. And though that clergy differed in their attitudes towards the anticipated Millennium, few were untouched by the anxiety it provoked. As they stirred up the people against George and his message, some accused him of being among the false prophets, "who privily shall bring in damnable heresies" that would appear in the last days.[23] Others, anxious to put an end to his disconcerting appearances in churches, especially with Parliamentary officers to support him, challenged him to engage in organized debates. That, however, was something that made him uneasy. "For the steeplehouses and pulpits were offensive to my mind," he claimed.[24] Though he clearly spoke convincingly to congregations and other public gatherings, the prospect of a formal confrontation with several Oxford-educated clergymen was too daunting to be considered.

Even when invited to speak in the church at Pickering, where the living was owned by Luke Robinson, Member of

Parliament, sympathetic Justice of the Peace, and one of the Commonwealth's leading men in Yorkshire, George still refused.[25] "I came to bring them off such things to Christ," he said. Later, with his hat very firmly on his head, he called on Robinson. "I told him I could not honour him with man's honour," he recalled. Robinson merely waved the potential insult aside – he was far more interested in the Inner Light – and like Durant Hotham, he invited the Leicestershire prophet into his study.

"I ... directed his mind to Christ, his teacher," George said, "and opened to him the parables, and how election and reprobation stood, and that election stood in the second birth ... " Though George Fox rejected predestination, he did not believe that all individuals were necessarily saved. Where the General Baptists believed it was the acceptance of free grace, for him, the elect were those who turned consciously to the Light. Those who refused were responsible for their own damnation. Robinson, already sympathetic, made it clear he was impressed. What his feelings were when his own minister, appointed by him to the Pickering living, abandoned it for the Inner Light and to follow George Fox, he did not say.

As he travelled on through Yorkshire, at some point George had cause to take up Durant Hotham's offer of aid. At Ulrome, when a minister punched him after insisting he leave his church, a word back to Cranswick ensured that the man was bound over to the next Quarter Sessions. For George, such a response was reassuring, showing that he did indeed command influential support. His opponents, however, viewed it with a resentment that fuelled their fear and increased their hostility, both towards him and towards the Children of Light.

Both erupted devastatingly at Gainsborough. After returning briefly to Balby, George made his way back to Nottinghamshire, holding meetings on either side of the Trent. At Gainsborough, he found the town in an uproar, seething with tensions after another of the Children had declared before a packed crowd in the market. As his own appearance provoked a fresh clamour, he was jostled into a supporter's house by an agitated crowd of Children, Seekers, Baptists and

Puritan ministers. And there, before the whole company, George Fox was accused once again of claiming that he was Christ. Moreover, yelled the accuser, he had witnesses to prove it. George, it seems, thundered back: "I was moved of the Lord God," he said, "to stand up atop of the table and tell them that Christ was in them except they were reprobates."

Once again, the conflict lay in the collision between different natures and different interpretations of faith; those which resonate to the inner vision and intuition, and those which find fulfilment in words and precision. At the same time, adding to the already overheated religious passions were a variety of social allegiances and political affiliations, as well as millennial anxiety and years of civil war. When George called his Gainsborough accuser "Judas", and did so more than once, to his opponents it was simply more evidence that he was indeed the worst of blasphemers. As the ministers among them wrote of it to colleagues elsewhere, they became ever more determined that the Leicestershire prophet and his heretical Children should not speak a word in their churches.

Some time later, passing back into Yorkshire, George Fox and Thomas Aldam, who now travelled with him, found the church door at Warmsworth shut against them. Though it was eventually opened, the agitated minister was clearly prepared for trouble. "What have you to say," he demanded, "what have you to say?" Quoting from Matthew's Gospel, he too accused them of being "... false prophets, which come to you in sheep's clothing, but inwardly they are ravening wolves."[26]

No, it was neither himself nor his companion, George retorted, his temper rising, but the minister himself who was the false prophet. At that, the congregation, no doubt yelling "Blasphemer!", "Heretic!" and "Ranter!", hustled the two men from the church and then locked the doors against them. When finally the minister and his congregation emerged, however, they found George and Thomas waiting outside. Clearly George was unwilling to abandon one last opportunity to confront the minister's Calvinism, and to call his congregation to the Inner Light. Clearly, too, he also liked to have the last word. But it seems it was to no avail. After George called the minister a "Pharisee", the clergyman grabbed him and shook him. Then, said George, "the people run upon me and knocked me sore with their crab-tree staves and abused me sore and threw clods and stones at me."

In March 1652, after spending the early part of the year in the region around Balby: at Doncaster, Tickhill and Warmsworth, George was back at Lieutenant Roper's house at Stanley. With him were James Nayler, Richard Farnsworth, Thomas Aldam, and several others more recently convinced, including another former Parliamentary soldier, William Dewsbury. "We had a great meeting of many considerable men," George said. It was a meeting whose implications and consequences were far-reaching. "The Truth was wonderfully declared amongst them and the Scriptures and Christ's words and the parables were opened unto them and the state of the church in the Apostles' days and the Apostasy since; and the Truth was mightily opened to them that those great men did generally confess that this Truth must go over the whole world."

That "many considerable men" – "great men" – were involved in the Stanley meeting, its purpose quite clearly to assess the current situation and consider future strategy, and that it took place at Lieutenant Roper's house, suggests the involvement and backing of at least some of George Fox's influential supporters. That Thomas Aldam attended at all, also suggests that powerful voices were raised on his behalf. For Thomas, subject to a charge brought by the aggrieved minister at Warmsworth, was travelling under guard to his trial at York. Intriguingly, both he and his military escort attended the Stanley meeting, while although the warrant also included George Fox, he was never apprehended.[27]

Quite what was meant by "the whole world" is not clear. The Stanley meeting may simply have been part of the ongoing effort to subdue and re-educate the north. It may have been the beginning of an attempt by an influential group of sympathizers aligned to broadly Seeker views to spread a certain interpretation of the Christian faith more widely. It may have had ramifications for a particular political faction within the Commonwealth. Equally, it may have been the case that when George Fox wrote his *Journal*, after so much else had taken place, he transposed what came later onto the meeting at Stanley. Or perhaps it was always his intention to convince the whole world. Whatever decisions were taken, within weeks, he was carrying his message and his mission towards a new and distant horizon.

Late in the spring of 1652, together with Richard Farnsworth, George Fox crossed the Pennines into Lancashire. Yet as they followed the packhorse trails that wound over gorse-covered slopes and slippery falls of scree, where but for the curlews and the buffeting wind all was silence, George's excitement was clearly tinged with apprehension. He knew that great things lay behind him, and that since leaving Derby Gaol his fortunes had changed. But, though he saw this as sure evidence of God's providence, there seem to have been times when he gazed on the hills towering impassively above him, when he wondered if the task ahead was too much even for his profound convictions and powerful frame. Committing himself to fasting and to prayer, as he and Richard left the mountains for the fell country near Clitheroe, he looked anxiously for a sign.

"As we went I spied a great high hill called Pendle Hill," he said. Rearing above the rough moorland, the hill's bulk loomed massively. Above it and around it, sunlight gleamed behind swathes of silver-streaked cloud. Like Lichfield earlier, the hill beckoned. And once again George knew he had no choice but to answer. "I was moved of the Lord to go atop of it," he said. This time, however, rather than leaving perplexing questions in its wake, the experience would be numinous, ecstatic and far-reaching.

As he heeded the hill's voice, George also knew that he must answer it alone. Insisting that Richard remain behind, and refusing to break his fast, he set off across the rugged country that lay between Pendle and himself. Reaching the hill, he began to climb. Struggling on paths where the stones slipped from beneath his feet, he grabbed at thorn bushes to haul himself upwards. Though the day was cloudy, it was hot, and as sweat coursed down his back and thighs, eventually he threw off his leather coat and his hat. Finally, with his breath heaving and his throat parched, he reached the empty summit. As he stood there alone, the world about him was hushed. Nothing moved but the grass, stirred into constant motion by the ever-murmuring wind.

Narrowing his eyes and peering into the far distance, he glimpsed a shining that he guessed was a great expanse of water. Beyond it, on a horizon of hazy blue, wrapped in many-layered veils of cloud, he saw the rise and fall of distant hills. "Blow ye the trumpet in Zion, and sound an alarm in my holy mountain," echoed the words of the prophet Joel, "let all the inhabitants of the land tremble: for the day of the Lord cometh, for it is nigh at hand."[28]

"Atop of the hill I was moved to sound the day of the Lord," George said. Atop the hill, and gazing towards those blue hills and the glimmering sea, he also experienced a moment of profound vision. "The Lord let me see atop of the hill in what places he had a great people."

Making his way down the same stony path of his ascent, to the place where he had tossed away his coat and hat, he discovered a spring of water trickling into a basin of rock. Bending towards it, and scooping the sparkling liquid into his hands, he washed his face and drank his fill.

Later that day, he and Richard found lodgings at an alehouse, where as the evening wore on, they fell into conversation with the landlady. As they told her of the day of the Lord, and how Christ was now come in his Spirit to teach his people, she urged them to write it all down.

That evening, standing alone beside the reedy banks of a broad river, and gazing on a landscape awash with summer moonshine, there was another numinous moment.[29] "And the Lord opened to me," he said, "... and let me see a great people in white raiment by a rivers side coming to the Lord." Beholding them, George saw the people of the Revelation, of the book he knew so well: "a great multitude, which no man could number, of all nations, and kindreds, and people, and tongues [who] stood before the throne, and before the Lamb, clothed with white robes, and palms in their hands."[30]

Next day, the landlady (George called her "the Ale wife woman") promised to copy the paper and spread it throughout the countryside.[31] That she did so was confirmation to him of the reality of his vision. It also made him all the more impatient to reach that distant land of blue hills and water, and after parting from Richard, he passed alone along the Ribble Valley and headed north into the winding dales of North Yorkshire.

"I ... declared freely and largely the word of life to the people," he said, "and ... passed up the dales warning people to fear God and declaring his truth to them." Just as on the eastern side of the Pennines, in the isolated farmsteads and scattered villages he found many people alienated from the orthodox Puritan church. Many of them, just as he had also expected, were members of separatist groups, some highly organized, others much looser. Almost all were unsure just what the future held, but from the messages that passed between them, they knew they were neither unusual nor alone. In the early summer of 1652, those messages also spoke of a man from the south, so that as George followed closely behind, he often found a bed made ready and a meeting waiting expectantly to hear him.

Like dissenters elsewhere, the faith of the Dales separatists was interwoven with resentments at perceived injustices and with social aspirations, some of which found an outlet in political action. In Dentdale, and Garsdale, and Grisedale, shortly before George arrived there, a decision by several substantial tenant farmers to withhold their tithes had escalated into a tithe strike covering all three valleys.[32] John Burton, one of the ring-leaders, opened his house at Stonehouses for George Fox to speak. Yet, though the Dales folk listened carefully, and though the speaker almost certainly promoted his own opposition to tithes, few were ready to be convinced. It must have seemed a disappointing beginning.

Garsdale, however, was also home to Major Miles Bousfield, perhaps a Parliamentary officer whose name was given to George by his powerful associates at Stanley. In turn, the Major directed him to another influential local man, Richard

Robinson, whom he knew would also be sympathetic. "As I was passing along the way," George recalled, "I asked a man which was Richard Robinson's; he asked me from whence I came and I told him, 'From the Lord'."

Robinson welcomed George Fox eagerly. In turn he escorted him to Gervase Benson, former mayor of Kendal and another Justice of the Peace, whose home at Borrats near Sedbergh, across the county border in Westmorland, hosted a local Seeker congregation.[33]

Next day, Whit Sunday, 6 June 1652, when he spoke at that Seeker meeting, George sensed that he was about to enter the landscape of the vision at Pendle. On the following Wednesday, the Westmorland market town of Sedbergh was thronged to overflowing. From many miles around, those who would find masters, and those who would find servants, flocked to the yearly hiring fair. In the narrow streets, shepherds mingled with cowmen, ploughmen with wheelwrights and smiths, and parlourmaids with milkmaids and kitchenmaids. At the same time, young men and young women eyed each other speculatively.

As people gradually became conscious of the tall weatherbeaten man striding powerfully among them, who called on them to follow him, once again there was an excited buzz of anticipation. The prophet of Leicestershire is come, who preaches the Day of the Lord. As word spread, a gathering crowd followed him along the cobbles. By the time he reached the church, so large had it grown that he climbed into the branches of a tree to make himself heard. Then, with a mass of faces gazing up at him, he spoke for hours. "The Lord Christ Jesus was come to teach his people himself," he declared, "and bring them off all the world's ways and teachers to Christ, their way to God."

Standing in the crowd, and paying very close attention, were two leaders of another local Seeker congregation: 34-year-old Francis Howgill, a yeoman farmer from nearby Greyrigg, and 22-year-old John Audland, a linen-draper from Crosslands.[34, 35] Like Richard Farnsworth and Thomas Aldam, both men had begun their journey of faith as zealous Puritans, who then moved among Independents and Baptists before finally finding their way to the Seekers. Like many other Seekers, they were also convinced that a time of great revelation drew near. "As soon as I heard him declare that the Light of Christ in man was the way to Christ," Francis Howgill said later, "I believed the eternal word of truth, and that of God in my own conscience sealed to it."[36]

In the charismatic preacher from Leicestershire, who held the crowded Sedbergh churchyard spell-bound, both men saw someone who not only shared their own convictions, but who seemed able to give shape to them in a way that was both powerful and unique. Later, after seeking him out, they urged him to join them on the following Sunday, when they led the preaching at a great separatist rally on nearby Firbank Fell.

During the intervening four days, as George stayed as a guest at the home of Thomas Blaykling, who with his son, John, was also a member of the same Seeker congregation, others of their number called on him. Listening to them, and learning of many similar groups spread over the fell country of Westmorland and Cumberland, he realized that he had indeed stepped into his vision. When Sunday finally dawned, he knew that if the harvest was to fall to his hand, every word he spoke should reach the minds and the hearts of all who heard him.

Many years later, Thomas Camm of Preston Patrick, a boy of twelve at the time, still recalled that day vividly. "And upon ye first day following," he said, "G:ff:, being Accompanied wth the sd John Blaikling, went to ffirbanke Chappell, where ff: Howgill & John Audland preached in the fore noone to a seekeing and religeous people ther seprated from the Comon way of Nationall worshipe."[37]

As George stood with his back to Firbank Chapel, and looked out over the Fell, he saw a vast sweep of moorland stretching away into the blue distance, a country transformed constantly from dark into light by the solemn passage of enormous cloud shadows. On that morning in 1652, it was also alive with humanity, as whole families arrived from every direction for a day of preaching, prayer and fellowship. By the time they had greeted old friends and then settled themselves alongside them, George judged that over 1,000 people were gathered on the fell-side. Meanwhile, mingling with the sound of human voices, the low tones of adults and the eager shouts of children, was the occasional cry of a curlew, the distant bleating of sheep, and the ever-present sigh of the wind. Sometimes, adding his shape to the cloud shadows, an eagle sailed watchfully across the sky.

At midday, after Francis and John had preached to them, the people paused to eat their dinners of bread and cheese, to search out more old friends, and to hear news of other, more distant communities. George himself had come fasting, and withdrawing from the people and their country feasts, he took only some water scooped from a stream. Then, once again employing that sense of the dramatic that is possessed by so many charismatic people, he made his way to a high rocky outcrop and then sat there alone. Clearly he had no doubt that having placed himself so prominently, in time eyes would turn to him, his Sedbergh churchyard audience would point him out, and the whole crowd would move expectantly closer.

When he finally judged that he had attracted sufficient attention, and also created a powerful tension, he stood up, atop his rock, entirely confident that a thousand pairs of eyes rested upon him. Then he spoke for three hours, passionately and convincingly, his voice ringing across the fells. The day of the Lord was at hand, he declared, when the old world would burn up as a parchment in the fire. "I opened the prophets and the figures and shadows," he said, "and turned them to Christ the substance, and then opened the parables of Christ and the things that had been hid from the beginning, and showed them the estate of the Epistles how they were written to the elect ... "

Furthermore, he said, the days of the false church, the church of the Apostasy, with its hireling priests and its tithes, were over and done. For the days were now come to fruition, and he, George Fox of Leicestershire, a prophet of God, had come to the Seekers gathered on Firbank Fell, in the Commonwealth of England, in the year 1652, to announce that their seeking was at an end.

Christ was now come to his people, he said, and he urged them to renounce the past with its ungodliness and corruption, and to enter the church that now lived within them, "that they might all come to know Christ their teacher, their counsellor, their shepherd to feed them, and their bishop to oversee them, and their prophet to open to them, and to know their bodies to be the temples of God and Christ for them to dwell in."

By the time George Fox declared his message on Firbank Fell, he had travelled more than miles from Derby Gaol. Clearly there were human forces behind him, the Seekers who had contacted him earlier and then promoted his campaign, and the influential men who were presumably part of the same network, and who had welcomed him and then passed him to others of their fellowship.

But George himself was also a driven man and he would not have stood before the Westmorland Seekers unless his own determination and convictions had carried him there. Through his own diligent searching he had found an expression of faith that set him free from depression and anxiety, and which at the same time answered the need created in childhood that he walk in purity. Recognizing the power of his vision, and convinced that it was no more than the Truth, he was determined to oppose the church that created in others the anxiety he had suffered himself, and also to share with those others the liberating message of the Inner Light.

Gazing on the sea of eager faces before him, hearing the wind, and seeing the fells awash with summer sunlight, George Fox surely had no doubt that he was carried on the breath of the Spirit. Nor could he have been in any doubt that he was indeed destined to see the Apostasy overturned, and that when the true Christian Church was restored first in England, apostles from the elect nation would then carry the message of the Light into the furthest corners of the earth.

CHAPTER SIX

Children of Light

You will say, Christ saith this, and the apostles say this, but what canst thou say? Art thou a child of Light, and hast thou walked in the Light, and what thou speakest, is it inwardly from God?"

George Fox,
St Mary's Church, Ulverston, July 1652

O N A DAY LATE IN JUNE 1652, George Fox and a companion strode purposefully along a dry and dusty road. Behind them it wound away north-eastwards, passing the southern tip of Lake Windermere before continuing on towards Kendal. Ahead it stretched south through Lancashire's Furness peninsula, until finally it met the narrow strip of water that separates the mainland from the long island of Walney.

A mile south of the market town of Ulverston they left the road, and with their backs to a ragged growth of hawthorn, they settled themselves on the sun-warmed grass. Before them stood a tall three-storeyed house. Its walls were of dun-coloured plaster and its roof-tiles of grey slate, while the glass in its stone-mullioned windows gleamed faintly green. Clustered about it, in a satisfying patchwork of varied shapes and earthy hues shot with the brilliance of summer flowers, was an array of kitchen-gardens and orchards, stables, byres and barnyards. Swathed in dappled shadow and airy light, the whole complex seemed fused into the drowsy fell country that lay about it.

As George Fox gazed on the peaceful scene, behind him lay two extraordinary weeks, that had further confirmed his Pendle vision and then eventually brought him to this quiet spot in Furness.

When he had finally stepped down from his rocky pulpit on Firbank Fell, his face raw from the moorland wind and his throat parched, he had found a great press of people waiting for him. Some were eager to know of his travels in Yorkshire, or his days among the Nottinghamshire Baptists, or his year in Derby Gaol. Others shared accounts of intense spiritual experiences, or spoke of convictions similar to his own. Others still asked if he truly believed that the time the Seekers awaited was come.

Eventually, late in the afternoon, as the last of the crowd made its way homeward, together with Francis Howgill and John Audland, George made his own way across the sweet-smelling country to Crosslands, John's house near Preston Patrick. It was there that something occurred that George highlighted later in his Journal. "And there came John Story to me ... and, said he, 'Will you take a pipe of tobacco,' saying, 'Come all is ours.'" At that time John Story was a young man of 22, and perhaps influenced, as young people often are, by the most colourful of prevailing attitudes.[1] However, George was anxious that his words should suggest something specific. "I saw he had a flashy, empty notion of religion," he added. He also made it clear that although he was a non-smoker, in a gesture of goodwill he touched John's pipe to his lips. Having thus implied that John Story was once a Ranter, while he, George Fox was always a conciliator, he left his words to do their work.

At John Audland's house he also learned more about the region to which he had been directed. Like parts of Yorkshire, it was a land of rough country and harsh climate, whose grudging soil yielded only small crops of oats, barley and beans. During the first decades of the century, which had seen an increase in England's overall population, the north-west, unable to support larger numbers, had been devastated by famine.[2] Later, between 1646 and 1650, desperately poor harvests had not only meant no bread, but no seed for following years. Exacerbating such poverty was the disruption caused by civil war; in areas where administrative services had broken down, where no Justices of the Peace oversaw poor relief, whole families were driven to starvation. In Cumberland, in 1649, some 30,000 families went hungry.[3]

Born of such a land, where remote villages were also isolated by snow for many winter weeks, the people were tough and independent. Given to drawing their own conclusions, many had rejected the national church with its harsh doctrines and ruinous tithes for a separatism that answered a yearning for social justice and individual worth.

The group which included Francis and John had first come together under the ministry of Thomas Taylor, an Oxford-educated clergyman, who like many of his colleagues could not reconcile his conscience with the forms and doctrines of the Church of England. Shortly before George's arrival in the north-west, however, overcome with reservations, he resumed the practice of infant baptism. Unable to reconcile that with their own rejection of ordinances, his congregation requested that he leave them.[4] Nevertheless, led by Francis and John, they continued to meet, and it was at their chapel at Preston Patrick, just south of Kendal, that on Wednesday, 16 June, George Fox arrived to address their regular monthly meeting.

Many had travelled huge distances to be there, from Sedbergh, Kendal, Underbarrow, Grayrigg and Hutton in Westmorland, from Yealand and Kellet in Lancashire. Though most would also have been on Firbank Fell, that huge crowd had encompassed many shades of opinion and commitment. The monthly meeting, by contrast, comprised the region's most decided separatists, men who were also the leaders of their congregations.

Clearly a plan had been formulated earlier. And clearly Francis and John were convinced that George Fox was indeed a man awaited by the Seekers, sent to proclaim the advent of the truly spiritual church, and to gather a new band of apostles. If they were to establish a base in the north-west, however, it was essential that the leaders at Preston Patrick should also be convinced. Once again, Thomas Camm recalled the event:

> J:A: would have had G:ff. to have gone into ye place or pew Where vsiually he & the preachr did sitt, but he refuised, & tooke A back Seat neare the doore, & J.C: satt downe by him, where he satt sillent waiteing upon God about halfe an hour, in wch time of silence ff H seemed uneasey, and pulled out his bible, & opened it, and stood up severall times, sitting downe againe and Closeing his Booke, A dread & ffeare being upon him yt he durst not begin to preach. After the said silence and waiteing, G:ff stood up in the mighty power of God, & in ye demonstration thereof was his mouth opened to preach Christ Jesus, the Light of life ...

"A nottable day," Thomas concluded, "Indeede never to be forgotten by me ... "[5] Nor was it forgotten by those who sat about him. By his own silence, George identified himself with his hosts. By his dramatic lengthening of that silence, however, with its consequent implication that he reached greater depths and would thus deliver a message all the more profound, then just as on Firbank Fell the previous Sunday, he drew every mind to himself.

Moreover, not only did he also convince them that his message was from God, and that he was a leader they could trust, he also spurred them to action. Within days, the leaders at Preston Patrick were opening George's way in all the towns and villages that were their homes.

At Kendal, Westmorland's largest town and a centre of the region's woollen manufacture, he preached in the town hall. As he then headed west into the Lakelands, and then south towards Morcambe Bay, walking alongside him were many of his new companions. Striding through that country of high peaks, deep water and wide glimmering sands, filled with enthusiasm and convinced that a time long awaited was come, they were surely in no doubt that they were the apostles of a new age, come to restore an ancient truth to a troubled and hungry land.

On Sunday, 20 June, George approached Staveley, to the south of Lake Windermere. By now, he had been almost three weeks in the region, and news of his successes had spread. That he had captivated the Seekers probably evoked little surprise among Puritan ministers, for like their colleagues elsewhere, they believed that once orthodox Protestantism was abandoned, individuals were open to heresy of all kinds. That he might seduce their own congregations, however, was another matter entirely.

Thus, Staveley's minister, Gabriel Camelford, watched with satisfaction as his churchwarden, John Knipe, led his fellows in dragging the intruder from their church and then hurling him over a wall into the graveyard. The intruder himself was furious at being denied. Later, after discovering several members of the congregation in the local alehouse, where they spent the hours between morning and afternoon service, he declared his message to them there.

The achievement inspired him to hurry three miles to Lindale, where he arrived in time for the afternoon service. But there, though given leave to speak, he received another rebuff. This time, however, Captain Adam Sandys, local constable and one of the congregation's leading men, simply dismissed George's message with a few humorous words.[6] Though the congregation may have sniggered, George was not amused. "I...admonished him," he said, "of his lightness and of his jesting." Clearly, in the opinion of the son of Righteous Christer, there was no room for light-heartedness in the realm of faith. Any encounter with it probably made him uneasy, rousing those deep insecurities that had once driven him from Atherstone Fair. Unable to bend, unsure how to respond, he projected his anxiety onto Sandys. "It was not seemly for a great professor as he was," he said stiffly.

Despite the rejection at Staveley and Lindale, that so many of the region's Seekers flocked to him doubtless reassured him that his was the true faith, and that his opponents were creatures of the Apostasy. Like those in Yorkshire, many of the north-western converts were countrymen, shopkeepers and small merchants. Many were also young, eighteen, nineteen, in their 20s or early 30s. That some of the youngest, nineteen-year-old Edward Burrough of Underbarrow and eighteen-year-old Ambrose Rigge of Grayrigg, were cast out by their families, perhaps seemed of little consequence. After all, George first left his family when he was nineteen, while James Nayler believed himself called quite unambiguously to leave a family which also included a wife. Perhaps it also seemed of little consequence that parents saw their children as seduced by fanatics, or that families were torn apart. For had not Jesus prophesied that "a man's foes shall be they of his own household"?[7] Were not his disciples men who "forsook all, and followed him"?[8] Much like those men of Galilee, England's Children of Light fixed their eyes on their mission and the future, rather than on the everyday present, suddenly so colourless and insignificant.[9]

Yet, though many of the Westmorland Children were young, and workaday yeomen and shopkeepers, numbered among them were Miles Bousfield, Richard Robinson, and Gervase Benson, men as influential and powerful as those "considerable men" who not many weeks earlier had convened the meeting at Stanley. Now, as he gazed on the grey-roofed house, surrounded by its orchards and barns, George Fox was clearly hoping that another considerable man would shortly be among his supporters.

Judge of Assize of the Chester and North Wales Circuit, Attorney for the County of Lancashire, and Vice-Chancellor of the Duchy of Lancaster, the 54-year-old Thomas Fell was not only a prominent man in the north-west, but one whose network of contacts reached into the governing heart of the Commonwealth.[10] Many were established years earlier, during a legal training at Gray's Inn among men who went on to produce the Petition of Right and the Grand Remonstrance, and who then overthrew the bishops and defeated the king.

A supporter of the Parliamentary cause, in 1645, Thomas became a Member of Parliament for Lancaster. Between 1647 and 1649, however, possibly to avoid the potential repercussions of conflict with the king, he absented himself from Westminster. Thus, when Charles was tried and executed, his name appeared on no warrants. Nevertheless, he remained on intimate terms with men far more prominent, most notably, John Bradshaw, the man who presided at the king's trial. A fellow Gray's Inn student, Bradshaw was now not only Thomas Fell's immediate professional superior, but as President of the Council of State, one of the most senior men in the Commonwealth.

That Thomas Fell was shrewd was demonstrated by more than his earlier absence from Westminster. As much in need of money as the monarchy it replaced, the Commonwealth had maintained a policy instituted by the Long Parliament in 1643 for the confiscation and sale of Royalist properties.[11] Since appointees to the resultant county boards of sequestration were not only supporters of the Parliamentary cause, but also local men, it was perhaps not surprising that many used their privileged knowledge to acquire such properties at advantageous prices. Since his appointment in 1643 to his own local committee, and as Thomas Fell judiciously added to his family holdings, Swarthmoor Hall was becoming one of the largest and richest estates in Furness.[12]

Thomas Fell was also regarded as a man with an interest in religion. As a leading Puritan, his name headed the lay list of a Presbyterian classis established in Lancashire in 1646. Since he also leaned towards Independency, he was clearly also in favour of toleration. Together with his much younger wife, he was also well known for receiving travelling ministers and itinerant preachers. Thus, it was with considerable optimism that George bade farewell to his companion, and prepared to knock on Thomas Fell's front door.[13]

The Judge, however, was not at home, he was away on the Welsh circuit and would not return for some weeks. His wife was also absent, although expected home later that day. Nevertheless, with traditions of hospitality to be observed, George was ushered by a servant into the house. No doubt believing the coincidence to be a happy one, the same person then ushered him into the presence of the local clergyman, who by chance had also come to call.

One look at William Lampitt told George all he needed to know. For in the vicar of Ulverston he saw a man very like Nathaniel Stephens, an Oxford-educated Puritan, secure in his faith, at home in his parish, and confident of his patron, Thomas Fell, who had almost certainly presented him to the living. Like Nathaniel, William was also a man with the courage of his convictions. Though three times imprisoned by Royalists, who on each occasion had sequestered his possessions, he had neither renounced his beliefs and allegiances nor abandoned his ministry.[14] Thus, he was not easily intimidated. Like his patron, William leaned towards Independency, while as a close friend of Paul Hobson, one of the Army's most prominent Particular Baptists, he was also wedded firmly to Calvinism. As such, he could never agree with George Fox.

Nevertheless, although William Lampitt had doubtless heard of the Leicestershire prophet's exploits, perhaps from Gabriel Camelford or Adam Sandys, his first impression of the intense 28-year-old was probably of a young man who held his errors in good conscience. Indeed, something of the sort seems to have encouraged him to reach out a hand of friendship. The combination of Calvinism and an Oxford education, however, was too much. "He would have owned me," George said later, "but I could not own him ... he was so full of filth." Later, after debate descended into argument, George called William Lampitt a Ranter. On the contrary, the clergyman evidently replied, the only Ranter present was Mr Fox.

Like William Lampitt, Margaret Fell had heard reports of a turbulent stranger, and confessed later that she was intrigued.[15] When she arrived home to find him sitting in her parlour, however, it was a shock. So too were the breathless accounts of her over-excited children, of raised voices, and of their clergyman leaving without his customary well-mannered goodbyes. The person of the stranger was perhaps even more of a shock. Taller and broader than most other men, his long hair straggling, his leather suit travel-stained, and his blunt and sometimes broken phrases delivered in broad country Leicestershire, he was a combination quite unlike any other preacher that had come knocking at Swarthmoor's door.

Moreover, not only was he not the least deferential, but he showed not the slightest remorse, neither for the commotion caused earlier, nor for the tensions abroad in the previously tranquil house. That evening he declared his message to Margaret and her children. Afterwards, she invited him to spend the night at Swarthmoor Hall.

Margaret Fell was the daughter of John Askew, a local man she described later as a gentleman, whose family had been Furness landowners for several generations. In 1632, when she was between seventeen and eighteen years old, she married Thomas Fell, then a rising barrister of 34.[16] Since then they had produced eight children, and although one died in infancy, the surviving six girls and one boy were all healthy and strong. The eldest, named Margaret after her mother, was a young woman of nineteen. After her came Bridget at seventeen, fifteen-year-old Isabel, fourteen-year-old George, ten-year-old Sarah, five-year-old Mary, and then the baby, Susannah, who was two.

Years later Margaret described her marriage as a happy one. Yet though husband and wife shared a common concern for their family, and a commitment to Bible reading and family prayers, Margaret also recalled that like so many others in her turbulent age, this had failed to satisfy. For 20 years, she confessed later, "I was inquiring and seeking."[17] Moreover, not once in those years had any of the numerous preachers welcomed to Swarthmoor ever assuaged her restlessness.

On the day after his encounter with George Fox, William Lampitt returned to Swarthmoor. Perhaps during the previous night he too was restless, concluding finally that he was called to counter a dangerous heresy. But when he challenged George Fox, this time with Margaret Fell present, and sometimes commenting, it became clear that something had changed. Moreover, as the discussion continued, so did William's alarm mount, both for the souls of the Fell family, and for his reputation as their minister. Yet, later, he surely reassured himself that all was not lost. Or as George put it, that Margaret Fell "was not wholly come off" from her existing religious convictions.

Days later, one set aside for national penitence and public worship, Margaret invited her guest to accompany her to Ulverston's parish church of St Mary. When he reached it, however, he refused to step inside. For a while, he paced nearby fields, then he returned to the churchyard. Whether he had a plan of action, or whether it was the sound of "priest Lampitt … singing with his people", something finally propelled him through the door. Then, before the sermon was even begun, he stood on a seat and claimed the right to speak. "And he that was in the pulpit," Margaret recalled, "said he might."[18]

He began with a verse from Paul's Letter to the Romans, that circumcision is of the heart, and not of the letter.[19] As he spoke, all but unconsciously, Margaret Fell stood up in her pew. "And then he ... opened the Scriptures ... " she said. As he did so, it was as if she heard them anew. For their words, George declared, spoken by Christ, by the prophets, and by the Apostles, were words they themselves received from God. "Then what had any to do with the Scriptures," he asked, "but as they came to the Spirit that gave them forth?" Looking around, his eyes rested on the congregation, apprehensively silent since Margaret rose to her feet, and then on Margaret herself. "You will say, Christ saith this, and the apostles say this," he continued, "but what canst thou say? Art thou a child of Light, and hast thou walked in the Light, and what thou speakest, is it inwardly from God?"[20]

"This opened me so, that it cut me to the heart," Margaret recalled, "and then I saw clearly we were all wrong." So overpowering was the insight, that she wept for all to see. "We are all thieves," she said, sitting down in her pew, "... we have taken the Scriptures in words, and know nothing of them in ourselves."[21]

"God was come to teach his people by his Spirit," George declared, "and to bring them off all their old ways, religions, churches and worships ... " Furthermore, he said, pointing accusingly at William Lampitt, such men as he "were out of the life and the spirit that they were in that gave them forth."

For some, that was too much. "Take him away," roared local magistrate, John Sawrey.[22] But, as men moved to do so, another voice stopped them. "Let him alone," Margaret Fell commanded, "why may not he speak as well as any other?"

"Let him speak," William Lampitt agreed. Later, George accused him of deceit, that his agreement was merely pretence. But, William Lampitt, not a cowardly man, was in an impossible situation. For not only did the wife of his patron demand that her house-guest be obliged, but he also had no idea of what might be Thomas Fell's position regarding George Fox. Equally it might be added, with the benefit of his mysterious fortune, George Fox had no reason to depend on others for his living.

That night, he spoke again at Swarthmoor. Seated before him, as well as Margaret and her children, were William Caton, the fifteen-year companion to George Fell, Thomas Salthouse, Judge Fell's agent, and two maidservants, Mary Askew and Ann Clayton. Later, with the exception of George Fell, they would all add their names to George Fox's following.

For a moment, however, later on that warm night in July 1652, a pressing unease settled on Margaret Fell. "I was struck into such a sadness," she said, "I knew not what to do, my husband being from home."[23] Brought up to be a wife, mother and mistress of a gentleman's household, for 20 years, often during Thomas Fell's absence, Margaret had successfully fulfilled such a role. But, she also lived at a time when wives, no matter how capable, were expected to defer to a husband's wishes and judgement. Quite on her own accord, however, she had welcomed a most controversial evangelist, and then made her support for him clear to her neighbours. Thus, at some point she almost certainly asked herself how her husband would react. Given subsequent events, however, part of her unease was linked as much to the person of George Fox as to his message.

By the next morning, the sadness was conquered. And in this, Margaret proved herself a woman of extraordinary resolution. For, without consulting her husband, she had made up her mind to commit herself totally to the doctrine of the Inner Light. "I saw it was the truth, and I could not deny it," she said later; "... it was opened to me so clear, that I had never a tittle in my heart against it; but I desired the Lord that I might be kept in it; and then I desired no greater portion."[24]

Given such strength of character, it would be surprising if George Fox did not see in Margaret a potential that perhaps initially surprised him. For it was almost certainly Thomas Fell whose support he had hoped to gain. Equally, as well as the truth of the Inner Light, and the unsettling attraction of

George Fox, Margaret perhaps also saw an opportunity to set free within herself capabilities hitherto unrealized.

Whether the intention was to summon supportive voices, or to pre-empt events, it was Margaret who posted a letter to Richard Farnsworth in Yorkshire, calling him to Swarthmoor Hall and the return of Thomas Fell. George Fox meanwhile continued his evangelistic campaign. He was in Grisedale, close to the tithe strikers of Dent, when a message from Margaret told him that Judge Fell was come home. She also warned him that their meeting would be fraught.

After the Welsh circuit, Thomas Fell went on to London. Making his way home, and anxious to reach Swarthmoor by the swiftest route, north of the county town of Lancaster he set out to cross Morecambe Bay. It was a route he had travelled many times and in the fourteen miles left exposed by the receding tide, he knew the safe paths among the quick-sands and the channels where the sea sweeps in to engulf the unwary. But, before he was barely halfway, he was intercepted by men from Furness.

"A great disaster was befallen amongst his family," they told him. They were seduced by "witches", evil men who even now persuaded them to abandon their Christian faith.[25] When the troubled man finally reached Swarthmoor, it seemed that the reports were true. For not only were two male strangers living in his house, introduced as Richard Farnsworth and James Nayler, but the whole atmosphere of that house was decidedly and extraordinarily changed.

Angry words followed. Only when the two offered to leave, but begged that they first be allowed to speak, was the Judge a little pacified. Then, still suspicious that he was somehow deceived, he allowed his wife to persuade him to his dinner. Apprehensively, she sat alongside him. "And whilst I was sitting," she said, "the power of the Lord seized upon me: and he was struck with amazement and knew not what to think... And the children were all quiet and still, and grown sober, and could not play on their music that they were learning, and all these things made him quiet and still."[26]

Later that evening, clearly by some pre-arranged plan, the

Leicestershire prophet returned to Swarthmoor Hall. "[M]y husband was sitting in the parlour," said Margaret, "and I asked him, if George Fox might come in, and he said, Yes... So George came in without any compliment, and walked into the room, and began to speak."

If Thomas Fell was offended by the lack of deference, he chose to ignore it. Rather, he simply listened to all George Fox had to say. "[H]e spoke very excellently," Margaret recalled, "... and he opened the night of apostasy since the apostles' days, and laid open the priests and their practices in the apostasy." Indeed, she said, "if all England had been there, I thought they could not have denied the truth of those things."[27]

Was George Fox the man that Luke Robinson of Pickering had recently commended to the men of the Parliament? Thomas Fell asked eventually. George agreed that he was. Shortly afterwards, Judge Fell retired to bed. Next day, despite a visit from William Lampitt, he offered the Hall as a place where his wife and her new companions might worship God in their own way.

On the following Sunday, as Swarthmoor's first Quaker meeting met in the Hall's parlour, Thomas Fell, together with his clerk and groom, attended service at St Mary's.[28] Thomas Fell, experienced lawyer, shrewd politician and shrewd acquirer of property, was used to sizing up people and situations. Moreover, from Luke Robinson, he must have heard details regarding the considerable men at Stanley. He must also have recognized that since his wife was utterly convinced by George Fox's message, relationships and loyalties at Swarthmoor had changed. In those early weeks, with the whole house in a state of heightened religious excitement, and emotions as yet unsuppressed, there must surely also have been huge tensions at large.

At some point they evidently drove George from the house. Desperate for his presence, Margaret and several others begged him to return. "Our dear Father in the Lord... our souls doth thirst and languish after thee... O thou bread of life... take pity on us, whom thou has nursed up with the breasts of consolation. O our life, our desire is to see thee again that we may be refreshed ... and so have life more abundantly ... "[29]

Even in an age where language could be extravagantly emotional, it was an extraordinary letter to write to a man of 28. It also indicates something of George Fox's charisma, and its effect on those who believed that he was indeed sent to them by God.

Margaret also included another message with the first: "My own dear heart," she said, to a man she had known for only a few weeks, "though thou has shaken the dust off thy feet at him, who would not receive thee, nor is not worthy of thee ... do not leave us or forsake us, for our life and peace is in thee." If her husband was the man referred to, then not only had harsh words been spoken to George Fox, but in her commitment to her new faith, Margaret was evidently prepared to side with its prophet rather than her husband. That postscripts were added by four of her daughters, encouraging George's return and referring to him as "dear father" and "the fountain of life", suggests that Margaret marshalled them deliberately on her behalf.[30] Clearly she was determined that George Fox should remain at Swarthmoor.

That he did return, and then stayed, also suggests that the one "not worthy of thee" was to some extent at least, reconciled to his presence. Years later, when reviewing much early correspondence, George noted that the individual referred to "was not long after convinced".[31] Certainly in his official capacity, Judge Thomas Fell protected George Fox and others from persecution. According to his family, he also left his study door ajar that he might hear Swarthmoor's Children at worship. Towards the end of his life, he also abandoned Sunday service at St Mary's. He left no indication, however, of his motives or of his own private thoughts on the subject.

William Lampitt, meanwhile, was determined to combat both George Fox and the growing band of Seekers turned Children of Light. Seeing them undermining the religion of the Word, the man who leaned towards Independency rallied his Presbyterian colleagues. "And though Lampitt had been at variance with most of the priests before," said George, "yet against the Truth he and they all joined together."

William Lampitt's fears, however, were not only fuelled by events in Furness, but by reports reaching him from all over the north. From their newly acquired base at Swarthmoor, George Fox and his comrades preached throughout all Westmorland. Further afield, at Malton in Yorkshire, the preaching of a certain Jane Holmes led newly convinced shop-keepers to witness to their faith both publicly and extrava-gantly, with a bonfire of vanities. Thomas Aldam, still captive in York, wrote of it to George. "She was moved by ye Lord to cry throw the Towne," he said, "but afterwards there was a mightie worke amongst them, many shaken...some shope keepers was caused to burne a great deale of riboning of silks and braveries..."[32, 33] Flung into York Gaol, Jane relayed her story not only to Thomas, but to Elizabeth Hooton, arrested earlier for speaking against a minister at Rotheram.[34]

From Selby came news of similar events. This time, the cat-alyst was William Dewsbury.[35] George Canby, then a young Selby apprentice, recalled the day that William came to the home of Richard and Elizabeth Tomlinson, his newly con-vinced employers. "And then the said Elizabeth Tomlinson was made to goe Out into the Streets in the mighty power of ye Lord, which carryed her almost off her feet, and her Testimony was, 'Repent! Repent! For the day of the Lord is at hand; Woe to the Crown of Pride: Woe to the Covetous Professors...'"[36]

In Wakefield too, many were "wrought on", said Richard Farnsworth, who returned home to Yorkshire later 1652. At Stanley, he said, such a multitude gathered, "very many from Leeds, and some from Wakefield, who had not been with us before," that it seemed to him "that the world is all on a fire."[37]

Moreover, very prominent among the crowds, Richard said, were men of the New Model Army. In Lancashire too, they gathered to hear George Fox. "I...had a great meeting in the street of soldiers and people," he said of a Sunday in Lancaster, "and declared the word of life..." Days earlier, he added, on a market day in the same town, "I spoke through the mar-ket...and declared the day of the Lord...and against all deceitful merchandise, and preached righteousness and Truth ... "

Almost certainly, many of those soldiers still wore the sea-green ribbons of the Levellers, and yearned to see England become a land where justice prevailed and where poverty and inequality were overthrown. In the Children of Light, with their rejection of worldly hierarchies, their opposition to tithes, and their denunciations of cheating merchants and deceitful priests, it seemed they had found champions they could trust. To many native northerners, however, support even by the Army's foot-soldiers for George Fox merely confirmed that he was in league with the occupation. To others, it was a reminder that the Army was the breeding-ground of the sects who threatened the nation with anarchy.

Just as elsewhere, the conflicting mixture of longings, expectations, fears and anxieties created huge stresses. Bound up with them, among those who believed implicitly, and those troubled at other levels of consciousness, was the knowledge that they lived in the decade prophesied as heralding the Millennium, the apocalyptic climax where all things would be changed.

In such a heightened state of tension, anxiety often found its outlet in argument, belligerence, hysteria and violence. In Kendal, George said, "the people began to fight some for me and some against me."[38] In Lancaster, he was dragged from the church and stoned along the streets.

Even at Ulverston, despite the support of the Fell family, there was violence. Or perhaps there, more than anywhere else, aggression was exacerbated by rumour and gossip. On the sands, Judge Fell had heard allegations of witchcraft, while George himself sometimes referred to dark tales: "that I carried bottles and made people drink of my bottles, and that made them to follow me ... "[39] Inevitably, there were also rumours concerning the relationship between George Fox and Margaret Fell: "she took G.F. in her Husband's absence," claimed a northern opponent later, "into her Husband's House, if not into his Bed ... "[40]

"All the people in the steeplehouse were in an outrage and

an uproar," George said of an incident at Ulverston Church. It was a day set aside for a public lecture and it drew a vast crowd, much of it intent on supporting or opposing the controversial George Fox. That George intended to speak in such a debate, clearly shows that by now a growing confidence had overcome his earlier reservations. Before anyone spoke, however, John Sawrey asked if he intended to speak according to the Bible. "I stranged at him for speaking so to me," George said, for in his view, every word he spoke was underpinned by Scripture. "I told him," he added, "that I would ... bring the Scriptures to prove what I had to say, for I had some thing to speak to Lampitt and them ... "

What he said, however, and what others said, provoked an argument which, just as in Kendal, became a fight between opposing factions. "People tumbled over their seats for fear," he said. Hauled down from the bench where he stood, he was dragged from the church and into streets which had become a battleground. "And the blood ran down several people so as I never saw the like in my life." Even Judge Fell's fourteen-year-old son was tossed headlong into a ditch. "Knock out the teeth of his head!" people screamed, as the boy floundered in the muddy water.

Separated from his friends, and surrounded by a mob, George was beaten to the ground. Once again, however, his size, his physical strength and his indomitable will served him well. Struggling to his feet, he held out his arm and challenged his attackers to hit him again. "He hath spoiled his hand," people gasped, after a local stone-mason struck a great blow with a walking staff. But, "after a while," George said, "the Lord's power sprang through me ... I recovered my hand and arm and strength in the face and sight of them all."

Though his courage transformed some attackers into admirers, it had no effect on John Sawrey. In October, he and George Toulnson, a former mayor of Lancaster, issued a warrant for George's arrest on a charge of blasphemy. The main charge, based on signed witness statements, was that he had affirmed himself equal with God. It was also alleged that he had publicly declared baptism and the Eucharist to have no significance, advised people against reading the Bible, claimed authority to judge the world, and that he was as upright as Christ. As he rode to the Lancaster Quarter Sessions to answer the charges, it was in the company of Thomas Fell, one of three men appointed to hear the case, and proof perhaps, that some of the scandalous rumours were unfounded.

In the courtroom, despite every bench being packed with the region's clergy, it also became clear that neither Thomas Fell, nor his colleague, Colonel William West, would allow evidence that could not be substantiated. "It seems you did not hear those words spoken yourself," the bench was forced to point out, over and again, "though you have sworn to it."

Later, when George spoke in his own defence, his words were measured and careful. "That was not so spoken," he said frequently, while also pointing out that his actual words were confirmed by Scripture. "He that sanctifieth and he that is sanctified are all of one in the Father and the Son," he replied to the allegation that he considered himself equal with God, "...this the Scripture doth witness."[41] As for sacraments, while nothing in Scripture commanded "the sprinkling of infants", he certainly agreed that the bread and wine taken by the saints was the body and blood of Jesus.

Judging the world was also the prerogative of those saints, and would be confirmed by a glance at 1 Corinthians 6. Moreover, some additional Bible study would reveal that "all teaching which is given forth by Christ is to bring the saints to perfection, even to the measure, stature, and fullness of Christ ... "[42]

When Colonel West eventually asked if George had anything further to say, he seized the opportunity. "The Scriptures were given forth by the Spirit of God," he said, "and all people must first come to that Spirit in themselves, by which they might know God and Christ ... and ... the holy Scriptures." At that, his opponents leapt up. The letter and the spirit were inseparable, insisted John Jacques, vicar of Bolton-le-Sands. If that were indeed so, the bench observed dryly, "then they might carry the spirit in their pockets as they did the Scriptures."

Following the dismissal of the case, the Children's northern

opponents drew up a petition to the Council of State, accusing
George Fox and James Nayler of seducing wives from their
husbands, children from their parents, and all of them from
their religion.[43] In response, the two men addressed the
Council themselves. As they did so, they were most certainly
aware of the influence wielded by their military and political
supporters in the north. They were certainly equally aware of
Thomas Fell's friendship with John Bradshaw, the Council's
powerful President.

As they refuted the ministers and justices who opposed
them, they also pointed out, perhaps with advice from Thomas
Fell and William West, that most of them were "men that never
drew a sword for the interests of the Commonwealth of
England, perhaps against it."[44] Thus they reminded the
Council that in the conflicts of the 1640s, and unlike men such
as James Nayler, those Presbyterians who now made allegations against the Children of Light, had themselves sided with
the Royalist and Scottish supporters of tyranny.

Later, as a freezing winter settled upon the north, George
relieved his anger at those who opposed him at Ulverston. "O
people consider," he warned the townsfolk, "God hath given to
every one of you a measure ... liar, drunkard, whoremonger,
and thief and who follow filthy pleasures ... Therefore mind
your measure, for nothing that is unclean shall enter into the
Kingdom of God ... "

To those who followed William Lampitt, who "leads you
into the ditch ... if ever your eyes come to see repentance and
own the light of Jesus Christ in you, you will witness me a
friend of your souls ... " Otherwise, he said, "when you are in
the ditch together, both teacher and people, remember ye were
warned ... "[45]

George Fox and Margaret Fell, meanwhile, discussed how
Swarthmoor might become an effective base for evangelists,
an administrative centre for the north, and a repository and
distribution centre for literature. Swarthmoor's mistress, confined there by responsibilities to household and family, would
ensure that records were maintained and information was sent
to wherever it was needed.[46]

In some of the letters that arrived at Swarthmoor at this time, the Children also referred to each other as "Friends". Thomas Aldam used it in letters written from York, and Richard Farnsworth from Wakefield. Thus, by the winter of 1652, it seems the term was in use.[47] It was probably also based on the words of Jesus in John's Gospel, "Ye are my friends, if ye do whatsoever I command you."[48] Believing that their message was also commanded by him, sometimes the Friends spoke of themselves as the Friends of Truth.

In the spring of 1653, James Nayler and Francis Howgill, both charged the previous November with blasphemy, were released from Appleby Gaol. As the news reached Swarthmoor, so too did other news arrive from London. On 20 April, accusing Members of treachery, and backed by armed troops, Oliver Cromwell had dismissed the Rump, the truncated remnant of the Long Parliament elected nearly thirteen years before.

Fearing that a free election would see a majority of Presbyterians returned, or even of Royalists, the Army's Council of Officers considered two forms of government. The first, proposed by John Lambert, was for a body similar to the Council of State, but with powers limited by a written constitution. The second, proposed by Major-General Thomas Harrison, was quite different, a ruling body of seventy selected "Saints" whose inspiration was the Jewish *sanhedrin* described in the Old Testament.

In May, with some modifications, Harrison's scheme was accepted, and in the name of Lord-General Cromwell and the Army, letters asking for suitable nominations were sent to Independent churches throughout the country. William West and John Sawrey were among those nominated for Lancashire. Meanwhile, rumour suggested that the new Parliament, scheduled to convene in July, was at last planning to transform England into a truly godly society. It was even said that the hated tithes would finally be abolished.

George Fox, meanwhile, in the spring of 1653, could certainly reflect on his own success. If at times it appeared more than he had originally anticipated, it was also probably no more than he expected Providence to provide for a prophet.

Since entering the landscape of his vision at Pendle, everything had been fulfilled. He had indeed encountered a great people, who had not only welcomed him, and hailed him as a leader, but who had gathered around him as apostles. Moreover, while he had also found a home, his first since Fenny Drayton, it was one which not only excelled in substance and comfort, but which seemed set to become the base of a great movement. Now, as the leader of that burgeoning movement, he could rest in his new home, while also considering how he might take his people forward into the future.

CHAPTER SEVEN

Newes Coming Up Out
of the North

...you are hatching mischief in your minds, and hatch the Cockatrice eggs: But the Saints of the most high God are coming to break them to pieces...

George Fox,
Newes Coming up out of the North,
Sounding towards the South (1654)

" ... *b* E BOLD AND VALIANT for the Truth..." George Fox exhorted the Children of Light.[1] As the spring of 1653 became summer, George Fox, James Nayler, Margaret Fell and those other men and women who had committed their lives to the Children of Light, extended their campaign in the north. Encouraging them were George's "epistles", the idea inspired perhaps by Paul of Tarsus, and begun two years earlier.

Though the 29-year-old George could be both belligerent and obstinate, as he grew in experience, so too did his vision mature. In the manner of the mystic, although he clearly reflected on ideas, he seems to have relied as much on sudden bursts of insight as on any sequence of logical thought. He seems also to have flung his words onto the page, writing or dictating "as in a rapture", and then rarely revising and certainly not cutting his many repetitions. Yet, within the torrent, sometimes almost obscured, lay profound truths and words of great power.

Remember, he exhorted the Children, their message was for everyone; there was no eternal decree that predestined only a select few for salvation. Moreover, since salvation was a potential carried by all, they were to disregard worldly appearances, and speak as best they could to the light within: "... keep within your own Measure," he said, "seeing over that which is without, answering that of God in all."[2]

He reminded them too, that bringing people to the Light involved a spiritual battle. "For many Deceivers are entred into the World," he said, "... and if it were possible they would deceive the Elect ... " But, he continued, once the choice was made and laid hold of, salvation was gained. "In the Light," he said, "the Elect do dwell, which the Anti-Christs, Deceivers, and false Prophets are turned from ... that Light which they do hate, the Children of Light dwell in, the Elect."[3] Moreover, he assured them, "this will be witnessed Measurably with Thousands, who are growing up out of the Fall, and coming up out of the Grave ... "[4]

Coming up from the grave, he implied, was as much a process of self-realization as it was an assurance of eternity. Indeed, as he spoke of "the Power of an Endless Life, which does not change", the two appeared intimately linked.[5]

Since the days of his own first painful journey within, since the months in Derby Gaol, he clearly continued to reflect on the experience of the Light that became also the Refiner's Fire. The insights he gained, and the conclusions he reached, he almost certainly understood as coming by the spiritual gift of discernment. In a later age, though many would understand them in a similar way, for the most part their views would be additionally informed by the insights of psychology. Other individuals, entirely secular, would dismiss any suggestion of a spiritual component. Nevertheless, however the process is understood, there seems little doubt that George Fox now recognized that by sitting in meditative silence, alone or with similarly minded others, it is possible for individuals to open themselves to a process that brings painful memories and disturbing thoughts to light. Furthermore, that by allowing the encounter to take place in an atmosphere informed by love, the way can be opened for healing and the achievement of wholeness.

He also recognized that the process was often painful. "Friends," he said, "stand all naked, bare and uncovered before the Lord."[6] Yet, he knew that it ultimately led to truth. "Stand still in that which is pure," he continued, "after ye see your selves; and then Mercy comes in. After thou seest thy Thoughts, and the Temptations, do not think, but submit; and then Power comes. Stand still in that which shews and discovers; and there doth Strength immediately come; And stand still in the Light ... Your strength is to stand still, after ye see your selves; ... and then Strength comes from the Lord, and Help, contrary to your Expectations ... "[7]

George also appeared to accept that each individual possessed gifts that were uniquely theirs. "Every one in your Measure wait upon God," he advised, "who ... leads his Flock unto the Green Pastures, and fresh Springs he opens daily ... " Nor did he believe that the Children were to be complacent. Unlike those who maintained it was enough to believe oneself saved, he insisted that the Children of Light were to reflect their faith in action: "... and none of you be Sayers (only)," he said, "but Doers of the Word ... "[8]

Nor, as is proved by his ready acceptance of Elizabeth Hooton and Margaret Fell, did he see faith in action as limited to men. "The Lamb of God, the Son of God," he said, "is but one in all his Males and Females, Sons and Daughters ... Stand up ye Prophets of the Lord ... quench not your Prophecy ... that over all the Contrary ye may reign ... seeing over that which is without, answering that of God in all ... "[9] And that answering, he said, applied as much to those who persecuted the Children, as it did to their friends.

"Dear John," he wrote to a Quaker currently in prison, "the Everlasting Arm of the Lord hold thee up, and break all thy bonds asunder ... And pray for thy Enemies, for the Lord to open them and their hearts, and see themselves and thee."[10] Whether the bonds were those of John's prison, or those of an inner despair, George knew from his own experience that even in courtrooms and gaols, hearts and minds could be changed.

So too did many of his comrades. During his trial at Appleby, James Nayler spoke of the voice that called him from his Yorkshire plough. As he did so, Anthony Pearson, one of the presiding magistrates, felt a quite unexpected response. Later, and perhaps with the encouragement of Gervase Benson, who sat with him on the bench, he travelled to Swarthmoor to meet George Fox.

Justice of the Peace in three northern counties, the Lancashire-born Pearson was another man with powerful friends.[11] Though only 25, he had served briefly as secretary to Sir Arthur Haselrig, Member of Parliament, member of the Council of State, former governor of Newcastle, and a man of huge influence both in the north-eastern counties and in London.[12] No doubt it was partly with an eye to Haselrig's possible patronage, that George Fox welcomed Anthony Pearson to Swarthmoor.[13]

While Haselrig never became a supporter, weeks after his visit to Swarthmoor, Anthony Pearson offered his home, Ramshaw Hall in County Durham, as a base in that county for the Children of Light. James Nayler, John Audland, Edward Burrough and Francis Howgill all took advantage of it later in the year.

In response, the region's Presbyterian clergy mounted a furious campaign of opposition. In *The Perfect Pharise under Monkish Holines*, five Newcastle-based ministers accused the Children of hypocrisy in their claims to perfection. They also alleged that by the doctrine of the Inner Light, the Friends proved themselves not merely Arminians, but the Catholic Antichrist in new form.[14] Though George Fox had been accused of Catholicism before, it was now additionally reinforced by his insistence that the Children be doers, not merely sayers, a view that seemed to affirm the Catholic belief that good works contributed towards salvation, as opposed to the Protestant doctrine that it was achieved through faith in Christ's redeeming sacrifice on the cross. "[A]mong the priests is a fire kindled: they are all in an uproar," said Edward Burrough; although, he added, throughout the whole county of Durham there was an "abundance convinced of the Truth."[15]

George Fox, meanwhile, together with several comrades, among them James Lancaster of Walney Island, headed north into Cumberland. At Bootle, ten miles from Ulverston, they were joined by Anthony Pearson, on his way to the Quarter Sessions at Carlisle. Forewarned of their coming, and seemingly part of a wider mobilization, the parish minister had drafted in colleagues from London.[16] Whatever was the content of his sermon, however, so incensed by it was George Fox, that instead of waiting until it was finished, he interrupted it in mid-flow. In so doing, by once again contravening the Act of Mary Tudor, forbidding interruption of services, he gave his opponents their opportunity. "So they hauled me out," he said, "and people were mighty rude, and one gave me a great blow on the wrist with a great hedgestake."[17] When they were ordered to surrender the culprit to a local constable, however, the congregation refused.

Determined to maintain their challenge, to the authority of the minister and presumably to his Calvinism, the Children returned for the afternoon service. When George finally stood up, however, and perhaps at Anthony Pearson's instigation, a figure of authority stood alongside him. "In the name of the Commonwealth," said the constable, the congregation were warned to keep the peace. Thus, once again, it was clear to all that George Fox was very publicly supported by the occupying power.

At Cockermouth, 30 miles further north, it was made clear once again. In the town, George had found soldiers from the Parliamentary garrison at Carlisle, together with their wives, waiting for him eagerly. Eager too, though less for his message than for a sight of the man whose reputation was spread through the country roundabout, was a huge crowd of local people. "People having notice of it," George said, "... that there came above a thousand people, which was like a horse-fair."[18] Later, when the crowd's mood grew threatening, "the soldiers told them we had broken no law, and then they were quiet." To the resentful northerners, however, such an intervention was surely further proof that the Children of Light were allies of the occupation.

Late in July, the party reached Carlisle. Close to the Scottish border, and in a region of Royalist sympathies, the city was of huge strategic importance to the Commonwealth. Clearly it was also of strategic importance to George Fox, and with much of the Army remaining radical in its politics, its huge military garrison was the primary focus of his campaign.

Relying on that sense of the dramatic that had served him so effectively before, he waited until Carlisle's Saturday market was a seething mass of activity, before staging his first striking appearance. "I stood a-top of the cross in the middle of the market," he said, "and said the mighty day of the Lord was upon all deceit and ungodliness and wickedness, and that they were to lay away all their deceitful merchandise and keep to 'yea' and 'nay', in all their dealings."[19] Anyone with Leveller sympathies would have felt their hearts lift at such words. Opponents, meanwhile, saw only a religious fanatic and a political subversive. Many of Carlisle's inhabitants also saw a civilian cohort of their oppressors.

Days later, as he successfully gathered groups of radical Baptists from among the regiments to his own fellowship, and the convinced troops summoned more of their comrades by the beating of drums, tensions in the city began to mount. On the following Sunday, though warned against it by Carlisle's magistrates, George declared in Carlisle's St Mary's Cathedral. "A dreadful power of the Lord there was amongst them in the steeplehouse," he said, "that the people trembled and shook, and they thought the steeplehouse ... would have fallen down." But as he declared, and as the troops in the congregation encouraged him, outside, an anti-government demonstration surrounded the building.

"Down with these round-headed rogues," the mob chanted, as they hurled barrage after barrage of stones. Eventually, Carlisle's governor, Major-General Charles Howard, sent a party of musketeers to order the troopers to quell the riot. Shielding George Fox, who was certainly the man the mob looked for, they then fought their way back to their barracks.

Charles Howard, a former Captain of Cromwell's Lifeguard, and a Member of the Nominated Assembly for Carlisle, might possibly have been sympathetic to George Fox. With his city in uproar, however, and with "stones ... and cudgels, in the steeplehouse, and ... in the streets, and swords drawn", his concern was to prevent riot becoming rebellion.[20] When Carlisle's magistrates issued a warrant for the arrest of the man responsible for the disorder, Howard was unwilling to forbid them. Nor was he present when the town's Puritan ministers questioned George Fox:

And they asked me if I were the son of God [said George].
I said, "Yes,"
They asked me if I had seen God's face.
I said, "Yes,"
They asked me whether I had the spirit of discerning.
I said, "Yes", I discerned him that spoke to me.
They asked me whether the Scripture was the Word of God.
I said, God was the Word and the Scriptures were writings; and the Word was before writings were, which Word did fulfil them."[21]

On 1 August 1653, George Fox was imprisoned as a blasphemer, a heretic and a seducer. Although he had countered the same charge successfully at Lancaster, he had been convicted three years earlier in Derby. A second conviction would render him liable to the full penalty under the Blasphemy Act; to be banished from the Commonwealth, and if refusing to depart, to be executed by public hanging. As he waited for the Assizes, rumour swept the country that George Fox would surely die.

Yet, when the Assizes came, and then went, and despite a demand from Anthony Pearson, George was not brought before the court. Perhaps, the authorities feared to create a martyr, or to open the way to a flood of similar cases.

On the departure of the Assize judges, however, the prisoner was ordered out of the gaoler's house and thrown into a dungeon. Like Derby, he said, it was a foul place, "where men and women were put together ... in a nasty and very uncivil manner, which was a shame to Christianity."

Yet, though the dungeon was dark and "exceeding lousy",

those people for whom George Fox was an inspiration insisted on visiting him there. One was Gervase Benson's wife, who each day passed George's dinner through a rusty iron grill. Another was James Parnell, a young man of just fifteen, and disowned by his parents for his association with the Children, who walked alone from Colchester to meet George Fox.

Meanwhile, others pressed for George's release. Anthony Pearson and Gervase Benson wrote to Carlisle's magistrates; so too did George from his dungeon. Margaret Fell, meanwhile, urged Colonel West to use his influence in the Nominated Assembly. "Hearing that a young man was to die for religion at Carlisle," George said later, "they writ down to the sheriff and magistrates." But by the time the letter arrived, and no doubt uncomfortably aware that George Fox had the backing of powerful men, after keeping him seven weeks in gaol, Carlisle's magistrates had set him free.

Though ridiculed by opponents, who named it the Parliament of Saints, the Nominated Assembly boasted significant achievements.[22] Since its opening session in July, it had passed some 29 ordinances dealing with a range of administrative, financial and social matters. Among them were the compulsory civil registration of births, marriages and deaths, greater protection for lunatics and their estates, and provision for the relief of impoverished debtors.

Though the Assembly had split on several issues, when the religious radicals, headed by Major-General Thomas Harrison, drew up proposals to abolish the Court of Chancery, to codify the common law, and finally to abolish tithes, opposition among conservatives, both in the Assembly and in the Army, began to mount. For such proposals struck at the power of the establishment – the church and the legal system alike – as well as at the fundamentals of property.[23] And as the Levellers had been left in no doubt, when the rich and powerful spoke of liberty, they did not generally include the poor.

Equally disturbing were the beliefs held by some of the Assembly's radicals. Like Harrison, many were Fifth Monarchists, a sect who maintained that Christ's 1,000-year reign, which they saw prophesied in the Revelation, would begin in 1656, less than three years thence.[24] Unlike others with similar beliefs, however, Fifth Monarchists believed themselves called to establish a theocratic regime in which godly discipline would be imposed on the unregenerate mass. From information supplied by agents, the Council of Officers was convinced that all over the country caches of weapons were being stockpiled in readiness.

The threat to the law and to tithes, and the beliefs of Fifth Monarchists, were too great to ignore. On 12 December, at a meeting of which the radicals knew nothing, the Assembly agreed that "it was requisite to deliver up unto Lord-General Cromwell the powers which they received from him."[25] Anyone protesting was driven from Westminster by armed soldiers. Three days later, the Council of Officers accepted the "Instrument of Government", a written constitution drafted by John Lambert.[26] Under its terms, a Lord Protector, assisted by a Council of State and backed by a standing army, was nominated as head of the Commonwealth.

On 16 December, Oliver Cromwell, the man able to command the widest loyalty, was installed as Lord Protector for life. Provision was also made for a single-chamber parliament, constituted on a representative basis, with the power, after a regulated delay, to pass bills against the Protector's will. Under the Instrument's religious clauses, the contentious issue of tithes was hedged: they would remain in place until a more satisfactory arrangement was devised. While liberty of worship was guaranteed, it did not extend to prelacy or Roman Catholicism, nor to those who practised "licentiousness" under the cover of Christianity. Nor was this tolerance to be abused, either in undermining the liberty of others, or in disturbing the public peace.

To the men and women at Swarthmoor, it was clear that the Children of Light, so often found in the midst of riotous assemblies, could be restrained under the Instrument's provisions. Nor could it be ignored that the catalyst for the dissolution of the Nominated Assembly was the proposed abolition of tithes, an integral part of the Children's message.

Though part of their objection was that tithes were taken by men "which do us no Work, whom we have not hired", it was also derived from the belief that since Christ was now come, he had thus put an end to the "first" priesthood, that began with Aaron, brother-in-law to Moses, and which had continued throughout the Apostasy to the Puritan ministers of their own time. "And so we cannot uphold Tithes, and such as take Tithes," George insisted, "who act against Christ Jesus, his commands, and deny him to be come ... in Life, Doctrine and Power."[27]

Thus, an affiliation to the Children of Light inevitably meant a rejection of tithes. Almost equally inevitably, as the fury of parish ministers descended upon them, and as magistrates rushed to support their ordained colleagues, the property of the defaulters was seized in lieu, while those unable to meet the demands were flung into gaol. And, if that were the case, said George, the Children must go bravely. For, "those who hale you before Magistrates for Tithes, and Maintenance, when they do you no work", were obeying neither the commands of Jesus nor the requirements of justice. Whereas, "we who suffer goods to be spoiled Joyfully" did so for "Christs sake, the unchangeable Priest ... and the new Testament's sake."[28]

Going to their imprisonment equally bravely were those who for conscience's sake refused to remove their hats in courtrooms. Their rejection of the "proud flesh" that sat on the bench, however, generally resulted in a charge of contempt. So too did their refusal to swear oaths. To the Children, it was quite clear that when Jesus in the Gospels said, "Swear not at all", he meant what he said. They also saw it as integrally linked to his subsequent statement: "But let your communication be, Yea, yea; Nay, nay, for whatsoever is more than these cometh of evil."[29] In their view, when a follower of Jesus gave his word, it was also his bond. That their opponents should offer them a Bible to swear on was an insult, implying that a book carried more weight than the Word made flesh, who had now come to teach his people.

So, as the Children refusing tithes kept their hats on in court, others wore them as they carried their message into churches all over the north of England. Indeed, said George, "there were few steeplehouses ... but Friends were moved to go to them and warn them of the mighty day of the Lord."[30] As they did so – though their opponents mobilized, and many individuals saw the Children as Ranters, Levellers or Catholics in disguise, as witches or as agents of the occupying Army – the message of the Light, the courage, and sometimes the sheer bravado of its evangelists, drew ever more English men and women into its fold.

"Thousands of people a-top of a hill," George said, recalling a meeting in Cumberland, "... as many as one could well speak over, there was such a multitude." Again, it is difficult to estimate precise numbers. Though some surviving documents speak of thousands, enthusiasm often makes crowds seem larger than they are. However, it is certainly clear that the numbers were again significant, and they certainly alarmed the leaders of other sects, as well as England's government.[31]

In 1653 and 1654, however, the Children's leaders called a series of meetings which, although they themselves may not have been thinking quite so far ahead, laid the foundation for what would eventually become a unified and structured movement. Adding to the longstanding monthly meeting at Preston Patrick, in the East Riding of Yorkshire, William Dewsbury settled a general meeting whereby representatives of smaller meetings nearby might come together every three weeks.[32] At such meetings, he said (his view endorsed by George Fox), "one or two who are the most growne in ye power and life & pure discerning in ye truth" should be chosen as overseers.[33] In the West Riding, established by Richard Farnsworth, and in Cumberland, settled by what George Fox referred to later as Elders, similar meetings were also established and met every four weeks.[34, 35]

Meanwhile, the numbers continued to grow. "And so great a convincement there was in Cumberland, Bishoprick, Northumberland, Yorkshire, Westmoreland and Lancashire," said George, "and the plants of God grew and flourished so by heavenly rain ... "[36] Neither George Fox, Margaret Fell, nor any of their comrades doubted that such rain was the mark of

God's favour. It underscored everything they believed, that theirs was the true revelation, and that they were called to overturn the Apostasy and to restore the true Christian Church. Equally clear to them was that George Fox had been led to the north by God, so that in that remote country the first fruits might have the time and space to take root and grow strong. Now, with their numbers increasing, and a coherent organization emerging, it was time to carry the message into the world.

In November 1653, Gervase Benson wrote to his comrades at Swarthmoor from London. "There are many hereaways inquiring after Friends in the North," he said, "and the Truth made manifest in you."[37] In the spring of the following year, after walking to London from Westmorland, John Camm, father of young Thomas, and Francis Howgill were shocked by the city. "The pure simplicity is lost," they lamented, "...lust and pride and all manner of filthiness such as cannot be declared."[38]

Perhaps the 30-year-old George Fox also found his thoughts returning to the London of 1644, the city under a chain of darkness. As he and his comrades prepared to carry the message of the Light into the nation, in *Newes Coming Up Out of the North, Sounding towards the South*, he issued a warning of what was to come:

> ... O England! is it not now among you where any Prophet is sent into this great Citie Sodom and Gomorrah...to cry against the deceitfull merchandize, to cry against this false worship that God never commanded, to cry against oppression and unjust dealing...your drunkenness...your blasphemy, cursed speaking and oppressing one another, and to cry against you who rule not the Countrey with Justice, and keep not all in order, justice and equity... Wait all you captivated ones that lie in prison...for Salvation is Coming to you...the mighty day of the Lord is coming, the dreadful day is coming, the glittering sword is drawn...[39]

By the summer of 1654, as plans for the southward mission were finalized, it was agreed that George would oversee every book used on the Children's behalf. "I doe Rejoyce," wrote Thomas Aldam, "to heare that the wisdom of god doth soe

Order that all Bookes may come to thy hand, to bee vewed bee fore they bee printed."[40] Thus, the child deprived of education had become a man who not only produced epistles for his own growing following, but one who considered, corrected, and endorsed the work of others.

In his *Journal* George claimed that 70 Children took part in the mission to the south, the number of evangelists that Luke's Gospel records as having once been sent out by Jesus.[41] Though the number was later disputed, it was clearly a sub-stantial force, while the arrangement that they travel in pairs seems certainly to have been based on that earlier enterprise.[42] Among them were Francis Howgill and Edward Burrough to London, John Camm and John Audland to Bristol; Richard Hubberthorne and George Whitehead of Orton to Norwich; and John Story of Preston Patrick and John Wilkinson of Hutton to Wiltshire.

With them they carried a paper by George Fox. "All Friends that speak abroad," it said, "see that it be in the life of God ... with which life you come to reach the Light in every man, which Christ enlightens every man that cometh into the world withal ... "[43]

Behind them, Margaret Fell, who in October 1653 gave birth to another daughter, named Rachel by her parents, would ensure the safekeeping of reports and letters sent back to her. She would also maintain a fund collected by the Children at Kendal for furthering the work, for the support of evangelists, the printing of their books, and if necessary, their maintenance in prison.[44]

Making their way south, neither George nor his comrades made any secret of their aim: the restoration of the true church, and the transformation of England to a nation where civil righteousness and personal virtue were paramount. Indeed, *Newes Coming Up* was already distributed on London's streets and passed there from hand to hand. But, as the evan-gelists strode on, so too did rumour hurry through the land. The Children of Light, people said, the fanatical Quakers, were planning to storm London, to attack godly ministers and cause riot in churches just as they did in the dark regions of the north.

At the same time, watching the Quaker missionaries closely, was Secretary of State, John Thurloe.[45] A lawyer, civil servant and passionate supporter both of the Commonwealth and Oliver Cromwell, he had became director of the Protectorate's spying and intelligence network in the previous year. It was a post he excelled at, increasing the number and efficiency of English agents in foreign governments and in Charles II's court-in-exile, and also establishing a cryptology department to break secret codes. He also ran agents throughout England, who as well as infiltrating most of the sects, received information from a large body of informers.

Thus John Thurloe knew that in 1653, emissaries from Morgan Lloyd, the Independent minister of Wrexham in North Wales, had visited Swarthmoor to meet George Fox. He knew too, that Morgan shared the beliefs of the Fifth Monarchists.[46] He was also aware that two of Fox's Children had then travelled to Wrexham, and that after establishing meetings in Cheshire, one of them, Richard Hubberthorne, had received a six-month prison sentence.[47]

Furthermore, his agents also reported back to him on the various activities of the south-bound evangelists. He knew, for instance, that in June, two women, Elizabeth Fletcher and Elizabeth Leavens, had called people to repentance at Oxford. He knew too that after being arrested and then punished under the Elizabethan Vagrancy Act by being stripped and whipped from the town, Elizabeth Fletcher had gone on to provoke a riot when she walked naked through the city as a sign against the divinity students.[48] They were hypocrites, she claimed, who would one day by stripped of their profession by God.

Nor was Elizabeth alone among the Children in such behaviour. As the son of a clergyman, John Thurloe certainly knew that their inspiration was the prophet Isaiah, who once walked naked as a sign to Egypt and Ethiopia.[49] Some reports also described Children who walked naked with lighted candles or bunches of weeds in their hands, testifying against a formal religion they saw as a cloak for hypocrisy, and against worldly vanities they regarded as dangerous folly.[50]

More immediately troubling to John Thurloe perhaps, was

that the target of such behaviour was sometimes Cromwell's Protectorate itself, whose failure to impose a godly society, just like the Commonwealth before it, would very soon incur divine wrath. Indeed, one William Simpson had declared at Oxford that his nakedness was a sign "to ym yt the day was neare att hand, even att ye Dore, in wch ye Lord would stripp ym naked & bare, both from ye Rule & authority they then were vnder in this Nation, & allso from yt Covering of Religion … "[51] Thus, as the itinerants continued their disruptive journey south, Thurloe instructed his agents to be extra vigilant.

Making his own way through Yorkshire, Lincolnshire and the Derbyshire peaks, where two of Margaret Fell's daughters arrived to travel with him, George visited individuals who had numbered themselves among the Children since the 1640s. Some had subsequently gathered meetings around them, and now as men and women turned out to meet the man they knew only by hearsay, so too did many hundreds of others. For the days when George Fox was just one itinerant preacher among many were long past. Now, his was a name known all over England, and the curious, the hopeful and the already convinced, were eager to see and hear him for themselves. Reading reports of the huge crowds, John Thurloe's anxiety mounted.

Very eager indeed to encounter George Fox, were those who opposed him, many of whom were determined that he should not be heard: "… they yelled and made such a noise as if they had been come to a bear-baiting," he said on one occasion, "and … several times they thrust me off from the place I stood on with the crowding of the people together against me … " Some opponents also had old scores to settle.

Among them was Rice-Jones, still smarting perhaps from the confrontation at Derby. "And … his company," said George, "… fell a-prophesying against me that then I was at the highest and that after that time I should fall down as fast." Another time it was Ranters. "And the Ranters opposed me," he said, "and fell a-swearing." In response, George insisted that the Children obeyed Christ's command to "Swear not at all."

For John Thurloe, as much as George Fox, although for

different reasons, the issue of oaths was critical. For when Oliver Cromwell assumed the role of Lord Protector, many of those soldiers in the earlier crowds, who had subsequently become Children of Light, had refused the Oath of Allegiance demanded of all ranks. Some were discharged, others transferred to regiments in Scotland, deemed far enough away to neutralize their subversive potential. Nevertheless, to the Army and the civil power alike, the unknown question remained. If such men refused an oath of loyalty, perhaps they would also refuse to fight.

As John Thurloe considered the possibility, he also wondered if, though they might not fight for the Commonwealth, the Children of Light would do so for some other cause. With that uncomfortable thought in mind, he studied another of the Leicestershire prophet's inflammatory missives, *To All Who Would Know the Way to the Kingdom*, that had also reached London and was currently hawked up and down the streets:

> Now shall Zion arise … now is the Sword drawn, which glitters and is furbished … to hew down *Baal's* Priest, corrupt Judges, corrupt Justices, corrupt Lawyers … Oh ye great Men, and Rich men of the Earth! Weep and howl for your Misery is coming … Oh doth Oppression and Tyranny rule, that the Cries of the Poor are entred into the Ears of the Lord of Sabbaths! … The Lord is pouring out his Spirit upon all Flesh, that his Sons and Daughters might Prophesie up and down this great City, and none shall make them afraid, Crying for Justice, Crying for Righteousness, crying for Equity … [52]

If it were the case that George had indeed been supported earlier by a faction in the Army, then its power had waned with the establishment of the Protectorate. Moreover, the Protectorate also felt itself vulnerable, not only from Charles Stuart, from the radicals of the abolished Assembly, and from militant former Levellers, but also from the terrifying possibility that those disparate causes might one day unite. Thus in John Thurloe's eyes, his inflammatory language, his links to other fanatical groups, the support he commanded among the troops, many of whom no doubt remained committed to the

Agreement of the People, and indeed, the ambiguous nature of his message, all made George Fox a potentially dangerous man.

So too did the massive series of rallies planned for his native Leicestershire. It was surely no coincidence that he intended to hold them there. For although Leicestershire was situated at the heart of England, with roads leading conveniently to Bristol, London, Norwich and York, clearly George also had old and very personal scores to settle in his home county. Perhaps he hoped that all those who had rejected him, who were unable to answer his anxious questions, and maybe even those who demanded he pay for a drinking contest, would be drawn to witness his powerful presence, his accomplished oratory, and his acknowledged leadership among a mighty movement.

Crossing the Leicestershire border in January 1655, together with 25-year-old Alexander Parker from Bowland near Windermere, by the time he reached Swannington, thirteen miles north of Fenny Drayton, the countryside was alive with expectation. For converging on the town were hundreds of Children, among them some of the movement's most well-known names: John Audland, Francis Howgill, Richard Farnsworth, James Parnell and Edward Burrough.

When they finally turned their horses towards Fenny Drayton everyone expected trouble. Foremost among them was Nathaniel Stephens, who, like colleagues elsewhere, had drafted in Calvinist reinforcements. Moreover, as Fenny Drayton's minister of many years, and as a Puritan in a region of Puritans, he also knew he could count on the support of nearby congregations. Indeed, almost without his asking, people had turned out, ready to do battle. Perhaps Christopher Fox, meanwhile, was in two minds, angry at the son who had rejected his apprenticeship, his faith and his family, but eager to see the man who had made such a name for himself.

In the event, everyone appears to have been satisfied. "A great dispute we had with those priests," George said. For those who loved argument, with much quoting from the Bible

153

and plenty of personal insults,.then the hours of controversy, over what was meant by being "born again", or whether tithes were really theft, was an entertainment to be richly relished. When the ministers egged the congregations on, so that St Michael's echoed to the chant of "Prove it, prove it," George's great voice boomed forth great chunks of Scripture in support of his claims that ministers were deceivers, hirelings who served their bellies rather than Christ.

By the time a second meeting was convened a week later, Nathaniel had acquired another six clerical assistants, while anyone who missed the first event, arrived eager for the second. As the dispute began again, with each side quoting lavishly from Scripture, George claimed the ministers misquoted and were false prophets. "Take notice people," he warned the congregation. "Hold thy tongue, George," some of them yelled back. If some of them remembered him as an aloof young man, who always appeared to look down on them, then clearly they had no intention of supporting him now. Christopher Fox, however, was impressed. "Well," he said, banging his walking-cane on the ground, "I see he that will but stand to the truth it will carry him out."

Though the Children were violently shoved into each other in Fenny Drayton's streets, and although at least once, George was set on by his former fellow villagers – "a great heap of them fell down as they were carrying of me, and I under them," he said – the anticipated trouble was largely confined to words. A mounted patrol drafted in to keep order merely gathered names and issued warnings.

Weeks later, however, on 11 February 1655, just outside Leicester, George was arrested. When he learned of plots against Oliver Cromwell, he must have immediately guessed that he was among the suspects. He would also have learned that in an attempt to end the abuse of ministers in their churches, and the constant complaints of congregations, a Proclamation was in hand to bolster the terms of the Instrument of Government and to make it illegal to interrupt Christian ministers or assemblies.[53]

Colonel Francis Hacker, whose men apprehended him,

offered the prisoner the option of house-arrest in Fenny Drayton. "I told them I should go to meetings as the Lord ordered me," said George, "and therefore could not submit to that, but said we were a peaceable people." With no other option, Hacker sent George Fox to Oliver Cromwell.

On the way to London, he certainly learned more details of the Protectorate's fears. In the previous year, suspicions were aroused by a petition drawn up by the Leveller, John Wildman, questioning the powers of the Protector, and calling for a "free parliament" and a reconsideration of the Agreement of the People.[54] In January 1655, shortly after the dissolution of the First Protectorate Parliament, John Thurloe was also aware of a Royalist plot, and that Charles Stuart had moved to Middelburg in the Netherlands in expectation of crossing to England when the insurrection gathered force.[55] Believing it to be part of the feared Leveller–Royalist alliance, on 10 February, the day before George Fox was taken at Leicester, Wildman was arrested and sent to the Tower. Also in the Tower was Major-General Robert Overton, a radical republican officer arrested in Scotland.[56]

Despite an armed guard, and sometimes with their complicity, George proclaimed the Day of the Lord all the way to London. In the capital itself, where he was lodged "at the Protector's pleasure" at the Mermaid Inn by Charing Cross, crowds of curious onlookers flocked to catch a glimpse of him.

Many had read *The Way to the Kingdom*, and were eager to judge whether the author was as colourful as his words, or as dangerous as his reputation. Presbyterian preachers also arrived to counter the blasphemy of the Inner Light. Meanwhile, eager to increase circulation, news-book writers loitered to catch incautious words that might add further spice to the rumours that George Fox had seduced Judge Fell's wife, or that the enchanted ribbons he reputedly wore drove young women into frenzies.

At the Mermaid, as well as dealing with his various visitors, George would also have heard further details of Overton and Wildman's arrests, and of others that had followed. Among them was the Leveller sympathizer, Lord Grey of Groby, as well as Thomas Harrison and large numbers of fellow Fifth Monarchists.[57]

Whether or not he himself was involved was probably immaterial. His organization included many individuals who over the years had been part of the radical movement, his own writings were inflammatory, and as his association with Morgan Lloyd demonstrated, he mixed in dangerous company. While under detention at the Mermaid, reflecting on what was taking place in London and across the nation, he was almost certainly aware of what the consequences might be, should he or his followers be accused of involvement with anyone caught plotting against England's government.[58]

From his detention he wrote to Oliver Cromwell. "Be still, and in the counsel of God stand, and that will give thee wisdom, that thou mayest frustrate men's ends, and calm men's spirits, and crumble men under..." Thus, he made clear that he, George Fox, speaking as a prophet of God, supported the Protector's recent actions. He then went on to suggest that what was now under way in England was to the benefit of others elsewhere: "... feel his hand that is stretched out over the nations; for a mighty work hath the Lord to do in other nations, and their quaking and shaking is but entering..."[59]

Nevertheless, at the beginning of March, he learned that it was not sufficient, and that a nervous Protector demanded in writing that George Fox was a man who would not lift a sword against the Protectorate. "I, who am of the world called George Fox," said the prophet, implying that the spiritual realms knew him somewhat differently, "do deny that the carrying or drawing of any carnal sword against any, or against thee, Oliver Cromwell, or any man..." "God is my witness," he said, continuing to speak as one whose authority came from a divine source, "by whom I am moved to give this forth for the Truth's sake, from him whom the world calls George Fox; who is the son of God who is sent to stand a witness against all violence and against all the works of darkness, and to turn people from the darkness to the light, and to bring them from the occasion of the war..."[60]

But, though he opposed violence, and was a friend to peace,

he also implied, by referring to Paul's letter to the Romans, his support for any righteous secular power forced to "the occasion of the magistrate's sword, which is a terror to the evil doers who act contrary to the light of the Lord Jesus Christ, which is a praise to them that do well, a protection to them that do well and not evil."[61] By referring to "my weapons" that "are not carnal but spiritual", he also implied that where standards of righteousness were compromised, then George Fox, and by implication, the Children of Light, would oppose the transgressors.

Though the statement maintained that words and peaceful actions, rather than violence, would be used to uphold righteousness, addressed to the most powerful man in England, currently preparing to prosecute individuals who disrupted church services, it was a provocative message. So too, addressed to the man ultimately responsible for the nation's blasphemy laws, was George's reference to himself as the Son of God. The deeply religious Cromwell, however, was a man who not only enjoyed theological debate, but was also personally committed to religious toleration. On receiving George's communication, he almost immediately requested that he be brought to Whitehall.

CHAPTER EIGHT

Horrid Blasphemy

Resolved: That James Nayler, upon the whole matter, in fact, is guilty of horrid blasphemy.

House of Commons, Monday, 8 December 1656

"COME AGAIN TO MY HOUSE," said Oliver Cromwell, "for if you and I were but an hour in a day together we should be nearer one to the other." At their meeting on 6 March 1655, the two men talked at length. "And I spake much to him of Truth," George recalled. But, on one crucial issue, they could not agree. "And ... he said we quarreled with the priests," said George, "and I told him I did not quarrel with them, but they quarreled with me and my friends." Furthermore, George had protested, "the prophets, Christ, and the apostles declared freely, and ... against them that did not declare freely; such as preached for filthy lucre ... " But Cromwell would have none of it. Sternly, he reminded George Fox that the Instrument of Government not only enshrined religious liberty for all Protestants, but made it an offence to disturb others in their enjoyment of it.

Later, as George retraced his steps along Whitehall, Captain Drury of Cromwell's Lifeguard was sent to tell him he was set free. And, by the way, Drury added, "my Lord says you are not a fool." With his liberty assured, for the present at least, and only too aware of the Protector's determination to prevent disorder, George made his way to the City.

In 1654, two women of the north, Isabel Buttery and a

companion whose name is unknown, distributed *The Way to the Kingdom* on London's streets.[1] Together with Amor Stoddard, then resident in the city, Robert Dring of Watling Street, Simon Dring of Moorfields, and Ann Downer, a native of Oxfordshire, they established London's first Quaker meetings. Later that year, Francis Howgill, John Camm and Edward Burrough arrived to build on their success.

Eager to win converts, the group proclaimed their message unceasingly. The response, in the highly charged religious atmosphere of 1650s London, was evidently massive. "We have two or three meetings in the week," said Francis Howgill in September 1654, "but no place large enough."[2]

By March 1655, when George Fox arrived, a place large enough had been found. Part of the building, at Aldersgate, north of St Paul's, housed a tavern; and thus it was known by the sign for the Bull and Mouth that swung outside. "[W]e two go to the great meeting place which we have," Edward and Francis told Margaret Fell, "which will hold a thousand people, which is always nearly filled."[3]

Clearly it was also the case that, ignoring the Protector, part of that filling was through the deliberate plundering of other sects: "...our brethren were...at several meetings," Edward said in March 1655, "some at one and some at another, and some among the Baptists and gathered people."[4] In this respect the Children were evidently successful. "A great shatter is among all the forms and gathered churches," said Alexander Parker triumphantly.[5]

The dispossessed congregations responded with fury. "All the priests and all the gathered congregations in the city preach against us," said Francis Howgill, "and are bent in great rage, and print lies, and incense people much."[6] Others disrupted the Children's own assemblies. "[T]he room which was very large hath been filled with people," another London Quaker recalled, of days at the Bull and Mouth, "many of whom have been in uproars, contending one with another, some exclaiming against the Quakers, accusing and charging them with heresy, blasphemy, sedition and what not...others endeavouring to vindicate them and speaking of them more favourably ... "[7] Even the mighty voice of George Fox was sometimes hard pressed to be heard. "G. was at the great meeting place ... " Edward told Margaret, "and his voice and outward man was almost spent amongst them."[8]

Though concerned at the Children's aggressive evangelism, both the Protector and John Thurloe remained equally alarmed by their militant language. For it was clear that *The Way to the Kingdom*, as well as similar tracts written by George Fox's colleagues, were no less than criticisms of a government they saw as reneging on earlier ideals.[9] And even if the Children maintained that they spoke metaphorically, to a nervous administration their broadsides and pamphlets appeared provocatively incendiary. Moreover, with their references to drawn swords, and their graphic warnings to the rich and powerful, their words was uncomfortably similar to those of groups openly committed to violence.

Only minutes from the Bull and Mouth, at Christ Church Newgate and Allhallows Upper Thames Street, messages smuggled from two imprisoned leaders were read aloud to rapturous Fifth Monarchist congregations. One of those leaders, the Reverend Christopher Feake, arrested earlier in the year, had refused to provide assurances that he would not take up arms against the government. The other, the Reverend John Rogers, had been imprisoned since the previous year.[10, 11] Though once among Cromwell's most fervent supporters, since the dismissal of the Nominated Assembly, both had virulently attacked him.

Rogers denounced Cromwell as a liar and a hypocrite, accused his government of breaking all Ten Commandments, and prophesied that his regime would suffer collectively the fate of King Charles.[12] Feake named him the "Little Horn" of Daniel 7 and accused him of inhibiting the establishment of God's Kingdom on earth.[13] In the *New Non-conformist*, published and distributed by the Christ Church congregation, Feake also called the faithful to be ready to make "a standing Army for the King of Saints, in the time appointed of the Father".[14] Heightening such apocalyptic agitation was Anna Trapnel, Fifth Monarchist prophetess, who proclaimed regularly at Allhallows. In 1654, during a trance lasting several days, and in a torrent of rapturous verse which she claimed came by the Spirit, Anna predicted that the Lord would "batter" Oliver Cromwell and his hypocritical friends.[15]

At the Bull and Mouth, said Edward Burrough, "There are some brought under the power exceedingly, which strikes terror into the hearts of many."[16] The many, witnessing such scenes, reading George Fox's words, and observing their militant evangelism, were unlikely to see a great deal of difference between the Children of Light and the equally fervent Fifth Monarchists.

To the Children themselves, the crowds at their meetings, and the numbers convinced, simply confirmed that they were winning Christ's battle. However, as the evangelists travelled the country, and sent news of their achievements to Swarthmoor, their letters often contained details of comrades arrested and imprisoned. Sometimes the Vagrancy Act was employed, sometimes the Protector's proclamation against disturbance, and sometimes it was the refusal to swear oaths in court which made a Friend guilty even if innocent of the charge that first brought them. "M. Halhead and T. Salthouse are in prison at Exeter," Francis Howgill told Margaret Fell in the summer of 1655, in just one letter among many. "…Jas. Lancaster and Thos. Stubbs, and other Friends are imprisoned at Bedford."[17]

Among the travelling evangelists was George Fox, who on leaving London made his way through Bedfordshire and the counties south-east of London. Later, he remembered seeing soldiers question travellers at a military check-point near Rochester – a reminder, no doubt, of the tensions that lay heavy on England. Though John Thurloe's vigilance and the incompetence of its leaders had ensured that the Royalist conspiracy came largely to nothing, when a rising led by Colonel John Penruddock went ahead in the West Country in mid March, orders were issued that national security be tightened. In April, fearful that foreign Catholics would come to Royalist aid, all persons suspected of Roman Catholicism were henceforward required to swear the Oath of Abjuration, a form of words renouncing papal authority. A refusal to swear implied guilt.

The troops themselves, just as in the north, were also in

evidence at George's meetings. In Reading, he said, at a huge gathering held in an orchard, standing among a crowd which also included two of Margaret Fell's daughters, was George Bishop of Bristol, a Captain in the Army, who stood "with his sword by his side", and perhaps also wearing his uniform and officer's insignia. They had also been in evidence the previous year in Bristol itself, when John Camm, John Audland, Francis Howgill and Edward Burrough all arrived in the city. "We have here in Bristol most commonly 3000 to 4000 at a meeting," they reported, "The priests and magistrates of the city begin to rage, but the soldiers keep them down ... "[18] Just as in Carlisle in 1653, the radical troops of the New Model Army, many still clinging to Leveller sentiments, made their support very clear for the Children of Light. Meanwhile, at Reading, said George, "a glorious meeting it was", "and a great convincement of people there was that day, and people were mightily satisfied."

He himself was mightily satisfied by those Children eager to carry the message of the Light further afield. In 1654, James Lancaster, Miles Halhead and Miles Bateman, all of Westmorland, had visited Ireland. Early in 1655, Mary Fisher, a Selby servant girl, and her colleague Ann Austin, planned to cross the Atlantic to Barbados.[19] William Caton, together with his colleague John Stubbs, meanwhile, were considering a venture in Holland.[20]

Far less satisfactory were the reports of continued arrests, and passing through Colchester later in the year, George paid a visit to one of the captives. The prisoner was James Parnell, the young man who in 1653 had visited George in his own captivity at Carlisle.

For James it was his second time in prison.[21] But, while the earlier imprisonment had been for a few weeks only, after being charged in Colchester with riot, he was sentenced to many months in the town's grim castle gaol. That George visited him there suggests a fondness for the young man, as well as a desire to repay an obligation. That the nineteen-year-old James was small and slight, and apparently eager to fast, perhaps also roused a concern in his large and powerful leader that he was not well suited to the rigours of a harsh captivity.

Weeks later, George and Amor Stoddard rode into Cambridge. They found the town in uproar, with almost every student ready to hurl missiles and abuse at the man who represented such a threat to Calvinist orthodoxy. As they were forced to a halt, and as many hands grabbed his bridle, Amor's horse threw his rider to the ground. Overcome with rage, and filled by a mighty surge of power, George then stood up in his stirrups and declared over the heads of the mob.

As he spoke, tall above his fretting horse, the crowd momentarily fell back. "Oh!" cried the students, "he shines, he glisters!" To Amor and to the Children in the crowd, it was as if George Fox were Moses come down from Mount Sinai.[22] Though it was another of the incidents that George chose to highlight later, and though he certainly did so to remind his readers that he was the leader divinely chosen to overturn the Apostasy, clearly something unusual took place, one of those mysterious and numinous events that is beyond the realm of the ordinary.

It was also certainly the case that many of the Children did regard George Fox as England's Moses, sent to lead them to the promised land. That they did so, and that George himself agreed with them, would also be used against him in later years. However, though Edward Burrough, William Dewsbury, and several others, were men of powerful presence and preaching ability, none of them appear to have possessed the extraordinary charisma that made George Fox unique. None except James Nayler, the man who like George "heard a Voice", and whose preaching after Dunbar had caused the people "to implore that the whole work of salvation might be consummated in them."

From the day he first added his name to the Children, James was acknowledged a leader. Like George Fox, he was courageous and passionate, as well as a man whose powers of insight allowed him to discern the thoughts and compulsions of others. Unlike George, however, whose "abrupt and broken" expressions sometimes gave the appearance of rudeness, the Yorkshireman possessed an outward grace that almost immediately drew people to him. Moreover, unlike the big-boned

George, James was of medium height and build, while his regular features and ruddy complexion, framed by long sandy hair, were regarded by many as compellingly attractive.[23]

Arriving in London early in 1655, James quickly established himself at the centre of the Children's work. "James is fitted for this great place," Alexander Parker told Margaret, "and a great love is begotten in many towards him."[24] His charisma and good looks also made him a favourite at Whitehall. "Yesterday I had a meeting at a house called Lady Darcy's," James said in November; "many were there from the Court, some called Lords ... divers ladies, divers officers of the Army ... divers are brought to tears when they hear the Truth."[25]

Thus, it did not seem untoward, when in that same month George left London for Cornwall, that he should also leave James overseeing the Children's work. Yet when he recounted the event later in his *Journal*, he added a note of apprehension. "And as I parted from him," he said, "I cast my eyes upon him, and a fear struck in me concerning him."

But this was written with hindsight. Though it is nowhere expressed as such, that they had worked together since that first meeting at Stanley, and that James was among the first to be called to Swarthmoor, suggests that from the beginning the two men were friends. If that were indeed the case, then it casts another, and very revealing light, on George Fox's reaction to what occurred in the following year.

In the winter of 1655, meanwhile, as George rode alongside Edward Pyott of Bristol, another former captain of the New Model Army, and William Salt of London, none of them would have been in any doubt that England was now a nation under military rule. Behind the move lay fears of further Royalist uprisings, of Fifth Monarchist plots, and the suspected complicity of the other radical sects in both. Adding to it, however, was Oliver Cromwell's unease at the overall failure of the Western Design, the planned seizure of Spain's Caribbean colonies and the potential extension of Protestantism, that had finally convinced him that God was displeased at England's moral slackness.[26]

In October 1655, the country was divided into twelve

regions, each governed by a Major-General answerable to the Protector. Their first duty, working alongside existing authorities, was to maintain security by suppressing unlawful assemblies, disarming potential Royalist rebels, and apprehending thieves, robbers and highwaymen. Assisted by specially appointed commissioners, they were also to enforce a ban on horse-racing, stage plays, cock-fighting and bear-baiting, as well as the laws against drunkenness, sexual licentiousness, blasphemy and swearing.

Thus, in January 1656, the prophesied Millennium year, when George and his companions crossed the Tamar into Cornwall, watching them closely was Major-General John Disbrowe, the man responsible for the south-western counties.[27] Like the north, his region was one of Royalist and Catholic sympathies, as well as home to Penruddock's failed rising, and Disbrowe was uncomfortably aware that the slightest spark could ignite a blaze of disaffection. It was a discomfort considerably increased by George Fox's suspicious tactics. Robert Hawkin, a Cornish Quaker, recalled them later: "The ffirst yt came into ye County," he said, "was our antient & faithfull friend, George Fox ... accompanied with Edward Pyott, of Bristoll, and William Salt of London, and their manner was to Enquire for the honest and well inclined and those yt were of good Report whose Desires were To fear God."[28]

But, as Disbrowe's agents described how the Children first gathered lists of names, and then went from house to house with personal invitations to attend the meetings George Fox was scheduled to address, he wondered if the whole campaign was in fact a cover for insurrection. By the time George arrived at Marazion, rumour said that all public meetings in Cornwall would be banned. Nevertheless, determined to maintain his own programme, he prepared a message for the seven parishes close to Land's End. "The mighty day of the Lord is come and coming," it declared, "... the secrets of everyone's heart shall be revealed ... If you do this light hate, this will be your condemnation. If you do it love and come to it, you will come to Christ, which light will bring you off all the world and teachers and ways of all the deceivers in it."[29]

Eagerly, William Salt gave a copy to John Keate, clerk to local Justice of the Peace, Major Peter Ceely.[30] Hours later, just outside St Ives, while waiting for Edward's horse to be re-shod, the three Quakers were arrested. Marched into the town, they were confronted by Ceely himself, who, at the head of an agitated crowd, demanded to know if the subversive tract was indeed the work of George Fox. "Major Ceely said he was a magistrate," George recalled, "and then I told him he should show forth gravity, and sobriety, and his authority, and keep the people civil ... For the Indians were more like Christians than they." Furious at being lectured, Ceely ordered the three to swear the Oath of Abjuration. Dismissing a written alternative that George carried with him, endorsed earlier by Oliver Cromwell, he sent the prisoners under guard to Launceston.

They arrived on 22 January 1656. By March, as rumour swept the country that this time the Leicestershire prophet would certainly hang, supporters, opponents and those eager for a spectacle had all descended on the town. As the trial opened at Launceston's March Assizes, armed troops were stationed in the streets, while the Chief Justice, John Glynne, president of the court, required a bodyguard to force his way through the crowds.

The tension, together with the knowledge that the trial was watched carefully not only by John Disbrowe, but also by Oliver Cromwell, clearly agitated Chief Justice Glynne. So too did George Fox's obstinate and well-informed determination to challenge every statement, that eventually forced the court to abandon an obsession with the prisoners' refusal to remove their hats, and to finally produce the indictment. The defendants, it said, "who go under the notion of Quakers ... who have spread several papers, tending to the disturbance of the public peace, and cannot render any lawful cause of coming into these parts ... having no pass for their travelling ... refusing to give sureties of their good behaviour ... and refuse to take the Oath of Abjuration, &c ... "[31]

At that point, Major Ceely interjected: "... this man," he said, pointing at George, "... he went aside with me and told me how serviceable I might be for his design and that he could raise four thousand men in an hour's warning and involve the nation into blood and so bring in King Charles ... "[32]

But, though George Fox exasperated him, clearly Glynne did not believe Peter Ceely. In the end, he issued a heavy fine; twenty marks apiece for contempt, and no release until it was paid.[33] George, William and Edward, however, had absolutely no intention of paying. They were innocent men, and they demanded to be released.

Nevertheless, though there was no release, George's supporters were determined to express their solidarity. Several visitors, often bearing gifts of food, were natives of Launceston, while others, including an eager young man named Thomas Lower, travelled from surrounding towns. Others still came from much further afield. Among them was William Caton to discuss his evangelistic campaign in Holland, while John Stubbs and former Baptist, William Ames, both returned from the Netherlands, arrived seeking advice on carrying the message into Ireland, Scotland, and northern Europe.[34]

Meanwhile, Ann Downer of Robert Dring's Moorfields meeting, walked from London that she might be George's cook and secretary. Through her, he sent letters of encouragement to Quakers across the nation: "... be valiant for the Truth upon earth ... " he exhorted, "And this is the word of the Lord God to you all, and a charge to you all ... be patterns, be examples in all countries, places, islands, nations, wherever you come; that your carriage and life may preach among all sorts of people, and to them. Then you will come to walk cheerfully over the world, answering that of God in every one; whereby in them ye may be a blessing, and make the witness of God in them to bless you ... "[35]

Sometimes the visitors to Launceston also brought news of tragedy; the worst being the death of James Parnell at Colchester. Kept in a tiny airless cell high in the castle wall, compelled to use a too-short ladder and a length of rope whenever he collected his food, one day James missed his footing and crashed to the ground. Forced by his gaolors into a cell even smaller and more stifling, and fasting as a rebuke to such brutality, James died at the beginning of April. The verdict was suicide.

In July, as the Devonshire authorities used the laws against vagrancy to close their roads to Quakers, the flow of visitors also came to a halt. One of those stopped, and thrown with 25 others into Exeter Gaol, was James Nayler. Though James had proved a capable leader, his workload was increasingly affected by the tensions running high in London. Eventually, in March 1656, staggering under the pressure, he called on Francis Howgill and Edward Burrough to come to his aid. Some weeks later, they felt called to warn several London Children against excessive enthusiasm. On being reproved, one of them, Martha Simmonds, complained to James.[36] When he then refused to support her, she accused him of being no better than the priests she had previously abandoned. "I came to Jerusalem," she told him, "... and behold a cry, and behold an oppression."[37]

Reduced to tears, and obviously close to breakdown, James Nayler entered that landscape where reality becomes distorted. At the same time, Martha projected onto him all her wounded emotions. In July, she followed him to Bristol. Justifying herself with references to the Shunammite woman before Elisha, together with others she knelt in reverence before James Nayler.[38] Meanwhile, his tears and obvious confusion told his colleagues that his mind was unsettled. "My Deare J.N. is as one that is not," observed Richard Farnsworth, and in August he urged a visit to George Fox at Launceston.[39]

But, in Devon, James was arrested. And by the time George was set free in mid-September, under an amnesty which eventually included religious detainees elsewhere, James Nayler and Exeter Gaol were the talk of England. In the dark of the prison, it was said, James Nayler had raised his fellow captive, Dorcas Erbury, from the dead.[40] A huge outpouring of emotion followed, and with Martha Simmonds arriving to encourage them, some of Exeter's female prisoners, all singing, "Holy, holy, holy," prostrated themselves at James's feet.

In the filthy conditions, probably hungry and tired, Dorcas had almost certainly suffered a physical collapse that terrified her friends. Meanwhile, already severely overwrought, James had embarked on a fast, fortifying himself with nothing but an occasional pint of white wine. The heady combination, of anxiety, hunger, alcohol and sickness, exacerbated by a sense of martyrdom, was a potent breeding-ground for the outbreak of hysteria that took place.

George arrived in Exeter one week after leaving his own prison. On Sunday, 21 September, he joined the Quaker captives for worship. And there, with mounting agitation, he saw James and his male comrades wearing their hats during prayers. It was something entirely new; hats might be worn before the apostate world, but never before God. Moreover, the implication was obvious. If James Nayler was prompted to such an action by the Spirit, it had clearly bypassed George Fox. Equally, the situation confirmed what some had said earlier in London: "... its like there is an evill thing begot amongst ffriends in ye citie," Richard Roper told Margaret Fell, "ye same as was amongst the Church at Corinth divisions & strife & contention one saying I am of James another saying I am of ffrancis & Edward."[41] For George Fox, it was clear just what was taking place. On the day after the service, when James went to kiss him in greeting, George proffered his boot. "It is my foot," he said.[42]

From Swarthmore, an agitated Margaret addressed James. "I have heard that thou would not be subject to him to whom all nations shall bow," she said, reminding him of an assurance given earlier that he would not be the cause of divisions. "... I warn thee from the Lord God," she concluded, "... beware of siding with unclean spirits, lest thou be cut off for ever."[43]

Clearly, Margaret was in no doubt as to who was the prophet appointed to lead the world into the new age of the Spirit. The letter, however, discovered years later among her own papers, seems never to have reached James.[44] Another letter, from Hannah Stranger, one of his London supporters, did reach him, and unwisely, in retrospect, he put it in his pocket.

In mid-October, James and a group of supporters travelling through the West Country towards London, decided to enter Bristol, "in the manner of a sign".[45] Next morning, through a pelting autumn rain, a bare-headed young man led a horse on which sat James Nayler, whose own long hair hung sodden about a face gaunt with prison-pallor. Strewing garments before him, and chanting "Holy, holy, holy, Lord God of Sabaoth," were Hannah Stranger and Martha Simmonds, both up to their knees in mud.[46] When they were arrested, Hannah's letter was discovered. Addressed to James, it named him "the fairest of ten thousand," the "only begotten son of God". A postscript from Hannah's husband added, "thy name shall be no more James Nayler, but Jesus."[47]

With almost total silence from Bristol's Quakers, James was examined before the city's magistrates. Whether it was the heightened tensions of the Millennium year, the reputation of the accused, or the nature of the offence, they clearly felt unable to proceed. Very quickly, the prisoner was transferred to London and brought before a specially convened Parliamentary committee.

Observing on behalf of the Children of Light, Anthony Pearson was at first optimistic: "... wt will bee ye end of it," he asked, now that the Children's message was "testifyed before ye highest cort in ye nation, yt god himselfe is come down, to dwell with ye sons of men ... "[48] Furthermore, he claimed, apart from some very violent men, the whole assembly was satisfied with James's replies.

In this, however, he was mistaken. An attempt to combine Parliamentary government with the military rule of the Major-Generals, the Parliament of 1656, the second under the Protectorate, was designed to ensure political unity against all threats. Since Royalists were debarred from standing, the most serious threats were perceived as "discontented spirits" – that is, the political and religious radicals.[49] As by various means almost one third of those returned at the election were subsequently excluded, the bulk of the remainder were the most rigorous Puritans, many of them opposed to the toleration enshrined in the Instrument of Government, that "all shall be protected that profess faith in Jesus Christ".[50]

Nevertheless, the discussion that took place was wide-ranging and sometimes sympathetic: "... that which sticks most with me," said Colonel Sydenham, a Member for Dorset, "is the nearness of this opinion to that which is a most glorious truth, that the spirit is personally in us."[51, 52]

"If you hang every man that says, Christ is in you the hope of glory, you will hang a good many," observed Henry Lawrence, President of the Council of the State. "You shall hear this in every man's mouth of that sect."[53, 54]

That, said Major-General Skippon, a staunch Presbyterian, was the problem: "their principles strike both at ministry and magistracy."[55] Moreover, he said, referring to the Instrument, "it was never intended to bolster up blasphemies of this nature."[56]

In the end, Skippon's view prevailed, and the man who once fought valiantly for Parliament was condemned as a blasphemer, an imposter, and a seducer of the people. Though a motion for the death penalty was narrowly defeated, no one disagreed that punishment should be both public and severe.[57] "Either be strict in this or you do nothing," said the Lord Chamberlain, Sir Gilbert Pickering, "for certainly this of Quakerism is as infectious as the plague."[58]

Despite an intervention by Oliver Cromwell, and two public petitions, the sentence was carried out in January 1657. Watched by a huge crowd, James Nayler was pilloried at Westminster, and then whipped through London's streets to the pillory at the Old Exchange in the City. There his tongue was bored through with a red-hot iron, while a similar instrument branded him on the forehead – "B" for "blasphemer". Three weeks later, he was whipped through Bristol, and afterwards imprisoned in London.

Many of the Children staggered in shock. James's supporters, however, resentful at the leadership's very obvious lack of support for him, began a campaign of disruption. The leadership, meanwhile, denounced them as Ranters. "Persons of a loose ranting spirit got up," said George Whitehead, "and frequently disturbed our Friends' meetings in London, by their ranting, singing, bawling, and reproaching us, crying out against divers of our faithful ministers … viz. 'you have lost the power, you have lost the power.'"[59]

That George Fox was moved by such accusations is unlikely. Partly it was motivated by his resentment at the challenge to his leadership, and thus to his divine appointment.

However, the challenge also implied something more. In the view of James Nayler's supporters, the removal of the hat during prayer indicated that a movement committed to a rejection of ritualism, had in reality begun instituting observances of its own. And thus, inevitably, it was in the process of becoming an institution of the apostate world. James Nayler, by contrast, remained true to the purity of the Children's beginnings.

With that, however, George Fox could not agree. "And they raised up a great darkness in the nation," he said of James and his following. Ignoring the widespread extremism and aggression of the Children in general, as well as those "raptures" of his own youthful days, and indeed much of his own early message that had emphasized individual response to the experience of the Inner Light, he thus transferred onto James Nayler all responsibility for the wave of anti-Quaker hysteria that followed the events at Bristol.

"They meet in thousands in our county," complained a Member for Devonshire, as Parliament continued to debate the Nayler affair, "and will certainly overrun all, both ministers and magistrates."[60] Endorsing such views were a host of petitions, drawn up by the Children's opponents, and all urging Parliament to bring in a Bill to suppress the fanatical followers of James Nayler and George Fox.[61] Though Luke Robinson and other influential sympathizers were able to prevent the mention of Quakers by name, new clauses added to the vagrancy laws provided for the detention and expulsion of anyone unable to provide magistrates with good reasons for their presence in any given area.

For George, and for other leaders shocked and alarmed by the Bristol events, the hostile reaction was a catalyst for action. Moreover, though George's claims to earlier misgivings regarding James were certainly written with hindsight, the attempts by Edward Burrough and Francis Howgill to suppress London's enthusiasts suggest that by 1656, in an organization that now numbered its adherents in thousands, a process of reflection and realignment was already under way. Besides, it was also a continuation of a process that began when George Fox assured Oliver Cromwell that although his movement had received a new revelation, that would transform the world and its people, it presented no real threat to the existing order.

Emphasizing that point, George sent Epistles to the faithful Friends: "To the elect seed of God called Quakers ... Go not forth to the aggravating part ... let your moderation, and temperance, and patience be known to all men ... for that which reacheth to the aggravating part ... breeds confusion, and hath a life in outward strife ... "[62]

When he left London again in the spring of 1657, this time making for Wales, he perhaps considered that although 1656 had passed without violent eruptions from Fifth Monarchists, indeed with no Millennium, and had thus lifted an anxiety from England, on his own 32-year-old shoulders there was a new weight of responsibility. For, although the Inner Light remained at the heart of his message, his aim now was also to rally the disillusioned among his brethren and to confront those who supported James, while also seeking to refute those opponents who made capital from the events at Bristol.

As he visited meetings along his way, he was certainly also reminded of how the laws deprived the Children of their freedom. "Seldom under a thousand," he said, "in prison in the nation for tithes and going to the steeplehouses, and for contempts and not swearing and not putting off their hats." Among many recommendations made by a representative meeting convened at Balby the previous year, was that the Friends keep a record of such sufferings.[63] As 1657 wore on, so that accurate accounts might be laid before judges, and before the Protector, George recommended the process more widely.

When he crossed the Welsh border in June, it was to discover that reports of the huge numbers there who clearly sided with James Nayler were correct. Thomas Holme, one of his travelling companions, had described the situation earlier to Margaret Fell: "... the most of the Welshmen that ministered is gone out of the truth and hath believed a lie," he said; "... they come into our meetings and tumbles upon the floor, and when they can no else stop me from speaking one falls a-singing, and they sit in meetings in haircloth and ashes ... "[64] Seeing it for himself, George's anger burned against the man who had once been his friend. "And some that had run out with James Nayler did not come to the meeting," he said in Cardiff, "and I sent word to them that the day of their visitation was over; and they did not prosper no ways."

Late in the summer, together with Alexander Parker, James Lancaster, and Robert Widder of Over Kellet in Lancashire, George set off for Scotland. But, there, for the first time, he made little headway. Later, he linked it to the nation's profound commitment to Calvinism, running deeper than anywhere else in the British Isles: "... they had frightened people," he said of the Presbyterian ministers, "with the doctrine of election and reprobation ... that the greatest part of men and women God had ordained for hell, let them pray, or preach, or sing, and do what they could ..."

Yet, like Protestantism in England, the Presbyterian Kirk was intimately linked to Scotland's sense of nationhood. Moreover, since the beginning of the decade, the country had been occupied by an English army, men who spoke with accents very similar to those of George Fox. The nation's ministers were also well prepared, and having pronounced anathema on anyone seen welcoming the Quaker invaders, they petitioned for and obtained from the English military authorities in Edinburgh an order for George Fox's expulsion.

Though George ignored it, everywhere he met opposition. Moreover, even in the Army, where previously he had always found a welcome and gained converts, there were tensions. "Captain Davenport," he said later, recalling a Quaker officer in Scotland, "... who afterwards was turned out of his place for not putting off his hat and for saying 'thou' and 'thee' to them." Davenport's immediate superior, Colonel William Daniel, made the reason quite clear: such actions were hardly conducive to a fighting discipline.[65] Moreover, Davenport was not alone, and in his Journal George recalled that several junior officers and troopers were at that time discharged as a result of Quaker affiliations.[66]

Since 1655, when Quaker troops refusing the Oath of Allegiance were sent to Scotland, there had been accusations of disruptions to Presbyterian church services, and of irate local populations. Equally serious, as far the Army's commander in Scotland, General George Monck, was concerned, was the Levelling talk that threatened insubordination, and the even more dangerous talk of the rejection of all carnal swords. Though unwilling to undertake any wholesale purge, he remained uneasy regarding Quakers, and during George Fox's months in the region under his command, he backed any officer wishing to discharge such men from their regiments.[67]

In February 1658, George turned his face southwards. Back in the north of England, through Anthony Pearson he met Henry Vane, former member of the Council of State, who at various times had been among the most influential men in the Commonwealth, and who was also devoted to the cause of civil and religious liberty. Though briefly imprisoned in 1656, he had refused to modify his views, and on his release, he had continued to criticize the Protectorate. For although in 1657 Oliver Cromwell had declined the offer of the English crown, in the opinion of Henry Vane, any political system where one man ruled alone quickly became a tyranny as evil as that of Charles Stuart.

"Is this George Fox?" Vane said in surprise. "I thought he had been an elder man." George was then almost 34 years old, and knowing of him only by his reputation and his huge following, like many others, Vane had imagined that the man and his movement stretched back many years. Almost certainly, however, despite his guest's youth, he was eager to solicit George Fox's support for his own cause. But, whatever Anthony Pearson may have thought earlier, George Fox and Henry Vane did not agree: "... he grew into a great fret," George said later. However, since he also recalled that Vane had told certain friends that "if Anthony Pearson ... had not been with me he would have put me out of his house as a madman," it seems likely that Vane was not the only man in a fret.[68]

Late in May 1658, George attended a gathering that was described some years later as "a General Yearly Meeting for the whole nation".[69] The venue was Beckering's Park, the substantial Bedfordshire home of John Crook, another Justice of the Peace committed to the Children of Light.[70] It was, George recalled, "a glorious meeting" attracting almost 4,000 people who took every bed at every inn for miles around.

Although it may not have been the meeting's overall purpose, it is nevertheless clear that at some point it provided a forum whereby George attempted to limit the disruption caused by the Nayler affair, by reassuring those distressed by James's actions, and by pacifying those angry at their leadership's failure to support him. It seems that he also aimed to encourage a sense of unity, that would in future limit the possibility of any Friend feeling themselves open as individuals to fresh leadings of the Spirit.

"I was moved by the power and spirit of the Lord," he said, "to open unto them the promise of God, that it was made to the Seed, not to seeds, as many, but to One, which Seed was Christ; and that all people, both male and female, should feel this Seed in them ... "

In this, of course, he was reneging on his own earlier experience and teachings. But, despite his conclusions being to some extent linked to James's challenge to his leadership, and despite not being "an elder man", George Fox had travelled a long road since leaving Fenny Drayton in 1647. Almost certainly experience had taught him that if an organization is not grounded in some form of structure, while the winds of change might mould it into dynamic new shapes, they are equally likely to blow it entirely away.

"Friends," he said, "take heed of destroying that which ye have begotten." Moreover, although he had once been taken up in raptures, he had also seen where such enthusiasm could lead. "That which calms the spirit and cools the spirit goes over the world and brings to the Father," he said, "to inherit the life eternal, and reaches to the spirits in prison in all."

Moreover, he continued, if Friends truly desired to "reach that which is of God in everyone," and to do so with discernment, then they must do it quietly. "All the boisterous, and hasty, and rash, beget nothing to God," he insisted.

Finally, aware of the spirit of intolerance that was descending on England, he attempted to keep his movement safe:

"...Friends, meddle not with the powers of the earth," he warned, "keep out of all such things... Keep out of all vain jangling, for all that be out from the law... but all that be in the law, comes to the Lamb's power, in the Lamb's authority, who is the end of it, the law..."[71]

Reading the reports sent by his agents, it perhaps seemed to John Thurloe that George Fox was indeed advising the troublesome Quakers to moderate their excesses. Nevertheless, he couldn't help being suspicious. Especially when he considered the visit to Henry Vane, or when his eyes were drawn to one of the Leicestershire prophet's more recent pamphlets, *The Law of God, the Rule for Law-makers*, and to one sentence in particular: "[A]re not all foundations to be overthrown that is not according to that of God in every man?"[72] Yet, John Thurloe hesitated, and thus it was not until three days after most delegates had departed, that a troop of cavalry broke down John Crook's door and forced their way into his house.

George watched from the garden. "...I heard them ask what Friends were in the house..." he said, "And the soldiers and constables said I was the man they looked for, but they never came into the garden..."

George Fox, however, was not the only Quaker in John Thurloe's sights, or in England's gaols. In 1650 in Derby, one man had offered himself as a prisoner in George Fox's place. Now, however, in 1656, in a gesture of solidarity and to highlight injustice, over 200 Quakers publicly offered "to lie in the same dungeons where their friends lay, that they that were in prison might go forth and not perish in the stinking dungeons and gaols."

George also attempted to intercede on the captives' behalf with Oliver Cromwell. "I met him riding into Hampton-Court Park," he said, "...in the head of his life-guard." But, as he drew near, on Friday, 20 August 1658, it seemed to him that the man who had dominated England for so long was moving towards the landscape of eternity.

Two weeks earlier, Cromwell's favourite daughter, Elizabeth Claypole, had died of cancer. Already sick himself, her suffering and death had devastated him. Perhaps he spoke of it to

George Fox, for learning of Bettie's fear and depression, George wrote to her. "And she said it settled and stayed her mind," he said later. Perhaps the Protector also urged something similar for himself from the man who had a reputation for discernment and healing.

"Come to my house," Cromwell said, as George urged leniency for the suffering Quakers. But, when George arrived, Cromwell could not receive him. "And Harvey told me," he said, "who was one of his men that waited on him, that the doctors were not willing I should come in to speak with him."[73]

Ten days later, on 3 September 1658, Oliver Cromwell, Lord Protector of England, the man who despite very human failings had steered his nation through the surging tides of political and religious transformation, died at Hampton Court. Without him, the future ahead lay uncharted and uncertain. And, though he could not have known it, the following two years would also transform George Fox's perception of himself and his mission, and would also be the catalyst that transformed the Children of Light into the religious society through which they would move into the future.

CHAPTER NINE

The Good Old Cause

Where is the good old cause now? ... and what is become of it? In whose hands does it lie?

Edward Burrough, *To the Whole English Army* (1659)

"*F*RIENDS, MEDDLE NOT with the powers of the earth," George Fox warned the great Bedfordshire meeting, "keep out of all such things ... Keep out of all vain jangling." Issued to men and women who for years had been intimately involved with the religious and political upheavals of their nation, however, such advice was unlikely to be received everywhere kindly. Nor, indeed, was it advice he had ever shown much inclination for taking himself. Since leaving Fenny Drayton in 1647 he had rubbed shoulders with many influential men, while as leader of a major religious movement, and in believing himself a prophet of God, he had issued warnings, admonishments and counsel to the movers and shapers of England's destiny. He also remained convinced that the news that the Apostasy was ended and that Christ was now come to his people was to be declared to the whole world.

He had also several times addressed Oliver Cromwell, including in 1657 when he added his voice to those who warned the Protector against accepting the crown. However, like almost everyone else in England and in Europe, he was unprepared for the chaos that followed Cromwell's unexpected death.

Yet, at first, chaos had seemed unlikely. In September 1658,

Richard Cromwell, Oliver's eldest surviving son, a modest, retiring civilian, followed his father as "Lord Protector of England, Scotland, and Ireland, and the dominions thereunto belonging." Most of the subsequent loyal addresses echoed the sentiments of the Army, reminding Richard that his father, a man used mightily by God, would be remembered by all good men for asserting the liberties of God's people, for restoring domestic peace, for loving civil rights, and endeavouring reformation.[1] It was also the Army's fervent hope that the same Providence would enable Richard "to carry on that good old cause and interest of God and his people."[2]

"The Good Old Cause" was the name given by the soldiers of the New Model Army to the reasons they fought for Parliament in the Civil War, and why they then supported the Commonwealth. To many, despite his very human failings, it was also embedded in the person of Oliver Cromwell, a man who by virtue of military brilliance, a powerful and charismatic personality, and the forces of a revolutionary movement, had been thrust into the leadership of his nation. It was that same personality, plus a shrewd grasp of political reality, that in the face of criticism from left and right, and the aspirations of many disparate groups, had enabled him to hold a divided nation together.

With his passing, how exactly "God's people" were to be governed, and what was meant by the liberties, civil rights and reformation embedded in the good old cause, was to become a matter of profound difference. But though such differences began immediately to stir, in the dying months of 1658 they were not readily apparent.

Taking advantage of the peaceful transition, London's Quakers presented the Council of State with details of 115 of their comrades imprisoned around the country, plus the names of nine who had died. In response, a circular letter was sent to 34 prisons where Quakers were held, requesting particulars of their offences. Subsequently, and maintaining that Quakers were guided more by "a spirit of error, than a malicious opposition to authority", orders were issued for the release of 40 captives, with the possibility that more should follow. For the Friends, the response appeared filled with promise.[3]

Similarly promising was the peaceful election, after which, in January 1659, a third Protectorate Parliament assembled at Westminster.[4] At its opening session, after preaching on the text, "Mercy and truth are met together; righteousness shall look down from heaven", the Reverend Thomas Goodwin then expounded the virtues of toleration within a truly Christian state.

Despite Goodwin's optimistic words, however, the differences that Cromwell had held in check now began combining into power blocs. The Cromwellians, a conservative group of politicians and Army officers, generally supported a Protectorate. The Republicans, or Commonwealthsmen, whose aim was to restore the pre-Protectorate Commonwealth, included a Parliamentary faction led by Henry Vane and Arthur Haselrig, many junior Army officers and rank-and-file soldiers, Levellers, Quakers, Fifth Monarchists, some Baptists, and various others. Another group of senior officers, the "Wallingford House Party", so called since they met at the London home of Major-General Charles Fleetwood, favoured a form of government dominated by the Army.[5]

Opposing them all were those who favoured restoration of the monarchy. They too were divided. As well as those whose interests lay primarily with the king, there were Laudian Anglicans who loathed Puritanism in all its forms, and Roman Catholics who saw in the pro-Catholic Stuarts hopes for a toleration extended to themselves. Large numbers of Presbyterians also asked if Charles Stuart might represent their interests more successfully than Richard Cromwell. Eager to utilize their potential, Charles instructed the Royalist peer, John Mordaunt, to encourage alliances between Royalists and Presbyterians. He also instructed Mordaunt to promise future pardons to anyone, saving the regicides, willing to abandon the republic.

During the first weeks of the new Parliament, in the debates surrounding the Bill of Recognition for Richard Cromwell, the Parliamentary Republicans, led by Arthur Haselrig, and supported by Army radicals, presented an essentially Republican manifesto. Drawing on the ideals behind the Agreement of the People, it offered encouragement to all opponents of the Protectorate bar Royalists. It also represented the Protectorate as a betrayal of the Good Old Cause. Although disagreeing with their ultimate agenda, but hoping to utilize their influence and support, Wallingford House entered into an alliance with the Republicans.

On 2 April, the Army's General Council of Officers met in London. Its purpose was to present a petition regarding Army grievances: its long-overdue pay, and indemnity from prosecution for illegal acts committed during war by order of a superior officer.[6] However, to the dismay of Wallingford House, hundreds of junior officers were determined that it should also promote a radical agenda.[7] Reminding the nation that England's Army was called forth to defend the people's just liberties, together with demands for arrears and indemnity, the final petition proposed that the Army should assist Protector and Parliament in removing "the wicked" from their places, a barely concealed reference to all who opposed the Good Old Cause.[8] Together with a recommendation that all good-effected people should enjoy freedom of worship, the petition also observed that such freedom had been "of late much violated by Indicting and Imprisoning many of their persons".[9]

Almost certainly it was no coincidence that on 6 April, following two large meetings in London, the Friends presented another declaration to Parliament. This time it contained details of 144 Quaker prisoners, of 21 deaths, plus a summary of the persecution of 1,960 others over the previous six years.[10]

Once week later, 164 Friends gathered at Westminster to offer themselves as replacements for their gaoled comrades. This time, however, almost certainly seeing them as linked to the Army radicals, the response was hostile. Three Friends, Thomas Moore, John Crook and Edward Byllinge, were called into the Commons chamber and told that if they objected to imprisonment, they should cease disturbing godly ministers and frustrating busy magistrates. Meanwhile, those gathered at Westminster should go home.[11]

Two days later, and opposed by the Republicans, the Commons resolved that the Council of Officers should not meet without the consent of Protector and Parliament. Shortly afterwards, Richard Cromwell declared the Army Council dissolved.

On 22 April, Fleetwood's faction staged a *coup d'etat*. Richard was ordered to dissolve Parliament and entrust himself to the Army. Believing Fleetwood and the Republicans to be united, many voices were raised in support: "... if the Army (by the Lord's good hand assisting them) shall now begin where they left the work of the Lord, & faithfully carry on that Good Old Cause, There are a willing People, and their number not a few, who will stand by them with their lives and estates ... " The authors of the paper, delivered to Charles Fleetwood on 26 April, named themselves "A People who through Grace have been hitherto kept from the Great Apostacie of this day".[12]

Such overtures fuelled the fears of conservatives. Haunted by visions of Agitators in the Army, of the Agreement of the People, and of toleration for religious fanatics, once again they saw England on the highway to Münster. But, as April neared its end, the clamour for the Good Old Cause was joined by a call for the Good Old Parliament.[13] No other authority, it was argued, than that which had worked with the Army to establish the Commonwealth, could deal with the Army's grievances, and equally promote the Good Old Cause. Bowing to popular opinion, Wallingford House capitulated. On 7 May, the Rump of the Long Parliament, the remnant remaining after Pride's Purge in 1648, and replaced in 1653 by the rule of a Lord Protector, was recalled to Westminster.[14]

Swept along by a tide of euphoria, radicals across the land offered a host of suggestions. Edward Byllynge proposed that Parliaments be chosen by groups of united parishes, with religious persecutors disqualified both as members and electors. Like many others, he also suggested that harsh gaolers be dismissed, and that strong, warm and decent gaols replace filthy dungeons and stinking holes.[15]

Under the heading "Fifty Nine Particulars", George Fox also

presented recommendations. "Let no man be prisoned for tithes … let no man be put to death for cattle, for money or any outward thing … let all fines and amercements be given to the poor … let all the poor people, blind and lame, and cripples be provided for in the nation … " He also issued a powerful call for religious toleration and for an end to persecution: "He that will be Lord over a man's faith is in darkness … He that will Persecute people about Faith, be in the dead faith, and is out of that Faith which works by love and gives Victory … "[16]

But, though the Army high command had acquiesced to the restoration of the Rump, when Parliament made provisions for a new militia, they began to suspect that it was intended as a rival military organization.[17] With some of those nominated to assemble such militias being well known for radical opinions, conservatives saw the fanatics not only pressing recommendations on Parliament, but also being issued with weapons. In the view of Edward Hyde, chief advisor to Charles Stuart, it was a plot to mobilize all those opposed to monarchy.[18]

During the third week of May, as it attempted to define the limits of toleration, the Rump also appointed a committee to investigate cases of imprisonment for conscience and how the sufferers might be discharged.[19] Among many Quakers scheduled for release was James Nayler.

In the same week, Parliament refused to recognize the Protectorate. Two weeks later, following the resignation of Richard Cromwell, Charles Fleetwood was appointed Commander-in-Chief of the Armies of England and Scotland. A purge of Cromwellian officers followed, while others previously cashiered by Oliver were reinstated. As rumours abounded that many previously discharged Levellers, Baptists and Quakers would follow, while conservative fears mounted, radical hopes soared.

When Parliament then considered "how a more equal and comfortable Maintenance may be settled for the Ministry … than by Tythes", they soared higher than ever. In the north, the Friends threw themselves into collecting signatures for an anti-tithes petition; in some places they canvassed door to door. By the time it was presented to Parliament, over

15,000 individuals had added their names. Weeks later, 7,000 Quaker women throughout England signed a similar petition.[20]

But, while the Friends saw potential victory, their opponents were determined to thwart them. Among them was William Prynne, one of those pilloried under Laud in 1637, and who later, as a Member of Parliament for Cornwall, had supported Denzil Holles in his attacks on Independents and the New Model Army. Prynne was also fiercely opposed to the sects, and in his tract *Ten Considerable Quaeres concerning Tithes*, he maintained that nine out of ten signatories to the Quaker petition were in any case too poor to pay tithes. Moreover, he continued, behind the petition were the Jesuits who controlled most congregations of Anabaptists and Quakers, and whose aim was to destroy the Protestant ministry.[21] Fearful of antagonizing that ministry, the Rump shelved the issue of tithes.

William Prynne also had another grievance. Following the recall of the Rump, and being prevented from taking his seat, he had drawn up a list of 213 still-living members of the Long Parliament, who for various reasons were secluded, debarred from taking their seats.[22] The Rump, however, dared not remove the military guard from the Westminster door. For, were Presbyterians and Royalists to enter, the Commonwealthsmen would be hopelessly outnumbered.

Such divisions encouraged the Royalists, and during the summer John Thurloe learned of an insurrection planned for early August. As houses were searched and weapons seized, regiments around the country were put on alert. Meanwhile, as the militia continued to muster, in areas of particular vulnerability new companies were enrolled.

Though the Friends no doubt knew of George Fox's earlier warnings, they were perhaps also aware that he had contributed his own recommendations to the men in power. Moreover, in an ambiguous pamphlet entitled *The Lambs Officer is gone forth with the Lambs Message*, he also made it clear that a judgement was about to fall. "Guilty or Not Guilty," he asked tithing priests, "the Lamb and the Saints shall have the victory."[23]

Besides, many Friends were torn. Many had served in the

New Model Army; they were heroes of Naseby and participators in the Putney debates, and they could not rest easy when all they once fought for was threatened. "I can neither persuade them to it nor dissuade them from it," Alexander Parker wrote anxiously from Wiltshire, regarding Friends named as militia commissioners but uncertain how to respond.[24]

Others were more decisive. In June, Amor Stoddard was among several named commissioners for Westminster. In July, Thomas Curtis, a Friend at Reading and another former New Model Army man, was among those named for Berkshire. Many more were named for Cheshire, Cornwall, Devon and Gloucestershire, Worcestershire and Wiltshire. Others were named for Wales, while Edward Pyott was among those enrolled in Bristol.[25]

"The Quakers appear in great bodies in several places, and it alarms us," Viscount Mordaunt wrote to Edward Hyde. Nevertheless, he believed such alarm would soon be overcome. "[I]n a few days," he assured Charles Stuart, "we shall order it so as we hope we may be able to defend ourselves against the storm of Quakers and Anabaptists."[26]

Presbyterian ministers, meanwhile, encouraging the rebellion, whipped up fear of fanatics. The Quakers are up, they told their anxious congregations. In one Devon town, said a news-book report in July, "the crie for a while increased, and grew higher and higher, to wit, that the Fifth Monarchy Men, Anabaptists and Quakers were joyned together, not only to cut the throats of the Godly in that town, but the throats of the Godly in the nation."[27]

In the event, when the day arrived, only in Cheshire, led by William Booth, a secluded Presbyterian MP, did the rising go ahead. Rather than declaring for King Charles by name, however, seeking to undermine Rump and Army alike, Booth called for "a free parliament".[28] He also claimed that by raising a militia, the government would subject England to "the meanest and most fanatick Spirits of the Nation".[29] Booth's own forces, however, routed by John Lambert, were largely allowed to escape.

Early in August, George Fox was in London. As he listened

to heated debates in the streets, and read broadsides pasted to the city's walls, perhaps it was at this point that he saw the tide beginning to turn. *A Phanatique League and Covenant*, said one such broadside, in a parody of the earlier Scottish alliance. John Lambert, Thomas Harrison, George Fox, James Nayler, and many others, it maintained, were members together of "the Fanatick party within the Kingdomes (formerly so-called) of England, Scotland and Ireland, living under and submitting onely to the Government of one Prince, Belzebub, Emperor of the Infernal Region ... " Their aim: "to obstruct and abolish all Decency, Order, and Form whatsoever, on the Concernment of Church or State."[30]

Another highlighted London's resentment at years of Puritan morality. "The Quakers who are now flourishing," said a broadside purportedly issued by the *Maids of the City of London*, "and indeed even ready to affright us with their dismal looks; yet we bid defiance to all such as quake ... and all Conventickling congregations."[31]

At the end of the month, George left London for Reading. His host was Thomas Curtis, an old friend, but now commissioner for the Berkshire militia. Meanwhile, as factions pursued their disagreements, in mid-September, radical officers loyal to John Lambert drew up a petition to Parliament. In their recent victory, they said, they had clearly "been saved by the Lord, and have had a late view of his appearance as of old."[32] Being encouraged therefore to consider how his work might be furthered, they urged reform of the law, the enlargement of religious toleration, and the removal from office of all those who supported the Royalist rebellion. They also requested that John Lambert become second-in-command to Charles Fleetwood.[33]

When a second petition followed, fears mounted that once again Parliament would be expelled by the Army. Insisting that the Army be subject to Parliament, and having revoked Lambert's commission, Arthur Haselrig ordered trustworthy regiments to occupy Westminster. With most of the troops supporting him, Lambert then ringed the occupiers. On 13 October, by force of arms, he expelled the Rump.

In Reading, meanwhile, George Fox was collapsed in a black depression, that lay upon him for ten long weeks. "I ... was in great sufferings and exercises," he said later, "... for I saw how the powers were plucking each other to pieces." Later too, after years of statements by George that the Friends had always shunned political activity and were equally always committed to peace, he was accused of hypocrisy. Not only had many of his friends served in the militia, said Robert Rich, a one-time London Quaker, citing documents that he had seen personally, but he had actively encouraged them. Moreover, Rich continued, it was also George Fox's intention "to exalt himself over the Government of the Nation".[34]

Whether this was so, and as a friend and supporter of James Nayler, Rich had little sympathy for George Fox, it would mean that the depression was caused by more than an awareness of events spiralling out of control: "... thou wert for certain very busie in the year 1659," Rich accused, "in numbering thy people."[35] If indeed he had supported the militia commissioners, and Rich also supported a claim that he nominated various friends for the magistracy, then at some point George must have realized, probably devastatingly so, that no matter how many nominations were made, or "Particulars" sent, that in the game of power and politics, both he and the Friends were expendable. And perhaps, though pushed to the depths, was a realization that while he believed he spoke as a prophet, to many individuals he was simply another fanatic.[36]

His depression also fed an old bitterness. Set free in September, James Nayler had hurried to Reading. Later, he wrote to Margaret, far away at Swarthmoor, and widowed the previous year when Thomas Fell died in October. "I suppose you may have heard of my going to see our beloved G.F." he said, "... which in tenderness of love I did ... hearing he was not well."[37] G.F., however, refused to see him.

Meanwhile, in Scotland, after responding to a plea from Arthur Haselrig and demanding recall of the Rump, General George Monck announced that if necessary, he would replace the Parliament by force. Certain that Fifth Monarchists, Levellers, Quakers and radical Baptists could not be trusted to support him, he purged over 150 of them, officers and troopers alike, from his regiments.[38]

After promising that his troops would be paid, Monck issued *A Conference between Two Souldiers*, a propaganda publication downplaying the view that victory in war was a sign of God's favour.[39] A further publication, *Information from some Souldiers of the Parliaments Army in Scotland*, claimed that the self-serving officers in London were the tools of Anabaptist agitators.[40] He then highlighted, and sometimes exaggerated, reports that in the streets of London, common soldiers were attacked by apprentice boys and citizens, who blamed them, rather than the fanatics, for the ills of the nation.

The Council of State was dissolved late in October. In its place, the Army established a Committee of Safety comprised of Fleetwood, Lambert and John Disbrowe, plus others to be appointed. When Fifth Monarchists and Friends hurried to make nominations, rumour said that both had proposed Thomas Harrison, leader of a sect openly committed to violence.[41] In the same month, as assaults on Quakers increased, a Quaker shop in London's Tower Street was attacked when it dared open on a Sunday.

At the beginning of November, John Lambert led 12,000 men north to confront George Monck. Throughout November and December, at Newark on Trent, only miles from Elizabeth Hooton's home at Skegby, mobs wielding cudgels and knives hurled "wild-fire" and rotten eggs into Quaker meetings.[42]

Early in December, George Monck crossed the border and established his headquarters at Coldstream on the Tweed.[43] In Yorkshire, and now behind Lambert, who had reached Newcastle, Thomas Fairfax, the New Model Army's now retired commander, assured Monck of his support.

On 17 December, the Committee of Safety collapsed, leaving England with no government. As Monck threatened to march south, Vice-Admiral Lawson, stationed off the east-Kent coast, began moving ships towards the Thames. On the 27th, Charles Fleetwood recalled the Rump.

Recovered from his depression, George spent the final months of 1659 in East Anglia. Though a warrant issued in

Norwich for his arrest was not enacted, the mayor explained the reason behind it: "that the soldiers should not meet and so we should not meet ... our meetings would make tumults in the town."

It was hardly surprising. Fuelled by rumours that Quakers were arming to support John Lambert, anyone reading Monck's pamphlets or who listened to Presbyterian preachers knew just who was corrupting the Army.[44] Meanwhile, in London the attacks highlighted earlier by Monck continued. When a group of soldiers were set on by city apprentices, householders showered them with roof-tiles and ice from the gutters.

On 1 January 1660, George Monck began marching on London. On the same day, York surrendered to Thomas Fairfax. Days later, Fairfax urged Monck to restore the monarchy. Meanwhile, John Lambert's army, unpaid, and downhearted by weeks of heavy snow, either deserted to Monck or went home.

Seeing so much sliding away, Edward Burrough pasted another broadside throughout London. "Where is the Good Old Cause now?" he implored, "and what is become of it ... was not the Good Old Cause for liberty ... the just Freedom of all People ... what is become of it now? Is your zeal perished?"[45]

But, as Monck's army moved towards London, increasingly it was supported not only by opponents of radicalism, but by a population weary of confusion and fearful of conflict. Meanwhile, in London and all across the country radicals appointed earlier to the militia were removed.

Entering the city on 3 February, Monck found its tax-payers, many of them influential Presbyterian lawyers and merchants, refusing all payments unless it was to a full and properly elected Parliament. Throwing in his lot with them, and making his support for a new Parliament clear, he dissolved the Rump.

The night that followed was recalled by a young man named Samuel Pepys, who only weeks earlier had begun keeping a diary. "The number of bonfires," he said, "... at Strand bridge I could at one view tell 31 fires ... burning and roasting and drinking for rumps."[46] Among those plentifully plied with meat and ale, were the men of Monck's army. In the days that followed, they found part of their pleasure, as well as their duty, in attacking the fanatics their general had warned them against.

"I returned to London again," said George Fox, "when General Monk was come to London ... and some of the soldiers were rude ... "; "... they began to pull Friends out of the house violently," wrote another Friend of an attack by troops, "... yea they beat and abused Friends exceedingly in the streets ... they pulled me out ... knocked me down ... and tore all my coat."[47]

Amid the fall and rise of Parliaments, a reconciliation was finally effected between George Fox and James Nayler. Alexander Parker and William Dewsbury had both worked hard to melt George's unforgiving spirit, and though they cheered the event, in reality it was a miserable affair. Perhaps jealous of the charm that still sat so easily on even a mutilated man, George forced his old friend to kneel before him to beg his forgiveness.[48] Afterwards, he left London for the West Country and Cornwall.

Almost everywhere he saw evidence of the turning tide. Arriving in Bristol, he discovered that only the week before, the civil and military authorities had combined to drive the Friends from the orchard where for years they had been accustomed to meet. Desperate to rally them, George immediately called a public meeting at Edward Pyott's house just outside the city. Later, in a more optimistic frame of mind, he reflected on how the earlier violence had provided some valuable publicity. Those remaining in Bristol, he said, "said the city looked naked, the sober people were so gone forth to this meeting."

Two weeks after the roasting of rumps, George Monck oversaw the re-entry to the Commons of the secluded members, foremost among them, William Prynne and Denzil Holles. With a Presbyterian majority re-established, the long-delayed Presbyterian Ordinance of 1648 then went ahead. England and Wales was divided into classical presbyteries, the Westminster Confession of Faith was adopted, and arrangements were made to promote Presbyterians to significant parishes.

In March 1660, as a date was set for new elections, the Long Parliament, which first met in November twenty years earlier, voted its own dissolution. Meanwhile, in Fenny Drayton, where he visited his parents, George Fox was clearly no longer the rebellious youth of earlier years. At 36 years old, and the leader of a powerful movement, his opinion was now sought by those who had formerly spurned him. "Many asked me what I thought of times and things," he said.

On 4 April 1660, Charles Stuart issued the Declaration of Breda. While agreeing to defer the precise limits to Parliament, he outlined his initial terms for the restoration of the English monarchy. Among them were clauses concerning liberty of conscience: "... we do declare a liberty to tender consciences, and that no man shall be disquieted or called in question for differences of opinion in matter of religion, which do not disturb the peace of the kingdom, and that we shall be ready to consent to such an Act of Parliament as, upon mature deliberation, shall be offered to us, for the full granting that indulgence."[49]

Days later, John Lambert escaped from the Tower, where he had been confined by George Monck. When he called on supporters of the Good Old Cause to rally to him at Edgehill, for a brief moment, some individuals recalled the brave days of the New Model Army. Others saw the spectre of civil war. Few doubted, however, that the Children of Light would be among Lambert's ranks.

On Easter Monday, 22 April, as George spoke to a great gathering at Balby, "many thousands of people and Friends," he was suddenly interrupted. "Divide to the left hand and right hand and make way," shouted an officer, forcing his horse among the crowd. Behind him, with two trumpeters sounding the alarm, came a troop of horse and a phalanx of foot. "If he found either swords or pistols about any there," George told him confidently, "then let us suffer."

On the same day, in a ploughed field near Daventry, John Lambert, four troops of horse, and several field officers, surrendered to Monck's man, Richard Ingoldsby. No Friends, it seems, were among them.[50] Nevertheless, next day, after

George Fox, 1624 – 1691
There are no images of George Fox that can be said to represent
him with any certainty. The above is an artist's impression.

St Michael's Church, Fenny Drayton, Leicestershire.

George Fox was born in Fenny Drayton, a small village in rural Leicestershire, in the heart of the English Midlands. He was baptised at St Michael's and All Angels and attended church there in his childhood.

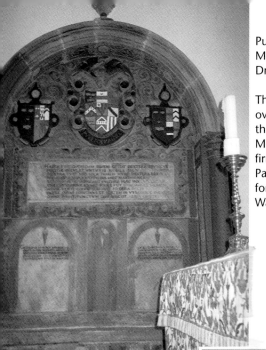

Purefey Family Monument. St Michael's Church, Fenny Drayton.

The Puritan Purefeys were overlords of large landholdings throughout the English Midlands. The family were firmly committed to the Parliamentary cause and fought for Parliament during the Civil Wars.

Pure Foy Ma Joye: Purefey Family Monument, St Michael's Church, Fenny Drayton.

The Purefey family moto – Pure Faith My Joy – may have inspired the young George Fox as he attended church each Sunday at St Michael's.

Pendle Hill, near Clitheroe in Lancashire.

"Atop the hill I was made to sound the day of the Lord." Atop the hill, on that same day, in the late sprint of 1652, as he gazed to the northwest, George Fox spied a land where the Lord had a great people waiting to be gathered.

George Fox's Pulpit from the site of Firbank Chapel. Here he delivered the message of the Inner Light to the Westmorland Seekers in 1652.

George Fox's Pulpit, Firbank Fell, Cumbria.

Firbank Fell, Cumbria.

There are words on the plaque that you can see on the rock. They say: "Let your lives speak." Here, or near this rock, George Fox preached to about one thousand seekers for three hours on Sunday June 13, 1652. Great power inspired his message and the meeting proved of first importance in gathering the Society of Friends known as Quakers. Many men and women, convinced of the truth, went forth through the land and over the seas with the living Word of the Lord, enduring great hardships and winning multitudes to Christ. June 1652.

In 1652 Swarthmoor Hall became the northern headquarters of the Children of Light, the name by which the Quakers were then known. In 1669, eleven years after the death of her first husband, Margaret Fell, the mistress of Swarthmoor, was married to George Fox.

The interior of Swarthmoor Hall, showing the original furnishings.

© The Religious Society of Friends in Britain

The Great Hall.

The main bedroom.

Staircase from entrance hall.

another large meeting, this time at Warmsworth, "as they passed through the counties," said George, "several [Friends] were taken up." What was their purpose in Yorkshire, they were asked, and why were they now leaving so hurriedly?

The Convention Parliament assembled on 24 April. Although in the election supporters of the Good Old Cause were heavily defeated, most of the 100 newly elected Royalists were to some degree dissenters from the Anglican Church. Thus, when the Declaration of Breda was presented to them, it was adopted with enthusiasm. When Royalist Members were added to Presbyterians who supported the king, there was also a majority for monarchy. On 1 May, despite some objections, the vote to restore England's monarchy was carried overwhelmingly.

"So God overthrew them," George said, "... and brought the King over them; who were always complaining that the Quakers met together to bring in King Charles." And that slander was unwarranted, he continued, for "Friends did not concern themselves with the outward powers." But, by the time he wrote those somewhat untruthful words, he was anxious to reassure that same king that such had indeed been the case.

Charles Stuart arrived in England at the end of May. But, though the crowds that welcomed him were hoarse with cheering, the king himself was wary. "Charles is of a pretty sober countenance," said Richard Hubberthorne, who saw him and his brother James enter London. Richard was also filled with foreboding: "... the great pride and vanity of those that brought him in is inexpressible," he said, "and he is in danger to be brought to those things, which he in himself is not inclined unto."[51]

Meanwhile, as George Fox continued to ride north, letters from London expressed fears that wholesale reprisals would eventually be taken against the pro-republican religious sects. Other reports spoke of continuing violence. In Cambridge the Friends' meeting-room in Jesus Lane was repeatedly stormed by townsfolk and students, who with "regard neither to old or younge men, or women with Child, but did very much abuse them by tearing there Cloathes, tumblinge and moileing

divers in the nasty and loathsome Channells in the streets ... "[52]
In Norwich, after smashing meeting-house windows, the city's
apprentices spat in the faces of male and female Friends and
then showered them with horse-droppings.[53]

Accompanied by Francis Howgill and Thomas Curtis,
George reached Swarthmoor in May. The absence of Thomas
Fell was perhaps disturbing. Moreover, since rumour of a sex-
ual liaison had been rife for years, that he now returned to
Margaret in her widowhood almost certainly fuelled them fur-
ther. The true state of affairs, however, is unknown.

What almost certainly did take place was discussion regarding the organization of the Quaker movement. Together with
Margaret, who as its northern administrator, and keeper of the
movement's archives, probably knew more of its concerns than
almost anyone else, George considered the meeting at Skipton
that followed three days after Warmsworth. Later he described
it as a general meeting of men Friends, attended by representatives "out of most parts of the nation ... about business of the
Church both in this nation and beyond the seas." Thus, although
the account is fragmentary, it seems to have been the first of
what could be called a truly representative general meeting.[54]

Together with a call for a collection to further the ongoing
work overseas, the Skipton meeting also considered an issue
that had been part of the Friends' work from the beginning,
the relief of their own poor, and sometimes provision for the
wider community. It was that issue, George recalled later, that
at Skipton transformed hostility into a somewhat grudging
admiration. Eager to observe the routing of many fanatics, a
number of local magistrates had arrived with the militia. But
"when they saw Friends' books and accounts of collections
concerning the poor," George said, "how that we did take care
one county to help another ... that the poor need not trouble
their parishes ... the justices were made to confess that we did
their work."

Almost certainly too, as the upheavals of the previous year
were discussed, and the reversal in fortunes of the religious
and political radicals, there was debate as to how the Quaker
movement would survive into the future.

What took place at the end of the month certainly threw the issue into stark relief. "It is a plot," George said, alerted by the anxious expression on Margaret Fell's face. Outside Swarthmoor's parlour door he was confronted by a gang of constables. "George Fox?" they asked.

That night, he was held captive at Ulverston. One of the guards, sitting squarely in a big fire-place, finally admitted that it was fears of witchcraft that placed him there. "They were afraid I would go up the chimney," George said scathingly. Next morning, after a night of wakefulness and insults, a guard of thirty horsemen, followed by a crowd of townsfolk eager for sport, escorted him through the town.

"Two took me by one leg," he said, "and put my foot in the stirrup, and two or three by the other, and set me behind the saddle on a little horse." Then, his captors beat the creature so unmercifully that it galloped and bucked, throwing George to the ground. Watching with ill-concealed delight was a group of his Ulverston opponents. "One wicked fellow," he said, "kneeled down and lifted up his hands and blessed God I was taken."

In Lancaster, after being questioned by the town's mayor, Henry Porter, the man who had ordered the arrest, and then committed to Lancaster Castle Gaol, it was only after repeated demands that George was allowed a brief glance at the Mittimus detailing the charges.[55, 56] To the best of his remembrance, he said later, it ran as follows: "That he was a person suspected to be a disturber of the peace of the nation, a common enemy to his majesty...a chief upholder of the Quaker sect, and that he, together with others of his fanatic opinion, have of late endeavoured to raise insurrections in this part of the country to the inbrewing of the nation in blood." Furthermore, the prisoner might only be released on the order of the king and his Parliament.

Whatever had been George Fox's position in 1659, five months in Lancaster Castle Gaol gave him time to ponder on the events that led to his captivity. Earlier, in his dealings with Oliver Cromwell, he had denied that he personally was a violent man. Now, he began to challenge more vigorously than ever the view that the Friends were religious fanatics committed to violence, while also insisting that they had always walked in peace. "All which is false," he said, answering the charges against him in a pamphlet addressed to King Charles, "and I do deny every word."

Indeed, he continued, he had been accused of these things before. "In the days of Oliver," he said, "I was taken up as raising arms against him, which was false ..." Careful now to avoid the heavily spiritual language he had used to the Protector, and with absolutely no reference to himself as the Son of God, he continued, "And I denied drawing a carnal weapon against him," he said, "or any man upon the earth, for my weapons are spiritual, that take away the occasion of war and which lead to peace."

Moreover, he said, although he was accused of enmity towards the king, that too was false, "for my love is to him and all men." Aligning himself a little closer to Charles Stuart, he continued, "And I can say it is of the Lord that he is come in, to bring down many unrighteously set up."

Furthermore, he insisted, "the Quakers are not a sect, but are in the power of God before sects were ..." And, "as for fanatic, which is furious, foolish, mad, and raging," the Friends were quite opposite, "... for we through patience and meekness have borne lies, slanders, and persecutions many years, and undergone great sufferings."[57]

Next, in an Epistle to the Friends, he addressed those downhearted by the end of many radical hopes, as well as those disturbed by what might be regarded as flaws in their leader's prophecies: "... and as concerning the changing of times and Governments," he said, "let not that trouble any of you, for God hath a mighty work and hand therein. He will yet change again, until that come up which must reign ... Therefore let none murmur nor distrust God ..."[58]

Margaret also lobbied on George's behalf. "Contrary to law," Judge Fell's widow told King Charles, not only had George Fox been denied bail, but when "a copy of his mittimus was demanded, which ought not to be denied to any prisoner ... it was denied him." Furthermore, she added, "I am concerned in the thing, inasmuch as he was apprehended in my house; and if he be guilty I am so too."[59]

Then, she hurried to London to petition Charles herself. Very shrewdly, and seemingly on George's advice, she was accompanied by Thomas Curtis' wife Ann, whose father, Robert Yeamans, a former Sheriff of Bristol, was hung in 1643 for siding with Royalist forces against Parliament.[60] Anxious to reward those who supported his father, Charles assured Margaret of his willingness to assist her. Though constrained by an agreement repudiating unilateral action in respect of the law, he nevertheless urged that a writ of *habeas corpus* be issued. With it secured, George was summoned to Westminster to appear before the Court of King's Bench.

At heart, Charles was in agreement with the Declaration of Breda. He also appeared genuinely interested to understand why the religious groups believed as they did. When Richard Hubberthorne gained access to him in June, he had listened to an outline of Quaker belief. "Well, of this you may be assured," he said finally, "that you shall none of you suffer for your opinions or religion, so long as you live peaceably, and you have the word of a king for it."[61]

In September, as George Fox set out for his trial in London, another man headed north. Though James Nayler had thrown himself back into the Friends' work, in the summer of 1660, he felt prompted to return to the family he had left in Yorkshire eight years before. Early in October he was mugged in a field near Huntingdon. Bound, gagged and grievously injured, he lay alone for several hours. Eventually he was discovered by a passer-by who knew of a Quaker doctor at nearby Kings' Ripton. It was in the doctor's house that James Nayler died, and in his burying-ground that his body was committed to the earth.

If the news of his old friend's death roused uncomfortable emotions, then George Fox kept them to himself. In this he might have been encouraged by what greeted him in London, that perhaps led him to reflect uneasily on the Friends' past extravagances and on their support for the Good Old Cause. "And when I came to Charing Cross," he said, "there were multitudes of people gathered together to the burning of the bowels of them that had been the old King's judges, that had been hanged, drawn, and quartered." Had not Judge Fell's old friend, John Bradshaw, not died the previous year, he would have suffered the same fate.

True to the earlier promise made by Charles Stuart, the Act of Indemnity and Oblivion, passed in August 1660, which restricted reprisals against most of those prominent in the Parliamentary cause, did not include the regicides. Arthur Haselrig, Henry Vane, and John Lambert, meanwhile, though not regicides, remained in the Tower awaiting trial.[62]

At his own trial, George listened to the charge that together with his fanatical sect, he was an enemy to King Charles and plotting another bloody civil war. If this were so, he replied, where were the accusers? When no one came forward, he publicly declared his innocence: "I stretched forth my hands, and said … I was as innocent and pure as a child, for I never learned the postures of war, and I loved all men; I was an enemy to no man."

Though one of the Judges, Sir Thomas Twisden, was unconvinced, two of his colleagues referred the case to the king and his Privy Council. When it was announced finally that George Fox was to be set free, the Secretary of State, Sir Edward Nicholas, issued the appropriate warrant. Emerging into the late autumn air, an innocent man, as he had always maintained, and perhaps reflecting on the fate of the regicides and the men in the Tower, George Fox was surely reassured that he and Margaret had acted with wisdom.

With the deaths of the regicides, Charles Stuart also breathed more easily. For he was eager that Europe should see him as a monarch committed to forgiveness, tolerance and liberality. His Parliament had already dealt successfully with the Army; after passing an Indemnity Ordinance, a special assessment was levied to pay soldiers their full arrears in return for swearing loyalty to the new regime. In August, after demobilization elicited virtually no resistance, the New Model Army disappeared back into the towns and villages of England.

Now, Charles hoped to deal equally successfully with

dissent. The religious settlement of the nation, however, was not a subject relished by the Convention Parliament. Indeed, with some relief the Members had delegated it to a conference of learned divines. But, when their conclusions were published in October 1660, it appeared that they too had avoided the issue.[63] Though happy to accede to the toleration expressed by Breda, they were equally content to avoid the pledges Charles had made earlier to the Pope and to Europe's Catholic monarchs, regarding the easing of restrictions on Roman Catholics. Thus, they proposed an interim arrangement: a mixed Episcopal and Presbyterian structure, to remain in force until a lasting settlement was concluded by a newly elected Parliament.

Nevertheless, towards the end of November, a Committee was appointed to examine the sufferings of Quakers. Thomas Moore, himself a former justice, represented the Friends before it. "You may go up," he was told; "it is the King's pleasure that you may come to him with your hat on."[64] Those whose memories were longer than Charles Stuart's, however, were more wary, especially regarding any oaths of allegiance. A letter to Edward Nicholas from a nervous official in Bristol expressed the fears succinctly: "I thought it my duty to acquainte you ... of the refuseall of all the Quakers, & those Anabaptists & Others (who are of very dangerous principalls & disaffected to his Maties interest & Gourmt) to take the Oathes aforesaid, they being very numerous in this City ... "[65] Rather like an earlier correspondent, the writer had then described huge meetings in his part of the country, sometimes involving up to 1,000 people, and lasting well into the night. He hardly dared imagine what might happen if such numbers were provoked into civil disobedience, or even into violence.

Eager to advance the cause of toleration, various dissenting groups proposed compromises. Baptists submitted a form of words they deemed equivalent to an oath, while from the Friends came an offer declaring that while they could not swear, they nevertheless accepted the king to be supreme magistrate and chief ruler. To his just commands they would at all times yield due obedience in the Lord, they said, while they would never plot against his person or the peace of the kingdom, and would also uphold by lawful means his just authority. Were that not possible, then they would suffer the consequences.

In the winter of 1660, George Fox must surely have considered the extraordinary changes of the previous months. Although he himself was a non-violent man, and had always advised peace, over the years he had clearly enjoyed mingling with influential men and being at the centre of events. Thus he had perhaps been far more caught up in the euphoria of 1659 than he cared to admit later. He had also realized, it seems, that in the new political reality of Charles II, both he and his movement would be wise to overcome some aspects of their history. However, in December 1660, he had every reason to feel optimistic. "Leave it to me," King Charles had said, when the Committee that discussed Quaker sufferings had requested an official document urging lenient treatment by magistrates.[66] Who could ask for more? Earlier, Charles had assured Richard Hubberthorne that the word of a king was binding. Now, it seemed that it was indeed so.

CHAPTER TEN

War on Terror

"He is one of the heads and chief ring-leaders," he said, nodding towards George Fox.

Former Parliamentary soldier,
Saturday, 12 January 1661

"*T*HIS MORNING NEWS was brought to me to my bedside, that there had been a great stir in the City this night by the Fanatiques, who have been up and killed six or seven men, but all are fled."[1] So said Samuel Pepys, the man who in February 1660 watched the roasting of rumps from Strand Bridge. Later that same morning, Monday, 7 January 1661, after leaving his lodgings, George Fox made his way to Whitehall. "And all the city and suburbs were up in arms ..." he said.

Rumour flew wildly. Some said Anabaptists had stormed the city; some said Fifth Monarchists, others said Quakers. Within hours, Sir Richard Browne, London's Lord Mayor, had ordered the militia onto the streets.[2] That evening, Samuel Pepys reported how he and his wife and brother were several times stopped and questioned.

Very soon, everyone knew what had happened. On Sunday night, following hours of passionate preaching, a Fifth Monarchist congregation in Swan Alley, Coleman Street, led by master-cooper, Thomas Venner, broke open hidden caches of weapons and then ran with pistols cocked and swords drawn into the streets. Weary with waiting for the Millennium,

bitter at the defeat of the Good Old Cause, and fired with religious fervour, they had convinced themselves that only bloody
insurrection would bring Jesus to them.

After storming St Paul's Cathedral, for an entire day they
fought off the King's Lifeguard and London's Trained Bands.
Eventually, after rushing twice through the city gates, and leaving havoc in their wake, they fled northwards towards
Highgate. On Thursday, convinced that Venner represented the
onset of a radical uprising, Sir Richard issued an emergency
proclamation. All meetings of Anabaptists, Quakers and Fifth
Monarchists were banned, while the conventicles where they
hatched their plots were to be demolished. "... [A]ll people
were against us," George said later, "and they cried, 'There is a
Quaker's house, pluck it down.'"

At the end of the week, Venner and his remnant were surrounded in the Highgate Woods. Shrieking their battle-cry,
"King Jesus and the heads upon the gate!" (the "heads" of the
regicides, displayed for all to see), they fought with manic fury
– slashing, hacking, stabbing and shooting, until all were
either captured or killed. When the bodies were removed, and
the captives led away, London's authorities and the king's ministers considered the week's events. Not a few drew compar-
isons with the Münster Anabaptists. Determined to prevent
further insurgency, they issued orders for mass arrests.

On Saturday night, when the door of the house where
George Fox lodged was opened by a maid, a gang of troopers
shoved their way inside. One of them, a former Parliamentary
soldier, recognized George immediately. So, too, did George
recognize him. But if their former acquaintance had once been
friendly, on this occasion there was nothing of comradeship in
the man's eyes. "He is one of the heads and chief ring-leaders,"
he said, nodding towards the Quaker leader.

On Sunday, George was interrogated at Whitehall. Released
later, and avoiding a party of musketeers he guessed were sent
to retake him, he made his way into the City. Everywhere, he
saw houses raided and their inhabitants taken away.
Everywhere, too, he saw suspicion and fear. "It was hard for
any to go up and down the streets to buy provisions for their

houses," he said, "either men or women, for they dragged men and women out of their houses, and some out of their sick beds by the legs." One man dragged from his sick bed, a Friend by the name of Thomas Patching, died shortly afterwards in gaol.

Other Friends were arrested as they attended meetings the following Sunday. He and Francis Howgill only narrowly escaped; "... we went to Mile End," he said, "but the officers had been there and would not suffer any meetings, and as we passed away there came a company of soldiers with muskets, and ... they followed us till we came near Ratcliffe, but we lost them in the streets, and so escaped their hands."

It was not until George Fox, Margaret Fell (still in the city following her visit to the king), Richard Hubberthorne and other leaders finally met at a secret venue in London, however, that they realized just how widespread was the action against those deemed a threat to the state. For despite talk of toleration, the counter-insurgency measures prepared by Sir Edward Nicholas were every bit as efficient as John Thurloe's had been earlier. Indeed, given that all charges of treason against Thurloe were waived on condition that his extensive knowledge was shared with the new regime, then almost certainly Nicholas' agents were also using the Republic's old files.

As the London leadership pieced information together, a picture began to emerge: all over the country constables were kicking down doors, forcing their way into homes, and dragging fathers, husbands and sons from their families. With no word of their likely fate, they were hauled away, interrogated, and flung into castle dungeons and city gaols. All groups considered sympathetic to the previous regime were included: Fifth Monarchists, Ranters, Levellers, Baptists, Republicans and Quakers.

In all, over 4,000 Quakers were taken: 500 in London, 400 in Yorkshire, 280 in Lancashire, 240 in Warwickshire, and at least 100 each in 11 other districts.[3] Among them were many of the movement's leaders: in gaol at Aylesbury were John Whitehead, a former Parliamentary soldier originally from Scarborough, and Isaac Penington, son of a former Lord

203

Mayor of London.[4] William Dewsbury was in York Castle, George Whitehead in the castle gaol at Norwich.

At the same time, the leaders realized that it was not only the prisoners who suffered. As Margaret produced a letter from her daughter, Bridget, and though Bridget wrote desperately of the Swarthmoor estate, it was an issue that in one way or another concerned prisoners and their families all over the country. If "they keep men in custody that should till the ground," Bridget said, "the time of seeding being now, it cannot be expected that we should be able to maintain them in prison, [and] hire our tillage at home."[5, 6]

As they themselves waited for the night-time hammering on the door, it almost certainly became clear to the leaders gathered in London that their earlier efforts to win the support of England's new Royalist rulers had been overturned by Venner's fanatical outburst. Whether or not they were involved in the events was quite beside the point. To the men who advised Charles II, their reputation as religious fanatics and disturbers of the peace, their long-time identification as Levellers and Ranters, their support for the Army *coup d'etat* of 1659, and for republicanism, all made the Friends of Truth a very potent threat.

Realizing that their prospects were bleak, and their options limited, they almost certainly agonized over their past, and over the right course of action for the present. They surely also considered their various dealings with King Charles, as well as George Fox's earlier reassurance to the deceased Lord Protector that he did "deny ... the carrying or drawing of any carnal sword against any, or against thee, Oliver Cromwell, or any man."

In the face of the mass arrests and detentions, they clearly felt called to issue a new and comprehensive statement. And whether the absence from their meeting of the more militant spirits of 1659 was deliberate, or merely fortuitous, is unknown. However, given the content of the document finally produced, the leaders obviously sought to speak for what they believed was the majority of their movement, men and women who were prepared to reject fanaticism, and repudiate violence, while at the same time remaining committed to the beliefs and behaviour that lay at the root of their faith.

On 19 January, Thomas Venner and his colleague Giles Pritchard were dragged on hurdles through London's streets, and then hung, drawn and quartered outside their Swan Alley meeting-house. Two days later, George Fox and his colleagues issued their declaration. A copy was sent to the king and his Council, while others were hawked on the London streets. Years later it would be known as the Peace Testimony.[7, 8]

"A declaration from the harmless and innocent people of God, called Quakers, against all plotters and fighters in the world ... " it began. "Our principle is, and our practices have always been, to seek peace and ensue it and to follow after righteousness and the knowledge of God, seeking the good and welfare and doing that which tends to the peace of all ... All bloody principles and practices, we, as to our own particulars, do utterly deny, with all outward wars and strife and fightings with outward weapons, for any end or under any pretence whatsoever. And this is our testimony to the whole world ... "

The declaration also answered the charge that the Friends might abandon this non-violent stance should they feel called, like Thomas Venner, to fight for the Kingdom of Christ: "... the spirit of Christ, by which we are guided, is not changeable," it said, "so as once to command us from a thing as evil and again to move unto it."

In a move that was new, and certainly very far from some of the statements issued two years earlier, the declaration also distanced the Friends from the view that God's Kingdom could in any case be established in the present world: "... the Lamb ... hath redeemed us from the unrighteous world," it said, "and we are not of it, but are heirs of a world in which there is no end and of a kingdom where no corruptible thing enters."

As it also denied the charge of sedition, it drew parallels between the sufferings of the Friends at the hands of unjust men, and the sufferings of Jesus. "We have been accounted as sheep for the slaughter, persecuted and despised, beaten ... " Moreover, it continued, rather than the Friends plotting violence against others, it was they who suffered violence, a violence provoked by "the worship of our God and in obedience to his requirings of us ... " Thus, it was made clear that the Friends were sufferers both for the sake of conscience, and on behalf of toleration: "For which cause we shall freely give up our bodies a sacrifice, rather than disobey the Lord."[9]

Among Friends seeing the statement for the first time, and disagreeing in part with its sentiments, some hostile reactions were tempered by the knowledge that elsewhere in the city the remainder of Swan Alley's congregation were dying that day at Tyburn. During the following week, the corpses of Oliver Cromwell, Henry Ireton, and John Bradshaw were ripped from their graves, dragged through the streets, and then hung on the Tyburn gibbet where the Fifth Monarchists had died.[10]

Among those unable to resist the grisly spectacle was George Fox. Shortly afterwards, as he laboured on a letter urging Friends to send accounts of their recent sufferings for presentation to the king, he may well have reflected on how the ideals of men and movements are so often tempered by their interactions with political reality. "My Dear Friends," he began, addressing his following, "In the innocent seed of God, which will plead its own innocency ... "

Like the Declaration some days earlier, the letter contained no fiery invective, no prophetic denunciations, and no apocalyptic visions. Instead, it reiterated that the witness of the Friends, like that of Christ, would be manifested through suffering. Indeed, George continued, although such sufferings were the product of an "unrighteous world", rather than being an encouragement to Friends to overthrow that world, they were "your portion" in it. Its reward, moreover, was also to be found in a future state. For the Friends of Truth were "inheritors of an everlasting kingdom that is incorruptible, and of a world and riches that fade not away."[11] Within a very few months, George Fox had travelled a long way from the man who sent his Fifty-Nine Particulars to the Parliament of a republican England.

Meanwhile, Margaret Fell and Thomas Moore, as well as many others, continued to lobby the king, pressing on him the accounts of Friends' sufferings, reminding him of the January Declaration, and also that before he died, Thomas Venner had absolved Quakers of involvement in the January events. Eventually, as a result of their efforts, in May 1661 there was a full liberation of the imprisoned Quakers. "And so the Truth," said George, "with great labour, travail, and care, came over all."

Once again, the Friends breathed more easily. Some among them also began to believe that the repression that followed Venner's uprising was yet another understandable reaction of a nervous, but essentially tolerant regime. Almost it seemed that the timely emphasis of their peaceful position had restored them to friendship with the king and saved them from further persecution.

Perhaps it was a sense of security that in August 1661 led George to write optimistically about the success of the Friends' foreign missions. "Things beyond seas are pretty well … and Truth spreads in the Barbados … in New England … in Holland and Germany … in Ireland … Robert Maylin is gone for Jamaica … John Stubbs and Henry Fell are gone towards the East Indies … "[12]

But it was in the very same month that one of the most successful evangelists, on his return to England, issued a challenge to George Fox that plunged the Quaker movement once again into the controversy provoked earlier by James Nayler. This time, the challenge came from John Perrot, a native of Waterford, a former Baptist, and a man who, very much like James, possessed considerable charisma and charm.[13]

It was in the late 1650s, after leading a party that between them reached as far as Constantinople, that John was for the second time arrested in Rome.[14] After being questioned by the Inquisition, and charged with speaking against the Pope and the hierarchy of the Roman Catholic Church, he was imprisoned in a lunatic asylum. There, as well as writing epistles to the Friends at home, all signed "John, the Prisoner of Christ", he also became convinced that he too was to speak out against what he saw as ritualistic and ultimately damaging behaviour.

"I have received by express commandment from the Lord God of heaven in the day of my captivity in Rome, viz., to bear a sure testimony against the custom and tradition of taking off the hat by men when they go to prayer to God, which they never had by commandment from God ... "[15]

Once again, the issue concerned revelation and thus who had received "the truth", and also what constituted a form or ceremony. And once again, it was expressed partly in terms of human dress as a powerful signal of an individual's relationship to God and to their co-religionists. When the freed John Perrot arrived in England in August 1661, bringing with him his message that was in direct contradiction to accepted practice, and which had already once been resisted, George Fox's thoughts must certainly have returned to Exeter Gaol and to an image of James Nayler at prayer with his hat on.

Ominously, just like James, John Perrot drew people to him: "... the refreshings of life in many, after his coming thither, insomuch as in meetings where he was ordered to be were much fresher than lately had been known," said Isaac Penington.[16] Others spoke of John's charm, humility and godliness, while also reflecting on a powerful vein of mystical spirituality that appeared to run through him. John himself, while recognizing the value of the organizational structure achieved, nevertheless insisted that after this period of consolidation, the Spirit once again moved freely. As he issued a call for the Friends to respond to its prompting, and not to set limits to their religious lives, he condemned the removal of hats during prayer, the by-now common practice of shaking hands to signal the end of meetings, and the view that meetings should be ordered at regular times.

To some Friends, John's words seemed to echo the excitement and purity of their movement's beginnings. To the 37-year-old George Fox, however, the inner turmoil produced by the challenge must have been enormous. For not only did it threaten the structure put in place since James Nayler's trial, but it surely reminded him yet again that he too once moved at the prompting of that Spirit that "bloweth where it listeth, and thou ... canst not tell whence it cometh, and whither it goeth."[17] Moreover, hadn't he once said that those who quenched the Spirit "were in confusion and deceit"?[18]

The hat issue, however, refused to die. In London, John's sympathizers, many of them former followers of James Nayler, resolutely upheld his position against George Fox's appeals for unity. Towards the end of the year, John was also welcomed with some honour by Isaac Penington at his home in Buckinghamshire.[19] As he went on to travel in the south-west of England and in Ireland, many Friends flocked to him, finding in him a spirituality and freshness of vision that seemed so absent now in their official leaders. Seeing his own vision, his years of labour, and his authority undermined, George Fox retaliated. As he did so, his newly acquired meekness fell away, and the Leicestershire prophet thundered once more. "Whoever is tainted with this spirit of John Perrot ... will be swept out of the camp of God's elect ... take heed that your memorial be not rooted out from among the righteous."[20]

But, as the Friends asked whether a revelation made once by the Spirit might later be changed by the Spirit, the political landscape around them continued its own process of transformation. Though much of the Good Old Cause was lost, and though definitions remained imprecise, by withstanding attacks from monarchy and military alike, Parliament had continued to make good its claim to be the representative of the people. Thus the monarchy of 1661 was very different from that which went to the block in 1649. On releasing the Quakers imprisoned after Venner's uprising, King Charles had insisted, "that he shall expect returns of Loyalty, and all due Obedience, from all such persons whose liberty is obtained hereby ..." Nevertheless, it was Parliament that was responsible for ensuring enforcement.[21]

The Cavalier Parliament, elected in the Spring of 1661, was of a very different political composition from the Convention Parliament that preceded it.[22] The House of Commons was overwhelmingly Royalist; nearly one quarter of Members had been punished by the Republic for their loyalty to the king, and many had lost land to sequestration. The House of Lords was dominated by elevations made by Charles II and by his father before him. Both Houses were deeply embittered by the experiences of the past two decades, and while vengeance was not a word they used openly, it was something they were determined to exact.[23]

Beyond the restoration of episcopacy, the Convention had largely avoided religion. The Cavaliers met it head on; they were under no illusions as to the crucial link between an individual's faith and their politics, and they were determined to destroy the power of Puritanism. All Members of Parliament, they decreed, were to be bound by a test, that of being seen taking the sacrament according to the rites of the Church of England. A Corporation Act, designed to limit the power of urban administrations, that during the Civil War had provided crucial funds to the Parliamentary cause, also required municipal officers to conform to the same test. Thus were dissenters barred from holding municipal office. At the same time, it also became a crime to gather more than twenty signatures to a petition, or for it to be delivered by a delegation greater than ten. A Licensing Act also re-imposed censorship.

With bishops restored to their seats in the Lords, and a diminished Presbyterian presence in the Commons, the way was open to enforce a religious settlement designed to nullify the radical gains of former years. As the Book of Common Prayer was returned to England's churches, with the support of the bishops, and overriding the objections of Presbyterians, it was also revised so as to restore ceremony and to overturn the theology of Calvinism.

In May 1662, having been discussed by Parliament and by the convocations of Canterbury and York, an Act of Uniformity received the royal assent. Under its provisions, all ministers and teachers were to abjure the Solemn League and Covenant, renounce the right of resistance, and like Members of Parliament, be seen to conform to the established practices of the Church of England. Though the framers of the Act insisted the intention was to prevent dissenters entering the ministry, they were more than aware that the consciences of many already within it would not allow them to remain. Subsequently, joining others removed shortly after the

Restoration, between 1,000 and 2,000 Puritan ministers were forced from their livings. Among them were Nathaniel Stephens of Fenny Drayton, William Lampitt of Ulverston, and Gabriel Camelford of Stavely. Largely at the insistence of Gilbert Sheldon, Bishop of London, not one appeal was upheld.

In his *Journal*, George Fox maintained that such consequences were the judgement of God on the Puritans, who had so signally failed either to adhere to their own rigorous moral standards or to impose them on others. He must surely also have seen it as resulting from their failure to heed his own message, and perhaps, although it would have been a most politically unwise conclusion to make public, that he and his movement were not taken more seriously in 1659.

In 1662, however, the Friends were equally a target of Cavalier and Anglican vengeance. In the same month that the Act of Uniformity became law, so too did the Quaker Act, aimed at limiting, if not eliminating, the largest of the troublesome sects.[24] Indeed, observed a member of the Commons, the Quakers were not only a numerous people, "but growing more numerous daily, – and upon the King's indulgence ... were very high and confident; and they met together in great numbers, and were of dangerous consequence, and prevailed much to the seducing of the King's subjects ... "[25]

Under the provisions of the Act, it became illegal in any way to maintain "that the taking of an oath in any case whatsoever (although before a lawful magistrate) was altogether unlawful or contrary to the word of God." It also became illegal for any group other than a household, numbering more than five people of sixteen years or upward, to hold a religious meeting not authorized by law. The penalty for a first or second conviction was a fine of £5 and then £10; the third was transportation to England's colony of Virginia.[26]

As a wave of arrests followed, individuals were dragged from their homes, while sometimes whole groups were seized at meeting-houses. In the capital, the arrests were ordered by Sir Richard Browne, who in the same year that he supervised the rout of Thomas Venner, was created Major General for

London. Eager to prevent similar outbreaks of terrorism to that of the previous year, he was determined that as many as possible of those labelled "fanatics" should be incarcerated in London's prisons. The City Bridewell, the New Prison at Clerkenwell, and the Clink and the Marshalsea at Southwark were all employed. Most prisoners, however, were sent to Newgate Gaol, which even more than some of the dungeons where George Fox had spent time, was regarded as "a place of infamy and great distress".[27]

In June 1662, there was yet another reminder that the Good Old Cause was defeated, when Henry Vane and John Lambert were finally brought to trial. Condemned as traitors, both were sentenced to execution. But, while Vane was beheaded on Tower Hill on 14th of the month, after appeals from both Houses of Parliament, John Lambert's sentence was commuted to life imprisonment. Arthur Haselrig, Anthony Pearson's old superior, had died in the Tower the previous year.

Though the Quaker Act was designed specifically to condemn them, when the first of some 140 London Friends emerged from Newgate at the end of June to stand trial at the Old Bailey, they found the Act set aside. Replacing it was another procedure, one far easier to apply, and which could equally trap Quakers, Baptists and all who refused on principle to swear oaths. It was also of considerable benefit to the state, which like the monarchy of Charles I, the Republican Commonwealth, and Cromwell's Protectorate, remained financially hard-pressed. Long before the main issue to be tried was reached, defendants were requested to take the Oath of Allegiance and Supremacy. Since it included a denial of the Pope's authority, failure to swear was tantamount to treason. The penalty, based on the medieval writ of praemunire, was forfeiture of the accused's estate, forfeiture of the king's protection, and imprisonment for life or at the king's pleasure, a term which might often be one and the same.

"Friends put forth in print the grounds and reasons why they refused to swear," said George.[28] But it made no difference. The authorities were determined to crush the sects, and with them the threat of radical republicanism. Having refused the Oath, the Quaker captives were returned to their prisons to await trial.

"In Newgate we are extremely thronged," wrote Edward Burrough, arrested in June along with John Perrot, "... near an hundred in one room on the common side amongst felons and their sufferings are great ... " In the stifling heat of summer, the poisonous air and the disease-carrying vermin reaped a bitter harvest. "Many have given up their lives in faithfulness in this place," said Edward sorrowfully.[29] Among them was Richard Hubberthorne, who had been arrested earlier at the Bull and Mouth. He was just 34 years old when he died.

For a brief moment in August, when the arrival in London of his new Portuguese Queen spurred Charles to clemency, those not regarded as ringleaders were set free. Days later, with no intervention by the king, they were rounded up and sent back to Newgate.

Meanwhile, as George Fox travelled the country, he was certainly very well aware that, if only by hearsay, his size made him almost instantly recognizable. He almost certainly knew too, that his arrest would be a coup for the authorities. Later, when he came to write his life-story, he recalled an incident that followed his arrival at the Broadmead Meeting House in Bristol in July 1662.

Although not arrested at the first of a series of meetings, it seems that very quickly, the authorities realized their mistake. "The next day they raised the trained band," George said, "and said they would hunt me out and they would have me." Fearing that his capture would provoke a collapse of morale, some Bristol Friends urged him to seek safety. "Divers Friends came to me and said I would be taken today, and desired me not to go to the meeting except I were eternally moved of God, for ... they would not have me taken." For if he were, they said, then their persecutors "would glory too much".[30]

Though urged to leave immediately, George resisted the plea. "I was moved to go back again and speak a few words," he said, "and stood up and told them that they might see there was a God in Israel that could deliver."[31] Only then, he said, did he slip out by a side door and disappear into a maze of winding lanes.

"It was the immediate hand and power of the Lord that did preserve me," he claimed. Back in Bristol, however, William Rogers, one of the city's leading merchants, remembered the incident too. Probably he did not think much about it at the time. Fourteen years later, however, when it resurfaced in his memory, he would use it against George Fox.

In 1662, however, as far as George was concerned, that he travelled on through Wiltshire and Berkshire quite unmolested simply confirmed that the Lord's power preserved him. Later, increasingly confident, he passed equally unmolested through the Midlands, until very early in September he came once again to Swannington in Leicestershire. It was there, as he was speaking to his hostesses, an elderly widow and her daughter, that quite without warning the front door caved in under the violence of the blows showered upon it.

"Put out the candles and make fast the doors," ordered Lord Thomas Beaumont, as with swords drawn and pistols cocked, his soldiers raced through the house.[32] After searching each room, they finally herded the family, their servants, a group of Friends who were found meeting secretly elsewhere in the house, and George Fox, into the main hall. Unlike Bristol, this time there would be no escape.

"I told them my name was George Fox," George recalled, "...and said I was innocent and pure and known over the nation."

"Aye, you are known the world over," Beaumont retorted, almost unable to believe that the man before him was the elusive Quaker leader.[33]

After a rough body search and finding nothing more incriminating in George's pockets than a comb-case, Beaumont left his men to guard the house. Next morning, the captives were marched into Swannington and proffered the Oath of Allegiance. "I told him I never took an oath in my life," said George. In fact he continued, "I would not swear my coat were my own, nor swear if a man took it off that he took it."[34]

In his *Journal*, George alleged that the number of captives was five. However, in another account written much earlier, he claimed it to be nine. Since the number was crucial in terms of the law, he may well have revised the number in his later account so as to suggest that no law was broken.[35]

Destined now for Leicester Gaol, and travelling through a countryside busy with the harvest, the party carried their Bibles open, quoting from them in their defence. The two women, both seated in a cart, also made a show of their spinning wheels, proof that they did not intend to lie idle in prison. "So we rid through the country to Leicester in that manner," George said, "... and declared how we were the prisoners of the Lord Jesus Christ for his name and his truth sake."

Although George Fox would always have maintained that he was a prisoner for Christ, and in many ways it was so, on the occasions that he was imprisoned earlier, it was also as a result of his determination to proclaim his message at the expense of others, and his insistence that he alone spoke the truth. At the same time, in the 1650s, as well as interrupting ministers and disrupting services, his comrades were also arrested for contravening the vagrancy laws, for failing to provide themselves with permits to travel, and for causing riot. Now, they were being persecuted incontrovertibly for their faith. Thus, as George Fox made his way to Leicester Gaol, more than ever was he a prisoner who demanded the right to speak and worship as conscience directed.

Once there, he almost immediately found himself defending the right of his comrades to do so too. On his arrival, he had discovered that when several Quakers already imprisoned attempted to keep their meeting, the gaoler, aided by his dog, dragged them out by their hair and then beat them viciously with a quarter-staff. "And so when the First-day came," said George, "I bid one of my fellow prisoners carry down a stool and set it in the yard." Then, he gave notice to every felon, and to all those imprisoned for debt, that there would be a meeting in the yard, "and any that would hear the word of the Lord they might come there." On Sunday, confronted by a huge crowd, and by the indomitable George Fox, the gaoler could do nothing but give way. When George was finally brought before the court, together with others he was indicted for refusing the Oath of Allegiance and detained for one month more in Leicester.

Meanwhile in London, the Newgate prisoners continued to suffer. Thomas Ellwood, a young friend of Isaac Penington, who had become a Quaker in 1659, and who was among a group herded away from the Bull and Mouth by soldiers using their pikes as a pen, described his days in the gaol: "But in the night we all lodged in one room," he said, "which was large and round, having in the middle of it a great pillar of oaken timber... To this pillar we fastened our hammocks... quite round the room... three storeys high. And under the lower rank of hammocks, by the wall sides, were laid beds upon the floor, in which the sick and such weak persons as could not get into the hammocks lay... the breath and steam that came from so many bodies... was enough to cause sickness amongst us."[36]

Towards the end of October, when rumours reached Henry Bennet, who that month replaced Edward Nicholas as Secretary of State, of a plot against the king by Quakers and Baptists, hundreds of suspects were rounded up and thrust into the gaol's overcrowded and stinking galleries: "...the trained-band men they came to the Bull," the London Quaker, Ellis Hookes, told Margaret Fell, "and laid hold of all the Friends they could... some very much beaten and abused... and that day they took abundance of Baptists; seven score I hear are to be brought... to Newgate."[37]

For a moment in December, when King Charles issued a Declaration of Indulgence, it looked as if the amnesty of August was to be repeated. Even more so when orders followed in January 1663 to release many sectarians from London's prisons. Those considered particularly dangerous, however, were exempted. Among them was Edward Burrough.

Unlike John Perrot, who had taken an option of voluntary exile in Barbados, Edward had elected to remain in England.[38] He died in Newgate in February 1663. He was 28. As his death drew near, he recalled the sparkling days of 1652, so full of optimism and purpose, and in their memory he wrote to the man who had been his inspiration. "Perfect love" was his, he told George Fox, "which is the love of a son to his father."[39]

In the same month, Parliament debated a request by the king, based on his earlier Declaration, that they prepare a bill that would allow him to suspend enforcement of the Act of Uniformity on an individual basis. The Members, however, were wary, for should they fulfil such a request, they would also provide a precedent that allowed the king to dispense with the law. While the Cavalier Parliament might be pro-Royalist, it had no intention of returning to Charles II the powers that their Puritan predecessors had stripped from his father. Moreover, only too aware that Charles was eager to lift disabilities on Catholics, neither were they prepared to allow any openings for an issue so potentially explosive.

On his release from Leicester, George Fox had set off once more to rally Friends around the country. He was now 39 years old, and apart from six periods of enforced idleness in England's prisons, he had travelled relentlessly for nearly twenty years. He was in Cambridge when news reached him of Edward Burrough's death in Newgate. To hear of another death was surely a blow, for it was yet another name to add to a list that was growing depressingly longer: James Parnell, Richard Hubberthorne and now Edward Burrough had died in prison. James Naylor had died at the hands of a violent man, while John Camm had died early in 1657, of a consumption aggravated by his constant missionary endeavours.

Thus, perhaps he was not particularly surprised, when in the spring of 1663, a female Friend arrived at his lodgings in Huntingdon in a state of near hysteria. "It being a whimsy got up into her head," he said, "and an imagination got into her head because Edward Burrough was deceased, that we should be all taken away." Though unable to deny the possibility, he felt he must reassure his followers. Once again, however, his message was a spiritual one. Once again there was nothing mentioned of the ideals that had motivated so many of them earlier; either of the Agreement of the People, or of the heady aspirations of 1659. "Friends," he wrote, "Be still and wait in your own conditions, and settled in the Seed of God that doth not change, that in that ye may feel dear Edward Burrough among you in the Seed... And so enjoy him in the life that doth not change, but which is invisible. G.F."[40]

Just as the Quaker movement itself was changing, it seems

that in the spring of 1663, as he travelled through England's southern counties, George saw something else beginning to change too. In Hampshire, in May, where he met Friends he had convinced on his way to Cornwall in 1656, an escape from almost certain arrest was due to the warning of a local well-wisher. "One of the world came to a Friend that was with me," he said, "and beckoned to him and told him the trained band was coming to break up our meeting."[41] Now that the Friends of Truth were the butt of so much official hostility, while at the same time behaving far less aggressively themselves, it seems that their fellow countrymen, rather than hurl stones and abuse at them, were increasingly inclined to regard them with sympathy.

As George continued to escape arrest, once again, he attributed his freedom to Providence. In Wiltshire, when constables arrived to break up the meeting he attended, reports of a nearby burglary called them away. Shortly afterwards he recounted the incident to Margaret Fell, who was herself embarked on what would eventually be a journey of 1,000 miles as she visited Quakers imprisoned throughout the land, supporting them, rallying them, and petitioning on their behalf.

In Cornwall, constables were hardly seen at all. In Somerset, although a search party arrived at his lodgings at two in the morning, and threatened to break down the doors, it seemed that George Fox was not their quarry. "You are not the man I look for," said one, lowering his sword as he gazed down on George Fox in bed. Once again, George told the story to Margaret, when they met shortly afterwards at Bristol.

Later in the summer of 1663, George moved into Wales. At a meeting near Pontymoile, where another had been held the previous day, once more his escape seemed divinely ordained. "In the middle of the meeting comes a bailiff," he recalled, "... and said they had been searching for the speaker at the house which I came from that morning ... So when the meeting was done I passed away; and he was in the yard and bowed to me but said nothing to me."[42]

Eventually, after passing through the Derbyshire Peaks and

meeting many old friends, at Cinder Hill Green in Yorkshire he also met Margaret again. Together with her daughters – Sarah, now 21, and Mary, now sixteen – she was finally on her way home to Swarthmoor. As she and George sat often by themselves, discussing the administration of the many meetings now established, the struggle against persecution, and how the captive Friends were to be supported, many of their companions looked on them and wondered. Others looked on and gossiped. Later, George travelled on alone throughout Durham and Yorkshire.

But, as the autumn mists gathered on the high moors and draped was among the trees, there was an anxiety etched on the faces of the northern Friends that spoke of something more than the Oath of Allegiance and a fear of praemunire. Finally, George discovered what lay behind it. "At York I heard of a plot," he said.

Late in 1662, northern supporters of the Good Old Cause, together with other individuals resentful at a host of new taxes imposed in the name of King Charles, began planning the restoration of the republic and a true gospel ministry. While they seized York and other northern towns, similar groups elsewhere would take control of other strategic urban centres and seaports.

But, just as had been similarly the case with George Booth and the Commonwealth, long before the foremost leaders left home on the night of 16 October 1663, government security forces knew almost every last detail of their plans. Many suspects had already been seized, while the forewarned county authorities had mustered the trained bands. By the time the Westmorland contingent led by Sir Robert Atkinson of Mallerstang, a former Parliamentary captain of horse and governor of Appleby Castle, reached the rendezvous at Kaber, a village north-east of Kendal on the road to Durham, it was clear that no reinforcements would arrive and that there would be no rising.

Piecing information together, it became clear to George Fox that among those arrested were republicans, Cromwellians, Baptists, a surprisingly large number of Presbyterians, and many Quakers. As the details became even clearer, it also became apparent that Francis Howgill, arrested in Kendal market in July, was among the suspects. Rumours from London, meanwhile, said that with Parliament convinced that the plot was hatched in the dissenting conventicles, there were further harsh measures planned against all non-Anglicans.

One man very eager to enforce such measures was Daniel Fleming, Justice of the Peace, passionate Royalist, and master of Rydal Hall near Grasmere, less than twenty miles north-east of Ulverston.[43] He wrote to his superiors:

> ... ye Quakers of whom wee have too many, this part of ye Country joyning upon yt pt of Lancashire where Geo. Fox & most of his cubbs are, & have been for a long time Kennell'd. Tho at present these psons are not much reguarded, yet I am confident ye first reall danger wee shall bee in will bee from them; for they are psons ye most numerous of any one opinion yt are here agt us, of ye closest Correspondencies (keeping constantly their meetings weekly within eight miles one of another throughout all this Countrey, if not England also) & they are such yt will do mischiefe ye most resolutely of any if Fox or any other of their Grand Speakers should but dictate it, unto them, wch some of ym halfe threaten already ...[44]

Moreover, said Fleming, he had it on very good authority that the said George Fox was currently in the north of England. Therefore, and in view of the danger he represented, he was personally offering a reward. He would present five pounds, he said, to anyone ready to assist in the notorious Quaker's capture.

CHAPTER ELEVEN

Prisoner of Conscience

And so they cryed take him away Goaler [*sic*]. And so I bid them
take Notice it was in obedience to Christs Commands yt I suffered.
George Fox, *Short Journal*

E ARLY IN JANUARY 1664, George Fox was
imprisoned at Lancaster. Since 1649, when he had been gaoled
at Nottingham, it was the seventh time he had been a prisoner
for his faith.

Following the abortive northern uprising of the previous
year, he had once again warned his following against anti-gov
ernment conspiracies. "I was moved to declare against all plots
and plotters," he said, "both public and private, and gave forth
a paper against plottings."[1]

Nevertheless, just as with Venner's rising earlier, in the mass
arrests that followed discovery of the northern plot, large numbers of Quakers were taken. Whether or not some of them
were actually involved, the Royalist regime plainly believed
they were. Indeed, later in the year King Charles assured Mary
Fell that "there were some Quakers in the last plot … he had
letters about it and their names."[2] There was certainly evidence
that among those involved were men known for their association with the Friends in earlier years, while with some of those
taken ready to accuse others, as the regime's security services
examined John Thurloe's old files, no doubt they felt able to
justify every arrest.[3]

Besides, even though the Quaker movement professed

peace, its size, its past history, and its resolute opposition to the state church and its authority, all made it a very potent threat. Thus, in the eyes of the state, not only did the Friends require constant surveillance, but at times of political tension their high-profile leaders could not be allowed to walk free.

"Friends came to me," George said of the days towards the end of 1663 when he passed into Westmorland, "and said would I come there to go into prison? For there was great persecution in that country..."

The knowledge that many prisoners had been taken with the help of informers, bribed with five shillings a day, led him to be wary. Very soon, he discovered it to be justified. Though during a visit to her Preston Patrick home he had cautiously refused her offer of overnight hospitality, next day Ann Audland's house was raided.

When he finally crossed the sands to Swarthmoor, he discovered that there too there had been searches, that men under the command of Richard Kirkby, Justice of the Peace, and master of nearby Kirkby Hall, had rifled the house, forcing doors and breaking open trunks in their efforts to unearth the Quaker leader.[4]

Later, George considered his best course of action. As a Royalist and a Member of the Cavalier Parliament, Richard Kirkby had little sympathy either for supporters of the previous regime or for the religious sects. Nor, having lost land to sequestration, had he cause to sympathize with any friend of the late Thomas Fell. And since news that George Fox was now at Swarthmoor had certainly reached him, no doubt his men would soon return. Deciding to forestall them, George went in person to Kirkby Hall.

On his arrival, he found the MP ready to depart for Westminster, and several local men, including Daniel Fleming, gathered to take their leave. Somewhat surprisingly, he also found Kirkby conciliatory. "He said," George recalled, "before all the gentry that were gathered together at his house, that as he was a gentleman he had nothing against me, but that Margaret Fell must not keep great meetings at her house that were contrary to the Act."

Even had Margaret Fell been prepared to comply, however, once Kirkby had left for London, his colleagues immediately took matters into their own hands. "I heard that there was a private meeting," said George, "of the justices and deputy lieutenants ... and that they had granted forth a warrant to apprehend me."

As soon as he heard of it, instinct told him to flee, to saddle his horse and be gone. Conscience told him to stay. Thus, when the troopers arrived, they found him waiting for them expectantly. Later, under guard, and accompanied by Margaret Fell, he was taken to Holker Hall, near Cartmel, home of Justice Thomas Preston. They arrived to find Preston surrounded by his fellow Justices of the Peace, an unofficial court convened in his great hall.

They began with the northern plot. And whatever was the reality of involvement by individual Quakers, and whatever it was that George Fox actually knew, he was nevertheless desperate to absolve the vast and innocent majority from implication. Of course he knew of the plot, he admitted, as did everyone, but no one he knew was involved.

Then why, his inquisitors persisted, had he written a paper warning against conspiracies? "My reason," George replied, "was because you are so forward as to mash the innocent and guilty together. I wrote to clear the Truth from such things, and to stop all forward foolish spirits from running into such things."

But the Justices would not be denied. Whatever George Fox might say, they believed Quakers to be implicated. And they also knew that they regularly contravened the Act of Uniformity. "You are against the laws of the land," they accused.

"No," George replied carefully, "for I and my Friends bring all people to the Spirit of God ... and this brings them into the well-doing which eases the magistrates who are for the punishment of the evil-doers."[5]

The gentlemen were unconvinced. Like the Cavalier Parliament, most were Royalists with long memories; in their view the troublesome Quakers, with their links to Levellers and to Oliver Cromwell's army, could never be loyal friends to King Charles.

One of their number, the Royalist landowner, Sir George Middleton of Leighton Hall, believed he had even less reason to be kind to any friend of Judge Fell. Not only had he lost land to sequestration, but later he would make allegations that after first inciting his tenants against him, Thomas Fell and William West had supported them through a series of legal battles that caused the Middletons to lose even more of their wealth.[6] When the interrogation turned to the subject of religion, Sir George was keen to provoke.

"You deny God and the Church and faith?" he enquired.

"Nay, I own God and the true Church and the true faith," George retorted, "but what Church doest thou own?"

Though it was no secret that many Middletons were Catholics, to have it flung in his face by George Fox, with the implication that the Oath of Allegiance could well ensnare them, was too much to be borne. "You are a rebel and a traitor," bellowed Sir George, his hand half reaching for his sword.

Despite his ambiguous position, it was George Middleton who then insisted that the Oath of Allegiance be put. When George refused it, he was ordered to appear at the Lancaster Quarter Sessions scheduled for 12 January 1664.

During the intervening weeks, George Fox and Margaret Fell received two significant visitors. One was their old friend Colonel West, who made it clear that the Oath of Allegiance would almost certainly be used to secure a conviction. The other was William Kirkby, brother to the MP, who, clearly suspecting that an illegal meeting was underway, arrived with a bevy of constables. After taking a list of names, and arresting those who refused to provide them, he reminded George that they would meet again shortly at Lancaster.

"And so at the Sessions in Lancaster I appeared," he said. "Peace be among you," he declared from the dock, addressing the assembled ranks of lawyers, the troopers who guarded the doors, and the townsfolk who filled the gallery. "Peace be among you."

"Silence in Court," roared the clerk.

After instructing his constables to remove George Fox's hat, Justice Robert Rawlinson, Chairman of the Court, demanded to know if the prisoner admitted to being a Quaker. "I told them quaking and trembling at the word of God I owned," he replied.[7]

When proceedings addressed the northern plot, and the requirements of the Quaker Act, once again George Fox robustly denied any involvement by members of his movement. "Our meetings are not to terrify the King's subjects," he said, "neither are we enemies to him or any man." Moreover, he said, after being asked to explain his attendance at so many large and illegal meetings, his reason "was to declare against plots".[8]

In that case, Rawlinson observed caustically, the accused would have no objection to taking the Oath of Allegiance. "I told them I never took an oath in my life," George said.[9] As everyone well knew, the Act contained provisions for such a reply. "So Rawlinson asked me ensnaringly whether I thought it was unlawful to swear," George recalled, "because in the Act that was made such were liable to banishment or a great fine that said it was unlawful to swear."

While the judge spoke, someone handed George a Bible. But, as his accusers saw him leaf through the pages, obviously preparing to quote Jesus' words in Matthew's Gospel, the book was snatched from his hand.

All he need do was repeat the words of the Oath, he was told. But of course he could not and would not. As he was led away, he turned to the court. "I bid them take notice it was in obedience to Christ's commands that I suffered," he said.[10]

Later that day, after many Friends followed George into the dock, ten of them also followed him into Lancaster Castle Gaol, to await the Assizes scheduled for March. "We proceeded smartly against the Quakers," a satisfied Daniel Fleming wrote to Joseph Williamson, assistant to Secretary of State, Sir Henry Bennet. One of the accused was praemunired, he said, George Fox and ten more were imprisoned for refusing the Oath, while another 60 were fined for unlawful assemblies. Furthermore, although Mrs Fell had attempted to use her influence with the local justices, it had come to nothing. "I doubt not but this proceeding against them will break their meetings & other designs in a short time," he added.[11]

Within days, Fleming's satisfaction turned to fury. Quite deliberately and provocatively, he told Williamson, and as soon as she arrived home from Lancaster, Mrs Fell convened a huge and defiant meeting of Quakers at Swarthmoor Hall. Since it was well known that she was behind most of the Quaker activity in the area, he continued, he was seeking the endorsement of his superiors to tender the Oath of Allegiance to her. If she refused it, as he expected she would, then she could be praemunired. Shortly afterwards, Margaret Fell was summoned to the Lancaster Assizes to stand trial with George Fox.

In London, meanwhile, the Cavalier Parliament and the Church of England fretted over their inability to curb dissent. For all its lack of success, the northern plot had proved that radicalism still thrived, while despite the Quaker Act and the Act of Uniformity, Quakers gathered at meetings, and Baptist and Independent ministers preached to eager congregations. Moreover, despite the censorship laws, Presbyterian polemic poured defiantly from the presses.[12] Haunted by the spectre of a resurgent republican movement fuelled by Puritan preaching, Royalist politicians began drafting a bill to outlaw completely the conventicles where they believed insurrection was hatched.

On 14 March 1664, at Lancaster's Lent Assizes, George Fox stood before Justice Sir Thomas Twisden, the judge who four years earlier had opposed his release in London. Twisden, however, like a number of other men in his profession, was opposed to the law being used as a catch-all against dissenters, and together with an uneasy certainty that George Fox intended to make a stand, it caused him to be agitated and brusque.

"Peace be amongst you," George said to the courtroom in general. Immediately his hat was hauled from his head. "Will you take the Oath of Allegiance, George Fox?" Twisden asked. For a moment, when the prisoner took hold of the Bible, the whole court fell silent. Had two months in Lancaster Castle

Gaol weakened the Quaker leader's resolve? But, as the prisoner began turning pages, a nod from the judge saw the offending book snatched from his hand. "Will you swear?" demanded an agitated Twisden, "will you take the oath of Allegiance, yea or nay?"

He was a loyal subject of King Charles, George protested, as well as a loyal subject of Jesus Christ, judge of the whole world. Moreover, he continued, a glance at King Charles' Declaration of Breda would prove the two loyalties not to be incompatible. Such words provoked some of his opponents to fury. For, it was suddenly very clear to them, that his experience of courtrooms, and much private study of the law, had enabled the weaver's son from Leicestershire to argue as effectively as any lawyer trained at Grays Inn.

Other observers, perhaps somewhat more sympathetic, may have found themselves reflecting on something quite different. For while George Fox still quite clearly believed that his truth was the only truth, the man who once abused ministers in their pulpits was now a spokesman for liberty of conscience.

"For it is in tenderness of conscience that I do not swear," George said finally, "in obedience to the command of Christ ... and for his sake I suffer, and in obedience to his command do I stand this day."

"I am a servant to the King," Twisden said wearily, "and the King sent me not to dispute, but to put his laws in execution."

Using his own knowledge of the law, George then claimed a statutory right to postpone his trial. Thereupon, he was returned to Lancaster Castle to await the next Assizes in August. Later, Margaret Fell, brought to trial for keeping illegal meetings, and likewise refusing the oath, after claiming the same right was similarly confined. Fifty miles away, Francis Howgill, accused of involvement in the northern plot, also claimed the right and was returned to Appleby Gaol.

In July, as George Fox turned 40 in Lancaster Castle, the Conventicle Act passed into law. Under its terms, all religious services, apart from those of the Church of England, were banned. Any person over sixteen caught attending such a service, where there were present five persons more than an actual household, was subject to an imprisonment relieved only by a rising succession of fines, followed by transportation as an indentured labourer to the colonies of Barbados or Jamaica. Only for transportation was a jury required to convict; for imprisonment, sentence could be pronounced by two justices. Furthermore, while all Nonconformists were to be treated the same, there would be no leniency towards those who occasionally attended an Anglican service. The Act was to remain in force until March 1669, when it would be reviewed.

On 29 August 1664, as the Court of Assize met once more in Lancaster, George Fox, Margaret Fell and several others were brought again to trial. Just as before, the proceedings began with the Oath of Allegiance. And just as before, Thomas Twisden brushed aside George's attempt to quote from the Bible.[13]

What he could not brush aside, however, were factual errors. Since January, the prisoner had studied the charge against him, and now he was determined to bring a mass of mistakes in the text to the attention of the court. So too was Margaret Fell. "And though Margaret Fell had some that pleaded for her," George said admiringly, "yet she spoke as much herself as she would."

Learning of the sympathy that her knowledge and boldness provoked, he nevertheless knew with a depressing certainty that he would neither receive such a hearing, nor the same concern for errors in the indictment. "They had the greatest envy against me," he said, "yet the most gross errors were found in mine."

Such errors led the Judge to criticize the clerks, the clerks to consult their almanacs, and George Fox to demand that the charge be declared invalid. "I desire nothing but law and justice at thy hands," he declared to Judge Christopher Turner, Twisden's fellow on the bench, "for I do not look for mercy." Assured that he would receive justice, George Fox enquired if he were then "free from all that ever hath been done against me in this matter."

The response was cautious. Indeed, perhaps both Twisden and Turner hated the inevitable sequence of events. But, like

George himself, they were perfectly aware of what would happen next. "You are free from all that has been done against you," Turner acknowledged. But as a tumult erupted on the public benches, among people uncertain whether to cheer or jeer, George admonished them. They would soon see how justice was done in England, he predicted.

Just as he knew it would be, the oath was tendered once more. And just as the Judge and everyone else knew, George Fox refused to swear. After once again exercising his right to defer the trial, he was returned to Lancaster Castle. But here Colonel Kirkby intervened. No longer conciliatory, angry that the prisoner's stand was provoking admiration, and embarrassed that his knowledge of the law made his accusers a laughing-stock, he insisted that he be treated more harshly. There was no cause for traitors such as he to be lodged in any comfort, where his friends could visit and whisper together to make plots.

"So I was put up in a smoky tower," George said, "where the smoke of the other rooms came up, so thick I was almost smothered, and could hardly see a candle sometimes ... and the wind and the rain came in on me, so that my shift was sometimes wet as muck, and so starved with cold and rain was I that my body was numbed, and swelled up with the cold ... and in this manner did I lie all that long cold winter."

Yet, despite the choking smoke and the bitter wind, in the chilly damp of his Lancaster prison George worked on an account of his life, beginning almost with his first imprisonment in the year 1649 at Nottingham. What exactly prompted him to begin, he did not say; instead he plunged almost directly into his narrative: "In Mansfield there came a Priest who was looked on to bee above all others ... " Perhaps, however, it was his incarceration at Lancaster, his seventh imprisonment, that caused him to reflect on his journey until that point, for in a brief introductory paragraph he says: "Here are some of his sufferings yt hee hath suffered by the world and their Professors, Priests, and Teachers." Clearly then the account was intended to highlight how a man committed to the service of God and of truth, was obstructed and abused by the forces of political, judicial and ecclesiastical injustice. Later, the account would be known to history as the *Short Journal*, and would also be used by its author as the basis for a much longer work.

As he worked on the account, mostly George dictated, for by now it was not only his lack of early education that hindered his writing. To his dismay, an occasional sharp spasm, first noticed some time before, had more recently become a series of fiery pains, both in his joints, which were also sometimes swollen, and wherever bones had been fractured in the savage attacks of earlier years. Though the agony was sporadic, he was filled with a dismal certainty that as time passed it would become more regular and more intense. As he willed himself to endure, and as he dictated letters to his comrades that urged them to stand fast in the face of persecution, he suspected that epistles of encouragement from a George Fox sick and in prison, were a far greater inspiration than a George Fox in health and at liberty could ever be.

In London, persecution centred on the most high-profile Quaker meeting house, the Bull and Mouth at Aldersgate, as well as on meetings held in the homes of Friends nearby, at Mile End, Clerkenwell and Spitalfields. South of the Thames, arrests were made regularly at the Horslydown meeting house in Southwark. Within a year of the Conventicle Act coming into force, over 2,100 Quakers from these five meetings alone were imprisoned.[14]

Elsewhere, from Cornwall to Cumberland, Quakers were marched from their meetings, through the streets, and into the gaols. Like George Fox himself, they went peacefully, holding their heads high, quoting from their Bibles, and announcing that they suffered for conscience and for Christ. One of those who saw such processions often was Samuel Pepys. "While we were talking," he said, describing the events of Sunday, 7 August 1664, "came by several poor creatures, carried by Constables for being at a conventicle. They go like lambs, without any resistance. I would to God they would either conform, or be more wise and not be ketched."[15]

Neither the Friends, nor the Baptists, nor Congregationalists, nor Presbyterians, however, had any intention of conforming. For all its many failures and disappointments, the Civil War was fought for the liberties of England, among them the right to speak and worship as conscience directed. Nearly two decades later, just as the Cavalier Parliament refused to surrender gains made by their Puritan predecessors, so were the Nonconformist sects unwilling to return to the status quo that preceded the fall of Archbishop Laud.

Frequently speaking on Nonconformist behalf was Richard Baxter, who in 1662 had been forced from his living at Kidderminister. The persecution shared by Nonconformists, however, had not lessened his opposition to Quakers, who in his view remained "proper fanatics, looking too much to revelations within, instead of the Holy Scriptures ... "[16]

He was, however, forced to admire them. For it was often the case, he said, that while other dissenters were supportive of their ministers persecuted under the Act of Uniformity, "and exhorted them to stand it out and preach till they went to prison", when they themselves suffered, their attitudes changed, so that "they did now think ... that secrecy was no sin."[17] This was not true, he said, of the Friends.

"And here the fanatics called Quakers did greatly relieve the sober people for a time", he said, "for they were so resolute, and gloried in their constancy and sufferings, that they assembled openly (at the Bull and Mouth near Aldersgate) and were dragged away daily to the common jail; and yet desisted not, but the rest came the next day nevertheless. So that the jail at Newgate was filled with them. Abundance of them died in prison, and yet they continued their assemblies still."[18]

Indeed, he said, the Quakers not only set a standard for all who refused to conform, but in a sense took the sufferings of all upon themselves. Eventually, the arrests made at the Bull and Mouth, at Mile End, at Clerkenwell and at Spitalfields, in the seventeen months following the introduction of the Conventicle Act, constituted 95 per cent of London's dissenting total.[19]

Had Richard Baxter or Samuel Pepys travelled to Reading, they would have witnessed scenes as distressing, and as inspiring, as those in London. There, the attacks were on the home of Thomas Curtis, George Fox's refuge in 1659, which served at the town's Quaker Meeting House. "Truly the rage of the wicked is not a little in this place," Thomas told his old friend in a letter of January 1665. It had begun even before the passing of the Conventicle Act, and largely at the instigation of Justice Sir William Armorer, friend and favourite of King Charles, many Friends were imprisoned. It was with pride that Thomas then went on to describe the fortitude of the Meeting's young people.

"Our little children kept the meetings up, when we were all in prison," he said, "notwithstanding that wicked justice, when he came and found them there, with a staff that he had with a spear in it, would pull them out of the meeting, and punch them in the back, till some of them have been black in the face."[20]

Though Richard Baxter felt compelled to refer to Quakers as "poor deluded souls", he also recognized how attractive their courage could be. "Yea, many turned Quakers," he said, "because the Quakers kept their meetings openly, and went to prison for it cheerfully … "[21]

In March 1665, one year after their first encounter there, George Fox and Thomas Twisden faced each other again at the Assizes in Lancaster. Just as before, the prisoner had studied the indictment, and having once again discovered many factual errors, he was eager to bring them to the attention of the court. This time, however, Twisden was in no mood to sympathize or debate. "Take him away, gaoler," he said crossly, almost as soon as George Fox opened his mouth.

Back in his tower cell, George waited for the summons to return to the court. But, as the hours passed, and then the days, he realized that he had been silenced. Later, he learned that the indictment was sent to London, where a series of embarrassed officials agreed that a charge containing so many errors would not stand. Nevertheless, as the state and its church sought to impose their authority, and to deny any opportunity of a challenge, especially from one whose example might inspire others, it was decreed that George Fox should no longer be allowed to appear in open court.

"So they would not let me plead to it," George said grimly. Equally distressing was the knowledge that he was praemunired, the sentence passed illegally in his absence from court.

Praemunired or not, as far as Colonel Kirkby and his associates were concerned, the rebellious George Fox was too potent a figure-head to remain in any region under their jurisdiction. Moreover, if he had his way, he finally informed George, the Quaker leader would be shipped to as remote a part of the earth as possible, somewhere from which he would never return. As it was, he was being sent to Yorkshire, to the gaol at Scarborough Castle.

When the day came, in May 1665, despite the arthritis that in the damp and cold of his prison had become acute, that made each movement a torture, George was dragged, barely able to stand, from his tower room. William Kirkby, the Colonel's brother, stood watching. Having refused to produce the order for the prisoner's removal, or to discuss the sentence of praemunire, he watched as the prisoner was half-lifted, half-thrown into the saddle. "And so they hurried me away," said George. "... I was very weak and hardly able to sit on horseback, and my clothes smelt so of smoke that they were loathsome to myself."

Surrounded by a military escort, George was hurried across the country. Nevertheless, as the news went before him, the people of Yorkshire turned out to watch him pass. As they did so, some among them remembered the Leicestershire Prophet of former years, the fiery preacher who strode their moors and dales proclaiming the Day of Lord. Now, however, they saw a sick man, who swayed in his saddle, whose clothes stank, and whose nose ran with cold. Also among the crowds were many Friends. Though they lifted their hands in greeting, and called out words of encouragement, some of them wondered if they would ever see George Fox again.

Grey, gaunt and jagged, and perched high on its sea-crags, Scarborough Castle stood exposed to the north wind that in winter came howling over the Yorkshire moors, and an east wind that drove in from the barren North Sea. As its gates closed behind him, and with his joints on fire after the long ride, George was barely able to carry his few belongings into the cell he had been allocated. Even his payment to his gaolers, he reflected, of 50 shillings for a dry room and a fire, had made no difference to where he was eventually lodged.

"The room being to the sea-side," he said, "and lying much open, the wind drove in the rain forcibly…and when my clothes were wet, I had no fire to dry them; so that my body was numbed with cold, and my fingers swelled, that one was grown as big as two."[22]

Cold and wet, and despite having paid for something better, he often went hungry. "A threepenny loaf served me three weeks and sometimes longer," he said. As for drink, all too often there was nothing but water.

Hungry, in pain from his arthritis, and often feverish with his nose running and his eyes and throat sore, he was also lonely. For although many Friends came anxiously to the castle gate, George Fox was allowed no visitors. Thus he faced the bleak prospect that with praemunire potentially a sentence for life, he might never leave Scarborough again. "So I was as a man buried alive," he said.

In April, the month before George Fox was sent to Scarborough, the inhabitants of St Giles, the poverty-ridden slum just west of London's city wall, began to fall sick. Very soon, all over the city, people spoke fearfully of violent fevers and headaches, of swellings in arm-pits and groins, ceaseless and painful vomiting, and most terrifying of all, flesh that turned purple and black. As the disease spread, horror turned to panic. Anyone with a house or relatives in the country fled, leaving Whitehall, the City and a series of grand new developments at Covent Garden and Leicester Square all but deserted.

In July, fearing that the many abandoned cats and dogs carried the disease, and as the death-toll reached 1,000 a week, the Lord Mayor ordered them destroyed. Later, the author Daniel Defoe estimated that 40,000 dogs and 200,000 cats were killed.[23] With their execution, London's huge population of rats, hosts to millions of parasitic fleas, multiplied by the thousand. So too did the plague's victims. Condemned to their forcibly sealed homes, with guards posted to prevent escape, all they could do was to scrawl on their doors the red cross of pestilence and a few words: "Lord have mercy!"

In scorching August, as deaths in London reached 6,000 a week, the epidemic ravaged Newgate Gaol. Though shuddering before the swollen purple flesh, and weeping at the chorus of groans, George Whitehead went regularly to the prison, as well as to the sealed homes of sick Friends. There, he washed and fed those he could, while for others he spoke words of comfort and offered up prayers. Other Friends too went among the dying. Gilbert Latey, once a tailor to the king's court, became treasurer of funds sent by sympathetic Friends in the country. Some of the money he used buy food that was passed through the windows of sealed houses, some he used to bribe guards that he might do so.

"I have been preserved well, but as a brand plucked out of the fire ... " Ellis Hookes, now Clerk to the Friends' London Meetings, told Margaret Fell in November, as he too ministered to the sick and dying, "for I have often laid down my head in sorrow, and rose as I went to bed, and not slept a wink for the groans of them that lay a-dying ... "[24]

Their heroism in the face of the deadly killer added to the respect the Friends were already winning for their stand against intolerance. Now, those who had once stoned them as fanatics, took comfort from the sight of those same men and women braving the plague-stricken streets.

Meanwhile, the ever-observant Richard Baxter also watched the progress of the plague. Later, he was also scathing: "... most of the conformable ministers fled," he said, "and left their flocks in the time of their extremity." Seeing congregations thus abandoned, "... divers Nonconformists, pitying the dying and distressed people ... resolved that no obedience to the laws ... could justify them for neglecting of men's souls and bodies in such extremities ... And that when Christ shall say, 'Inasmuch as ye did it not to one of these, ye did it not to me,' it will be a poor excuse to say, 'Lord, I was forbidden by the law.'"[25]

In the view of the Cavalier Parliament, however, obedience was all. So was the total suppression of dissent. That hundreds of Quakers were prepared to face imprisonment rather than abandon their meetings, reinforced their view of them as intransigent fanatics and potential rebels. When Baptist, Congregationalist and Presbyterian ministers not only grew bolder, but began making inroads into the congregations of absent Anglicans, once again it conjured uncomfortable memories of the past.

Like the Corporation Act, the Five Mile Act, which came into force in the autumn of 1665, was based on the view that dissent was largely an urban phenomenon. Therefore, in order to separate them from their congregations, the Act forbade dissenting clergymen from living within five miles of a corporate town.[26] "Those who will not be governed as men, by reason and persuasion," said Gilbert Sheldon, Archbishop of Canterbury since June 1663, "shall be governed as beasts, by power and force."[27]

In his lonely Scarborough captivity, George Fox had every reason to believe that he was not only being governed by power and force, but had become the butt of other men's frustration. Should any rumour reach his bored guards of plots against King Charles, or of restless discontent erupting into riot, then "often they threatened to hang me over the wall", he said. Eventually, before the taunts of the deputy governor, he declared the principle that governed his life. "So I told him," he said, "if it was what they looked for I was ready, being innocent of all stirrings and plottings, and I never feared death nor suffering in my life." As his gaolers realized that he meant what he said, at last they gave him their grudging respect. "That stopped them from threatening me any more," he said.

Eventually too, although the Friends who would have brought him most comfort remained forbidden, men and women driven simply by curiosity, and whose status gave them special privileges, were allowed unlimited access.

With a group of influential Roman Catholics, friends of Sir Jordan Crosland, Scarborough Castle's Catholic governor, he debated the infallibility of the Pope. Perhaps the group also debated the work produced in 1664 by William Prynne, *The Quakers Unmasked, and clearly detected to be but the Spawn of*

Romish Frogs, Jesuites and Franciscan Fryers, that continued to perpetrate the allegation that Quakers were among the secret agents of England's enemies.[28]

To the widowed second wife of Fernando, Baron Fairfax, father of Sir Thomas, George explained the Quaker doctrine of the Inner Light, and why the Friends used the singular "thee" and "thou" rather than the plural "you".[29]

On another occasion, Sir Jordan arrived with an excited party of influential Anglican ministers, powerful laymen, and fashionably dressed women. One of them, Dr Cradock, an Anglican minister since the days of Archbishop Laud, raised the contentious issue of Quaker marriage: "You marry, but I know not how," he said.[30] From Genesis to Revelation, George replied, he saw no one married by a priest; not Isaac and Rebecca, not Jacob and Rachel, not Boaz and Ruth. Rather, they took one another before God, in the presence of God's people – the example followed by the Friends. As for whether a priest was necessary, he said, if the reverend gentleman "could show me any instance, we would come to them to marry us."[31]

After Cradock also admitted that he had excommunicated many individuals who had abandoned the Anglican Church, George accused him of hypocrisy. "You left us above twenty years ago ... to the Presbyterians, Independents, and Baptists," he said, reminding Cradock of the days when Episcopalians were replaced by Puritans. "If you would have kept your principles alive," he continued, "you should have sent some of your epistles, homilies and evening songs to the old men that knew them, so that they could then teach them." And furthermore, he couldn't help adding, "Paul wrote epistles to the saints, though he was in prison."

Though the Friends were kept strictly away from their leader, he constantly filled their thoughts. For just as he had discerned earlier, the imprisoned figurehead of a persecuted sect was a far more potent symbol of repression, and potentially of resistance, than a free man could ever be. Moreover, this was clearly not a view that George held independently. The years of persecution had taught the Friends more than the effectiveness of passive resistance; they had also learned how to lobby on behalf of their imprisoned comrades as well as the potential advantages in raising public consciousness. As all over the land individuals campaigned on George Fox's behalf, adding to their voices were the pleas of many influential men. Among them was Sir Jordan himself, who over the months of George's Scarborough confinement, had found himself increasingly drawn to his prisoner. "I desired him that when he came to London," said George, "him being a Parliament man, that he would speak to Esquire Marsh...and some others...tell them that I was a prisoner, and for what."

Richard Marsh, a long-time supporter of the Friends, a long-time gentleman of the king's bedchamber and a man who clearly knew how to raise widespread awareness, had already publicly offered to walk 100 miles barefoot to procure the liberty of George Fox. Eventually, towards the end of August 1666, when the long campaign was finally successful, it was Richard Marsh, together with John Whitehead, who received the order of release from King Charles.

In Scarborough, George received a certificate of discharge, dated 1 September 1666, from Sir Jordan. He had been a prisoner of conscience for two years and eight months, much of it in almost solitary confinement.

Though his limbs were swollen, and though struggling onto a horse was agony, George was quite certain that his immediate mission was to rally the Friends. By going among them, by letting them see for themselves his physical presence, he would personally provide the assurance that prison, even sickness in prison, could be endured. Thus he would convince them that the cause of justice, righteousness, and toleration would finally prevail. Nevertheless, as he turned his face towards London, it was with a certain sadness. Among many Friends in prison, Margaret Fell remained a captive at Lancaster, and Francis Howgill at Appleby. Moreover, while he had been held in Lancaster and in Scarborough, there had been more deaths among his old comrades: John Audland in 1664, William Caton in Holland in 1665, while earlier in 1666, Richard Farnsworth was struck down by fever in London.[32]

As George turned his own face towards London, in the early

hours of the next morning, a fire broke out in the kitchen of a bakery in Pudding Lane. Left to itself, in the narrow street of timbered buildings, bone dry after a long hot summer, the fire spread. As it reached Fish Street Hill, that led down to the city's ancient wooden bridge, an east wind sprang up to fan the flames. Within hours, with the wind blowing ever stronger, warehouses full of oil, pitch, hemp and tar began to explode, and the stained-glass windows of churches to melt; the homes of the people, meanwhile, full of furniture and clothing, the tools of men's trades, and many lifetimes of treasured possessions, became violent and crackling bonfires.

Samuel Pepys, sleeping soundly as the fire took hold, was woken in the morning with the news that more than 300 houses were consumed. Later, from a vantage point by the river, he watched the city burn: "... we saw the fire as only one entire arch of fire ... an arch of above a mile long. It made me weep to see it. The churches, houses, and all on fire and flaming at once, and a horrid noise the flames made, and the cracking of the houses at their ruine."[33] Over three days, until the wind finally dropped on Wednesday, and watched by Londoners from their refuge north of the city on Hampstead Heath, St Paul's Cathedral, 89 ancient churches, 52 magnificent guild halls, and 13,000 homes were burned to the ground.

Making his own way towards the ruined city, George discovered that although his release made him a free man, in many eyes it did not make him a less potentially dangerous one. In Yorkshire, in Derbyshire and in Nottingham, it was clear that town watchmen had orders to find him and intercept him, while anyone suspected of harbouring him found constables wielding search warrants at their door. Yet, somehow he escaped arrest, sometimes walking straight past men whose description of the inflammatory George Fox was nothing like the grey-haired man with the swollen limbs who nodded briefly to them as they hurried to break up a reported illegal meeting.

Standing before her door in Fenny Drayton, watching George approach, Mary Fox was perhaps shocked by what she saw: the resolute stride and colour of youth now overtaken by a painful limp and prison pallor. Perhaps she also reflected on those stories she told so long before, of how the Lagos were of the stock of the martyrs. Christopher Fox had died some few years earlier, the precise date unknown.[34] Would he have been proud of his son? Or would he have regretted that some other course on his part had not sent George on a different path through life?

Later, the son told his mother how it was for him now. "I was so weak with lying about three years in cruel and hard imprisonments my joints and my body were so benumbed that I could hardly get on my horse, neither could I well bend my knees, nor hardly endure fire nor warm meat, I had been so long kept from it."

When George reached London in November, and picked his way over the still-smouldering waste, he was eventually confronted with the ashes and charred timbers of what had once been the Bull and Mouth meeting house. Though he most certainly grieved for it, and for the memories it had contained, perhaps he also considered that its fiery demise was somehow significant. For with its death, went the early days of the Children of Light, who declared fiercely and uncompromisingly that their truth was the only truth, and who denounced all who opposed them. What would be raised up from the ashes, although inspired still by the Inner Light, and still equally uncompromising, would be a movement strong enough to resist the fires of persecution, and to stand firm and to endure until the day finally dawned when every man and woman was allowed to speak and worship as conscience directed. Moreover, by virtue of the courage that prompted him to speak truth boldly, the indomitable will that gave the strength to endure, and equally the deaths of many former comrades, George Fox was emerging as the towering leader of the Friends of Truth.

CHAPTER TWELVE

Gospel Order

I exhorted all ye heires of ye power of God to take there possessions of ye gospell for that was ye authority of there meetinges.

George Fox,
Cambridge Journal, 1667

"*T*HOUGH I WAS VERY WEAK," George
said, recalling the dawn of 1667, "yet I travelled up and down
in the service of the Lord." As he did so, the world around him
continued to change. He had seen sedan chairs in London in
the 1640s, although they had not been much used. Now, they
were everywhere, the burly pole-men that ran with them
yelling, "Have a care sir, have a care!" as they drove pedestri-
ans from their path. Everywhere too were the hackney carriages, that had increased with the blessing of Oliver
Cromwell, but which multiplied dramatically in 1662 when
Charles II issued the first licences. Often more than ten at a
time might be seen waiting for hire at their public stand by the
Maypole Inn in the Strand.[1]

Sometimes, as George saw chairmen and coachmen open
their doors with a flourish and a bow, he could hardly keep
from crying out. For fashion, that had often seemed wayward
even in the days of the Commonwealth, was now more extravagant than ever. Almost every man seemed determined to sport
the elaborately curled periwigs made popular by King Charles,
while women appeared eager not only to display their bosoms,
but to deck themselves with as many ribbons, ruffles, and

frivolous flounces as possible. Even when they flocked to the fashionable Anglican churches on a Sunday, their purpose seemed to be to outdo each other in finery, rather than come soberly before God.

Only Nonconformists, it seemed – Baptists, Congregationalists, Presbyterians and Quakers – continued to wear the subdued costumes of Puritanism. But even the Nonconformists were growing bolder, although rather than an unashamed desire to decorate, theirs was an increasing determination to walk openly as conscience directed.

As had already been the case for years, many Nonconformists met in secret, sometimes laying tables with bread and cold meats as an alibi should constables arrive to investigate a reported conventicle. Yet though George Fox accused such folk of hypocrisy, and it was certainly true that the Friends were the most resolute in their stand against intolerance, as Richard Baxter observed, it was no easy thing for men to follow principle at the expense of their families.[2] Since the Five Mile Act forbade Nonconformist ministers to come within that distance of any parish where they once served, or of the city or corporation where they were born, then even the parish relief was denied them: "... it pierceth a man's heart to have children crying, and sickness come upon them for want of wholesome food," Baxter said bitterly.[3]

Yet, as he also observed in the plague year, many Nonconformist ministers had remained in the city. Moreover, where an Anglican fled, a Baptist or a Congregationalist sometimes stepped into his empty pulpit. When the Anglican eventually returned it was often to find that his congregation chose to follow the man who shared their danger, rather than him who abandoned them. In the following year, when the fire destroyed so many city churches, many Nonconformists kept their meetings even more openly, sometimes furnishing rooms as chapels with pulpits, seats and galleries.

Elsewhere in the country, avoiding the Five Mile Act, Nonconformist ministers able to support themselves began setting up in small villages. Others, especially those dependent for their income on the contributions of a congregation, sometimes established themselves in small unincorporated market-towns not covered by the Act, such as Manchester and Birmingham, and similar towns elsewhere.[4, 5]

Though such men were still hounded, their numbers, their confidence, and the support of their congregations all added fuel to a climate where persecution was increasingly opposed, and where the law consequently became more difficult to enforce. "God bringing good out of men's evil," said Baxter, "many resolved to preach the more freely in cities and corporations until they went to prison ... "[6] And, as ever more individuals made public witness, the congregations that the state sought to stifle grew inexorably larger.

In the 1650s, George Fox viewed other sectarian leaders as rivals, and their congregations as potential converts to the Children of Light. As the 1660s wore on, their renewed confidence, and their establishment of meeting houses and chapels, once again made them competitors for the soul of Christian England. However, by the time he arrived in London in 1666, he was also convinced that the continuing divisions within his own movement were as great a threat to its existence as the attractions of other sects or its persecution by the state. For, as the faction which had supported James Nayler and John Perrot continued to insist that each Friend should remain open to fresh leadings of the Spirit, the issue of whose was the true revelation refused to die. To the leaders, however, the individualism of the Naylerites and Perrotists, and the potential split they represented, could only produce anarchy. A month before his death in June 1666, Richard Farnsworth had called an urgent meeting of many leading Friends still at liberty. Given past experience, he told them, and the present activities of certain individuals, if their movement was to survive then its structure must be further strengthened and its discipline tightened.

Their conclusions were published as an epistle, *Testimony from the Brethren*, which was sent to all meetings, to be read aloud, and then kept for future reference. Although some voices were raised in opposition, the weight of the signatures gave the document immediate authority, among them Richard Farnsworth, Alexander Parker and George Whitehead.

These leading men, said the *Testimony*, "by the operation of the Spirit of Truth," had been brought to a serious concern for "the present state of the church of God; which ... hath not only many open but some covered enemies to contest against." Those "covered enemies", it alleged, were unruly spirits within their own ranks. Moreover, should their disruption be allowed to continue, it would lay waste everything so far achieved. Contrasting them with the vast body of Friends, so reassuringly "steadfast and constant", it was also made clear that the unruly not only lacked spiritual authority, but that they should no more be heeded than the persecutors of the world. Furthermore, said the *Testimony*, should they fail to submit to "the Spirit of Truth in the Elders", then they should be "rejected, as having erred from the Truth".

Hearing the words of their leaders spoken aloud by their Elders, and then seeing the document stored in a place of authority, within a very short time it came to seem to Friends all across the country that the *Testimony* was indeed an extension of the "word of life that hath been preached unto you from the beginning".[7]

It was a long way from the heady days of 1652, when the Malton Friends flung their finery onto bonfires and trembled for all to see, when Elizabeth Tomlinson ran into the Selby streets calling people to repentance before the Day of the Lord, and when Richard Farnsworth himself claimed "that the world is all on a fire." It was a great distance too from the days when George Fox denounced merchants at market crosses, and demanded that "hireling priests" demonstrate those same charismatic gifts that were so evident in the Children of Light. Nevertheless, when the *Testimony* was presented to him, he endorsed it wholeheartedly.

Thus, the Friends continued along a path that virtually every other surviving Christian movement had followed before them, that saw a retreat from a radical, charismatic and often apocalyptic enthusiasm which had brought them to birth, and over time to become sober, settled and conservative. By the mid-1600s the Friends' membership numbered some 50,000 men, women and children, and as meetings became settled, as young people matured, and as children arrived to be nurtured, the ardour that drove the evangelists of former years was often replaced by other considerations.[8] Though the Friends remained committed to the message of the Inner Light, and were opposed to the state church and its tithes, community and stability often assumed a greater importance than spiritual enthusiasm, passionate evangelism and fearless denunciations.

Besides, though the Friends continued to maintain their witness, the years of persecution had caused huge disruption. Since George Fox first preached his message in the Midlands, since the Seekers at Balby and Westmorland first welcomed him, many meetings had been settled and had prospered. But, although some of the county and general meetings were kept up, during the attacks of the 1660s many of those established under the Commonwealth either collapsed or became dormant. Many Friends were in prison, others had lost livelihoods and possessions. Nor were those who devoted their energies to caring for captives, or lobbying for their release, able to spare time for anything but the minimal administration required to maintain meetings deemed illegal.

In 1662, following a national collection for work overseas, supporting mission abroad had become the responsibility of the well-organized Friends in London. For, although many collections were maintained locally, with letters regularly intercepted, and informers on the lookout for plots, money transferred openly could be interpreted as funds gathered to fuel an uprising.

Equally detrimental were the constraints on travel. In the 1640s, during the turmoil of the Civil War, George Fox walked freely over the land. In 1652, after the convincement in Westmorland, his new comrades walked freely beside him. When Cromwell sought to limit their missionary journeys, when they were flung into town gaols and whipped as vagrants, the Friends still declared the message of the Light. But, in 1667, in an England dominated by a king, the Cavalier Parliament, and the Anglican Church, so many were in prison that the travelling ministry had virtually ceased. Moreover, among those prisoners were some of the movement's leading men. William Dewsbury had been in prison almost constantly since 1661; Francis Howgill remained a close prisoner at Appleby.[9]

By their regular worship the Friends contravened the law, while national and regional authorities often viewed them as promoters of subversive ideas and instigators of treasonable activity. In the face of repression, and in order for such a large and disparate movement to survive, it seemed increasingly necessary not only to create a firmer structure, but also to define what was meant by "Truth", and, inevitably, just who should be the definers. Inevitably too, it became necessary to silence dissident voices, so that, in the words of the *Testimony*, "nothing but what is sound and savoury, that will answer the witness of God in all people, (even in our adversaries,) may be exposed by us to public view."[10]

"The Lord opened to me," said George Fox, in the cold months at the beginning of 1667, "and let me see what I must do, and how I must order and establish the Men's and Women's Monthly and Quarterly Meetings in all the nation, and write to other nations, where I came not, to do the same." Such words were also written with hindsight. Although he was in a sense establishing meetings, many were those that had previously fallen into abeyance, while others were riven by the conflict that the *Testimony from the Brethren* was designed to suppress. It was also the case, that although women's meetings were established when he wrote the words of his *Journal*, the main focus of the Monthly, or district, Meetings of 1667 was men.

He began in London, where before anything new was established, any Friend regarded as "unruly", or who had once behaved divisively, perhaps by supporting John Perrot, was given the opportunity to recant. "So ... they were made to condemn and tear all their papers of controversies to pieces," he said of those who accepted the offer. Since the alternative was to be "rejected, as having erred from the Truth", it was only the diehards, it seems, who refused to return. "And judgement was set," George said, "and whole days we sat, wherein many condemned their former lives ... as may be seen in the books of condemnation."

In London, five new monthly meetings were established and added to a similar meeting already existing, their function to oversee and coordinate various smaller meetings, and to enforce discipline among meetings and members.[11] Almost immediately, at Horslydown, south of the Thames, the only meeting from which records survive, there were disciplinary issues to deal with. Some Friends had married before "hireling priests", some continued to wear hats during prayers, some visited astrologers, some had been seen playing ninepins, and some, so their colleagues alleged, were too fond of their ale. After some very close questioning, a shopkeeper among them also admitted to using false measures.

Late in the summer, George began the task of imposing what was now called Gospel Order on Friends' meetings elsewhere in the country. As he did so, he was often encouraged by stories of heroism in almost every locality. At Colchester, in the bitter winter of 1664, eight years after the death there of James Parnell, when their meeting-house was destroyed, Colchester's Friends gathered in the street outside. Each Sunday, as they stood silently before God, fingers and toes numb with cold, mounted troopers rode among them, kicking with spurred boots, lashing with pistol butts, and wheeling their horses so violently that men, women and children were hurled to the ground. Stephen Crisp, a signatory to the *Testimony from the Brethren*, who was at that time in the town gaol, wrote to Colchester's Mayor. The worship of God was more important to Quakers than life itself, he declared, and echoing the observations of Richard Baxter, he warned that meetings would not only continue, but that persecution would see numbers increase.[12]

Moving on through East Anglia into Lincolnshire, one of the Men's Monthly Meetings took place at the home of Robert Craven, a former sheriff of Lincoln. But, even the status of the host was not enough to dispel an air of apprehension. For with every meeting contravening the Conventicle Act, should the constables arrive, then the Friends knew they not only faced imprisonment, but probably a beating as well. They might well also be robbed of their possessions. When George visited

William Smith, a former Independent minister turned Friend, he learned that even sickness evoked no relief: "... ye constables and bailiffs had seized upon all William Smith's goods to the very bed he lay on," he said.

But though George himself avoided arrest, he could not escape the English weather. "We passed into Staffordshire over the Peak hills," he said, "which were very cold, it being snow and frost. And I was so exceeding weak I was hardly able to get off or on my horse." Yet, despite weakness and cold, he pressed on, driven by his need to settle the organization that was now so much a part of his life that he could barely imagine existence without it. "And so the Lord's power came over all," he said, "and all the heirs of it came to inherit it, for the authority of our meetings is the power of God, the Gospel which brings life and immortality to light."

In Cheshire, early in 1668, at the home of a female Friend, Jane Milner, George welcomed Margaret Fell. Though technically still imprisoned at Lancaster, and despite a praemunire imposed upon her, her status as a substantial landowner and the widow of Judge Fell allowed her privileges not granted to others. Earlier she had attended one of Cheshire's new Monthly Meetings, and now, in the privacy of Jane's parlour she greeted her friend of fifteen years.

Since the day that Margaret first gave her life to the Quaker cause, it had indeed allowed her to utilize and develop many strengths and abilities. In 1663 she travelled the country on behalf of the Quaker captives, while from 1664 onwards, a captive herself, she devoted herself to writing. Like George Fox, she also sought to overcome the Friends' reputation as religious fanatics and political subversives. "For I never did thee nor any other Man in the Nation any wrong," she told King Charles, "and so I may say for many more of our Friends that have suffered even until Death."[13]

Like George, Margaret also sought to transform the organization once determined to renew the world through a campaign of militant evangelism, into one that accepted suffering as a mark of Christian witness: "... keep faithful to the Lord God and his Truth," she wrote in 1664, "and make War in

Righteousness, and give your Backs to the Smiter, and your Cheeks to them that pull off the Hair; it is but for an hour, stand it out, the Lamb shall have the victory."[14]

During her imprisonment, she also wrote four books, among them *Women's Speaking Justified*. Using texts from the Bible to underpin her arguments, she highlighted the teaching and prophetic role of women in the Old Testament, and also showed how women took a leading part in supporting the ministry of Jesus. Moreover, Margaret said, quoting from the Acts of the Apostles, and from his own letters, when Paul of Tarsus advised the church at Corinth to "let your women keep silence", he referred to issues that were specific. It did not apply, she insisted, to women speaking in the power of the Spirit.[15, 16]

Over the many years that Margaret Fell and George Fox worked together as friends and colleagues, it would have been surprising if a woman of such strength and resource had not also influenced his thinking. However, from the day he first walked into her life, it is also clear that for Margaret, as she herself made clear to James Nayler, George was the leader to whom all others should defer. For George himself, the son of a woman "accomplished above most of her degree in the place where she lived", it also seems that in his relationship with Margaret Fell, a woman of power and intellect, and now head of the supportive family that he himself had always lacked, there were issues at work on a very deep level.

Whether those issues also led to the intimacy hinted at by others is unknown. But, certainly by the time George and Margaret met at Jane Milner's home in Cheshire, specific allegations had already been made: "... it is so reported among Friends," maintained the Yorkshire Quaker, John Harwood, "that the said George Fox and Margaret Fell did so carry themselves each to other, and walk so unseemly and indiscreetly at the house of Elizabeth Trott when they lay there, that she questioned their honesty." Though Harwood had fallen foul of George Fox in 1660, and was perhaps nursing a grudge, that he refers to rumours circulating among Friends before 1663, implies that he and Elizabeth Trott were not alone in their suspicions.[17]

Whatever were the Friends' opinions regarding George Fox, the change in the attitudes of "the world" that he had first noticed in Hampshire in 1663, was now beginning to make itself felt even in civil administrations. As Margaret returned to her cold room in Lancaster, and George crossed and re-crossed the Welsh border, an incident in Shrewsbury made it clear that in the governing bodies of towns there were serious differences of opinion regarding the laws against dissent. "The mayor and his officers," George said, "hearing of my being in town ... they took counsel together to imprison me, but some of them opposed it, thus the Lord confounded them."

In Radnor, rather like the incident at Skipton in 1660, it was a case of hostility being transformed into respect. Just outside a small market town, George and his comrades were surrounded by a gang of youths. As the mob closed in, their leader, a clerk to a local justice, urged them to violence. Only the unexpected arrival of a crowd returning from market saved the Friends from a beating. Shortly afterwards, as they went on their way, and as the road plunged into a hollow among dense trees, they encountered violence once more. This time, however, the intended victim was a young woman, one of a party of two women and two men beset by an armed drunkard who bellowed obscene threats while slashing wildly with his sword. "He would have ravished the young woman," George said.

When the attacker ran off, George caught his horse and sent it with the young woman to the nearest justice, that the criminal might be apprehended. Since the Assizes currently sat nearby, he also complained about his own would-be attackers. "And the justice rebuked his clerk and the others for abusing and disturbing us upon the highway," he said, "and they made entreaty to Friends not to appear against them at the Assizes." When the Quakers agreed, it was their compassion, as well as their willingness to brave danger to save others, that "did a great deal of good in the country, and stopped many rude people that had used to abuse Friends formerly."

Returning to London in the spring, and perhaps motivated in part by the rumours surrounding his relationship with

Margaret Fell, George considered the subject of Friends' marriages. Though it was one on which he had spoken before, despite all guidelines, the persecution that flung men into prison and tore families apart had taken a savage toll of human relationships. Moreover, there were still associations in many minds between sectarian religion and "unnatural" sexuality – promiscuity, collective debauchery, the seduction of innocents and deviance of all kinds. Allegations like those of Dr Cradock at Scarborough, that Quaker couples lived in sin, caused many Friends to marry before ministers in parish churches. Others followed their own desires as to partners. "For many had gone together contrary to their relations," said George, "and sometimes young, raw people had mixed with the world." Others still abandoned previous responsibilities. "Widows had married and had not made provision for their children before marriage again," he said.

Thus to ensure regulation for individuals, to strengthen solidarity within the organization, and to prevent the loss of young people to "the world", a new set of procedures was established. "It was therefore ordered," said George, "... that marriages might be laid before the Men's Monthly and Quarterly Meetings ... so that they might see their relations were satisfied and that they were clear from all others ... " Moreover, Friends arriving from one county to marry in another were henceforward obliged to bring with them a certificate confirming their eligibility to be wed.

Just as young people were to be regularly married, so too were children to be educated. "I came to Waltham and established a school for teaching of children there," George recalled. In the same months, at Shacklewell in London, he helped establish another, "... and ordered a women's school to be set up, to instruct young lassies and maidens in whatever things were civil and useful in the creation."

The schools themselves were part of a wider move by Nonconformists to provide education free from control by the state church, and also to ensure that their children acquired the knowledge and skill to allow them as adults to become self-supporting. Thus they would not only avoid future charges of vagrancy, but, debarred by the tests from municipal office, they could also establish themselves in mercantile trades and businesses. That George Fox played a role in the foundation of the Friends' schools, no doubt gave him enormous satisfaction.[18] For, like many individuals denied an education, and who feel the loss keenly, he was clearly determined not only to provide for others what he himself lacked, but also to be seen as doing so.

He was also determined to continue with the establishment of Gospel Order, and through the long summer days of 1668 he travelled on relentlessly, from Buckinghamshire through Oxfordshire to Gloucestershire, and then over the hills into Monmouth. It was there that once again he saw hostility become an admission that perhaps there was good in the Friends after all. At Monmouth, he said, after settling the Monthly Meeting, he had cause to "admonish and exhort such as did not walk as becomes the gospel." Though perhaps embellishing the response with more colour than it possessed at the time, his words evidently made an impression. "It made a great cry in the country," he said, "insomuch as the very justices said 'never such a man came into their country that had reconciled neighbour to neighbour and husband to wife, and turned many people from their loose lives.'" No longer, it seems, was George Fox a disrupter of families and an instigator of youthful rebellion. At the age of 44 he had become an agent of harmony and an apostle of obedience.

Late in the autumn, he returned to London, where Margaret Fell, released from Lancaster in June, waited for him. There, she recalled the August wedding of her daughter Mary to Thomas Lower, the Cornishman who in 1656 travelled to Launceston to support the imprisoned George Fox. It was the fifth marriage in the Fell family, but only the third to bring much happiness to Margaret. In 1660, George Fell, who, to her dismay, rejected the message of the Light, married a non-Friend, while in the spring of 1663, Bridget, who had married the previous year, died in childbirth.

The younger Margaret had also married in 1662. Her husband, John Rous, the son of wealthy sugar-planter in

Barbados, had become a Quaker while still on the island, both he and his father convinced by Mary Fisher of Selby, who with Ann Austin had arrived there in 1655.[19] Two years later, Isabel married William Yeamans of Bristol, brother to Ann Curtis, and son of the sheriff hanged in 1643 for opposing the forces of Parliament.

As they spoke of the Fell family, their weddings and the children that eventually followed, George and Margaret also discussed a marriage of their own. She had spoken to her daughters, Margaret said, and they were all in agreement. Only her son, George Fell, was opposed. Despite that, Margaret saw the way ahead clear. For George Fox, however, the union was not quite so straightforward. It was upon him, he insisted, and perhaps to Margaret's disappointment, to await God's indication as to when the event should take place. In the meantime, he intended to travel to Yorkshire, while after that, he would be crossing the sea to Ireland. Though he had already sent papers to the Friends' meetings there, his presence, he felt, would add weight to the first consideration in his life, the establishment of Gospel Order and the furtherance of the Friends.

In Yorkshire, he visited Durant Hotham, where they recalled together the days long before when an eager young evangelist passed through the country gathering followers. Later, he was welcomed by another old friend. "And when I came into Scarborough," he said, "the governor ... sent to me by one of his soldiers, and said surely I would not be so unkind as not to come to see him and his wife."

Shortly afterwards, hearing that Colonel Kirkby was sick of the gout, he was seized by a triumphant certainty that divine retribution was meted out upon his persecutor. But, at the same time, there was sorrow. From Appleby, where Francis Howgill had been imprisoned since 1663, the news said that his health was failing, and that he could not much longer survive.

In May 1669, together with four companions – Robert Lodge, James Lancaster, Thomas Briggs and John Stubbs – George approached the estuary of the River Mersey. It was a day of bright sunshine and high white clouds, a day when the wind from the sea seemed infused with the breath of the Spirit that coursed through the heart of an evangelist embarking for a distant land. So elated did George feel, that when he learned that the gout-stricken Kirkby had once again offered money for his capture, he simply laughed out loud. Riding on towards the ships, only one shadow lay across his path. In the freezing January cold Francis Howgill had laid down his life in Appleby Gaol.

Plunging into the troughs of the Irish Sea, rising high on the waves, and lurching from one side to another, the small ship battled her way towards Dublin. From her passengers, huddled into their cloaks and clutching their heaving stomachs, there came nothing but groans and the occasional curse. Apart from the crew, only George Fox stood on his feet. At the ship's prow, his face reddened by the wind, he strained for his first glimpse of a foreign shore. Yet, he recalled later, as blue hills appeared on the horizon, he was overcome with an enormous sense of dread.

Following the execution of Charles I, his nephew Prince Rupert had rallied Irish Royalists and Irish Catholics against the English Parliament. Subsequently, Ireland became a centre of Royalist activity and a potential power base for the then Prince of Wales, now King Charles II of England. In the late summer of 1649, after the suppression of the Levellers, Oliver Cromwell led the formidable English Army to Ireland. Early in September, as they stormed Drogheda at the mouth of the River Boyne, something took place that many English men and women preferred to ignore. Around 3,500 people were slaughtered – not only troops, but old men, women, children and many Catholic priests. Hundreds of survivors were subsequently transported to Barbados.

In the three-year campaign that followed, all Ireland was subdued, the surrender of Galway in May 1652 marking its final subjection to the Parliament of England. As a man of his time, and despite his understanding of the Inner Light, George Fox almost certainly shared the view of Oliver Cromwell, who saw the suffering of Catholic Ireland as divine vengeance on the agents of Antichrist who, in 1641, had unleashed their attack on Ireland's Protestants. Moreover, just like many other English Protestants, George almost certainly carried always in his mind the images from John Foxe's *Book of Martyrs*, where Protestant saints burned amid Mary Tudor's Catholic flames.

"The earth and the very air smelt with the corruption of the nation," he said, as he stepped ashore at Dublin, "... the corruption and the blood and the massacres and the foulness that ascended." Almost certainly his reference was to the 1641 slaughter of Protestants.

By 1669, when he arrived in Ireland, an uneasy peace lay on the country, that for Ireland's Quaker community meant less hostility than was suffered by their co-religionists in England. Though persecuted for non-payment of tithes, and sometimes hounded by the Irish Protestant church, the rigors of the Conventicle Act and the Five Mile Act largely passed them by. In this atmosphere of calm, their numbers had increased, and in the provinces of Leinster, Ulster and Munster, there were 30 settled and vigorous meetings.

Many of their members were emigrants from England, some of them part of successive attempts to "plant" Ireland with individuals both English and Protestant, who could thus be relied on for loyalty to England and opposition to her European Catholic enemies. Cromwell's conquest had also been financed by promises of plunder, and almost half of all Irish land was confiscated from its former owners to repay loans made by English civilians and to pay the wages of English soldiers. An Act of Settlement in 1652 had also cleared six Irish counties of their Catholic landholders.[20]

William Edmondson, one of Ireland's leading Friends, and part of this emigration, was both a staunch Cromwellian and also a former Ironside – a member of the cavalry troop formed in 1643 by Oliver Cromwell that had been the inspiration for the New Model Army. In the spirit of that disciplined and battle-hardened band, he named one of his daughters Hindrance and his youngest son Trial, and called relentlessly for tighter order in the Quaker Church. "I was made a thrashing instrument in the hand of the Lord," he said, "to thrash sharply, reprove and rebuke such as walked loosely." Thus, when George Fox arrived, bringing with him his plans for Gospel Order, Edmondson welcomed a comrade-in-arms: "...it pleased God to send His servant George Fox to set up Men's and Women's Meetings, and then I was eased," he said.[21]

George threw himself into the Irish work, setting up Monthly Meetings, urging tighter discipline, and admonishing those "hat-men" who continued to follow the ways of James Nayler and John Perrot. As he did so, however, Roman Catholicism, and the resolute devotion of the Irish nation to their faith, irked him to the point of obsession. Equally provoking was the attitude of the Irish Catholic priests, who rather than seeing George Fox as a prophet, appeared simply to regard him as yet another interfering Protestant Englishman.

"Some of the Papists was angry and raged very much," he declared, affronted at their disruption of his public meetings. Though such attacks were little different to those he once levelled at English Puritans, being the butt of such abuse himself roused him to fury. Defiantly, he issued a challenge guaranteed to give offence: "...friars and monks, priests, and Jesuits, and the Pope himself," should come forth, he declared, "and try their God, and their Christ, that they had made of bread and wine." When no response was forthcoming, he accused the Catholic clergy of being worse than the priests of Baal, who had at least been prepared to petition their wooden idols before Elijah and the multitudes of Israel.[22] "Baal's priest and people did not eat their god...and then make another," he added as a final insult.

Yet, even as he taunted Ireland's Catholics, he knew that England's secret service watched his own movements. One day, at an inn near Cork, and becoming uncomfortably aware that someone stared at him intently, he sensed his inward antennae stir. Presently, as he and his comrades mounted their horses, the same watcher asked casually where the party were bound. "And so he sang and went into the house as if he had got his prize," said George. Later, on reaching Limerick, he learned that his description had been circulated earlier – his height, his long hair, the type of hat he wore, even the colour and size of his horse. Now, having been informed of his whereabouts by the spy at the inn, the authorities would soon be closing in.

From the moment the Irish trip was first planned, George knew he took a risk. William Edmondson was not the only Irish Quaker who had once been a stalwart of the New Model Army, and with many men at Westminster quite unconvinced by the Friends' assurances of peaceful intentions, they watched for evidence of republican plots. Others, who saw England's chief enemies in the Catholic courts of Europe, were equally unmoved by George Fox's anti-Catholic tirades, remaining convinced that even if all Quakers were not themselves Jesuits, then they were certainly all in the pay of the Pope.

Nevertheless, despite the danger, George was ambivalent. On the one hand, he urged Irish Friends to be cautious, and had warned English Friends earlier not to write lest they betray his whereabouts. On the other, he was sometimes reckless to the point of folly. Indeed, perhaps it was also a folly that was sometimes quite necessary, to overcome the inner insecurities that still lived within him, and thus to reassure himself that he was indeed the confident man that he appeared to be to the world. Perhaps he also liked the edge that danger provided, that made everything seem so much more vibrant and alive.

In Cork, after the Friends there learned that a warrant was issued by the town's mayor for his arrest, they urged him to leave swiftly through the city's back alleys. But "the way was through the streets", George protested. That way was not possible, his fearful comrades assured him, for with it being market day, "the way was so slippery ... his horse could not stand."

With memories of his former appearances at England's market crosses suddenly fresh in his mind, George ignored all advice. To the dismay of his hosts, he rode out defiantly, first along Cork's main streets, then over the rotting vegetables and tossed-away food of the marketplace, and then right past the mayor's front door. As he did so, he was convinced that the mayor watched him. "There goes George Fox," he imagined him saying.

"Let the Devil do his worst," he said resolutely. As far as he was concerned, mayors and magistrates, Catholic priests, informers and spies were all part of that same enemy that had always been determined to hinder the spreading of Truth. Some time later, lying wakeful at a Friend's house in the north of Ireland, he believed he saw the Devil's purpose take shape. "A grim, black fellow," he said, "who was fettering of my legs with a cord, that I had much ado to preserve my feet from him." Next day, he felt that same power again: "the power of darkness at work strongly." That very evening, after reluctantly allowing his hosts to dissuade him from accompanying them to their meeting, one of them came back with disquieting news. "The Devil's messenger is come," he said; "he is staring up and down in the meeting."

Though that particular Devil's messenger was both "a Papist and a bailiff", come to serve a warrant, sometimes, rather than Catholics, the hostility came from Ireland's Protestants – English Episcopalians in the south, Scottish Presbyterians in the north. And sometimes, the fear that caused Friends to bar their doors at night was of Tories, Irish Catholic outlaws who raided English settlers and any native Irish they regarded as collaborators. George, however, was scathing. "Though there were tories up in several places of the nation," he said, "none hurt me but the judges, justices and priests."

Nevertheless, he was not taken captive, nor did he suffer any harm. Moreover, in the Irish Friends, he saw a freshness and vitality lacking from their persecuted colleagues in England. "The power of the Lord was so great," he said of many meetings held in Munster, "that Friends in the power and spirit of the Lord brake out into singing, many together with an audible voice." The sight and sound of it reminded him of the early days in Yorkshire and Westmorland. So too did the "mighty convincement" he saw taking place.

Returning to Dublin in August, he reviewed his first trip beyond seas. He had been impressed by the commitment and the ready welcome of Ireland's Friends, and especially by their eagerness to embrace Gospel Order. "A gallant visitation they had," he observed, "and there is a gallant spirit in them." If persecution in England could be brought to an end, then Friends there could surely recover the spontaneity and joy that had once been such a part of their own faith.

In the autumn of the year, after holding meetings in Lancashire, Cheshire and Gloucestershire, George arrived in Bristol. So too did Margaret Fell. "At Bristol," she said later, "he declared his intentions of marriage to me, and there was also our marriage solemnized, in a public meeting of many Friends who were our witnesses."[23]

Although George claimed that it was only during his Irish journey that he sensed the divine command, to almost everyone else the marriage clearly came as little surprise. Nevertheless, it was not everywhere welcomed. "There was a jumble in some minds about it," George said. Possibly it was a jumble provoked by the allegations of earlier sexual intimacy, and perhaps also by a view that it was somewhat late in the day to regularize something already in existence for years.

Whatever exactly lay behind the jumble, George clearly felt called to answer it; early in October he sent an Epistle on the subject to the Friends. His marriage to Margaret Fell, he maintained, a joining together by God, "was a figure of Christ and his Church – a mystical spiritual union". Moreover, he continued, it was a "figure of the Church coming out of the wilderness".[24]

As the marriage then went ahead, all the formalities, so clearly delineated in the new Gospel Order, were firmly adhered to. "I was moved to ask the children whether they were all satisfied and whether Margaret had answered according to her husband's will ... and if her husband had left anything to her for the assistance of her children; which if she married they might suffer loss therein ... "

Not only had she "doubled it", Margaret's daughters replied, they would not have George Fox even speak of such things. It was a reply which expressed the affection they obviously felt for the man they first called "father" in 1652, in the postscripts to their mother's passionate letter. It also suggests that they saw their family as one of faith, as much as a family united by blood. And, as indeed proved to be the case, although by her second marriage Margaret lost the ownership of Swarthmoor

Hall, her daughters, to whom it then passed, were eager that it should remain a home not only for their mother, but also for her new husband.[25]

On 18 October 1669, before a men's meeting at Bristol's Broadmead Meeting House; on 21 October, before a meeting there of men and women; and on 22 October, before a public meeting, the marriage intentions of the 45-year-old George Fox and the 55-year-old Margaret Fell were made clear. Many spoke on their behalf, among them Margaret's six surviving daughters, and her three sons-in-law. Also speaking at the meeting on 22 October was a young man by the name of William Penn, son of Admiral Sir William Penn, who against his father's express wish, had two years earlier become a Friend.[26, 27]

Subsequently, on Wednesday, 27 October, before a large company, the marriage itself took place. Clearly it was an extraordinary event: "... there was a mighty power of the Lord God among Friends," said a chronicler, "that did so overcome them, that there was many testimonies could not be taken, and ... G.F. had like to have fallen down, but that he laid his hand upon another, for he could not tell whether he had a body or not a body."

The new Margaret Fox, echoing her husband's belief that their marriage was a figure of the Quaker church, also prayed passionately: "ye Bride, ye Lamb's wife, whose light is of jasper stone, clear as crystal, whose firstborn of that womb of eternity is coming out of ye wilderness ... to be nursed and clothed with ye eternal free spirit of ye living God ... "[28]

Ninety-four witnesses then signed a certificate worded so as to make it clear that the marriage followed the ancient biblical practice of taking each other before God's people, rather than a "hireling priest". Thus, George Fox and Margaret Fell, after a friendship of seventeen years, were married. Whatever had been the true nature of their earlier relationship, they clearly intended that their union should be seen as an example both to the Friends of Truth, and to the whole world, as symbolic of the Quaker movement, a figure of the restoration of the true Church, and the embodiment of Gospel Order. How much it was also a union based on a mutual physical longing and a desire for a mutual long-term domestic companionship is debatable.

Ten days after their wedding, the newly married pair set out from Bristol on a road leading north. After an hour or two they reached the village of Olveston, where they parted company. "I passed on ... in the work of the Lord into Wiltshire," said George Fox. His new wife travelled on to Swarthmoor alone.

CHAPTER THIRTEEN

Resist in the Power of God

And why should any man have power over any other man's faith,
seeing Christ is the author of it?

George Fox,
Declaration against the Second Conventicle Act [1]

"AS I CAME UP THE STREETS in
London," said George Fox, recalling the dangerous days that
opened 1670, "the drums beat for every household to send
forth a soldier into the trained bands, to be in readiness, the
Act against seditious conventicles being then come into force."

Three years earlier, in 1667, Edward Hyde, Lord Clarendon
since 1660, Charles II's Chancellor since the Restoration, fell
from favour. The immediate cause was the defeat of England
by Holland in a war which virtually bankrupted the Crown,
and saw Dutch ships tow England's flagship away from the
Royal dockyard at Chatham. In the absence of Clarendon,
who, though overseeing the laws against dissent, had always
urged caution, the way was then opened for Archbishop
Gilbert Sheldon, and his allies in Parliament and Church, to
demand harsher measures against Nonconformists.

It was a demand fuelled by mounting frustration. For
despite the restoration of Anglicanism and the repressive legislation that followed, the sects that emerged from the Puritan
Revolution had no intention of returning to the Anglican fold.
Moreover, as Richard Baxter and others had so often observed,

in the face of persecution, both dissenters and their conventicles continued to increase.

However, it was not only Protestant Nonconformity that troubled Gilbert Sheldon. For once again, the spectre of absolutism and Roman Catholicism was at large in England's Royal court. During his Restoration years, Charles Stuart was cautious, but, as he felt himself increasingly secure, so too did he became influenced by the aura of power surrounding his fellow monarch, Louis XIV of France. Thus, he grew ever more determined to assert what he believed to be the divine right of a king to determine matters of politics and religion, and the lives of his own family. Like many of that family, including his brother, James, Charles was drawn towards Catholicism, provoking an anxiety in Parliament that was exacerbated by his marriage in 1662 to Catherine of Braganza, daughter of the Catholic king of Portugal.

Late in the 1660s, the financially insecure Charles opened negotiations with Louis. In May 1670, they culminated in the Treaty of Dover, where in return for a promise of regular payments and a share of the Dutch empire, Charles would support Louis against Holland. The treaty also involved two secret clauses: that England would suspend penal laws against Catholics, and that at an agreed propitious moment, Charles would announce publicly his own conversion to Roman Catholicism.[2]

Though the secret was maintained, Sheldon and many others were suspicious. He was also convinced that it was the king's connivance, part of a long-term plan to relax proscriptions against Catholics, that was responsible for the overall failures of the 1664 Conventicle Act. Thus in May 1670, as Charles finalized his treaty with Louis, he was also persuaded by Sheldon to sign a second Conventicle Act. Its aim was the "providing of further and more speedy remedies against the growing and dangerous practices of seditious sectaries and other disloyal persons, who, under pretence of tender consciences ... contrive insurrections as late experience hath showed."[3]

In order that the second Act should be more effective than

the first, transportation was dropped as costly and ineffectual, and the emphasis placed instead on ruining individuals financially and in undermining the solidarity that had played so consistent a part in Nonconformist resistance. The new Act would also be enforced without the safeguard of a jury, with a single Justice empowered to convict, and to levy fines of five and then ten shillings for attendance at an illegal conventicle.

Two new offences also carried more substantial fines: anyone preaching at a conventicle was to be fined £20 for a first, and £40 for any further offence, while harbouring a conventicle carried a fine of £20. Fines were to be recovered by distress, while informers were to be rewarded with a third of all fines levied, with the remainder shared between the king and the poor.

Dissenters too poor to pay would have their fines forcibly met by wealthier co-religionists. Justices were also empowered to issue orders for forcible entry into homes, for which purpose the militia was placed at their disposal. Writing to clerical colleagues, Sheldon was confident that the outcome of the Act would be to "the glory of God, the welfare of the Church, the praise of His Majesty's Government, and the happiness of the whole kingdom."[4] Others chose to disagree. The Conventicle Act of 1670, said the poet Andrew Marvell, was "the quintessence of arbitrary malice".[5]

George Fox exhorted the Friends to resist in the power of God, a resistance that was to be expressed through endurance. "If so be that the Lord do suffer you to be tried," he said, "let all be given up; and look at the Lord and His power, which is over the whole world, and will be when the world is gone ... "[6]

Then, he turned his attention to the Act. As he did so, once again it was a very different George Fox who spoke. No longer the Leicestershire prophet of former years, warning magistrates to "take heed whom you imprison" or else suffer divine retribution. Now, at 46 years old, his vision transformed by experience, and with arguments both measured and persuasive, he was at the forefront of the call for toleration.

"And why should any man have power over any other man's faith," he asked, "seeing Christ is the author of it?" Moreover, rather than faith being imposed by force, far better was it to obey the biblical commands. "And do unto all men as ye would have them do unto you," he said, "for that is the law and the prophets."[7]

But, the call went unheeded, and on 15 May 1670, the Sunday after the Act came into force, George Fox was arrested at the Quaker meeting-house in White-Hart Court, Gracechurch Street. He was pointed out by an Informer, greedy for his share of the fine. "There came an officer with a file of musketeers, and pulled me out," George said, "and the officer said I was the man he looked for ... and said he must carry me to the Lord Mayor."[8]

Watching was a huge crowd, drawn from their homes by the sight of the militia in the streets. But, whereas such crowds would once have bayed for sectarian blood, now, said George, they "were mighty moderate". Moreover, as they urged the troopers to "have a care of him", it was clear that they also wished George Fox to be well treated.

The informer was not so fortunate. Nor did George's own appetite for toleration stretch in every direction. When the man referred to "the good old religion", and thus gave himself away as a Catholic, George immediately denounced him. Moreover, while the crowd might sympathize with English Nonconformists, most English Protestants remained convinced that Catholics were in league with England's enemies.

"A Papist informer! A Papist informer," the crowd yelled, their attention diverted from Quakers to Catholics. As their mood of moderation also turned to one of aggression, George urged his attendant musketeers to rush to the rescue. Later, when he saw the unfortunate man steal away through an alley, hurriedly changing his periwig and coat as he went, perhaps he also recalled the dangerous days that followed Venner's uprising, when he and Francis Howgill slipped equally furtively through the London streets.

"Mr Fox," said Sir Samuel Starling, Justice and London's Lord Mayor, "you are an eminent man amongst those of your profession, pray will you be instrumental to dissuade them from meeting in such great numbers?" Anxious to avoid invoking a law with which he clearly disagreed, Starling then referred to Matthew's Gospel, where Jesus speaks of two or three gathered together in his name.[9] Could Quakers not then be happy that "the King and Parliament are graciously pleased to allow of four to meet together," he asked.

It was not to encourage his followers to meet in small groups that Jesus had so spoken, George pointed out, but to reassure them that though they were few, he still valued them. Besides, that was not the point. If Quakers were intent on plotting insurrection, then many groups of four might be far more effective than one huge multitude. "And would not this Act have taken hold upon Christ and his Apostles and disciples in their day," he asked, "who often met together above that number of four?"

Though he set the prisoner free, Starling requested that George Fox leave details as to where he might be found in future. He was "but a lodger in London", George replied. It was an important point, for although praemunire could mean imprisonment for life, the knowledge that a man had no property to call his own was at least a small deterrent to a law determined to strip individuals of their possessions.

As he left the court, George turned once more to Sir Samuel. "As I was going away," he said, "I spoke to the Lord Mayor, and told him he knew in his own conscience we were an innocent people and that the Act did not concern us."

Weeks later he was back on the road. And everywhere he heard reports of meeting-houses occupied by troops, of beatings endured by Friends who met in the streets, of their being dragged before magistrates and deprived of their belongings, of informers settling old scores, and of the tensions that arose when the richer were fined on behalf of their poorer brethren. Sometimes, he couldn't help recalling the Friend in Huntingdon, and her distress at the death of Edward Burrough. Perhaps she was right; perhaps the persecution would simply continue until not one single dissenter had anything left to call their own.

Adding to his anxiety was the knowledge that after being re-arrested at Swarthmoor, Margaret was imprisoned again in

Lancaster Castle. Indeed, in April, when he first heard the news, it almost certainly roused uncomfortable emotions. For having never before been linked by the bonds of marriage, he had perhaps not considered its implications of responsibility. Moreover, had he not allowed his wife to travel to Lancashire alone, to face her persecutors there, less than two weeks after they were wed?

Margaret's arrest, together with a renewal of the praemunire upon her, was partially engineered by her son. Angry that she should marry a man so far beneath her in status, George Fell had subsequently used her conviction in a bid to gain control of the Swarthmoor estate. Though George Fox wrote to his wife, advising caution towards her son, and assuring her that he was urging Mary and Sarah, her two daughters then in London, to plead with King Charles for her release, he did not offer to support her with his presence. Possibly it never occurred to him to do so, or perhaps the new Conventicle Act so absorbed his energies that Lancaster Castle seemed very far away.

However, making his way towards Oxford one day, he was forced yet again to confront the subject of his marriage. The catalyst was his encounter with Walter Newton, "an ancient Puritan", and neighbour to some of the Fox relations.[10] Why had George married so late in his life?, Walter asked, quite unashamed of his frank curiosity; "…as a testimony," George replied, repeating what he had already told the Friends, "that all might come up into the marriage as was in the beginning…out of the wilderness to the marriage of the Lamb."[11] Like some of the Friends, Walter was unconvinced. Wasn't the point of a marriage to produce children?, he asked bluntly. But such a blatant reference to the flesh made George uneasy. "I told him I never thought of any such thing," he said, "…and I judged such things as below me." Even as a married man, it seems, the thought of unashamed sexuality, even the conjugal pleasures of marriage, roused him to awkwardness and caused him concern.

Far away in her Lancaster prison, Margaret was equally pressed on. Convinced of the crucial necessity of turning to the

Light, that her son so resolutely spurned it evidently caused her enormous grief. Certainly it was a grief her son was aware of, for in letters written to him during his years as a student at Gray's Inn, and then as a resident in London, she constantly urged him to renounce his unrighteous behaviour. That both the behaviour and his subsequent hostility might have some justification evidently never occurred to her.

On the remarriage of his mother, George Fell inherited the estate at Marsh Grange, the Askew family property that Margaret herself brought to Thomas Fell. However, as he also attempted to gain Swarthmoor, which under the terms of his father's will passed to his sisters who so admired George Fox, he also enlisted the support of Richard and William Kirkby. Somehow, that speaks of a huge resentment. For not only had the youthful George Fell seen the affections of his mother and sisters transferred from his father and himself to George Fox, he had no doubt also been aware of the attendant unsavory gossip. Moreover, he had also seen his family home transformed into the headquarters of a people regarded as traitors by the state, and fanatics by many of his own neighbours.[12] In his own mind, George Fell probably thought of himself as betrayed.

"I continued [there] a whole year," Margaret wrote of her second Lancaster imprisonment, "and most part of that time I was sick and weakly."[13] She was then in her mid-50s, a mature age for the period, and although her extensive travels proved her to be robust and determined, at least nine pregnancies would no doubt have weakened her constitution and frame. It is also possible that Margaret's sickness was compounded by something she believed she carried within her. Although at 55 years old, it is highly improbable that Margaret Fox could have been pregnant, there is some evidence that she herself, as well as others, believed it to be so.

In July 1670, nine months after Margaret's marriage to George Fox, a female Quaker based in London wrote to William Penn. She referred to another woman, who had recently met with Margaret's daughter, Margaret Rous, "about her Mouther's Besenes, that is in order to Geat her relese." The reason, said the writer, was "Margrret Foxes Condeshon, & that she being weth child, & so nere ass she is her time beingen out," that her daughter was anxious to procure her liberty. Addressing her letter to Penn, who was then in Ireland, the writer committed it to the post. Shortly afterwards, it was intercepted by a government agent and sent to London. Later, it disappeared into an archive where it remained for over 250 years.[14]

Clearly no child arrived. Yet, rumours circulated for years in the north, even after Margaret's death. Later they were used by critics eager to undermine George Fox's legacy: "... whether the Spirit of Delusion, to whom they had given themselves up possess'd them," said one, "... that they were Abraham and Sarah, I know not, but it is very certain that they both persuaded themselves, that Margaret Fell, alias Fox, was with Child, and that the Lord would raise up a Holy Seed of them ... baby-clouts were prepared, the Midwife was call'd, and gave attendance for about a Month together, but there came nothing forth, all prov'd wind."[15]

Both Margaret and George Fox clearly saw their union as in some sense symbolizing the restoration of the true Church, and no doubt the "firstborn of that womb of eternity", that featured in Margaret's marriage prayer, was a reference to the Quaker movement. Nevertheless, as was the case with George himself, there are times when the flesh mirrors what is present, often subliminally, in the mind. For Margaret, married to the man she had perhaps yearned for over many years, who she believed to be the herald of a new age, it would not be surprising that she also yearned to bear his child. Incarcerated for her faith, and alienated from her only son, it would also not be surprising that she saw evidence to convince herself that her longings were taking shape.

As Margaret experienced her unsettling physical symptoms at Lancaster, elsewhere in the country the Conventicle Act continued its progress of arbitrary malice. After being stripped of their furniture, meeting-houses were padlocked. Sometimes they were demolished, while anything removable was taken away to be sold.[16] Meanwhile, everywhere there were informers, ready to reveal that a neighbour attended a conventicle, before pocketing their share of the fine.

But the men and women whose consciences drove them to defy the authority of church and state alike, and whose defiance had provoked Sheldon to increased persecution, would not be cowed. In some places Quakers met resolutely on the ruins of their meeting-houses; in others, they worshipped outside padlocked houses.

By August, the numbers outside the meeting-house in Gracechurch Street, which had escaped an attempt in the Lord Mayor's Court to demolish it, had swollen to many hundreds. In a letter to Sarah Fell, John Rous reckoned them in thousands. Although, he said, "by reason of the multitude of rude people who came mostly to gaze, it was more like a tumult than a solid assembly."[17]

On a day towards the middle of the month, at the very centre of the shoving, shouting throng, William Penn, now returned from Ireland, strove to make himself heard. Supremely confident, and with the well-bred good manners learned in the wealthy Penn home, when the watchmen sent to arrest him were unable to fight their way through the crowd, William politely offered to come to them later. "And so he and one William Mead, who is lately convinced," said John Rous, "went to them; they carried them before the Mayor, and he committed them for a riot."[18, 19]

In September the two men stood trial at the Old Bailey. Since the charge was riot, rather than contravention of the Conventicle Act, they were given the benefit of a jury. And as Judge Sir Samuel Starling, and the Recorder, Sir John Howell, attempted to force through a charge of guilty, it was to the jury that William Penn spoke. "Is this justice or true judgement?" he asked, defending his right to worship as conscience directed. "Must I therefore be taken away because I plead for the fundamental laws of England?"[20]

Inspired by Penn's arguments, encouraged by their foreman, Edward Bushell, and obeying their own consciences, the jury refused to convict. As a furious Howell openly declared his desire for harsher laws, Starling fined the jury and committed them to Newgate until it was paid.

Refusing to be brow-beaten, the jury also refused the fine

and demanded their freedom. As support for them mounted, and people spoke of English liberties once again under threat, the judicial system was thrown into turmoil. In November, after appearing before the Court of Common Pleas, Edward Bushell and his eleven fellows were set free on bail until a decision was reached.

Everywhere the talk was of William Penn and Edward Bushell. Eventually, it reached Margaret Fox, in her lonely Lancaster prison, where by now she not only grieved that no baby would be born, but also for the death of her son George, who died in October, leaving a widow from whom Margaret was estranged, and two surviving children.

Almost the only place the talk did not reach was a darkened room in the village of Enfield, just north of London, where George Fox lay silent and motionless, and where his carers whispered of death. The malady had come swiftly, earlier in the summer, as George travelled with Alexander Parker, John Rous and John Stubbs among the apple orchards of Kent. One morning, on a day of bright sunshine, as he gazed towards the distant spire of Rochester Cathedral, to his increasing horror he saw a thick and oily darkness, like the shadow of a malicious hand, creep first over Rochester, and then over the country all around. "A great weight and oppression fell upon my spirit," he said, "... much loaden and burdened with the world's spirits."

By the time he reached Hornchurch in Essex, he was barely able to speak. At Stratford, three miles east of London, he collapsed. "I lost my hearing and sight," he said. As anxieties once again seized on his flesh, a depression settled within him, blacker than any that had gone before. As the weeks passed, as he sunk into the depths, he lay in a state of physical suspension, all outward senses blocked, but with his inner eyes and ears painfully open. "I felt their spirits," he said of the people who gathered around him, "and discerned them, though I could not see them." In the world outside, rumour flourished and spread. The Quaker George Fox was struck down at last, it said. Finally, it said he was dead.

After almost two months, George indicated to Margaret

Rous, who had left her own family to devote herself to his care, that he should be moved to the home of a Friend at nearby Edmonton. Three weeks later, he demanded to be moved again, this time to visit the dying Amor Stoddard at Enfield. "I was moved to tell him he had been faithful as a man and faithful to God," he said, "and that the immortal Seed of life was his crown." Afterwards, carried into the nearby house of the widow, Elizabeth Dry, once again he collapsed.

Through the long winter, as 1670 became 1671, he lay in a darkness lit only by a candle at his bedside, and by visions that surged and flickered through his mind. As his anxieties took shape, the persecutors of the Friends were transformed into monsters. "The false prophets and priests, preached peace to the people if they put bread into their mouths ... but if not, they gnawed their flesh off to the bone and chopped them for the cauldron."

Adding to his distress was the news that sometimes broke into his consciousness, that at Bristol and at Preston Patrick the Friends wavered beneath persecution. Rather than stand boldly before locked meeting-houses, they met secretly in woodland glades and on barren hillsides.[21] In January 1671, rousing himself from his sickbed, he dictated a letter to Bristol. They must stand, he told the Friends there, they must stand!

Exhausted, he sank back into sickness. "So in my deep misery," he said, "I saw things beyond words to utter, and I saw a black coffin but I passed over it." Another time, he saw the vision of the Revelation. "Oh ye heavenly Jerusalem, the bride is come down, the marriage of the Lamb."

In yet another vision he saw himself walking through English fields with many Friends. Stopping them suddenly, he ordered them to dig. As they did so, the ground collapsed. "And I went down," he said, "and there was a mighty vault top full of people kept under the earth." Setting them free, he saw them step into the light. Then, he went on alone, descending ever deeper into darkness.

Entering a shadowy cavern, he saw at its centre a mysterious treasure; beside it, a motionless guardian. "And there sat a woman in white looking at time, how it passed away." But, when he lifted the treasure, time began to race. It whisked, he said. Suddenly too, there were footsteps. "There followed me a woman down the vault ... and she laid her hands on the treasure which was in my left hand," he said. Unlike her companion, this woman was all motion, vigorously, and perhaps dangerously, alive. "I clapt my hands upon her," he said, "and said touch not the treasure." Then he breathed more easily. "Time passed not so swift," he said.

As a prophet, as a liberator, George Fox had set men and women free from the oppression of harsh doctrines and the terrors of hell. So too did he yearn to set free the captives who languished in England's gaols. By his understanding of the Light, that came as the Refiner's Fire, he saw that individuals might be delivered from aspects of their natures that impeded their growth. Nevertheless, there was clearly something that he could not address in himself. Almost certainly it was implanted very early, probably when he was "taught how to walk to be kept pure". It was what took form in the youthful struggle against fleshly temptations, and in the need later to declare the physical part of marriage as below him. That throughout his sickness he demanded to be cared for only by "sober women", seems also to echo the vision of the cavern, a yearning for female contact, but a fear of its sexual potential. It is of course also possible that something relating to his marriage, "the marriage of the Lamb", had caused him distress. And though it was never mentioned by George, and there is no indication as to whether he knew of the situation in Lancaster Gaol, that news of the child who was not to be, had added to his inner turmoil.

Margaret Fox was set free in April. After many representations made on her behalf, King Charles finally pardoned her and overturned the praemunire. By awarding the "Estate of the said Margaret Fell, alias Fox, unto Susan Fell and Rachel Fell, the daughters of the said Margaret", he also attempted to settle the controversy over Swarthmoor.[22] That it should be so settled, however, while indeed appearing to conform to the wishes of Thomas Fell, was also in direct contravention to the will of the deceased George Fell, who left the estate he claimed as his own to his own infant son.

George Fell's death, and the conflict over property that was continued by his widow, almost certainly roused many ambivalent emotions in Margaret Fox. But had she expected to be sustained by the loving attendance of her husband, then again, she would be disappointed. After returning briefly to Swarthmoor, she then set out herself on the 300-mile journey to London. Eventually, at the fine new home at Kingston-on-Thames, of her daughter and son-in-law, Margaret and John Rous, she met with the man she had not seen since their wedding almost two years earlier.

She found him pale and weak, the evidence of his long winter's suffering still heavy upon him. Yet, for all the feebleness of his frame, the swollen joints that caused him to flinch, and the darkness that sometimes shadowed his brow, there was a determination in his voice and an eagerness in his eyes. Partly it was caused by the knowledge that the Bristol Friends had heeded his advice, and that having admitted their errors, they met once again outside their padlocked meeting-houses.[23] But, even more was it the result of something that caused him to forget his aching bones, his winter melancholy, and the endless persecution. For once again, he was planning a trip overseas.[24]

On 14 August 1671, Margaret Fox, William Penn and Gulielma Springett, step-daughter to Isaac Penington, stood on the Kentish downs above Deal. Peering out to sea, they could still just make out the hazy shape of the Industry, as the 100-ton ketch made her cumbersome way into the evening twilight. Earlier they had sailed on her from Gravesend, and although they prayed for fair winds and fine weather, when the captain of a man-of-war anchored nearby sent his press-master to search out recruits for King Charles' Royal Navy, the departing passengers had been filled with foreboding. "Being made sensible of the much leakiness of our ship, and length of our voyage," wrote John Hull, a Friend who kept a log of the journey, "out of compassion and much civility [he] spared us two of his own men."

George, meanwhile, perhaps disdainful of those among his

50 or so fellow passengers who, expressing such alarm at the leakiness, clearly failed to trust God's provision for his prophets, stood at the ship's prow and considered the Friends of the New World. From information received over many months, he knew that although John Perrot had died only three years after exchanging Newgate Gaol for voluntary exile in the Caribbean, he had given an enormous boost to all those already contaminated by the heresy of the hat. Now, as George and his comrades set out to establish Gospel Order in the Americas, he knew that an enormous task lay before him.

Eventually, as night gathered around the *Industry*, he himself gathered his companions for their first meeting on shipboard. All were committed and experienced Friends, and some George had known for many years. Robert Widder was at the great Preston Patrick convincement of 1652, while James Lancaster, convinced the same year, had travelled with George through Cumberland, and later accompanied him to Ireland. Thomas Briggs, who helped draft the *Testimony to the Brethren*, had also been part of the Irish adventure; as had John Stubbs, who had earlier carried the Quaker message towards the East Indies. William Edmondson, stern father of Hindrance and Trial, was eager to see Gospel Order established in the furthermost places, as was Solomon Eccles, a former music teacher who once walked naked through London's Bartholomew Fair in protest against the Oath of Allegiance. London mariner George Pattison, once fearlessly retook his ship from Moorish pirates, while John Cartwright of Stourbridge, had suffered for Truth in his native Worcestershire. George's step-son-in-law, John Rous, born in Barbados, would smooth the travellers' way when they reached their first landfall, and John Hull was most enterprisingly keeping a log of their voyage. Finally, of the party's two women, sitting alongside Elizabeth Miers was Elizabeth Hooton, now in her seventieth year, the eagerness of her eyes reflecting her great desire both to proclaim her cause and also to drink life to the full.

As the *Industry* ploughed through the heaving Bay of Biscay and then hugged the western coast of Portugal, and as the weather veered from fair to foul with unsettling unpredictability, there was much to see and to comment on. A Dutch merchant fleet bound for Virginia, to take on tobacco for the burghers of Amsterdam, led to observations on how the smoking habit, once the preserve of Ranters, had now become quite commonplace. Being hailed by a merchantman out of Lubeck, her crew eager to know whether France had declared war on Holland, led to speculation on the rumours that together with Louis XIV, their own monarch planned to attack the Protestant Dutch.[25]

Equally diversionary were the many strange creatures of the sea. "We saw several grampuses sporting themselves in the briny ocean not far from us," John Hull recorded, "and two great porpoises leapt a great height above water."[26]

"We took a dolphin, which made us a good broth," John reported later, as the *Industry* continued close to Portugal, "and is a very good fish to eat, and a lovely for variety of colours. It is very remarkable how several Friends were so soon raised up again that were ill." It was the nourishing dolphins, he maintained, together with the almost constant pumping of the Industry's leaky bilges by crew and passengers alike, that kept a large part of the company in health.

Despite a painful desire for it to be otherwise, among those unable to pump, and very far from health, was George Fox. For, as the weather grew more sultry, and as the *Industry* turned westward to cross the Atlantic, his much-abused body gave way. "While at sea his legs and feet swelled so much," said John, "as if the skin would break ... For he coming weak from London aboard, he did sweat exceedingly ... and all his body broke out into pimples ... so that what with his old pains, and former bruises in his joints ... he became very weak beyond words."

At the beginning of October, after almost two months at sea, when the *Industry* finally dropped anchor in Carlisle Bay, Barbados, it was clear that it would be some time before George Fox would travel far. Taken by coach to the plantation home of John Rous's father, Thomas, he lay in bed for almost three weeks, eating nothing and drinking only water flavoured with ginger:[27] "...yea my pains such as are beyond words or expressions," George said, writing home to his comrades in England, and asking that a copy be sent to Margaret. "I have been almost a month in this island, but have not been able to go abroad or ride out."[28]

Eventually, restored by the comforts of the substantial plantation home, and spurred on by his own indomitable will, he was increasingly filled with an optimism that urged him towards recovery. Much of it was inspired by what he learned from his travelling companions, now ranging widely through the island, who told him that all Barbados was stirred by the English Friends' presence.

They "have very considerable numbers at their several meetings," John Hull wrote home, "which are many both to place and time, and are the greater and fuller by reason that many of the world flock to them." However, seated alongside them on the meeting-house benches, he continued, were many, "as tis feared here too many", Quaker backsliders.

Yet, though the English Friends laboured hard, they were conscious of a restlessness in the assemblies, that all too often found expression in fidgets and impatient murmurs. "When will George Fox speak?" the crowds asked. "When shall we hear him?"

"I question not," John continued, "but that the Lord...will make him a choice instrument in his hand for much good unto them, even unto the blacks as unto the whites, for the blacks (as 'tis said) expect some good by his coming here."[29]

Almost as soon as Barbados was claimed for England by James I, its fertile soil attracted colonists eager to replace the island's forests with lucrative crops of cotton, tobacco and sugar. At first the land was worked by indentured white labourers, some of them inmates of England's gaols, while others were men kidnapped, often in Ireland, for the sole purpose of enslaving them.[30] But, in the 1630s and 1640s, they were joined by more than 20,000 black slaves from Africa.[31] As the years passed, as the European demand for sugar became all but insatiable, slave numbers increased dramatically. By the time of George Fox's arrival in 1671, the more astute planters had swallowed up smaller rivals and had given themselves over entirely to sugar and slaves.

Fertile Barbados had also attracted many Quakers, anxious to make a new life in the New World. By the 1670s, they numbered several hundred, and were the Island's second largest religious denomination. While some were counted among the poor, either as indentured labourers or unsuccessful farmers, others had become hugely wealthy plantation owners. Almost all of the wealthy were slave-owners, while their combined resources had financed the erection of the island's five meeting houses.[32] The wealth and success of the richest, however, did not overcome the unease that such large numbers of Friends aroused among the island's other white inhabitants. For as Quakers crossed the Atlantic, so too did the rumours and allegations that had always surrounded them, of religious fanaticism, anti-government plots, the denial of true religion, and of bizarre sexual practices.

Their unwillingness to support the island's militia also made Quakers seem untrustworthy, while a refusal to attend any religious services but their own not only made them appear aloof, but caused men to ask what it was they kept secret. That they set up similar meetings for their slaves, in an island where the total slave population vastly outnumbered Europeans, and where for some time there had been a seething discontent, suggested to some that Quakers encouraged slaves to question white authority, and perhaps eventually to rebel.

Many leading Friends in Barbados saw George Fox's presence, and the interest it aroused, as an opportunity to publicly reject the accusations aimed at them. Consequently, as soon as his recovery was certain, a delegation gathered at the Rous plantation to enlist his name and his help in their cause.

The result was a statement addressed to the Island's Governor, Colonel Christopher Codrington, to the Assembly of Barbados, and to other men of influence. Its intention was to reject accusations of fanaticism, clarify orthodox Quaker religious beliefs and explain Quaker attitudes to the slave population: "...many scandalous lies and slanders have been cast upon us," it began. Then, continuing the process that dated

from George Fox's first denial of violence towards Oliver
Cromwell, it proceeded to affirm that not only were the
Friends of Truth a God-fearing and peace-loving people, but
that their domestic arrangements and long-term aspirations
had much in common with those of their neighbours. Indeed,
so full of Protestant orthodoxy were its opening paragraphs,
dwelling at length on incarnation, resurrection, atonement,
and the sufficiency of Scripture; so absent was any mention of
perfection, innocency or the Fall; and so backed up was everything with careful biblical references, that even the sternest
Presbyterian would have found little to quibble with. While as
for "the lie they have cast upon us ... that we should teach the
negroes to rebel," the very opposite was the case. "For that
which we have spoken and declared to them is, to exhort and
admonish them to be sober and to fear God, and to love their
masters and mistresses, and to be faithful and diligent in their
masters' service and business ... "[33]

It was a theme which George found dovetailed nicely with
his views on Gospel Order. Well informed now of the charges
levelled against the Friends of Barbados, as he addressed their
gatherings he emphasized righteous living, a quiet and orthodox spirituality, and the good ordering of meetings. To end the
unsavory practice of Friends being buried "in their gardens",
he also recommended that the communities purchase suitable
burial plots.

He also spoke out sternly against the sexual laxity which
gave rise to the many scandalous reports, "as to marrying kin,
and of two wives at once, or two husbands". Marriage, he
pointed out, "was one man and one woman, not many".
Furthermore, regarding marriage, those coming to it should
not only make their intentions clear, but should do so several
times; twice before the women's meetings, and twice before
the men's. As in England, Friends were also required to ensure
that certificates were provided proving their freedom to marry.

Addressing the subject of black slavery, he reiterated the
theme of the earlier document. Perhaps to expect otherwise,
and in light of the huge contribution made by Quakers to the
eventual abolition of the Atlantic slave-trade, is to impose

hindsight on a situation which appeared very different at the time. Most Quakers in seventeenth-century Barbados saw the island as an escape from the persecution they suffered at home. While almost certainly aware of the reality of slavery – the horror of the ships and the abuses that often took place on plantations – they were also anxious to prosper and be held in esteem. Though George Fox's recommendations today seem naive, he was a product of his time, and he almost certainly believed he was promoting the growth of a godly and harmonious community. Overseers should be instructed to deal mildly and gently, he said, while Quaker slave owners should consider setting their slaves free after 30 years' servitude. In the interim they should "train up their slaves in the fear of God, so that with Joshua, they may say, 'As for me and my house, we will serve the Lord.'" [34, 35]

Though opposition remained, especially among the Island's large population of Baptists, and among Friends refusing to make peace with Gospel Order, George Fox's paternalistic attitude to slavery, and his desire to restrain the wilder elements among his own fellowship, clearly won an increased acceptance for the Friends among their white neighbours.

It was an acceptance that also found expression among the Island's leading men. During his Rous plantation convalescence, George had already received "many considerable persons" of the world. [36] While such calls may well have been prompted by concerns regarding the Friends' beliefs and practices, having seen them subsequently allayed, both in writing and from the lips of the man himself, those same considerable persons were clearly prepared to treat him as the elder statesman of a large and influential movement.

Later, several of those persons also attended his public meetings. One of them, a Justice of the Peace, rode fourteen miles across country to do so. Another, a Lieutenant-Colonel Lyne, in a statement echoed by several of his fellows, confessed how after hearing George Fox, his views had subsequently altered. "Now I can gainsay such as I have heard speak evil of you," he said, "that say you own not Christ nor that he died, but now I perceive that you exalt Christ in all his offices ... " [37]

Moreover, after Governor Christopher Codrington welcomed George Fox to his table, the General Meeting of Friends that took place the same week was unexpectedly awash with the quality. "His kind reception with the governor," John Stubbs told Margaret, "did give a sound among the officers, both military and civil, throughout the island … and that not of the least rank, as colonels, and justices, and judges, and captains, etc., came to this General Meeting, hearing that thy husband would be at it."[38]

In January 1672, it was with some reluctance that her husband left Barbados for Jamaica. Again, the voyage was eventful. On one occasion, the rope that stabilized the mainmast snapped in a storm; on another, so rapidly did water sweep into the ship, that not until a quick-thinking carpenter leapt overboard to hammer a leak full of oakum, did the colour return to the passengers' faces. "She's as tight as a dish now," he reassured them, grinning as he broke through the green water in a shower of foam.[39]

Eventually, as Jamaica finally appeared blue on the horizon, some of the Friends recalled that in 1655, it was as part of Oliver Cromwell's Western Design, the bid to strip Catholic Spain of her American colonies, that the island was seized for England. So too did they recall that leading the attack was William Penn's father, Admiral Sir William Penn, then a faithful servant of the republican Commonwealth.

Since then, the colony had attracted more than 15,000 settlers, and among them George Fox found a welcome that encouraged him to set up seven new meetings. "Not a mouth was opened against us," he said, "and when we were to go away they said it was a pity that such men should go out of the land."

One woman who did not go out, was Elizabeth Hooton. "Elizabeth was well upon the Sixth day of the week," George said, "and deceased the next day about the eleventh hour, in peace like a lamb." As Elizabeth was lowered into the Jamaican earth, with her went part of George Fox's past, the days of revolution and the Children of Light. At 47 years old, he had travelled a long way from the day he walked into the village of Skegby. Now he was becoming an elder statesman, a man whom the leaders of England's overseas colonies sought out. As they did so, clearly they found something to admire. Though he still spoke brokenly, and probably still in broad Leicestershire, native intelligence was transformed into a wisdom born of experience, while uncontrolled passion had become a confidence born of achievement. Now, as he headed north through the Caribbean and then past the long coastline of Florida, he carried that experience, wisdom and confidence with him towards the mainland of America.

CHAPTER FOURTEEN

The Wild Woods of America

I desired them to speak to their people, that God is setting up his tabernacle of witnesses in their wilderness countries, and his standard, and setting up his glorious ensign of righteousness.

George Fox, *Journal*, 1672[1]

"WE INTEND TO PASS FROM hence about the beginning of the next month," George Fox wrote to his wife in February 1672, "and we shall pass towards Maryland, if the Lord please."[2] When he learned later that a frigate rejected as too costly, was boarded and robbed by a Spanish fleet, he saw it as proof that his alternative choice of a ketch at ten shillings per passenger was indeed divinely inspired.

But, for days the ship made no headway against the wind, that blew her back constantly to Jamaica and flung her wildly flapping canvas into the heaving sea. Eventually passing north from Florida, the weather remained violent, "high winds and blustering weather, and rain and great storms in the night."

Finally reaching Cheasapeake Bay in the middle of April, it was to be greeted once again by great storms. In the midst of the tumult, however, once more George saw the divine hand at work. For when a small vessel capsized and her terrified passengers were hauled aboard the ketch, they turned out to be "men and women of account", among them a lawyer, a former sheriff, and a clerk of the Maryland court. "We had a fine meeting with them on the sea," George said, reflecting on how providentially they were rescued from certain death that they should hear his message of life.

Though on shipboard his flesh had succumbed once more to sickness, when his feet stood finally on mainland America, and with a task waiting ahead, he felt energy flowing and urgency take hold. Arriving at West River, Maryland, towards the end of April, he found himself in a major centre of Quaker life in the North American Colonies. The meeting itself was thronged, and within hours it was as if he relived the London days of 1667, when Gospel Order was first settled. "A brave men's meeting and women's meeting, we had," he said, "and established several women's meetings and men's meetings." That "most of the backsliders came in" was due partly to groundwork already laid by John Burnyeat, a Cumberland Friend who crossed the Atlantic in 1670, partly to a desire for unity, and partly, as elsewhere, to an awareness that the alternative was to be "rejected, as having erred from the Truth."

As in Barbados, the presence of George Fox also drew the region's leading men. "There came to it," George said of the West River meeting, "five or six Justices of the Peace, and a speaker of the Assembly and one of the Council, and several other considerable men of the world."

Crossing Chesapeake Bay, he continued to impose Gospel Order, this time in meetings along the shores of the Choptank River. Once again, "there were two justices of the peace and several men of quality" in attendance. But he couldn't resist reaching out further. "It was upon me from the Lord," he said, "to send for the Indian emperor and his kings to come to me the First-day's meeting." Silently, from out of the forest, they eventually arrived, the "emperor" at first, and later the same day, "the two Kings also came with some of their Cockarooses."[3]

Watched by many intrigued and anxious eyes, the Native American leaders – emperor, kings, and their subsidiary chiefs – and the prophet from Leicestershire summed each other up. The Americans were copper-skinned, dark-eyed, and clothed in their native buckskin; the Englishman, fairer and weather-beaten, and no longer the wearer of leather breeches, wore the sober costume of Puritanism. Yet, for all their outward difference, in the other, they evidently saw something that was alike – perhaps men who stubbornly refused to deny their truth no matter what the world might threaten. In the evening, George declared his message. "What I said to the kings and emperor," he said, "I desired them to speak to their people, that God is setting up his tabernacle of witnesses in their wilderness countries, and his standard, and setting up his glorious ensign of righteousness."

Disturbing news, however, forbade him to linger. For although Maryland's Friends seemed largely happy to accept Gospel Order, and although the excitement of George Fox's presence had allowed many of their backsliders to slip home almost without comment, this seemed not to be so elsewhere. As soon as the West River meeting was done, James Lancaster and John Cartwright left for New England, while the doughty William Edmondson thrashed his way through Virginia. Things in those places, said George, "were much out of order".[4]

At its root, said John Burnyeat, lay the ideas propagated by John Perrot. Moreover, at the half-yearly meeting at Oyster Bay, Long Island, held the previous October, George Dennis, a recent arrival from England, had openly attacked George Fox.[5] Desperate to prevent further damage, George, John, two other Quakers and two native American guides, set out overland towards New England.

"We passed all along through the woods," said George, "... and swimmed our horses over Sassafras River, and went over ourselves in canoes; and from thence we came to the Bohemia River, and swimmed over our horses, and went over ourselves in canoes." At night, surrounded by the alien snuffles and grunts among the trees, "sometimes we lay in the woods by a fire, and sometimes in the Indian cabins."

"Through the bogs, rivers and creeks we passed," he said, "and the wild woods, where it was said it was never known before for any man to ride." Yet though the adventure sometimes reminded him of his first days on the road in England, it was a relief, after two long weeks, to see a highway and a tidy group of homesteads.

But there was no time to linger. He must press on. "We

came to Gravesend on Long Island," he said, "and the next morning we set forward, though we were weary, to Oyster Bay." There, in mid-May, at a meeting lasting over six days, he met Friends from Oyster Bay, Gravesend, Flushing, and other settlements nearby. Just as he expected, "some of the bad hat spirits" were there too. Most of the men and women who came to meet him, however, were eager to be reassured. Like the Friends in Barbados, many were refugees from persecution, and whilst privately some might yearn for excitement and fresh leadings, on the whole they longed for security and prosperity. Confronted by George's physical presence, and by the force of his personality, almost all Friends, he said, were ready to embrace Gospel Order. As for George Dennis, said John Burnyeat, rather than holding fast to his convictions, he not only "began to fawn upon George Fox", but also began transferring blame onto others.[6] While, as for any "hat spirit" daring to speak out, they were "judged down and condemned", said George.

Driving themselves on, the party made a 200-mile sea voyage to Rhode Island. When the world there turned out to hear him, it wore a very different face to anything George Fox had encountered before. Founded in 1636 by Roger Williams, a Cambridge-educated clergyman and religious refugee, the colony was a response to the intolerance of Puritan Massachusetts where, since the 1630s, evangelists from other Christian traditions, including the Friends, had been imprisoned, tortured and sometimes executed.[7] Rhode Island's policy of official toleration, by contrast, had made it a haven for all non-Puritans. But, though Williams was a public force for tolerance, he was also opinionated and volatile, his differences with Massachusetts being as much personal as political. When he eventually fell out with Rhode Island's Friends, then taking advantage of the colony's essentially democratic political structure, several stood for election and won political office.

Thus when George Fox arrived in 1672, the governor, the lieutenant-governor, and several members of the judiciary, were all Friends. Welcomed into the Newport home of Nicholas Easton, the Colony's new Quaker governor, and being respectfully served tea by a neat parlour-maid, he couldn't help contrasting it with the night in 1664 when he faced Thomas Preston and his Cavalier cronies at Holker Hall.

Another long series of meetings followed, this time, with the colony's leading men not only observing, but fully participating as Friends. Watching them, George surely caught a glimpse of what might be the future for England if only toleration were to become a reality. It was a vision that blazed even brighter at the home of Newport's founder, William Coddington, when George attended the wedding there of two young Quakers.[8] The joyful young couple, the substantial house, and the prosperous, confident company, was yet another example of how a new country, free of Europe's long history of conflict, could offer Friends a great hope for the future.

Such inspiration and such fellowship were not easy to abandon. "It was somewhat hard for Friends to part," George admitted, as towards the end of July, New England's Quakers finally bade each other farewell.[9] He himself sensed that his work there was done; he had set up men's and women's meetings, dealt with dissidents, who in his old way he sometimes labelled Ranters, and seen a vision of a future where toleration and Gospel Order flourished. Leaving John Burnycat, John Stubbs and John Cartright to continue work in the region, he then turned his face to the south.

Briefly he made landfall at Shelter Island, on the east coast of Long Island, its name reflecting the haven created there for persecuted Friends by its proprietor, Nathaniel Silvester. It was in that haven, one rainy night, that he found himself part of another novel gathering.

"I had a meeting at Shelter Island among the Indians," he said, "and the king and his council, with about one hundred more Indians with him, and they sat about two hours, and I spoke to them by an interpreter that was an Indian ... and they said all was truth, and did make a confession of it."

That their understanding of the Spirit seemed so close to his own encouraged him further. "I have set up a meeting among them," he said, "once a fortnight, and Nathaniel Silvester is to read the Scriptures to them."[10]

Such success, among native Americans and Europeans alike, and the vision of a tolerant future, produced such a youthful vigour in George Fox that his comrades could barely reconcile it to their bloated companion of the *Industry*. "I met with thy dear husband again," William Edmondson told Margaret, after meeting George on Shelter Island, "and he was very well, I have not seen him more healthy and cheery of some years."[11]

But, as George continued south, the weather that tossed him so violently earlier, returned to harry him again. Sea fogs obscured his ship's passage, vicious tides dragged her off course, and gales so battered her that it was not until the end of August that he and his companions stepped onto the shore of New Jersey. In the circumstances, that a region close to their landfall was known as Purgatory seemed very appropriate.

A place of dense woods and a hundred deceptive slopes, it was there that John Jay of Barbados was thrown by his horse to the ground, with his neck twisted at such an unnatural angle that his companions swore he was dead. "They laid him on a tree," George said, "... and I took him by the hair of his head, and his head turned like a cloth, it was so loose, and I ... set my knees against the tree ... and put my hand under his chin and behind his head, and raised his head two or three times with all my strength, and brought it in ... then he began to rattle, and afterwards to breathe."

From his words it does seem that at some point in his life George learned how to manipulate dislocated bones. But, just as with the distracted women of England, little remains beyond intriguing fragments to indicate just what might have been the foundation and extent of his knowledge. John Jay, however, survived, and next day, his neck wrapped in a linen cloth, he rode alongside George Fox. George, meanwhile, buoyed up by success, declared the Day of Lord in every native American village, just as he had once declared it to the yeomen of England.

By September, he was back in Maryland, where Quaker meetings and the world turned out to welcome him. Early in October, when he arrived at Tred Avon Creek for the General

Meeting of Maryland Friends, so many boats thronged the water that a local justice remarked that it was become just like the Thames.[12] Rather like London itself, the rain also poured down for days. But, despite grey clouds, the people evidently went away satisfied. "They said they had never heard the Scriptures so clearly opened before," he continued, "for said they, 'He hath them at his fingers' ends, and as a man should read them in a book and hold it open before him.'"

The man who opened the Scriptures so clearly, however, still could not rest. With his time in America now passing swiftly away, he was desperate to establish more meetings, restore more backsliders, and touch more native hearts. Continuing south, by land and by water, and drenched by ever more rain, in the middle of October, he reached the settlements around Chesapeake Bay, the site of his first landing, seven months before. Then, passing briefly through Virginia, he headed into north-eastern Carolina.

After the heavy Quaker presence of Maryland, and the prosperity of Rhode Island, sparsely populated Carolina seemed alien and strange. "A wilderness country," George called it, a place of dank bogs and November dreariness.[13]

By December, he had been soaked so often, from the water slopping in canoes, or from wading through swampy streams, that the optimism that had so filled him at Newport now wore thin. Nevertheless, it was often at moments when he came close to despair, that an unexpected dazzle of light restored the indomitable spirit. "And there was a doctor that did dispute with us," he said of an event near Cone-oak Bay, "which was of great service and occasion of opening much to the people."[14] In the face of the doctor's denial that the Light was to be found in all, George called on a native American to speak.

"I asked him," he said, "whether he would not do to others what he would not have them do to himself, and whether there was not something within him that did tell him of it?" When the man agreed that it was so, George used it to shame the doctor, to show that God welcomed everyone to his fellowship, and also no doubt to underline the truth of his own message.

"They say we are a thousand miles from Boston

southward," he said not long afterwards, "... all which we have travelled by land and down bays, and over rivers and creeks, and bogs and wildernesses." Though he would not travel so far north as Boston, the thought of the long trek ahead was daunting. For despite knowing "that the truth spreadeth ... and many people [were] made tender", he was growing weary of the endless travelling on horseback and by canoe, of dense woods and wide rivers, and of being constantly dirty and cold. It was a weariness exacerbated by constant pain, for the winter cold seemed to be armed with teeth, eager to gnaw at his joints and his poorly mended bones. When the snow came in December, and ice made the trails more treacherous than ever, every jolt set the teeth snapping more viciously. Sometimes, waking by a flickering fire in the night, he had the odd sensation that he dozed by the hearth at Swarthmoor. Then, seeing the white flakes whirling, and hearing wolves howl in the distance, he returned to his damp bed in the woods of Virginia.

Finally, in January 1673, he reached the Patuxent River once more, where James Preston, a Maryland Friend, welcomed the tired and bedraggled party into his home. "Very weary were we," said George. Two weeks later, when James's house, "by reason of a careless maid servant, was burned down to the ground," every single item, "our boxes and our clothes, my great chest, and James Lancaster's chest," were lost. "There we lay three nights by the fire on the ground," he said bitterly. Sometimes it seemed that he was hardly destined to sleep in American beds, only on her cold bare earth.

But, within days of the fire he was back on the frozen roads of Maryland. Indeed, how could his heart not soar when despite the weather, "with hard frost that some had like to have lost the use of their hands", so many Friends turned out for him. As he spent March and April in Maryland, American Friends, the "world", and leaders of the native people all flocked to hear him. But, among the Friends, there was also a sense of impending loss. For as they saw him planning his homeward voyage, they knew they would not meet him again in this world. Finally, in mid-May, at the four-day General Meeting for the whole of Maryland, he outlined for the last time his vision of Gospel Order. "We discoursed about the church of God," he said, "...and the mighty presence of the Lord over all was seen, blessed and praised be his name for ever."

The *Society of Bristol*, battered by the heaving Atlantic, dropped anchor in her home port in June 1673. George Fox had been away from England for almost two years, and for a while the teeming wharves and raucous English voices were as alien as a native American cabin had seemed long months before. Alien too was the city's week-long St James Fair in July, where the thronging crowds seemed so intent on pleasure it was as if they could hardly drink it deeply enough. When their imbibing also included drinking their king's health, it was often with smirking allusions to royal mistresses, and with many glasses raised to the people's favourite, Nell Gwynne, who unlike the barren queen, in 1670 had borne Charles a son.[15]

On his arrival, George wrote immediately to Margaret. She arrived with two daughters, Sarah and Rachel, and her son-in-law, Thomas Lower. William Penn, married to Gulielma in the spring of 1672, arrived too, as did many others, all eager to hear news of America and to exchange it for that of their own land. In November 1671, they said, a ruling was issued on the Bushell case, that no English jury could in future be punished for its verdict. Thus, William Penn and Edward Bushell between them had established a principle guaranteed to become a bulwark of English liberties.[16]

In March the following year, when King Charles issued a Declaration of Indulgence that enabled licensed dissenters to worship openly, and Catholics to do so privately, it had also begun to seem that persecution was nearing its end.[17] Behind it, however, were Charles' own leanings towards Catholicism, and the promises made in the 1670 Treaty of Dover to Louis of France. Two days after the Declaration, as an Anglo-French armada sailed towards the Dutch coast, a French invasion force crossed the Rhine towards Holland's land frontier. The Dutch, however, responded unexpectedly. Abandoning their republican principles, they made William, Prince of the House of Orange, their ruling Prince. Under his leadership, the English fleet, commanded by the king's brother, James, Duke of York, was repelled, while on land, after convincing his fellow-countrymen to flood their rich farmland by breaching their own dykes, William drove the invaders from Dutch soil.

Though many dissenting ministers applied for the licences offered by the Declaration, the Friends, with no formal ministry as such, had refused to participate. Instead, as they redoubled their efforts on behalf of their gaoled comrades, King Charles eventually granted a Grand Pardon to 491 prisoners.

Their names, written on skins of vellum with the king's Great Seal attached, were carried all over England, from one gaol to another, by George Whitehead. Among the captives who emerged was William Dewsbury, imprisoned almost continuously since 1661. Among them too were several non-Quakers, including the Baptist, John Bunyan, whose earlier books criticizing the Friends had been answered by Edward Burrough and George Fox. Now, it was his former antagonists who welcomed John Bunyan to freedom after twelve years of captivity in Bedford Gaol.[18]

But, for all the licences, and freedom for captives, in the end, the Declaration came to nothing. In February 1673, after another disastrous naval campaign against Holland, and as determined to resist royal absolutism as their Puritan predecessors, a furious Cavalier Parliament forced Charles to break the seal on the Declaration with his own hand.

Encouraged by the Prince of Orange, the Dutch presented the Anglo-French alliance as a Catholic conspiracy. Meanwhile, as the Anglican Church warned of the Catholic menace, the English population grew increasingly hysterical over French Catholic designs on Protestant England.

In March 1673, Parliament passed a Test Act, whereby England's government, civilian office-holders and military commanders, were all to be Anglicans; the "test" being their willingness to take Anglican communion publicly. They were also to take an additional oath denying the doctrines of Catholicism. Forced swiftly from his position as Admiral of the Fleet was James, Duke of York, who in the late 1660s was received into the Catholic Church. In 1673 James also married for the second time, his first wife, Clarendon's daughter, Ann Hyde, having died two years earlier. That his new wife was the Spanish princess, Mary of Modena, fuelled growing fears of a Catholic monarchy. William of Orange, by contrast, appeared the very model of a Protestant prince.

Had the Test Act and the Oath been the only discouraging news to greet his return, then George would simply have willed himself to endure. But, just like many others before him who sought to stamp out heresy, he was discovering that what he had attempted to suppress had sprung up more vigorously than ever.

The *Spirit of the Hat* was a work published anonymously, but widely believed to emanate from the London Quaker, William Mucklow. Its title also made clear that an item of clothing was now universally recognized among Friends as reflecting a certain religious position. Referring disparagingly to "Foxonian Unity", the book claimed that Gospel Order would not only "deprive us of the law of the Spirit" but "would bring in a tyrannical government: it would lead us from the rule within to subject us to a rule without." By implication, George Fox and his colleagues, rather than being servants of the Spirit, were motivated by self-seeking and a desire to control others.[19]

After spending so many months combating division in the Americas, to be greeted by it so virulently on his return home was galling for George Fox. When his colleagues assured him that an Epistle issued by the national Yearly Meeting in May, and signed by many leading Friends, had not only addressed the issue of disaffection, but was welcomed all over the country, he would have liked to believe them and then put the matter behind him.

That, however, would not be the case. Not only was the Epistle not everywhere welcomed, but in some cases it had fuelled other resentments. Indeed, such was the case in Westmorland, heartland of Quakerism's birth, where those meetings that had met secretly to avoid persecution were deeply resentful at the censure received from visiting ministers arriving to bring Gospel Order. Chief among the critics were John Story and John Wilkinson, who had often travelled together as evangelists, but who in 1672 had become joint leaders of a party of disaffection.

Riding northwards through a West Country summer, George's thoughts were often in the Westmorland of earlier days. In a village in Wiltshire, however, he was suddenly brought into the present by the strident voice of Nathaniel Coleman, a Friend who made it very clear that he spoke on behalf of many others.

"Was it not the command of God that a man must rule over his wife?" Nathaniel demanded. "Did not the apostle say, 'I permit not a woman to teach?'"[20] So, "where did we read of women elders and women disciples," he asked, and was it not "an abuse to the elders to set up a women's meeting?" It was surely an uncomfortable moment.

Shortly before leaving for America, George had issued a circular letter, basing it on the practice of women's meetings already established in London and Bristol, and advising the establishment of others. This was, he said, "so the women may come into the practice of pure religion, which is to visit the widows and the fatherless and to see that all be kept from the spots of the world."[21]

During his absence, Margaret Fox's Bristol-based daughter, Isabel Yeamans, together with other female Friends, had established a new monthly meeting of their own in the city. They had also set up procedures for visiting the poor and infirm, for inaugurating a fund for them, and for overseeing local apprenticeships, part of a national development urged by George Fox in an Epistle of 1670. The response was swift and hostile. Led by William Rogers, Bristol's male Quakers ordered their female colleagues to renounce both meeting and procedures, and to do nothing further unless endorsed by what was described as the "unity of all". Though for the sake of that unity the women agreed, the episode left a sour taste in the mouths of Bristol's Friends.

Responding later to Nathaniel Coleman and others who thought similarly, George stated that humanity lived in a fallen world. But, though referring to the restoration made by Christ, his words were ambiguous, once again seeming to refer to some future state, rather than to his original message of a return to the innocency that preceded the Fall. Though he also mentioned the female prophets of the Old Testament, and the reference in the Book of Acts that both sons and daughters would prophesy, when he pointed out that the Dorcas of Acts 9 is described as a disciple, he also suggested that her role was the teaching of "good things" to younger women rather than to all.[22, 23]

From the first stirrings of the radical movement, women played a significant role. In the 1640s, Baptist women had preached in the first conventicles, Leveller women organized on behalf of John Lilburne, and Anna Trapnel was heard with respect. Elizabeth Hooton was the first of many women in George Fox's following who braved hardship and danger to proclaim the message of the Light. George himself had always encouraged women, and also worked in close partnership with the woman who later became his wife.

Although William Rogers, Nathaniel Coleman, and others like them, were particularly strident, even George Fox's own circular letter suggests that by the 1670s Quaker women were increasingly being viewed as helpmeets and carers, and with a role to play largely among women, rather than as the bold evangelists of former years. Indeed, it seems to have been yet another part of the process where in the interests of unity and survival, a singular and revolutionary vision was becoming smoothed into the garments of acceptability.

Towards the end of summer, George met Margaret and her daughter Rachel at the Rous home at Kingston. Later, they travelled together to Rickmansworth in Hertfordshire to be with William Penn. There, as he discussed the controversies shaking their movement, George also re-read William's pamphlets written to answer the *Spirit of the Hat*. As he did so, he may well have considered the differences between William Penn and the first generation of Friends.

Though his father, the Admiral, was then a servant of the Commonwealth, William was a child during the upheavals of the 1650s. Thus while he doubtless understood the substance of the debates, the religious fervour and the political passion were probably quite alien. Though he spoke out boldly in the law-courts, and went to gaol rather than disobey his conscience, it would be hard to imagine the wealthy, well-educated and cultivated William Penn emulating James Nayler's entry into Bristol.

Leaving Rickmansworth, George and Margaret Fox and Rachel Fell, together with Thomas Lower, set off towards Lancashire. By now it was late autumn, and the sudden sharp gusts that sent brown leaves scurrying awoke all the old pains in George's bones and the joints of his fingers and limbs. Recalling those nights in the American woods, he found himself yearning for winter evenings close to the Swarthmoor hearth and nights in a feather-bed.

Yet, whenever his horse crossed a bridge, or plunged through a ford, his heart grew cold. "And I had a vision when I was lying in my bed at Kingston," he said. "I saw that I was taken prisoner, and I saw also that I rid down into a deep steep water, three times and up again." Contemplating another bleak prison, awash with rainwater and filled with smoke, he hoped that it might not be before he reached Fennry Drayton. For Mary Fox's eldest son was summoned to a woman convinced that her last days drew near.

"And when I heard she was dead, it struck me," said George, "for I did in verity love her as ever one could a mother."[24] But Mary died without her son beside her. In mid-December, only miles from her, he was arrested. George Fox was a danger to the public peace, claimed the writ issued by the Worcestershire justice, Henry Parker, and intent on stirring up trouble. "There has of late been several meetings … to the number of four hundred persons and upwards at a time," it continued, "upon a pretence of exercise of religion." At one of these meetings, it said, held at Armscott, over 200 people had congregated to hear the said George Fox, who together with his companions, had failed to provide satisfactory reasons for his presence in the area. Since neither Mr Fox, nor Mr Lower, who insisted on accompanying him, were prepared to provide sureties for their attendance in court, both were consigned to the county gaol at Worcester. Both would also appear before the next Quarter Sessions scheduled for January 1674 at Worcester.

Not surprisingly, in Worcester prison, George's thoughts turned towards his mother. Though doubtless often overcome with good intentions, he had seen her rarely since he left home in 1647; that she died without him at her side seems also to have filled him with guilt. Clearly, it was also a guilt that he was eager to dispose of, and a doctor's letter stating that the news of George's arrest "struck her to the heart and killed her" enabled him to lay the blame squarely on the Worcestershire judiciary. "So these wicked justices God will judge," he said, "who hindered me from visiting her according to her motherly and tender desire."[25] In his cell he had a vision that reassured him that his mother understood. "I saw her in the resurrection and the life," he said, "everlastingly with me over all, and father in the flesh also."

The imprisonment brought a number of leading Friends to Worcester, who as they began a campaign for George Fox's release, discovered that many local justices now sympathized with them. But despite it, Henry Parker was determined to find the prisoner guilty. Moreover, was it not preferable to send two Quakers to prison, than for everyone who heard them to be fined for attending an illegal conventicle? he asked. Faced with the prospect of dragging 200 local men and women before the court, his colleagues bowed to his opinion.

"You Mr Fox are a famous man," observed Justice Leonard Simpson, chairman of the court, after George spoke in his own defence, "and all this may be true what you have said. But, that we may be better satisfied, will you take the Oath of Allegiance and Supremacy?"

Just as expected, George Fox refused. Yet, he was nevertheless anxious to prove himself a loyal subject. "I do own and acknowledge the King of England to be lawful heir and successor to the realm of England," he said, "...and as the Oath of Supremacy, I deny the Pope and his power and religion, and abhor it with my heart."

Though George was returned to Worcester Gaol, the Friends, with years of experience now in fighting legal battles, continued their campaign for release. Both at Worcester, and in London, and led by George Whitehead, Ellis Hookes and Thomas Moore, they called for a writ of habeas corpus.

Thomas Lower, meanwhile, though set at liberty, elected to remain with the man he referred to as "father". Motivated partly by a desire to see justice done, it also stemmed from a concern for George Fox's health. Though the older man struggled to hide his distress, Thomas, who had trained earlier as a doctor, was not deceived. Meanwhile, his brother, Dr Richard Lower, a physician at the royal court, added his voice to those who petitioned on George Fox's behalf.

Late in January 1674, habeas corpus was finally achieved. Summoned to appear before the Court of King's Bench in London, and passing along roads deep in winter mud, George and Thomas arrived at the beginning of February. The proceedings, however, were mired in complexity. Moreover, when George saw his accusers out-manoeuvre the counsel hired by his London colleagues, it added to a burden that had oppressed him since the day he was first cast into Worcester Gaol.

That it concerned deep emotions made it hard for him. For his usual practice was to bury such things, ignoring them until they returned in dreams, in visions, or most extremely, in his flesh. "Dear Heart," he wrote to his wife in February, "Thou seemedst to be a little grieved, when I was speaking of prisons, and when I was taken thou began to fall upon me with blaming of me." Knowing that he courted arrest by speaking at great meetings, knowing he was ill, and after so much time apart no doubt wanting him to herself, perhaps his wife had urged that for once he should avoid making himself so conspicuous. If so, then George totally failed to understand. "Why could not thee be content with the will of God?" he asked her reproachfully.[26]

Though he sent Margaret a peace offering, "as much Spanish black cloth as will make thee a gown", the will of God seemed to be that George Fox be returned to prison.[27] After a series of demands by Henry Parker to the court in London, the prisoner was sent back to Worcester in March.

In April, he appeared again before the Worcester court, this time before Justice Christopher Turner, who had sat with Thomas Twisden in 1664 at Lancaster. When George once again refused the Oath, Turner simply referred the case to the Quarter Sessions at the end of the month. But he also looked closely at George Fox. Though he still had little sympathy for Quakers, the prisoner's condition shocked him into action.

"The justices have promised that I should have my liberty in the town," George told Margaret, "and lodge at a Friend's house till Sessions."[28] Weeks later, Justice Sir Thomas Street, MP for Worcester, and President of the Court, not only had no sympathy for the defendant, but was furious that a vast number of England's Quakers should dare to throng his courtroom in support of their leader. One might almost think, he said testily, that it was they who represented justice and not the judges appointed by law. Crossly, he sent their leader back to gaol. But, as he did so, those justices who had expressed their sympathy earlier, now intervened. "Yet within two hours," said George, "through the moderation of some of the [other] justices, I had liberty given me to go at large till next Quarter Sessions."[29]

Interpreting "at large" very liberally, George attended Yearly Meeting in London. However, true to his word, he was back in Worcester when the court resumed in July. There, Justice Street took his revenge and praemunired him for refusing the Oath of Allegiance. With the prospect of life imprisonment once again looming, George addressed the man who pronounced the sentence. "You know we are a people that suffer all things and bear all things," he told him, "and therefore you thus use us because we cannot revenge ourselves, but we leave our cause to the Lord."

In August, Margaret arrived from Swarthmoor, her anger long subsided and desperate now to care for a man whose health was deteriorating daily. Together with Thomas Lower, she went over errors in the indictment that George had already identified, and together they pleaded for the sick man's release.

Yet, no matter how hard they struggled, it seemed that their efforts were doomed. "I seemed to myself to be amongst the graves and dead corpses," George said.[30] Nevertheless, he was not yet destined for death.

In October, Margaret went alone to London to beg King Charles for George Fox's release. She had rather wasted her time, Charles told her somewhat carelessly. He could certainly set her husband free, but only with a pardon; something which Mr Fox's continual protesting of his innocence made impossible.

Meanwhile, in Worcester the intransigent George Fox was grappling with the ongoing division provoked by John Wilkinson and John Story. Since the previous year, the controversy had reached huge proportions, and backed openly now by supporters in Westmorland, at Bristol and in Wiltshire, the dissenters made their views clear.

Among them was their opposition to separate women's meetings, and also to women having any responsibility for decisions regarding Friends' marriages, a call George had made first in Barbados. They also objected to details of disciplinary actions being kept on record, and to Friends being obliged to submit testimony in writing before taking any public action. And while not exactly admitting that they had avoided the full consequences of persecution, they insisted that it was the duty of other Friends to understand and be lenient.

In January 1675, despite his failing health, a desperation to hold the Quaker movement together led George to invite Wilkinson and Story to Worcester. When they arrived, he immediately lost his temper. Overhearing, though kept at a distance by his father-in-law, Thomas Lower knew that offence would be the inevitable result. He told them, he said, in a letter to Margaret, "if they continued in that spirit they were in he must bear as great a testimony against them as ever he did against the priests."[31] Unconvinced and unrepentant, the two men rode away leaving an exhausted and equally unrepentant George Fox behind them.

In the same month, a further writ of habeas corpus

summoned George again to London. But as Thomas reached out to seize it, the opportunity began to slip away. The last date for the appearance was at the end of the court's term on 12 February, but when he attempted to find the sheriff of Worcestershire, whose signature was required on the writ enabling George Fox to travel, he discovered him to be absent. When finally located, he claimed the document would take far longer than a few days to complete.

Having threatened and cajoled the sheriff, and with the writ finally signed, when Thomas then attempted to find seats on the London stage-coach, he discovered every one to have been booked weeks in advance. And he was perfectly certain that no way could the ailing George Fox ride a horse 90 miles over the winter roads of England. After posting a surety of £100 that made him George Fox's keeper, Thomas eventually found a private coach to carry George, himself, and a Clerk of the Peace all the way to the capital.

They arrived on 8 February. Three days later, George appeared before four justices of the King's Bench. After listening to counsel, they pointed out that the case should have been brought to them sooner. Next day, the final day of the legal term, after considering everything that had passed since the first arrest at Worcester, and after being fourteen months a prisoner, George Fox was set at liberty by Lord Chief Justice Sir Matthew Hale. "Thus," he said, recalling his Kingston vision, "from December 1673, was I kept a prisoner, tossed to and from Worcester to London, and from London to Worcester again, three times."

A free man once more, he and Margaret took the stage-coach to Kingston. But, almost as soon as they reached it, he began fretting. From Worcester Gaol he had written a paper in support of women's meetings set up earlier in Westmorland, and now he must read everything that was contributing to the acrimonious debate.

In May, when he attended the Yearly Meeting, despite joy at his presence, the whole event was marred by what had taken place earlier in the month. To the distress and anger of many Friends, including many in Westmorland, John Story and John

Wilkinson and their supporters, now numbered in hundreds, had established a separate meeting for business at Preston Patrick. Controversy had now become a breach.

Though George was desperately sad, when he left London some weeks later, with Margaret and her daughter Susannah beside him, his route was virtually a royal progress. At every stage, and sometimes lining the road, the Friends of Truth waited to greet him. All gripped his hand, while many were in tears.

For the eighth time now, George Fox had suffered imprisonment for the right to speak and worship as conscience directed. While in the 1650s, he went to prison as a volatile and somewhat incoherent young man, in the 1670s it was as the acknowledged leader of a large, powerful and international movement. That so many of his own following campaigned on his behalf, and then turned out to greet him, is proof that his words, actions and sufferings were on behalf of many thousands of men and women for whom he was an inspiration in their own struggle against oppression. In the process, however, his health was broken. By the 1670s, and probably on the *Industry*, it is clear that the arthritis that caused him constant pain had been joined by the condition known to his century as dropsy, the swelling of soft tissues due to the accumulation of excess water. Today it would be likely for its cause to also be identified, possibly congestive heart failure.

On Friday, 25 June 1675, the party reached Lancaster, where Thomas and Mary Lower, Sarah Fell, Leonard Fell and James Lancaster waited to ride with George over the sands. Carefully, they ranged their horses alongside his own, anxious to prevent any fall. Later that day, 23 years after he first hammered on Swarthmoor's front door, George Fox dismounted in its stable-yard. Walking into the parlour where he had once preached to Margaret and her children, where he had declared his message to Thomas Fell, and where James Nayler and Richard Farnsworth had crowded to hear, he sat down in a chair by an open window. Closing his eyes, he was aware of nothing more than the birds in the garden, the scent of roses and the distant smell of the sea.

CHAPTER FIFTEEN

My Holy Element

> ... a very large meeting, exceeding throng ... So I am in my holy
> element and holy work in the Lord ...
>
> George Fox to his wife, 1677

A<small>T SWARTHMOOR, GEORGE FOX</small> allowed his abused body to rest. He was 51 years old, and for 32 years, since leaving Fenny Drayton in 1643, rarely had he been still. Only in the enforced idleness of England's prisons was the urgency that drove him confined.

But, now, just as in the mysterious underground chamber of his vision three years before, time seemed to pass slowly. From a garden chair, he watched the brown leaves fall as the autumn of 1675 passed into winter. From a high window, he saw the distant fells shrouded in silence and snow. By an open door, he felt the warm breath of spring, and marvelled as green shoots became a yellow glory of flowers.

Being cared for so lavishly was unique too. Though for years his friends had welcomed him to their homes, at Swarthmoor, Margaret and her daughters were determined that he be indulged. "And thou shouldst buy us a cask of wine, of what sort thou judgest father likes best," Sarah instructed her mother earlier, "... also some anchovies, some olives and two larding needles, and some oranges and lemons, and what else you should think fit."[1]

And should idleness seem hard to bear, then the fire in his joints when he moved, or the breathlessness that overtook him on the stairs, that caused him to stoop forward and pause, soon forced him back to his novel and reluctant retirement. Relieving the days, however, were a stream of visitors, some of them Friends, others rather more surprising.

Early in 1676, Colonel Kirkby sent constables from Ulverston to warn Swarthmoor's Quakers that they must no longer hold their meetings. "For if we had," George said, "they were commanded by him to break them up." Yet, though the meetings continued, no constables arrived. When Kirkby himself came to call, it was to welcome George into the county, and to reminisce about the days when he was his host's great persecutor.

Among the Friends making the long journey to Lancashire was William Penn, who arrived in April 1676 to find a fat sheep slaughtered and roasted in his honour. Others, travelling south from Scotland, sometimes brought news of a young convert who, even more than William Penn, was the son of a wealthy and aristocratic line. His name was Robert Barclay; and in 1663, having returned from the Scots Theological College in Paris, well grounded in Latin, Greek and Catholic theology, he had embarked on a religious quest that three years later led him to the Friends.[2] His education, as well as his convictions, also led him to write on the Friends' behalf. In 1670, he published *Truth clear'd of Calumnies*, a carefully argued reply to an anti-Quaker tract.[3] Six years later, he produced a work unlike anything the movement had ever seen. For his comprehensive defence of the Quaker position, *Theologiœ Vere Christianœ Apologia*, was written entirely in Latin.[4]

It was the language so consistently criticized by Protestants ever since Wyclif, in that it prevented ordinary people reading for themselves the words at the root of their faith. Such obscurity had also been opposed by the youthful George Fox, when he attacked the Oxford- and Cambridge-educated ministry and their claims to knowledge and insights denied to others. He had opposed it too in a response to a proposal by Oliver Cromwell in 1657, to establish a university college at Durham. Hebrew, Greek, Latin and the Seven Arts, he maintained, were all irrelevant to teachings inspired by the Spirit.[5]

Whether Robert Barclay's work provoked discomfort in George Fox, or a secret stirring of pride, the book in some ways reflected the continuing controversy within the Quaker movement. For part of the opposition to the removal of hats and the shaking of hands was that they were a form of ceremony, ritualistic behaviour denied by Protestantism as being superstitions perpetrated by Antichrist, the Latin-dominated Roman Catholic enemy. Also opposed was any tendency to superiority in education or experience. In the *Spirit of the Hat*, which had vilified the collective discernment of Elders as "Foxonian-unity", the author had also accused the leadership of dominating every meeting by their own confident and lengthy ministry, leaving "all the rest to come as hearers, neglecting the gift in themselves, only waiting upon their lips."[6]

In the spring of 1676 – and the reason for William Penn's presence at Swarthmoor – an attempt had been made to reconcile the divisions within the movement. The meeting, lasting over four days, took place at Draw-well, John Blaykling's home near Sedburgh, and while, despite the entreaties of William Penn, George Fox would not attend, William himself, Margaret Fox, Sarah Fell and Thomas Lower were all present. So too were John Story and John Wilkinson, William Rogers of Bristol, and several others.

At first, as each individual spoke carefully, it seemed that some sort of resolution might be achieved. But, gradually, it became increasingly clear that even if that were eventually to be the case, it would not be achieved easily. While both sides regretted the anguish their movement suffered, equally they insisted that it was they who acted in response to the Spirit. In conscience, therefore, they could only conclude that the other was mistaken. Nevertheless, as the meeting broke up, John Story promised to remain open to the Spirit's leading. Welcoming his decision, William Penn and Margaret Fox voiced the hope that it might lead him to abandon the separate meetings.

The two Johns then made their reluctant way to Swarthmoor. Still smarting from the meeting at Worcester, they resented the imperious summons to attend the man they regarded as having betrayed the message of the Light. Even more, as they left him, did they resent the lecture they had received. They were in great spiritual danger, he told them, and in laying themselves open to adverse forces they not only put themselves at risk, but the movement of which they still claimed to be a part. Thus, they should return to God's people, put themselves at the service of Truth, and disband their separate meetings forthwith.

In this, however, George Fox would be disappointed. Though the Yearly Meeting of Ministers in May echoed his plea, neither John Story nor John Wilkinson felt able to comply. By midsummer, John Story was rallying support in the south, while John Wilkinson and eleven others sent out nationwide a document defending the separatist position. From Bristol they were supported by William Rogers, who produced a version of the Draw-well proceedings sympathetic to the separatists.

As he did so, William Rogers also chose to recall certain misgivings he had suffered in 1662 at Bristol. That George Fox had avoided arrest, he claimed, was due less to the workings of providence, and rather more to a carefully planned campaign of avoidance. Thus, he cast George Fox into the very same role as the Westmorland Friends who once met so secretly in the woods.[7]

George Fox and his supporters strenuously denied the accusation. Moreover, George also chose to recall that the Friends at Bristol had urged him to remain free. "They would not have me taken," he said, "for they [the authorities] would glory too much if I were taken."[8]

It is quite possible that in the 1660s, during the persecution that followed Venner's uprising and the northern plot, there were indeed anguished debates over whether a leader should remain free to travel, coordinate and inspire his movement, or whether he would best serve the cause by sharing the sufferings of his comrades. But, whatever was the case regarding Bristol, and indeed elsewhere, that George Fox went to prison so many times for his faith, that he suffered such hardship there, and that when he finally emerged he was broken in health, though not in spirit, seems to prove beyond all reasonable doubt that he was not the hypocrite that William Rogers alleged him to be.

Partly in response to such allegations, and partly in response to the whole huge and bitter controversy, it was at Swarthmoor during his long convalescence that George began the account of his life that would later become his *Journal*. That he had produced a shorter version during his imprisonment at Lancaster, also suggests that writing an autobiography had been on his mind for some time.

Indeed, he had every reason to believe that it was of importance for the future. He had, after all, lived through some of the most tumultuous times in England's history. That the *Journal* in its original form is also compelling, taking the reader directly into the world of the seventeenth century, and into the mind and personality of its author, also suggests that in life, George was something of a raconteur, who loved to tell stories and to see others listening spellbound.

As he began his account, he also gathered together the many hundreds of letters, pamphlets, broad-sheets and epistles, that since the early 1650s had been sent to Swarthmoor and stored there by Margaret Fell. Then, reading every word, he sifted, organized, amended and perhaps also destroyed.

On some documents he noted that he had read them and approved them. On others he added comments. "This was sent to G.F.", he wrote, at the base of Margaret's passionate letter of 1652, "and he came back again to them that sent for him, and he that he shaked the dust of his feet against, was not long after convinced."[9] Then with the edited archive and his earlier account from Lancaster both aiding his memory, and with Thomas Lower writing at his dictation, George Fox addressed the future.

However, it was also his intention that the future should read an account of the origins of the Quaker movement that was biased towards George Fox and the supporters of Gospel Order. Thus he cast such individuals in a favourable light, while at the same time throwing doubts on their opponents and minimizing their roles. There is also no doubt that he not only wanted to be the hero of the story, but was probably quite convinced that the God he served would more than endorse such an effort.

"I saw he had a flashy, empty notion of religion," he said of John Story, recounting the pipe-smoking episode at John Audland's house in 1652. Of a great debate at Derby in 1655, when James Nayler's ecstatic supporters ran through the streets yelling, "A Nayler, a Nayler hath confuted them all", he implied that James's success was due to his own prompting. "I was moved to bid him go on," he said, "and that God Almighty would go with him and give him the victory." He also suggested that he was forewarned of the disastrous events at Bristol. "A fear struck in me concerning him," he said, recalling the day he left James to continue the work in London.

While physical inactivity might frustrate him, the reward of being rooted meant that his comrades knew where to find him. "Upon my bed, in the nighttime, I saw a vision that I was with dear George Fox," recalled John Banks, a Friend who returned in 1677 to his home at Cockermouth with an arm he could barely use. Since in the vision he had apparently expressed the belief that George's touch would heal him, he made a painful journey to the Quaker leader at Swarthmoor. "We walking together silent," he said, "he ... lifting up his hand, he laid it upon my shoulder, and said, 'The Lord strengthen thee within and without.'" Some time later he told George that the very same evening the arm regained its full strength. "John, thou mended," George replied. "Well, give God the glory."[10]

Though he was perhaps aware that unlike John Banks' arm, he did not mend so well, as the spring sunshine of 1677 grew gradually stronger, George finalized the plans he had been making during the second winter of his recuperation. "A male pillion and braces and three girths for father," Sarah Fell wrote carefully in her accounts, "and mending his saddle."[11]

Late in March George set out for London. Though the blustery weather made his horse restless, her rider could only travel slowly, and as he passed along the road to Ulverston, with Margaret and Rachel beside him, there were many individuals who looked on the worn features and crippled hands and recalled the aggressive young man of 1652 with his determined face and long loping stride. Perhaps Margaret Fox recalled that young man too, as she parted from her husband at Draw-well, and watched him ride away. Though he had stayed with her for almost two years, she was probably aware that it was sickness that detained him, and that while he welcomed the oranges and wine, the soft beds and her own companionship, he would not really miss them, nor would the memory of them be enough to bring him back.

"... [G]reat storms and rain," he wrote to her from York, the writing that of his young servant, Edward Haistwell, "but by the power of the Lord I went through all ... yesterday ... a very large meeting, exceeding throng ... So I am in my holy element and holy work in the Lord."[12] On the move, among the crowds, drawing their attention to himself, and at work for the passion that drove his life, was where even in sickness, George Fox always yearned to be.

Travelling on through the rain that drenched men and horses and found its way into every item of baggage, the party's progress was slow. At times, they managed barely five miles a day, while George's poor health often forced them to rest for days at a time. During such respites, at inns or the homes of sheltering Friends, he sometimes reflected that unlike so many previous journeys, there was a notable absence of constables seeking to arrest him. Was he no longer considered a dangerous man? he wondered. Perhaps that thought saddened him a little, for that he loved to be at the centre of events, and always on the move, suggests that despite his support for orthodoxy and order, something within George Fox yearned after the days when all England was turned upside down. Yet, though the authorities were clearly wary of creating a martyr of George Fox, persecution certainly had not ceased.

Though Nonconformity no longer struck all hearts with the fear once provoked by Thomas Venner or the northern plot, Roman Catholicism continued to do so. And while England might just about have forgiven the popular King Charles his unfortunate liaison with Louis XIV, it had not forgotten that behind the relationship lay Louis' desire to increase French and Catholic power. When that memory was linked to the failure of Charles's queen to produce an heir – many bastards left no one in any doubt of the king's potency – then powerful anxieties were set loose.[13] For with Catholic James as heir apparent to the throne, and his Catholic princess the potential mother of Catholic offspring, then Protestant England felt itself painfully at risk. And to many English Protestants, the only way to counter such a risk was that Mary and Ann Stuart, James's Protestant children by his deceased first wife, should not only succeed him, but do so sooner rather than later.

By the time George arrived in London in May 1677, the name of Princess Mary Stuart was on everyone's lips. So too was that of the Prince of Orange. Linking them together were the policies of Thomas Osborne, the man who succeeded Clarendon in influence and power.[14] Created Lord High Treasurer in 1673, and Earl of Danby the following year, the pro-Dutch, pro-Anglican Osborne had not only salvaged the royal finances, but had concluded a treaty with Holland that abrogated Charles's commitments to King Louis. The fifteen-year-old princess, offered as wife to William of Orange, was the cement to a pro-Protestant, anti-Catholic alliance.

There was no alliance, however, within the Quaker fold. At the end of the Yearly Meeting in June, when 66 ministers issued a document condemning John Wilkinson and John Story, among those withholding their names were some of the movement's leading men. One of them was George Whitehead, who made it clear that to sign such a document would compromise his own effectiveness. That the bearer of the Pardon of 1672 should express such a view, had surely influenced many others, who subsequently had not added their names.

When passions on both sides were partly responsible for a decision by the Westmorland Quarterly Meeting to withdraw meetings for worship from the homes of separatists, it was clear that for all the promises made at Draw-well, no healing was in sight. Despite their differences, and despite conducting business separately, all Friends had hitherto worshipped together. Now, it seemed the schism was complete.[15] That the Westmorland separatists referred to "excommunication" made it all the more bitter.

But, as George Fox fretted over internecine conflict in England, an attack on him arrived from America. Its author was Roger Williams, the ousted governor of Rhode Island, who, having studied George's book, *The Great Mistery*, published in 1659 to refute criticisms of the Quaker movement, had then produced his own comprehensive denunciation of the man and his message.

During a summer month spent at Worminghurst in Sussex, where William Penn now brought up his family, Roger Williams' book, *George Fox Digg'd out of his Burrows*, claimed almost all of its namesake's attention. It also claimed the attention of several other leading Friends: Robert Barclay; George Keith, who like Barclay was a Scotsman and a scholar; and John Burnyeat, who had taken part earlier in a debate with Williams at Rhode Island. As they worked on their answer, naming it *A New England Fire-Brand Quenched*, they also finalized arrangements for an extension of Gospel Order, not this time in America, but across the North Sea.

Towards the end of July, with a day of departure fixed and passages secured, George consigned several cases of books, the collection of many years, into the safe keeping of London Friend, Edward Mann. Later, he sensed his spirit quickening. As far back as 1651, he had believed that a great body of Friends would rise up in northern Europe.[16] Although that had not yet been the case, as a result of the evangelism of the 1650s small meetings had been settled in Germany and Holland. In the years that followed, Quaker merchants domiciled in those lands had sometimes added to their numbers, or sometimes founded new meetings of their own. That the Dutch meetings were now mired in the controversies currently disrupting England and America was hardly a surprise, yet as he set out to impose Gospel Order upon them, George also hoped that the openings might appear that would bring his greater vision to birth.

In the third week of July 1677, the travelling party assembled at Harwich. As well as George Fox, William Penn and Robert Barclay, there was also George Keith and his wife Elizabeth, as well as Margaret Fox's daughter, Isabel Yeamans, who had been widowed three years earlier. Among others in the party there were also three Quaker merchants, William Talcot and John Furly, of Colchester, both with trade links in northern Europe, as well as the hugely wealthy George Watts from London. Finally, standing proudly alongside them was Edward Haistwell, who as scribe to George Fox, would record the journey for history.[17]

Unlike the journeys in the Americas, throughout the 30-hour voyage to Holland the wind barely breathed, while all that was to be seen were the gulls swooping low over Harwich and their Dutch cousins echoing them at Brielle. Yet, as the party travelled on immediately to Rotterdam, and George found himself in a land where English was not heard in the streets, nor used as a first language at meetings, perhaps Holland also seemed alien and remote. For just as had been the case among the native people of America, every sentence must first be repeated in Dutch by Jan Claus, the translator secured by Ben Furly, John's Netherlands-based brother. Then, just as if everything happened in slow-motion, when signs of understanding finally dawned on the listeners' faces, the whole process was to be gone through again.

During the party's first days in Holland, their travelling in that low-lying land seemed to happen in slow-motion too. Mostly, it was by water, on long barges hauled by placid horses, who plodded the flat towpaths that stretched on towards flat horizons, mile after uneventful mile. "...[T]ook boat and passed to Delf Citty," Edward wrote at his master's dictation, "and walked thorow ye Citty, and took boat againe to Leiden Citty... took Boat to Harlem Citty..."

In Haarlem, at the home of their host, Dirk Klasen, and roused from the reverie induced by level land and unchanging horizons, George Fox and William Penn engaged in a series of Dutch meetings. "Ye Lord gave them a blessed oppertunity," Edward inscribed later, "not only with Respect to ffrds but many sober baptists and professors." They were indeed sober, George reflected, contrasting the placid Dutch with his own rowdy fellow-countrymen, and equally as polite as the undemonstrative men of Rotterdam had been earlier. Would the General Meeting scheduled for Amsterdam over the first few days of August – the first of its kind among Dutch Friends – be equally sedate? he wondered.

At that meeting, neither George nor William Penn moderated their words, making very clear what they considered to be expectations on all Friends everywhere. Once again, they dealt with the structures of meetings – quarterly, monthly, men's and women's – as well as with marriages, education, and modest, orderly behaviour. "Be it known to all men that the Power of God, the Gospel, is the authority of all our men's and women's meetings, and every heir of that power is an heir to that authority." Thus stated the first of a list of decisions made by the General Meeting, and recorded by William Penn.[18]

Though at the Amsterdam meeting there had been slight stirrings of unease, and some murmurs of dissent, just as elsewhere, and to the English party's satisfaction, some who had formerly abandoned the orthodox fold, made clear their decision to return. After the meeting, the party went to the home of John Lodge, an English resident who had confessed some time earlier that the spirit of the hat had almost been his undoing.[19]

Reviewing the proceedings, and the establishment of the neatly structured hierarchy of meetings, George reflected that he had achieved in Amsterdam exactly what he had set out to do. Yet, as he considered the affluent Dutch and English merchants who chiefly made up the Friends' meetings, and saw them warned against the heresy of the hat, perhaps he couldn't also help thinking of the men and women of the early 1650s, who abandoned all worldly possessions to preach the message of the Light. Moreover, while he had had no regrets that the meetings of Friends were largely placid, in Amsterdam, just as in Rotterdam formerly, the lack of disputation at the many public meetings he addressed continued to cause him unease.

At such meetings, he noted, though he and William Penn spoke on issues that were certainly contentious – the Fall, and the restoration of the church of the Apostasy – and even though each audience had admitted to "severall opinions, as Baptists, Seekers, Socinians, Collegions, & Brownists", barely a voice was raised in argument. Yet, it was hardly surprising.

For so much of Dutch radical Protestantism – its General Baptists, its Waterlander Mennonites and others – bore so many similarities to the beliefs of England's Quakers that there was little with which to disagree. Indeed, there were so many similarities, that it virtually precluded the possibility of convincements.

In the second week of August, the larger part of the party set out for Germany. That time and infirmity prevented him from accompanying them, was a bitter disappointment to George Fox. For entrusted to Isabel Yeamans and Elizabeth Keith was his letter to Robert Barclay's distant cousin, Elizabeth, Princess Palatine of the Rhine, Abbess of the Protestant women's convent at Herford near Bielfeld, and the correspondent and inspiration of the French philosophical thinker René Descartes.[20] Both Robert himself and William Penn had met Elizabeth earlier, and both praised her great intellectual and spiritual gifts. But now, the man who once braved wild moorland in mid-winter, and who had boldly confronted Oliver Cromwell, must wait for some other hand to bring a reply from the intriguing but distant Elizabeth.

With most of their companions gone, George, Edward and Jan Claus travelled on together, by boat, and by wagons belonging to local Friends or hired at inns. On reaching Alkmaer, 50 miles north of Haarlem, they encountered for the first time a Dutch Friend who had suffered persecution. His name was Willem Willems, a shopkeeper and their host. For daring to trade on a day in 1665, he told them, declared a fast to the Lord that the Dutch people might pray for the success of their arms in the then war with England, he was fined three guilders. Following his refusal to pay, his home was raided and property to the value of 150 guilders was carried away. Not so very different from similar episodes in England, George reassured him. "And on ye 11: day G ff writt a pap to all yt persecute ffrds for not observing their fast dayes," Edward inscribed proudly.

A week later, midway through August, Edward was less sanguine. "I being sick stayed at Embden," he wrote, desperately frustrated at being forced to remain there in the substantial merchant home of Jan Claus' father-in-law. Days earlier the party had crossed the Zuyder Zee into Friesland, where they travelled along the coast to Harlingen, before turning inland towards Emden on the border of Eastern Friesland. It was there, as they drew close to the frontier, that Edward had witnessed a change in the party's reception that alarmed him.

Both Embden itself, and the eastern province, were home to many Quakers, and unlike their colleagues in Holland, over the previous years they had suffered a bitter persecution. Moreover, earlier in 1677, several had been banished. On the frontier, for the first time on their journey, the party were stopped and searched, George Fox especially arousing considerable suspicion. Now, despite George's reassurance that he had faced and survived such perils many times before, Edward saw his master heading into an uncertain landscape without his faithful servant to protect him.

George and Jan Claus now continued alone. Their eventual destination was Friedrichstadt, in Holstein, and that there would be many similar detentions and interrogations before they reached it, they had no doubt at all. It was also the case, that though languages might vary, the cocky aggressiveness of uniformed troops towards civilian suspects regarded as inconsequential was the same the world over. And so, George pointed out, after their fifth detainment, was the most effective response: an unyielding and self-confident awareness of one's legal rights in all circumstances. He had also decided to take up Edward's pen, for despite the pain in his crabbed fingers he was determined that the account should not suffer. It seems too, that he also sensed something moving within him, and that at 53 years old, travelling towards unknown horizons, he once again felt himself a prophet, a man anointed by the Lord, who moved at the divine command.

"I declared to him and ye people ye truth," he said of a Burgomaster at Oldenburg, "and warninge them of ye day of ye Lord." He declared it again at Bremen where he lodged at the Sign of the Swan, and also when he and Jan mingled among the crowds on a ferry forging its way across a great river. But, as he stepped onto its further bank, he was aware that his inward antennae forewarned him of danger. For, just as in days gone by, something struck at his life.

"Wee hyred a wagan," he said, "and travelled in ye Bishopp of Munstrs Country, to Clostersevie; the people of this Country are dark: and ... I declared ye Lords truth to them and warned them of ye great and notable day of ye Lord." Was the enveloping darkness that pressed so heavily upon him a memory of what once happened in this land?, he wondered. A previous Bishop of Münster had decreed the massacre of John of Leyden's followers, and for months afterwards, the fires that burned Anabapists alive had lit up the nights.

Eventually, about the third week in August, George and Jan Claus arrived in Friedrichstadt. The travelling was hard, at almost every town they were questioned, the rain poured down relentlessly, and often failing to find Friends, or a bed at an inn, they were forced to spend their nights huddled on the rough straw of stables. Yet, despite it, George was feeling better than for years. "Ye Lord made all well," he said contentedly, "blessed bee his name for Ever."

Overflowing now with the power of the Spirit, and even more in his holy element than ever, he encouraged the Friends of Friedrichstadt to establish Gospel Order in their meetings. At the same time, he also found himself encouraged by them. Most were Dutch, and having settled in the region to escape persecution at home, they had discovered belatedly that their new overlord, the Duke of Holstein, not only resented them, but urged his magistrates to issue writs of banishment. "But they (the magistrates) said they would lay down their offices before they would do It," George reported admiringly, "for they (meaning ffrds) had come to yt Citty upon matter of Conscience."

"The Lords power, seed, and Life was set over all," he said, as leaving Friedrichstadt's Friends established on Gospel Order, he and Jan began the long journey back to Holland. Once again, there were beds to be found each night, wagons hired each day, and soldiers to be confronted, resisted and passed by. Shortly after passing through Hamburg, where they were joined by John Hill, an English Friend bound for

Amsterdam, George was arrested, hauled to a nearby barracks, and interrogated for hours. Despite the month being August, nor did the weather do anything but grow more dismal and wet. Yet, more than ever, now George seemed restored to the energy and vigour of his youth.

"We passed to a great watr," he said, as unable to find lodgings, the party continued in heavy rain across the wild heath country near Lüneburg. Towards midnight, with the road deep in shadow, and the moon shining fitfully among racing clouds, they reached a swollen river, overflowing its banks and bearing branches and tangled roots in its frantic, swirling rush.

When the driver of their wagon refused to go on, George took up the reins. "I drove ye Wagan thorow," he said triumphantly. But, the prophet from Leicestershire would not pass through easily. "Ye water, being so deep and ye Stream so strong," he said, "yt It carried one of ye horses off his Legges from ye other, and hee was going down ye stream." But, while Jan Claus and John Hill quailed before a looming disaster, George Fox, who once drove his master's beasts to Atherstone fair, saw how he might overcome. Ignoring the rain streaking icily down his back, he ran along the river-bank barking out orders. "I called to ye Waggoner," he said, "and to ye men yt held ye wagan with Cords, that It went not down ye Stream, to pluck ye horse up to them; and so hee Recovered his Legges, and at length thorow much difficulty wee got to ye Bridge." They also eventually got to a town where once again, they found no bed, only a pile of straw. His clothes soaked, his heart pounding, George dropped down upon it and fell fast asleep.

Once again, it seems, George Fox's flesh bowed to his spirit. But rather than being laid low, sunk into depression or numbed by paralysis, this time it was filled with a preternatural energy. In a situation where all progress seemed doomed, the vision that drove him swept aside everything that stood in its path – the raging storm, the fearful companions, and the threats from arthritis and dropsy alike.

Twenty-four hours later, he was ready to press on. Zeal infused him, sunbeams shot fire from a million raindrops, and the Day of Lord must be declared. Jan Claus and John Hill could barely keep up. "There was souldiers and people drinking and playing at Shuffleboard," he said, when the party reached Oldenburg again, "and ye Shopps were open & they were traiding one with anothr though It was ye first day of ye week." Indignantly, he took the people to task. "I was moved to speak to ye people ye truth," he said, "and to warn them: of ye Judgements of God."

"I take a Journal again as followeth," Edward Haistwell wrote, restored in the first weeks of September to his position as secretary to George Fox. He had been more relieved than he liked to admit when his master walked through his Embden door, and not a little awed by the aura of power about him and the brilliance of his eyes. When the restored party later crossed the frontier into Friesland, where they rejoined their comrades, perhaps Isabel Yeamans was rather more troubled than Edward at the frantic pace now set by her stepfather.

After bidding farewell to Isabel at Amsterdam, as she and others of the party returned to England, and as September became October, and chilly winds ruffled Holland's canals, George threw himself into a round of frenetic activity. Day after day there were meetings – sometimes two, frequently three – at which he often spoke for hours on end. At other times he travelled by boat or wagon to towns nearby, leaving early and returning late. Together with William Penn, he also spent several days at the Hague. "Ye Hage," Edward inscribed, "...is accounted ye greatest village in ye world, and ye Prince of Orange Court is there." Though their purpose was to meet one of Holland's most senior judges, and to urge the cause of toleration, almost certainly they also reflected on the likelihood of Prince William playing a role very soon in England. And if that was the case, how would Holland's Protestant prince regard the English Friends of Truth?

Rather more immediately, as news of the English Friends' presence spread, the benches of the Amsterdam meeting houses were crammed more densely than before. Moreover, scattered liberally among the city's Dutch residents, were people from much further afield. Some were individuals unable to relate to the dominant faith of their homelands, and who in fear of persecution were driven to seek shelter elsewhere. Some were travellers, who in pursuit of business, scholarship, or simple curiosity, were drawn to tolerant Holland. "There came a great high Priest; who had belonged to ye Emperor of Germany, and anothr Germa[n] Priest," Edward noted regarding two such visitors. To them both, George declared the truth that was at the heart of his message. Though "they might know God and Christ, & his Law & Gospell," he told them, "they should never know It by Studying, nor by philosophy, but by Revelation, and Stillness in their minds by ye spirit of God." They went away well satisfied, he said. On another occasion, there was "a Doctor of Polland at ye meeting, who was banished out of his Native Citty for Religion." He too, Edward noted later, writing at his master's dictation, went away content.

At the same time, as the English Quakers became more familiar, the subdued response that had first greeted them, now changed to something that reminded George far more of home. Returning to Amsterdam after one of his many brief absences, he found that the city's Baptists had marshalled their forces for attack. Led by "one Gollanus Abrahams", they heckled during his declarations, muttered ominously during his prayers, and then demanded that charges of heresy and blasphemy be answered.

The mounting hostility and argument, as well as his encounters with seekers at meetings, and victims of persecution elsewhere, all encouraged him to set down his thoughts. "And whilst G ff: was at Amsterdam hee writt severall Bookes in Answer to Priests, and others to ye Clearing of truth," Edward wrote proudly, after taking down pages of his master's dictation. Later, as an epistle was sent to the magistrates of Emden, chastising them for their lack of Christian charity in their persecution of the town's Quakers, Oldenburgh and Hamburg received messages of warning, regarding ungodliness and the Day of the Lord. To Baptists and Lutherans, meanwhile, went details of the Quaker message, while to the Friends at far away Danzig, unreached by road but constantly in mind, went words of encouragement.

Finally, however, though Amsterdam's meetings remained

crowded and contentious, among the city's Friends there was much clasping of hands, promises of letters, and many tears. Eventually, when the Dutch Friends who accompanied the party to the Harwich-bound packet-boat said their very last farewells, they also said goodbye to one of their own number. Gertrude Dirk-Neison, a wealthy widow who had hosted the party earlier in her luxurious Amsterdam mansion, had decided to travel with her two children to England.

For Gertrude, her decision was one which for a few hours at least, she regretted. "Wee had Contrary winds," Edward noted, "and a great storm ye most pt of ye time, wee were at Sea & ye Vessell was so exceeding Leaky, yt two pomps went both day and night." Only George Fox, who despite all other ailments, apparently knew nothing of seasickness, gazed on the heaving waters without fear and with a quiet stomach.

But, though he exulted at the power of the wind and the sea, when he stepped ashore in Harwich on a blustery October evening, he could go no further. For the body that had served his eager spirit so well when confronted by a raging torrent in Germany, now betrayed him in England. Forced eventually to follow his comrades in a hired wagon, his aching limbs resting on hastily loaded bales of straw, he reflected bitterly that only very old men were transported thus.

Yet, in Colchester, where nearly 1,000 Friends waited to greet him, and as he spoke to them for several hours, he sensed the weariness ebbing away. By the time he reached London, and taking possession once more of the precious books, he felt almost as if he travelled on the breath of the Spirit. Every day there was another opening to preach, another meeting to settle, a Friend to encourage, and an epistle to write. Early in November, he preached for hours at the meeting-house in Gracechurch Street; and then attended the Meeting for Sufferings, founded earlier in the 1670s to provide legal information and employ defence counsel for persecuted Friends.[21] In mid-month he addressed meetings at Devonshire House, the building in Bishopsgate purchased to replace the old Bull and Mouth. A week later, he went by stage-coach to Shacklewell, home of the school he had helped to found in 1668, where he gazed with pride on the young women who bent studiously over their books and needlework.

From London he went on to the Rous home at Kingston, where he corrected the proofs of *A New England Firebrand Quenched*, wrote letters, and travelled to meetings in the country roundabout. Afterwards, in Buckinghamshire, he called on Isaac Penington at Amersham, and Alexander Parker at Jordans. In Berkshire, however, with Thomas Curtis at Reading, though they reminisced over the days in 1659 when Thomas sheltered his friend through his depression, there was now a distance between them. Both Thomas and Ann had involved themselves in the ongoing Quaker controversy, and though they had attempted to mediate at the tense meeting in Worcester Gaol, since the condemnation issued in London in June, both had come out strongly for Wilkinson and Story.

In February 1678, having travelled through Marlborough and Chippenham, where hundreds of Friends turned out to see him, and with so many sometimes riding alongside him that he was barely able to remember their names, George reached Bristol. So too did John Story, to debate with George, while William Penn and William Rogers jointly attempted to arrange meetings where the Friends of the city could finally put their differences to rest. But, wrote the faithful Edward Haistwell, there was "no stop". Indeed, he reported, not only were the meetings "very contentious", but it was also quite evident that John Story took particular exception to William Penn.

Leaving Bristol in mid-March, having stayed longer than he intended, George was once again back on the road. For he was in his holy element and the Lord's work could not wait. It took him first to Cirencester and Cheltenham, then to Tewkesbury and then to Worcester, where for one evening only, William Dewsbury arrived to greet him. But, the hours passed too swiftly, and as they parted, the comrades of many years promised that one day soon they would set time aside to recollect, review and make plans for the future.

At the end of May, George was back in London for the Yearly Meeting. "It was very Large and glorious," Edward noted, "and many heavenly Testimonys were born to the Truth and G ffs were taken down in Caractrs and afterwards writ out at Length." It was a proud time for Edward, to see other scribes busily taking his master's words, just as he had done himself on the placid canals and long roads of Holland. But, there was also sorrow, for after many months, Edward Haistwell's service with George Fox was done. "And ye 24:d (comonly called midsumer Day)", he wrote, "I took Leave wth my Dear & ever Loving Mr G: ff: and came to London, and he passed (visiting ffrds) to Enfeild to Edwd Mann's house there."

As Edward turned his footsteps to London, his master, after staying awhile with Edward Mann, took the public stage-coach to Hertford, arriving there in July. Early one morning, he boarded another, this time bound for the north country. It was a slow progress. Often, the pain in his joints laid him so low that he rested for days, sometimes at inns, sometimes in Quaker homes. On the days that he travelled he sometimes took out the Dutch New Testament, presented to him in Holland, and struggled to reconcile the foreign text with the words he knew so well. But, mostly he gazed out upon the passing landscape of England, and allowed his memories to keep him company.

Since leaving the north almost two years earlier, he had indeed been in his holy element, surrounded by people, feeding on his need to be at the centre of events, and using what was essentially his genius for inspiring, for organizing, and for imposing his will on a huge and disparate movement. But though his spirit was on fire, and though at moments of crisis it threw off the burden of disability, at 54 years old, his body could no longer carry him. Thus he returned to the place where he knew he would be welcomed and indulged. He arrived at Lancaster in September 1678. Riding to meet him, escorting him across the sands, and then helping him dismount in the Swarthmoor stable-yard, once again Margaret Fox welcomed her husband home.

CHAPTER SIXTEEN

All Stand Steadfast

All children of New and Heavenly Jerusalem, that is from above,
and is free, with all her holy spiritual children, to her keep your
eyes.

"An Epistle of George Fox's,
written with his own hand, and left sealed up..."
(in *Journal*, Bicentenary Edition, vol. ii, pp. 527–9)

"*F*RIENDS, KNOW WHAT the Lord doth
require of you, and all have a Sense of that in your Selves, that
he doth require; which is, to do Justly, and to love Mercy, and
to walk humbly with God."[1]

In September 1678, George Fox had arrived once again sick
and exhausted at Swarthmoor. But, though there were
oranges, anchovies and wine in abundance, though there were
soft beds and leather-backed chairs, and though there was a
family to welcome and indulge him, his thoughts lay with the
movement that was his life.

Unable to rest, he continued to address the Friends in the
series of Epistles begun so many years before. With his own
painfully twisted fingers barely able to grip a pen, no doubt he
often called on the services of Thomas Lower, his scribe of the
Journal, who since 1676, when he purchased the property, had
lived with Mary and their children at the old Fell property of
Marsh Grange.[2]

Whether during his visits there George played the grandfa-
ther to the two Lower daughters, Margery and Loveday, in his

Epistles he certainly assumed the air of a bishop or pastor to his flock. While in the 1650s, his phrases had thundered with denunciations culled from Isaiah and sparkled with the images of Revelation, now at 54 years old, he seemed far more at home with Paul of Tarsus. Perhaps it was not surprising, for just like the Apostle to the Gentiles himself, it seems that issues of unity, good order and sound practice were among his weightiest concerns.

For despite all attempts at conciliation, the controversies within the Quaker movement refused to die. Moreover, in 1678, to the dismay of George Fox, George Whitehead, William Penn and the other leaders opposed to the separatists, tracts written earlier by James Nayler and John Perrot were republished.[3] It was those two who had been the true messengers of the Light, claimed the faction that continued to uphold them. Calling on the Friends to reject Gospel Order and for each individual to open themselves to the Spirit, they urged them to abandon George Fox. Desperate to hold the movement together, George issued calls for unity.

"As to unity," he wrote in 1679, "it makes all like it self, that do obey it: Universal, to live out of the narrowness and self, and deny it: so it brings all into Oneness, and answereth the good Principle of God in all People, and brings into Humility, and the Fear of the Lord, which is the beginning of his Wisdom."[4] Moreover, he said in another Epistle of the same year, "the Eternal Living God of Truth, he is a God of Order, and is not the Author of Confusion, but of Peace in all the Churches of the Saints."[5]

Although George Fox clearly recognized that a constant rejection of structure leads almost inevitably to chaos and ultimately to collapse, perhaps there were times, especially at Swarthmoor, and on nights when the pain of his arthritis kept him from sleep, when he felt the chilly breath of James Nayler's ghost on his face. For although it was George's commitment to unity and order that ensured the survival of the Quaker movement, and although it is not easy to define or quantify spiritual experience, something does seem to have been lost. For clearly the Inner Light that so powerfully moved

James Nayler and John Perrot, that came as a blinding revelation and a consuming fire, was very similar to the experience of the youthful George Fox. And again, although it is impossible to know, somehow it does not seem likely that the many wealthy merchants who were now part of the movement, men such as William Talcot and John Furly, who travelled with George to Holland in 1677, shared that same numinous and ecstatic vision.

At some point too, George seems to have abandoned the earlier fascination with the link between the inner life and outward wellbeing and wholeness. Or if he had not, he did not dwell upon it at any length in his writings. Perhaps as Gospel Order became paramount, with its need to impose orthodoxy and combat schism, such considerations either faded from his mind or were too uncomfortably linked to the highly spiritual message of his earlier years. Rather than looking into the self, and bringing to light what was found, it seemed increasingly needful now to avoid the contamination that came from without: "... this religion," he said of the Quaker Church in 1678, "must be above the world, that keepeth from the spots of it ... "[6] Or perhaps it was all too uncomfortably linked to the mysterious cavern of his vision of 1671, to the passive woman who watched time pass slowly, and to her far more disturbing sister who caused it to whisk. For, although the advice contained in George's later Epistles and writings would produce sober and God-fearing men and women, it certainly did not encourage anything that would cause the pulse to race and the emotions to tremble.

"... [T]he aged Men must be sober, grave, temperate, sound in Faith, in Charity and in Patience," he said. At the same time, while he never deviated from the view that women shared in the gifts of prophecy, preaching and teaching ability, they were to be exercised within clearly defined limits. "And the aged Women likewise, that they be in Behaviour, as becomes Holiness, not false Accusers, &c., but to be teachers of good things; and that teach the younger women to be sober, to love their Husbands, and to love their Children, and to be chaste, keepers at home, good, obedient, &c ... "[7]

Yet, ambivalent as always, while he warned his followers against the contamination of the world, he himself could not keep away from it. And, though he urged women at least to be keepers at home, he was certainly not made for domestic life. Indeed, in what was to be a marriage of 22 years, less than five were spent with his wife.

Clearly, Margaret knew George Fox well when she finally married him in 1669. But physical longing and pleasure in the loved one's company sometimes induce a blindness to their true nature. Perhaps she had believed he would change, and certainly her outburst at Worcester indicates a frustration at always being second in George Fox's affections. Although later she maintained that they had both bowed to the will of God, there is a wistfulness to her later justification of their long separations that suggests she would have liked things to be different.

"And though the Lord had provided an outward habitation for him," she said, "yet he was not willing to stay at it, because it was so remote and far from London, where his service most lay." As for herself, she said, "my concern for God and his holy, eternal Truth was then in the North, where God had placed me and set me." This being so, she continued, "we were very willing, both of us, to live apart some years on God's account and His Truth's service, and to deny ourselves of that comfort which we might have had in being together."[8]

Being so involved in the events of their turbulent times, certainly neither Margaret nor George Fox himself would have been aware of just what a driven man he was. For though clearly his achievements were extraordinary, both as the prime force behind the foundation and survival of the Quaker movement, and as a figurehead in the struggle for toleration, there is always the sense that the anxiety that first manifested itself in childhood remained with him to the end of his days. That for his whole life he remained a homeless wanderer, also suggests that he was never entirely at home with himself.

He left Swarthmoor in March 1680. Whether he too suffered a passing wistfulness as he parted from his wife is unknown. Nor whether he paused to look back, wondering if he would ever return. Far more likely was it, that as he turned his face towards London, as he moved into his holy element, his heart quickened and his spirits soared. Moreover, during his eighteen-month recuperation at Swarthmoor, dramatic events elsewhere had once again intensified the persecution of dissent.

In 1678, it was alleged by Titus Oates, son of one of the Civil War's more famous Baptist preachers, and by Israel Tonge, a fiercely anti-Catholic clergyman, that Jesuit priests working secretly in London planned to overthrow King Charles, replace him with his Catholic brother James, and forcibly return England to Catholicism.[9] By the time the "popish plot" was discovered to be a fabrication, 24 innocent people had been executed, a Second Test Act had been introduced, and after seventeen years the Cavalier Parliament had finally been dissolved. The crisis also led to a demand that James, Duke of York, be excluded from the royal succession.

The demand was led by Anthony Ashley Cooper, Earl of Shaftesbury, a nobleman opposed to Catholicism and who equally promoted the cause of dissent. Dissent, moreover, was also a cause that was growing in power and becoming increasingly vocal. For while men such as William Talcot and John Furly might not welcome ecstatic visions, they certainly believed that they and their interests were entitled to economic and political representation. Moreover, echoing the demands of the Puritans before them, and insisting that the creators of their nation's wealth should share in its government, by 1678, despite the Corporation Act and all the tests, many powerful dissenters had gained leading positions in the administrations of urban centres.

Together with Shaftesbury, such men formed part of a burgeoning political movement. Seeing themselves as representing the people, and favouring the green ribbons once worn by the Levellers, their programme was Exclusion, relief for dissenters, and a contract theory of government, a theory which allowed the people to set aside a King.[10] Meeting in London's fashionable new coffee houses, they were known as Whigs, the name taken from the Whiggamores, Scottish Presbyterian rebels of 30 years earlier.

Opposing them were those who supported the king, the Anglican Church, and the doctrine of divine right. Like the Whigs, they too met in London coffee houses. They were known as Tories, after the bandits that George Fox dismissed so lightly during his 1669 visit to Ireland.

In the election of 1679, where candidates campaigned on Exclusion and relief for dissenters, many people made partisan choices: were they Whigs or were they Tories? Among those favouring the Whigs was William Penn, now widely regarded as the leader among the Quakers, and who made no secret of his support for his friend Algernon Sidney, a republican theorist and the Whig candidate for Guildford.[11]

When a Whig majority was returned, and King Charles saw divine right and the Stuart dynasty threatened, within two months he dismissed the Parliament. However, just as had been the case in the 1640s, when Charles I dismissed the Short Parliament, the people of England were not prepared to tolerate a monarch behaving in such an arbitrary and high-handed manner. Calling on the electorate to choose men of industry and courage who would maintain civil rights and favour liberty of conscience, William Penn was among those who threw themselves into the campaign for the calling of another Parliament.[12]

By the time he reached London in the summer of 1680, in time for the Friends' Yearly Meeting, George Fox would have found the city in a state of tension very similar to that of his first visit 36 years earlier. For just as in the 1640s, the language of liberty was heard in opposition to the Crown. This time, however, it was Shaftesbury rather than John Pym who dominated the Parliamentary cause, while the hugely popular Duke of Monmouth, Charles' illegitimate Protestant son by his mistress, Lucy Walker, was seen by some as an emerging Cromwell. When the second Whig Parliament passed an Exclusion Bill and introduced legislation granting relief to all Protestant dissenters, and was subsequently dissolved, and when the streets then echoed to the shouts of Whig demonstrators, it did indeed seem as if the 1640s were about to repeat themselves.

Quite unlike the days when George arrived in London

knowing only one Baptist uncle, however, the city was now the administrative hub of the organization which he himself had inspired. The centre of that hub was Devonshire House in Bishopsgate, a huge and busy building that was full of meeting rooms and committee rooms, as well as attics that were home to several poor Friends.[13]

It was at Devonshire House that the Second Day Morning Meeting of men ministers met each week, to oversee the printing and distribution of literature, the settling of new meetings in and around London, and to discipline ministers considered to be "walking disorderly".[14] It was there too that the Meeting for Sufferings met, that was founded to supply counsel for Quakers brought before the courts, but which as the Friends grew increasingly experienced in the law, had become ever more sophisticated.[15] By 1676, a full Meeting was held before the beginning of each law term, its members consisting of London Friends, members of the Morning Meeting and at least one Friend from each county. In the intervals a smaller committee dealt with issues of pressing urgency.

In the Spring of 1681, as elections were held for another Parliament, the Meeting for Sufferings sent a letter to Friends encouraging their support for Whigs. "As we ought not to be discouraged in our endeavours for the relief of the oppressed by any present disappointments, so we desire that all Friends who are in capacity ... may appear and make what good interest they can, in this election of Parliament men, for sober, discreet and moderate men; such as live in love with their neighbours, that are against persecution and popery, and that deport themselves tenderly to our Friends."[16]

In the same year, and rather as Edward Haistwell had done earlier, once again a journal was kept on George's behalf.[17] The record for 1681, however, is a brief few pages, while that of 1682 is non-existent. Nevertheless, he was certainly at Devonshire House in 1681, and both there and elsewhere he must have taken part in some of the debates regarding the parliamentary election. Quite what his personal opinion might have been is not clear. He was certainly opposed to persecution, but in his own writings he continued to promote the view developed in the 1660s, that the Friends were to endure suffering as part of their Christian witness. "Dear Friends," he wrote to a group of Quaker prisoners in Surrey, "Who suffer for your Testimony ... I am glad to hear of your Faithfulness, and of your standing for the Church ... wheresoever ye are, in Prison, or out of Prison, where two or three are gathered ... there is a church ... "[18]

Perhaps the thought of the Friends supporting a Whig political programme brought back too many uncomfortable memories of 1659, of his Fifty-Nine Particulars and the ambiguous role of the Lamb's Officer. Perhaps he was also uncomfortably aware that in 1678 the allegations of his seeking political office for his followers in 1659 had finally appeared in print, detailed for all to see in *Hidden Things Brought to Light*, the book written by James Nayler's supporter, Robert Rich. As for the language of liberty, there again it seems that George Fox was wary of returning to the political arena that had led to his 1659 breakdown: "... true Liberty is in the Truth," he said, "... which gives Victory over that which separated man and Woman from God, and by which they have access to God again ... the true Liberty is in the Truth, which if the Truth hath made you free, then you are free indeed ... "[19]

Nevertheless, when a third Whig Parliament was elected, again on a programme of Exclusion and relief for dissent, freedom of any kind seemed to be slipping even further away. As King Charles once again dissolved the Parliament, this time Shaftesbury was arrested and briefly imprisoned for treason. Even more ominously, and with alarming parallels to the 1620s, Charles refused to call another Parliament. As he attempted to suppress the charters of corporate towns, he also began to purge Whigs and dissenters, often one and the same, from the magistracy and the militia.

At the same time, an Act of Queen Elizabeth originally designed to suppress sixteenth-century separatists, was now used against the Presbyterians, Baptists, Congregationalists and Quakers of the 1680s. Under its terms, any person over sixteen present at an unlawful conventicle, who on conviction failed to conform within three months, would forfeit their estate and be banished. Refusal was on pain of death. Dissenting meetings were to be treated as unlawful under the Act, and thus became a riot or unlawful assembly under Common Law, entailing a fine or imprisonment.[20]

Hundreds of dissenters were arrested; in London many were flung into Newgate, while the meeting houses now alleged to be home to Whig plotters, rather than the Fifth Monarchists of former years, were once again stripped of their furnishings and padlocked. Like many of those earlier separatists, and like the Independents suppressed by Archbishop Laud, Shaftesbury and many leading Whigs fled to the safety of Holland.[21]

As the fury of the State descended on dissenters, though it may not have motivated George Fox to eagerly endorse political action, it certainly roused that spirit in him that refused to be cowed and which rose to a challenge. Rather like the stormy night in Germany when he was confronted by a river in full flood, the swollen body and the painfully gnarled joints were marshalled in support of his determination to resist oppression.

"I was moved to go to Gracious Street meeting," he said of a day in March 1683, "and they set a guard that kept us out in Lombard Street and another at Gracious Street gate, and kept us out in the street and I stood upon a chair and spoke largely to the people many weighty truths ... and there were thousands of people ... " Once again the crowds turned out, partly for the spectacle, and partly to see for themselves the determined resistance that had endured now for so many years and the man whose name had virtually become legend.

Being at the forefront of a struggle, at the centre of the crowds, seems to have filled George with an energy that all the restful days of Swarthmoor were unable to provide. Just as he had stood on the chair at Gracechurch Street, so too did he appear at the many other venues that the Friends had acquired or built throughout London. One day he was at the Savoy, at the building that formed part of a small colony of Friends that nestled in a courtyard close to the Strand.[22] Sometimes he was at The Peel, a meeting house in Peel Court, Clerkenwell.[23] Sometimes he crossed the Thames to be at Horslydown.

In the summer of 1683, perjured testimony was used to implicate a number of prominent Whigs in the Rye House Plot, that was allegedly to assassinate the king and his brother and to bring down the monarchy. Among those executed was Algernon Sidney, the candidate at Guildford supported earlier by William Penn.[24] However, though persecution became ever more bitter, and as the Friends continued to meet outside their padlocked meeting houses, it was also very clear to George Fox that even among those who carried out the work, there was very little heart for repression. "When I had spoken about three quarters of an hour," he said of a meeting at Gracechurch Street in August, "one of the Constables came and took me by the hand, and said I must come down ... I asked them if they were not weary of this work, and one of them said, indeed they were."

And though he was loath to admit it, and though his spirit was eager, so too was George Fox weary. Sometimes after speaking he slept for hours on beds provided for him at the homes of London Friends. Increasingly, however, he left the smoky city to spend days or weeks in the fresh air of the country with wealthy members of the family that had so long been his own. Sometimes he took a river boat along the Thames to the Kingston home of John and Margaret Rous. Sometimes it was a stage-coach into the leafy lanes of Essex. In 1681, William Mead, the man who in the 1670s had made history with William Penn and Edward Bushell, married Sarah Fell. By then, the Fenchurch Street linen-draper, who had also been a widower for two years, was a wealthy man, and shortly after the wedding he bought a country estate, Goosehays, or Gooses, near Barking. It was there that he and Sarah welcomed the ailing George Fox.

Sometimes, however, it was not only George's own health that took him to his family. In January 1683, when John and Margaret's daughter, Bridget, was struck down by smallpox, George was called urgently to Kingston. By now, his reputation as a healer had taken him to many sickbeds, and gazing on the Rouses' little girl, it was evidently clear to him that the shadow of death lay heavy upon her. Nevertheless, when her distraught mother begged again for his presence, "though I was satisfied," he said, "through her tenderness I went."[25]

In London too, his healing powers were in demand. "James Claypole was mighty sick of the stone," he said, "in such extremity that he cried out like a woman in travail ... I spoke to him and was moved to lay my hand upon him and desired the Lord to rebuke his infirmity." Later, he said, after James Claypole fell asleep, "his stone came from him like dirt."

But, though others responded to his touch, George Fox was a man for whom there was no healing and whose infirmity was clear for all to see. It was also one which his enemies used against him, accusing him of becoming a gross and indolent man, who spent his empty days sleeping and guzzling. When the Cambridgeshire Quaker, Ann Docwra, visited her leader in London in 1683, they were allegations she was determined to refute.

"I found him sitting down to dinner," she said, "his meat was upon the table; it was only a piece of very salt beef as big as a man's fist – it was cold meat ... I had heard before ... that most of his diet was salt beef when he could get it and wormwood stamped and squeezed into his beer." Ann then went on to describe George Fox's appearance. "He was pretty tall of stature and a very great-boned man in my judgement; but his face was not so fat as some fat men's faces are by much. His hands were stiff and swelled, so that he could not write well ... His limbs were stiff; I could perceive that by his rising up and sitting down. It is likely his body was swelled; I have heard him speak to that purpose. He wore loose garments ... but I could perceive that he was somewhat burly."[26]

Nevertheless, determined to resist dropsy and arthritis alike, throughout 1684, when over 1,300 Quakers were imprisoned, George was regularly at the Meeting for Sufferings.[27] In March he visited the prisoners in Newgate. More often now he also spent time with Francis Camfield, a Friend whose London home was close to Hicks Hall, the Middlesex Sessions House in Clerkenwell where many of the Friends' cases were tried.[28]

Yet though he pushed himself on, the days when he was unable to rise easily from his bed or from a chair were increasing. "And on the 1st day of the week ... G.F. was not very well, and unfit to go forth," said his diarist in October. Nevertheless, there was no time to be idle. "So he had Mark to write some things for him at Benjamin Antrobus's." Mark Swanner, the assistant to Richard Richardson, the Friends' General Secretary, frequently assisted in this way, and perhaps the opportunity to spend time with the legendary leader was worth what might otherwise have been his Sunday rest.

Disturbing George's own rest, and adding to the fatigue caused by speaking outside illegal meetings and visits to Newgate, and to the stress of preparing for court cases, were the internal problems that continued to plague the Quaker movement. Constantly during the year his diarist refers to meetings called to discuss "the Jersey business", the contentious question of the ownership of parts of New Jersey that had eventually come into the hands of a consortium of Quakers led by William Penn.

At the same time, although John Story had died in 1681, and without him John Wilkinson's own ardour appeared to fade, another adversary had stepped into their place. Francis Bugg, son of a wealthy Suffolk wool-merchant, had once been a Quaker, but in 1680, having rejected his former convictions, and with all the fervour of those who believed they were grievously misled, he spent the next 30 years attacking his former comrades.[29] In 1683, though accepting that the Friends often led the way in their willingness to suffer for their convictions, like Wilkinson, Story and William Rogers, he also insisted that he was opposed to any new innovations, especially the women's meetings, that were clearly not sanctioned by the Bible. Nor could he accept the role of the movement's leaders "in making Laws, Orders, Directories, and Prescriptions to bind the Consciences of their Brethren to the Observation of this, that, or the other Ceremony or Practice in Religion."[30]

While Bugg also accused the leaders of sitting in judgement on their fellows and of persecuting James Nayler and John Perrot, it was George Fox for whom he had a special antipathy. It was Francis Bugg who accused George Fox of gluttony and sloth, of an ignorance that amounted virtually to illiteracy, and who also promoted allegations of sexual impropriety.[31]

Given Margaret Fell's letter of 1656 to James Nayler, and others in a similar vein that Bugg liked to quote, there was clearly substance to his allegation that George Fox regarded himself as "One greater than Moses, a Prophet indeed".[32] Nevertheless, while George certainly did believe that he was commanded by God, and while such a belief may have led him to behave in a manner that was authoritarian and overbearing, among his supporters he inspired admiration and respect. Some, such as Ann Docwra, were also inspired to confront opponents on his behalf. Moreover, despite the accusations, George Fox was clearly no sluggard.

In June 1684, after receiving a delegation of Dutch Quakers in the previous month, he paid another visit to Holland. Once again, several substantial Friends accompanied him, including his old associate Alexander Parker. It was another round of travelling, between Rotterdam, Amsterdam and Haarlem. Although this time there was no trip to Germany and no swollen rivers to cross, there was a reunion with Gollanus Abrahams. Finding him far more accommodating than before, George claimed that his former adversary had renounced his aggressive stance. Or perhaps, by his sixtieth year, experience had also made George Fox a far more conciliatory man.

In Furness, in the north of England, however, there was little of conciliation, and in October 1684, there were "distresses made at Swarthmoor", to add to George's already high levels of stress. Fined under the Conventicle Act, "for my speaking and praying in my own house", Margaret was deprived of almost all her livestock. Particularly galling was that the beasts were removed "under colour of I am a widow although I showed them ye King's warrant...which owned me Margaret Fox." Galling too was the loss of a particularly choice ox that the Kirkbys had taken for their own table.[33]

Subsequently, the 70-year-old Margaret travelled to London. It was the second time she had made the long journey since George's own arrival in 1680, having spent three months with him in the summer of 1681. Arriving now in November

1684, she petitioned James, Duke of York for his help against the Kirkbys.

By the time Margaret returned to the north in March 1685, James had become King. Whatever Charles Stuart's real intentions had been – and no doubt he really had intended to act wisely and do justly – the growth of dissent, its demands for toleration and its increasing politicization, all so contrary to much of his own nature and to the aspirations of his supporters, led him inevitably towards the absolutism that had destroyed his father. Moreover, his official opposition to toleration was increasingly at variance with a large body of English opinion that no longer regarded Protestant dissenters as either rebels or traitors. However, since in most Protestant minds English Catholics remained firmly wedded to the nation's enemies, it was only on his deathbed that Charles admitted that years earlier he had been received into the Catholic Church.

His brother James, however, now King James II, had never made any secret of his faith. He went openly to Mass, and perhaps unwisely, included many Jesuits among his entourage. Nevertheless, when a new Tory-dominated Parliament met in May, he acquiesced to its demands and issued assurances that he would support the Church of England. But James was also eager to repeal disabilities on Catholics, and with them, those on Protestant dissent. To the Friends, it seemed an auspicious beginning, especially so as, following a petition to James in March, detailing 1,460 Quaker prisoners, an assurance was received that discharges would follow.[34]

In their perception of James, the Friends were correct; he was indeed genuine in his desire for toleration, even if largely on behalf of his own co-religionists. However, although neither he nor the Friends could have known it, it was his eagerness to promote toleration, that though it would swiftly bring it into being for Protestants, would also lead to the downfall of the Stuart dynasty. And in both, although unwittingly, James would be aided by the Friends.

At first, however, toleration seemed to slip further away than ever. In June 1685, the Duke of Monmouth landed at Lyme Regis, calling for annual parliaments, toleration for dissent, and for English Protestants to unite against Catholic James. But though 4,000 men of the West Country rallied to him, they were disorganized, outnumbered and eventually out-manoeuvred. As Monmouth was executed in London, 300 of his supporters suffered similar fates in the West Country, while hundreds more were transported to the West Indies as indentured labourers.

In the same year, perhaps to discourage political involvement, George Fox published a long tract regarding liberty. "God pouring out of his Spirit on all flesh," it began, "... all are to walk in the liberty of this holy, pure, peaceable, gentle spirit of God, that keeps in humility and in tenderness and kindness ... the fruits of which is love and peace &c."[35]

Meanwhile, by the time Parliament reconvened in November, having been adjourned during the Monmouth crisis, it was to discover that, contrary to law, James had appointed a number of Catholics to the armed forces. Fuelling English Protestant fears as to James' ultimate motives were events in France, where only the month before Louis XIV had revoked the 1598 Edict of Nantes, that granted French Protestant Huguenots the right to worship freely. Subsequently, as French Protestant churches and schools were closed, an exodus began of Huguenots seeking shelter in Europe's Protestant states. As it also became clear that on behalf of Catholics, James intended to repeal the Corporation Act and the Test Acts, Anglicans and Tories saw the menace of international Catholicism on the one hand, and that of Whig and dissenting ambition on the other.

To the Friends, however, it really did seem that their fortunes at least were indeed set to change. In 1686, as James fulfilled his promise of the previous year, 1,000 Quaker prisoners were released. Among them was William Dewsbury, who in 1678 had once again been imprisoned in Warwick.[36] Moreover, often adding to Quaker hopes was the special relationship that some of their leaders appeared to enjoy with the king. Both William Penn and Robert Barclay had royal connections, while for some years William had been especially close to James. Though opponents of the Friends were sceptical, seeing Penn's friendship with a man who encouraged Jesuits as further evidence that Quakers were secret agents of the Pope, Penn consistently encouraged James' inclination for toleration.

As he did so, he was encouraged by his own achievements in America. Over the previous two years, on land granted to him earlier by Charles II in lieu of a debt owed to his father, William Penn had established a colony where he intended religious toleration to flourish.[37] On his return to England, it was at his suggestion, and through his persuasion, that in 1687 James II issued a Declaration of Indulgence.

In response, and led by William Penn, a delegation of Friends presented King James with a document of thanks drawn up by that year's Yearly Meeting. "We cannot but bless and praise the name of Almighty God who hath the hearts of princes in his hand," it began, before thanking James for "his kingly compassion, thus to commiserate our afflicted condition", and for "his kingly word" that the indulgence would continue throughout his reign.[38]

It was perhaps ironic that such an address, that saw religious indulgence as the gift of kings, rather than the right of all people to worship as conscience directed, should have been presented by an organization once associated with the Levellers. It was indeed a long way from the years of revolution. Moreover, although some Baptists were prepared to similarly thank James, not all dissenters shared the Friends' sense of gratitude or relief. Not least since James had acted as an absolute monarch, rather than one working in harmony with his Parliament.

Moreover, when James subsequently set about removing over 2,000 Anglicans from prominent positions in the judiciary, civic corporations and the universities, in order to replace them with Catholics and dissenters, the resulting Protestant alarm, that included that of many dissenters, was summed up by the Marquis of Halifax. An alliance of dissenters and Catholics, he argued, "of Liberty and Infallibility", was surely a paradox.[39] It was also a paradox that led many dissenters to refuse the political appointments offered.

Unaware of the growing unity of the Protestant opposition,

or perhaps unperturbed by it, when James reissued his Declaration in 1688, he ordered that it be read from every Anglican pulpit in the land, and circulated by each Anglican bishop. When the Archbishop of Canterbury, supported by six other bishops, demurred, they were arrested and placed in the Tower. When a son was then born to James and Mary of Modena, Catholic succession and Catholic oppression seemed inevitable.

As the bishops were acquitted by the courts, unbeknown to James, a deputation of leading Whigs and Tories issued a formal invitation to William of Orange that he should invade England in order to "investigate English liberties."[40] Though William issued a formal acceptance, as his English supporters were perfectly well aware, with Louis already mobilizing against Holland, and with the prospect of a potential Catholic alliance between France and England, William's plans were already well advanced.

Calling for a free and lawful Parliament to be assembled as soon as possible, William of Orange landed at Torbay in Devon on 5 November 1688. As he then moved towards London, the North and the Midlands rose to support him. Two of James' leading generals, John Churchill and the Duke of Grafton, also defected to his cause.[41] By the end of the year, James, his wife and his infant son, had fled. Early in 1689, after accepting a Declaration of Rights drawn up by Parliament, William and his wife Mary Stuart, James' eldest daughter, were invited to rule England as joint Protestant monarchs.

In the spring of 1689, the London Friends took a chamber at Westminster. There, the leaders examined the text of a Bill currently before Parliament, that would finally establish the basis of religious toleration in England.[42] George Whitehead, William Mead, and another Friend, John Osgood, appeared on behalf of the Friends before the Grand Committee that sat to consider the Bill.

As the dawn approached for which so many people had suffered, and for which so many had died, and which some had given up all hope of ever reaching, George Fox's health continued to deteriorate. Sometimes, he said, he reeled and then collapsed in the streets, losing all track of events until he returned to himself again in the nearby home of a Friend, where the faces of those who had led him there, oddly distant and awry, gazed upon him anxiously. Nevertheless, with all London in a ferment, and optimism brightening the air, he could hardly keep away from Westminster.

On 19 March, says his diarist, "he took coach to James Beech's at Westminster, there to meet with Friends about their business with the Parliament." On the 20th he was at Westminster all day. On the 21st, "he had a great deal of discourse with Sir Robert Knaper, a Parliament man."[43] Throughout the remainder of the month, interspersing it with attendance at the Meeting for Sufferings, and meetings for worship at the Savoy meeting house, he was backwards and forwards constantly to Westminster. On the 27th, after Sir Robert attended George Fox at James Beech's house, "afterwards he went to the Friends chamber near the Parliament house where many friends came to him and Lord Carbery came to see him and had discourse with him." Sir John Vaughan, Lord Carbery, imprisoned earlier at Newgate under the Conventicle Act, now spoke in the Parliament on behalf of the Friends.

Though he was clearly ailing fast, "very weary and weak", George could not abandon the city. On 12 April, "... he took coach to Westminster Hall to see after Friends business with the Parliament." Next day he was there again. He was there on the 15th, the 16th and the 17th. On 28 April, with the subject of persecution very much on his mind, he wrote an Epistle to the Friends at far away Danzig, "who were under great persecution", as well as a paper "to the magistrates, their persecutors". On 15 May, he was at a meeting in Berkshire. "Pretty many Friends met there about Reading," said the diarist, "fitting their amendments upon the Bill of Indulgence."

Days later, William and Mary signed into law the Act of Toleration, that granted freedom of worship to all Protestant Nonconformists: Baptists, Congregationalists, Presbyterians and Quakers. They were also allowed their own places of worship, teachers and preachers. For Protestants in England there would be no more court cases, no more fines, no more prison sentences, no more deaths in custody, and no more padlocked meeting houses. After centuries of oppression, and of struggle, persecution for religion had come to an end.

At the end of the month, accompanied by Margaret Rous and her daughter, Ann, George took the stage-coach to Kingston. There, alternating between the Rous home and that of Francis Holden, another member of Kingston's Quaker meeting, he spent the last lingering weeks of summer in the peaceful country beside the slow-moving Thames. He was still there in August when "the King's Surgeon", perhaps a physician sent by King William, called to see him. Yet, whatever the surgeon said, or did, it would have made little difference. Perhaps knowing this, George had already made his will. Later, in the autumn, as chilly winds drove the leaves from the trees, he moved to Essex to spend the winter with William and Sarah Mead.

In December, 61 years after the *Petition of Right* was presented to Charles I, William and Mary signed a Bill of Rights that guaranteed regular Parliamentary elections and sessions, freedom of speech within Parliament, and for the processes of law to be established by Parliament and to be free from interference by the sovereign. It also guaranteed that only through Parliament could taxes be levied, and that all subjects had the right to petition the sovereign without fear of prosecution.

Throughout 1690, in the novel climate of toleration, and in meeting houses now free from padlocks and armed troops, George often incorporated the many experiences of his long life into his ministry. "He declared for a long time of many particulars," said his diarist, recording a meeting at Tottenham, then a village north of London, "viz., how they that wait upon the Lord renew their strength – Christ given for an ensign to the gentiles who is the Captain of their salvation, therefore exhorted them to stand to their colours and ensign – how people become leaky vessels viz by not giving attention to the Light – how natural arts and sciences and all outward learning and knowledge may be bought for money but the gift of God is not to be purchased ..."

In the spring, Margaret Fox, now aged 76, arrived in London once more and remained until June. Later, as summer once again turned into autumn, both in London and in the country George Fox found a welcome among the many friends who clearly found great joy in the presence and conversation of a man who loved to tell a story, who carried healing in his hands, and whose experience was virtually second to none.

Very early in 1691 he was back in London. On several days at the beginning of January he attended the Meeting for Sufferings. Perhaps as he glanced through the huge archive stored at Devonshire House, he recalled the many occasions when he had stood in the dock in England's courtrooms, first as the aggressive young prisoner of Nottingham, and increasingly as a confident and self-assured fighter for the toleration that had now been achieved. On the 11th he was at Gracechurch Street, where he had so often stood high on a chair that he might speak over the heads of the soldiers who blocked the people's way to their meeting house. Later that day, feeling unwell, he went to one of the Quaker houses in White-Hart Court.

"... [H]e said he thought he felt the cold strike to his heart as he came out of the meeting," said his diarist, "but was pretty cheery with the Friends that came to him there." When the convivial crowd finally departed, then just as he had so often done before, George lay down on the bed to rest. Yet, for some reason he could not get warm. The cold that had struck him, now rested within him. Nor could he rise from the bed. "I was with him most of the time," said Robert Barrow, a Friend from Lancashire, "wherein he spoke many living powerful sentences, to the tendering of the company present. There was no sign of any great pain upon him, neither did he ever complain."

Three days after taking to his bed, George Fox died. "George shut up his eyes himself," Robert continued, "and ... lay as if he had fallen asleep – one would have thought he had smiled."[44] Later, in his own tribute to George Fox, the Preface to the *Journal*, William Penn expressed something similar: "So full of assurance was he," he said of George Fox, "that he triumphed over death; and so even in his spirit to the last, as if death were hardly worth notice or a mention; recommending to some with him, the dispatch and dispersion of an epistle, just before written to the churches of Christ throughout the world."[45] Thus, the man who had faced down opposition for years, who had proclaimed his message fearlessly, and who had endured and then triumphed over eight bitter imprisonments, faced the last journey with the same courage and hope

"The 16th of ye 11 month," said his diarist, "he was Buryed from Grace Ch: street where there was a very Large Meeting the house and yard well peopled, & a great Many Testimonyes Borne Concerning him ... " Afterwards, as six Friends carried the coffin, behind them, "three and three in a rank, as close together as they could go, – that the other side might be left clear for the citizens and the coaches," 4,000 Quakers followed George Fox's corpse through the streets of London to the dissenters' burying ground at Bunhill Fields. Watched by a huge crowd, the convinced and the curious alike, the coffin was lowered into the earth.

Epilogue

...be patterns, be examples in all countries, places, islands, nations, wherever you come...

*T*HOUGH IT SEEMED a short walk for those who followed George Fox's coffin from Gracechurch Street to Bunhill Fields, in reality it was a journey that had begun 66 years earlier, in 1624, in Leicestershire. Since then, it had taken George Fox through the most tumultuous years of England's history. It commenced at a time when religion and politics were intimately linked, when to do anything but follow the version of faith imposed by the state was illegal, and when parliaments were called and dismissed by a monarch who believed himself appointed by God and whose will could send men and women to prison and to their deaths. It was a journey that saw the calling of the Long Parliament, the decisive victory at Naseby, and the epic struggles that finally ensured that the English people would be represented by their Parliament. It also saw the return of religious dissenters from overseas exile and the emergence of others from a radical underground. It then saw both groups demand the right to worship freely and openly as conscience directed. At the same time, it saw ordinary men and women calling for an Agreement of the People that would establish the right of all people, rich and poor alike, to take a share in the government of their country. Though these things were then at their beginning, they laid the foundation for future parliamentary representation, freedom of speech and a much wider religious toleration.

When George Fox first preached his message, he believed himself called by God to re-establish in England the true

Christian Church of the Apostles, and to impose his own truth on all people. In the course of his life, although he retained his belief in the reality of the Apostasy, and in his own divinely appointed mission, the power of events propelled him to a position where he finally became a man who upheld freedom of conscience for all people. Yet, just as had been the case in 1643 when he first left Fenny Drayton, in many ways he reflected his own turbulent times. One part of his consciousness remained locked in the medieval past, which saw God as partial, favouring certain people and nations above others, and fighting on their behalf. Another part of George Fox moved into the future, where men and women would recognize their common humanity and also share a belief that God's Kingdom is open to all.

A time of such tensions was not an easy place to inhabit. It drove England to civil war, and then to a violent repression that was overcome only at a huge cost in lives and livelihoods. And as a product of such tensions, and living within them, George Fox was not an easy man. On the one hand, he believed himself a prophet; on the other, he began to speak the still-unquantified language of liberty. Holding the two together made him restless, stubborn, overbearing and aggressive. At the same time, his example set people free from the fear of the world, while his message set them free from the fear of eternal damnation. Though he clearly provoked huge antagonism among his opponents, to his supporters he was a man of courage and insight, while to his own comrades, he was a true friend and a righteous man. To rouse powerful emotions, love or hate, but rarely indifference, is often the way with the movers and shakers of this world, men and women who leave their lives and their work as a monument behind them.

The Quaker movement is clearly George Fox's monument. It is today, however, in many ways a very different organization from the one he first inspired. Long gone is belief in the Apostasy and in a return to the perfection that existed before the Fall. Moreover, very soon after George Fox's death, a retreat from the world, and a fear of its corrupting influence, led to a sharp decline in the movement's numbers. The 50,000 or so of the late 1600s became 39,000 Quakers in England and Wales by 1715.[1] Nevertheless, there were always men and women who remained determined to combat injustice, to transform their world, and to leave it a better place than they found it. From the mid-eighteenth century onwards Quakers played a leading role in all areas of social reform, among them the abolition of the Atlantic slave trade, and the reformation of prisons. With the Peace Testimony as their inspiration, they have consistently opposed war and also worked in the area of conflict resolution.

In many ways, George Fox's *Journal* is a monument too. In 1685, he requested that all his Epistles, notes and letters, together with "ye great Jornall of my Life, Sufferings, Travills and Imprisonments", should all be gathered together and printed. Ironically, perhaps, in the new Quaker environment that he himself had helped to bring into being, his own rough edges, self-aggrandizement and earthy phraseology were no longer considered suitable. Thus, Thomas Ellwood, the friend of Isaac Penington, and later of George himself, and who had once been secretary to John Milton, was given the task of refining George Fox for nice ears. From 1694 until 1911, therefore, it was a much smoothed and edited George who spoke to the generations that followed his own. In 1911, however, the original manuscript was republished by the Cambridge University Press, and with it the possibility to return to the world of seventeenth-century England, and to catch a glimpse not only of George Fox, but of all our ancestors as they lived out their lives in that strange land of the past that is at once so alien and yet so familiar.[2]

Sadly, in those years when the Quaker movement, and indeed Western Christianity in general, shunned the thought that human hands might channel the power of healing, much of the evidence that George Fox was also a healer was lost. In 1932, however, a small catalogue was discovered that also contained a reference to a "Book of Miracles". Though the book itself has disappeared, the catalogue cites a few words relating to each of 150 cures attributed to George Fox, not only of "distraction", or of kidney stones, but of the many ailments that afflict humankind.[3] Thus, even more do we catch a glimpse of this extraordinarily charismatic individual who travelled the roads of England and the wild woods of America, healing the sick as he also proclaimed the Day of the Lord.

Just as the later years of the twentieth century saw a renewed interest in the healing arts, so too did it see a longing for self-knowledge and self-awareness. And to this longing, in his early experience of the Inner Light, perhaps George Fox has a message that speaks down the centuries to all people who yearn to know themselves, and through that knowledge to flourish and grow. Whatever each individual's understanding of the divine might be, perhaps in the Inner Light there is a path to healing and wholeness. "Stand still in that which is pure," he said in 1652, and perhaps now to the twenty-first century, "after ye see your selves; and then Mercy comes in ... Stand still in that which shews and discovers; and there doth Strength immediately come; And stand still in the Light ... Your strength is to stand still, after ye see your selves ... and then Strength comes from the Lord, and Help, contrary to your Expectations ... "[4]

Equally, and perhaps both are uniquely linked, there is a message to a world where once again conflict on the basis of faith is all too common. Again, no matter what each individual's understanding of God, or the Light, might be, it seems that George Fox speaks very powerfully to the fractured world of the twenty-first century.

"And this is the word of the Lord God to you all, and a charge to you all ... be patterns, be examples in all countries, places, islands, nations, wherever you come; that your carriage and life may preach among all sorts of people, and to them. Then you will come to walk cheerfully over the world, answering that of God in every one; whereby in them ye may be a blessing, and make the witness of God in them to bless you ... "[5]

Notes

Chapter 1: Pure Faith My Joy

1. The original manuscripts used for the compilation of George Fox's *Journal* are known today as the Spence MS. After George Fox's death in 1691, on the instructions of the Second Day Morning Meeting, and in accord with George Fox's own wishes, a committee of the Society of Friends in London undertook the publication of his *Journal* and other writings. The editor was George's friend and colleague, Thomas Ellwood, a former secretary to John Milton. At the time of editing, however, the organization that had grown from the movement which George Fox helped to bring into being had changed considerably from its early years. Not only was its membership far wealthier, and what might be termed today as "middle-class" than the first Friends, but they were also anxious to become an acceptable part of the political and social landscape of their time. Thus, the text produced by Ellwood removed much of what might in 1694, the year of publication, have embarrassed or offended the Friends of that time. Ellwood's text was published in 1694 and then in several editions, down to the eighth, or Bicentenary Edition in 1891. In 1911 the original Spence manuscript was used for a new edition, published verbatim and literatim in two volumes by the Cambridge University Press under the editorship of Norman Penney. This is known as the Cambridge *Journal*. All quotations attributed to George Fox in this book, unless otherwise stated, are taken from the Cambridge *Journal* of 1911. In this I am indebted to the Cambridge University Press who have allowed me to quote extensively, and also to transcribe the text into modern English. However, since the first sixteen pages of the Spence MS are now missing, all quotations attributed to George Fox down to page 88 of Chapter 4, unless otherwise stated, are taken from the eighth, Bicentenary Edition, 1891, between pages 1 and 50.

2. William Penn, Preface to George Fox's *Journal*, Bicentenary Edition, 1891.

3. For details of such prefixes see Kishlansky, 1997, p. 26.

4. Kishlansky, 1997, p. 28.

5. Robert Mason was rector of Fenny Drayton from 1606 until 1638.

6. George Purefey, 1605–61, succeeded to the titles and estates in 1628 on the death of his father, another George Purefey. It has been suggested that George Fox was named in their honour. So too, judging from accounts of Fenny Drayton's inhabitants during this period, were an enormous number of other boys. That George Purefey's mother was Dorothy, suggests that George Fox's sister was named for her. (See Pickvance, 1970.)

7. If George did maintain contact with his father, he did not refer to it. Christopher Fox died some time before 1664.

8. From the manner in which George Fox's bequests appear, it seems that Dorothy died before her brother. (Note 2 to p. 353, on p. 490 of Cambridge ii.) Katherine appears to have been either unmarried, or to have died without children. (Notes 4, 5 to p. 352 on p. 489 of Cambridge ii.) John Fox (d. 1718) was survived by one son, George, 1662–?. He had one son, Joseph, and five grandchildren. (Note 6 to p. 352 on p. 490 of Cambridge ii).

9. For this information I am indebted to local historian, John D. Austin, and his pamphlet of June 2006, "George Fox and Fenny Drayton".

10. For comments on George Fox's awareness of phonetics, and the suggestion that he might have suffered illness as a child, I am indebted to Laura Stokoe, whose MA in Early Reading Skills was the result of a desire to assist her dyslexic, but artistically talented, son.

11. William Penn, Preface.

12. William Penn, Preface.

13. Pickvance, 1970, p. 9.

14. Koenigsberger, H. G., Mosse, George L., Bowler, G. Q., 1989, p. 194.

15. A new Act of Supremacy in April 1559, designated Elizabeth "Supreme Governor of the Church in England".

16. The term "Anglican" as such was not really in use until some time after the Restoration of 1660. For the sake of brevity it is used sometimes in this book to replace "Church of England".

17. Kishlansky, 1997, p. 74.

18. Koenigsberger, H. G., Mosse, George L., Bowler, G. Q., 1989, pp. 194, 198, 352.

19. Edward Coke, 1552–1634.

20. Kishlansky, 1997, p. 126.

21. Jacobus Arminius, 1560–1609.

22. John Pym, 1584–1643. Pym died of cancer in 1643.

23. Sir John Eliot, 1592–1632. Eliot died in the Tower of London, where he was imprisoned by Charles I.

24. Memoirs of Edmund Ludlow, ed. C. H. Firth, 2 vols., 1894. Quoted in Fraser, 2002, p. 44.

25. Further information about Cartwright, Fenn and the Warwick *classis* may be found in the Victoria History of the County of Warwick, OUP, London 1969, in the article on "Protestant Nonconformity" by Clarke, Celia B., Lancaster, Joan C., Rose, R. B. & Tomlinson, Margaret.

26. Pickvance, 1970, p. 15.

27. Pickvance, 1970, p. 16.

28. Pickvance, 1970, p. 22.

29. The Act of Uniformity of 1559 made church attendance compulsory on Sundays and holy days.

30. See Pickvance, 1970.

31. The family crest and motto may be seen at St Michael's and All Angels, Fenny Drayton, Leicestershire, on the wall to the left of the altar.

32. William Penn, Preface.

33. Braithwaite, *The Beginnings of Quakerism*, CUP, 1955, p. 29.

34. Joseph of Arimathea was a wealthy disciple of Jesus of Nazareth, who, according to Matthew 27:57–60, requested permission from Pontius Pilate to take Jesus' dead body in order to prepare it for burial. He also provided the tomb where the body was laid. Joseph is also mentioned in parallel passages in Mark, Luke and John, but nothing further is heard about his later activities. In legend, however, he visited Britain, the most far-flung region of the Roman empire, bringing with him the cup of the Last Supper. It is this legend, woven into Celtic mythology of a magic cup, that eventually produced one of the story cycles of the Holy Grail.

35. Croese, G., 1696, p. 14.

36. For an example see Baxter, Keeble, ed. 1974, p. 80.

37. Genesis 1:1–2; Isaiah 9:2; Joel 2:28; John 1:4–5; Revelation 21:1–3.

Chapter 2: A Glimpse of Sion's Glory

1. William Penn, Preface.
2. Punshon, 2001, p. 38.
3. William Penn, Preface.
4. Docwra, 1699, pp. 44–47.
5. Atherstone Fair was held each year by a charter granted to the Manor of Atherstone by Henry III in 1246. The Fair was essentially a hiring fair and lasted over three days beginning each year on 7 September. It was known as the Statutes Fair, or "the statutes". As a hiring fair the Statutes lasted until the nineteenth century, and possibly to 1920. Those seeking work would stand with the tools of their trade – a rake, a mop, etc. – outside the Angel Inn, which still stands (its present façade is a restoration) in Atherstone's marketplace. Brenda Watts and Eleanor Winyard, *History of Atherstone*, Mercia Publications, 1988. I am indebted for the information to Lorna Dirveiks of the Atherstone Heritage Centre.
6. Tolmie, 1977, p. 17. The conventicle in question was the Henry Jacob Church, where a William Pickering, possibly George Fox's London-based uncle, was among those arrested.
7. Tolmie, 1977, p. 47.
8. Hill, 1973 ed. Winstanley, Gerrard, *The Law of Freedom and Other Writings*, p. 27.
9. The "Grand Remonstrance" was passed by a margin of 159 to 148.
10. The Five Members were John Pym, John Hampden, Denzil Holles, Sir Arthur Haselrig and William Strode. A Member of the House of Lords, Lord Mandeville (the future Earl of Manchester), was also to be arrested.
11. Gardiner, S. R., *History of England*, new edition, 10 vols., 1883. Quoted in Fraser, 2002, p. 97.
12. Hill, 1991, *The World Turned Upside Down*, p. 22.
13. For the corroboration by George's parents see Chapter 4, page 91.
14. Many of the books which refer in any depth to George Fox speculate on the origin of his mysterious fortune. None have ever reached any firm conclusion.
15. Technically the outcome of the first battle of Newbury, in September 1643, was a draw. Parliament, however, claimed it as a victory.
16. For more information on this subject, see "Sin and Hell", in Hill, 1991.

17. Barnet Chase.

18. Hill, 1991, p. 33.

19. Milton, *Complete Prose Works*, i, p. 526. Quoted in Capp, 1972, p. 37.

20. Goodwin, *Sions Glory*, 1641, pp. 5–6.

21. Thomas Edwards' books were: *Reasons Against... Toleration*, published in 1641, and *Antapologia*, a response to the *Apologeticall Narration* published by the leaders of the new Independent churches as a statement of belief.

22. Although the three parts of Thomas Edwards' *Gangraena* were not published until 1646, by 1644 he was collecting his material. He would also have known of a good many incidents similar to those described later in his book. Therefore, on the basis that he would have used some of this information in his weekly lectures at Christ Church Newgate, I have taken the liberty of putting words taken from *Grangraena* itself into his mouth somewhat earlier than he put them into print.

23. The Magisterial Reformation was so called since it was effected with the help of "civil magistrates", i.e. the civil power, comprising both national and local nobility and politicians.

24. *Gangraena*, 1646, Part ii, p. 27.

25. *Gangraena*, 1646, Part iii, p. 95.

26. The doctrine of the Fall is related to the Creation stories in the Book of Genesis which hold that when Adam and Eve, the first man and woman, disobeyed God by eating fruit from the forbidden tree of the knowledge of good and evil, they fell from a state of innocence. For this they were expelled from their first, perfect home, the Garden of Eden, and were subsequently forced to labour on the earth to sustain their existence.

27. *Gangraena*, 1646, Part i, p. 84.

28. *Gangraena*, 1646, Part i, p. 120.

29. *Gangraena*, 1646, Part i, p. 77; for Antinomianism see Chapter 4.

30. William Pickering, as a member of the JLJ Church, is mentioned in Transactions of the Baptist Historical Society (TBHS), vol. 1, 1908–9, p. 214, note 12. In TBHS, vol. 5, 1916–17, p. 69, there is a reference to an earlier statement of a Pickering who was a London General Baptist. This may well be the same man, although the reference dates from a period prior to the most recent research into the JLJ Church. Certainly, the JLJ congregation of which the William Pickering arrested in 1632 was a member, were not Arminian Baptists.

31. The two Baptists in question were under the command of Major-General Lawrence Crawford. One of them was Lieutenant William Packer.

32. To Major-General Crawford, 10 March 1643. Abbott, 1937, Vol. I, p. 278.

33. Tolmie, 1977, p. 125. Such liberty of conscience was based on acceptance of the Bible as the Word of God, and belief in the Trinity.

Chapter 3: The Light

1. "To my noble Friends, Sir William Springe, Knight and Baronet, and Maurice Barrowe, Esquire, etc.", 29 August 1643. Abbott, 1937, p. 256.

2. The "Declaration of the Army", issued on 14 June 1647. As well as calling for a new Parliament to be elected on a wider franchise, the Declaration also stated the Army's right to be involved in the settlement of the nation.

3. "For the Honourable William Lenthall, Speaker of the Commons House of Parliament", 14 June 1645. Abbott, 1937, p. 360.

4. This branch of the family spelled their name "Purefoy".

5. Later William Purefoy was among those who signed the death warrant of Charles I.

6. Clarke, Celia B., Lancaster, Joan C., Rose, R. B. & Tomlinson, Margaret, 1969, p. 373.

7. Baxter, Keeble, ed. 1974, p. 49.

8. Baxter, Keeble, ed. 1974, p. 49.

9. Clarke, Celia B., Lancaster, Joan C., Rose, R. B. & Tomlinson, Margaret, 1969, p. 373.

10. William Penn, Preface.

11. George Fox does not provide much in the way of dates for this period in his life. Nor are his memories of the period described as if they follow a sequence. At some point he returned from London to Fenny Drayton, where he was then based for some time. He seems to have moved backwards and forwards, staying away for a while and then returning to spend periods at home. He states that he left home again at the beginning of 1647, which by the calendar then in use would be the spring of the year.

12. Nathaniel Stephens studied at Magdalen Hall, Oxford, and graduated with a BA in 1626, and an MA in 1628. He went on to become curate at Fenny Drayton, working with Robert Mason until 1638 when Mason retired, after which Stephens was

probably in overall charge. He took refuge in Coventry in 1642 and returned to Fenny Drayton in 1645. In 1659, he became rector of the parish. He was described by contemporaries, although not by George Fox, as "moderate and fair" (*Dictionary of National Biography*).

13. In 1644, Hastings captured one hundred clergymen and their supporters who had attempted to reach Leicester in order to sign the Covenant there. They were rescued by Parliamentary forces.

14. Nathaniel Stephens published his book on Revelation in 1656. Entitled *A Plain and Easie Calculation of the Name... of the Beast*, it included a preface by the highly respected Edmund Calamy, an indication that Stephens' work was well respected. It also discouraged fanciful speculation regarding the Apocalypse. Five years earlier, in 1651, Stephens published *A Precept for the Baptism of Infants Out of the New Testament*, a defence of infant baptism, directed specifically against the growing Baptist movement, while in 1658, he defended the Calvinist position against Arminianism in *Vindiciae Fundamenti, or a threefold defence of the Doctrine of Original Sin* (*Dictionary of National Biography*).

15. This is possibly the same Mr Craddock who was among the 30 or so ministers who took refuge after 1642 in Coventry. See Clarke, Celia B., Lancaster, Joan C., Rose, R. B. & Tomlinson, Margaret, 1969, p. 373.

16. In 1644, the Puritan authorities at Westminster passed an act banning festive celebrations as superfluous to fundamental Christian belief. Although in 1646 the House of Commons dutifully sat on Christmas Day, many people ignored the ban.

17. The Elizabethan Act of Uniformity, 1559, which made church attendance compulsory on Sundays and certain holy days, was still officially in force. It was a powerful weapon not only for enforcing religious observance, but in disseminating the ideology of the state. It was also a means of discovering Roman Catholics and sectarians, and perhaps of discouraging them. It was also a useful means whereby the minister and the lord of the manor could note any absences from home of their parishioners.

18. 1 John 3:14.

19. Acts 7:48–50.

20. 1 John 2:27.

21. Luke 1:46–47.

22. Oliver Hooton, Box A, Portfolio 10 (LSF).

23. "The Newcastle Propositions", so called as they were negotiated at Newcastle-upon-Tyne.

24. The first demand for the disbanding of the New Model Army followed a decision to send additional English troops to Ireland. The Independent faction in Parliament proposed sending regiments of the New Model Army. Seeing an opportunity to be rid of the NMA, the Presbyterian faction demanded that it be disbanded and an entirely new force raised for Ireland.

25. *A Glimpse of Sion's Glory*, 1641.

26. The term "agitator" did not have the modern meaning of "troublemaker". The role of the Agitators was to lobby (agitate) on the Army's behalf.

27. Charles agreed to the establishment of Presbyterianism in England on condition that he and his family retained the Book of Common Prayer and the rites of the Church of England.

28. "The Declaration of the Army". See earlier, p. 57.

29. The Agreement consisted of four clauses: that the people's representatives, the Members of Parliament, should be elected in proportion to the population of each constituency; that the existing Parliament be dissolved in 1648; that future Parliaments be elected biennially and sit every other year; that the biennial Parliament, consisting of a single elected House only, should be the supreme authority in the land. Furthermore, Parliament was not to interfere with freedom of religion, press men into military service, or prosecute anyone for their part in the recent war. Nor was it to exempt anyone – rich or poor, nobles, churchmen, or commons – from the ordinary course of the law, while all laws it passed should be for the common good.

30. Many people believed that Charles escaped from Hampton Court with the connivance of Oliver Cromwell.

31. In December 1647, Charles secretly negotiated the "Engagement" with the Scottish Covenanters. Under its terms, a Scottish army would invade England on behalf of the king, in return for which Charles promised to impose Presbyterianism in England for a three-year period and to suppress the Independent sects. In addition, Scotsmen were to be guaranteed greater influence in the government of England with a view to eventual union of the two kingdoms.

32. Fraser, 2002, p. 283.

33. Jakob Boehme was first published in English in May 1645 (Aylmer, pp. 218–19).

34. Malachi 3:2–3.
35. John 1:1–14. See also Ephesians 5:1–8.

Chapter 4: The Prophet of the Lord

1. Genesis 3:24.
2. In 1664, during his trial at Lancaster, the Judge commented on George Fox's loud voice: "thou speakest so loud, thy voice drowns mine, and the Court's; I must call for three or four criers to drown thy voice; thou hast good lungs" (Cambridge, ii, p. 58).
3. *Gangraena*, Part I, p. 73 (the first of two pages in Part I that are numbered "73"). The term "Roundhead" was coined shortly before or during the Civil War to describe supporters of Parliament. Supporters of King Charles were already labelled "Cavaliers". Although not all Puritans wore their hair closely cropped, that some evidently did so was an obvious contrast to the long ringlets fashionable among men at the royal court. The term Roundhead was used throughout the Civil War and up until the Glorious Revolution of 1688 to describe the political radicals, particularly those committed to republicanism. For George Fox's own comments on his hair, that was "pretty long", see Cambridge, i, p. 207.
4. Ephesians 6:10–20.
5. "Being born again, not of corruptible seed, but of incorruptible, by the word of God, which liveth and abideth for ever" (1 Peter 1:23).
6. *Short Journal*, p. 3.
7. In 1646, the "Westminster Confession of Faith" was sent to the English Parliament to be ratified, and also submitted to the General Assembly of the Scottish Kirk. In 1647, the Church of Scotland adopted it without amendment. The House of Commons, however, returned it to the Assembly requesting that it be accompanied by a list of proof texts from Scripture. In 1648, with the omission of some sections and chapters, it was eventually accepted by Act of Parliament as the "Articles of Christian Religion". In the following year, in Scotland, the Confession was ratified by an Act of the Scottish Parliament, again without amendment. At the restoration of the monarchy in 1660, and of the Anglican episcopacy, both Acts were nullified. When William of Orange replaced James II on the throne of England in 1688, he gave permission to the Scottish Parliament to ratify the Confession once again.

8. From the beginning of the Quaker movement there were constant allegations that Quakers were Jesuits. One of many who propagated such a view was William Prynne, who in 1664 published *The Quakers Unmasked, and clearly detected to be but the Spawn of Romish Frogs, Jesuites and Franciscan Fryers, sent from Rome to seduce the intoxicated Giddy-headed English Nation*.

9. The Blasphemy Ordinance was passed in May 1648, after a debate of two years, and against the opposition of the Independents and their allies (Tolmie, 1977, p. 135).

10. In 1618, James I offended Puritan sensibilities by formally issuing the Declaration of Sports. The catalyst was a conflict in Lancashire between the gentry, many of whom were Roman Catholics, and the Puritan clergy. The declaration gave permission for dancing, archery, leaping and vaulting, and for "having of May games, Whitsun ales and morris dances, as well as the setting up of May-poles, together with various other sports". This was to be done on the understanding that it did not conflict with divine service or with the decoration of the church by women. Bull and bear baiting was prohibited on Sundays, and as far as the common people were concerned, so was bowls. Although James at first ordered the parish clergy to read the declaration from the pulpit, so strong was their objection to amusements on Sunday that he was forced to withdraw. In 1633, after Charles I ordered the republication of the Declaration, and then insisted upon the reading of it by the clergy, many were punished for disobeying the command. When Charles was overthrown, Puritan prohibitions against sports and games on the Sabbath again prevailed until Charles II was restored in 1660. That they were largely ineffective is underlined by George Fox's words regarding holy-days, and by his insistence that such strictures be obeyed in a godly nation. See *Journal*, Bicentenary Edition, i, note on p. 39.

11. The average age at conversion in the early years of the Quaker movement was 26. While a few were younger, some were older, in their early to mid-30s. See Reay, 1985, chapter 1.

12. In his *Journal* (Cambridge, i, p. 389), George Fox says that in the early years, Quakers were nicknamed "Children of Light". It was a term that was also used by the Quakers themselves. For example, see Aldam to Fell, 1654, Swarthmoor Colln, iv, 89 (LSF), and James Nayler, *Works*, p. xliii. For its usage by George Fox, see his Epistles of 1653 "On Marriage" and "To all Friends, concerning the Light etc." It was, of course, the famous question he asked in

Ulverston Church (see Chapter 6). I have used this designation in the early chapters, as it seems likely that this was widely used for a sect of religious enthusiasts for whom the Light was a central part of their theology and preaching. After the crisis caused by James Nayler at Bristol in 1656, when the sect began to question some of its earlier excesses, I have begun to use the term "Friends of Truth", a term that, once again, was used by Quakers themselves. Following the Restoration, when the sect attempted in an organized manner to shake off its reputation for fanaticism, I have used "Friends of Truth" more regularly. I have also used "Quakers" throughout. Although George refers very early on in his *Journal* to "Friends", he did not of course begin working on his memoir until the 1670s, when the term was in common use. However, since it was used in letters dating from the early 1650s, it was clearly in use by then.

13. King Charles was secretly planning to escape from his then captivity on the Isle of Wight, and his intention was to spin out the negotiations for as long as possible. He was also sending secret instructions to the Earl of Ormonde, who was negotiating for support from Irish Catholics on the king's behalf, telling him to disregard anything he conceded whilst in captivity.

14. By removing the MPs who still favoured a negotiated settlement, the Purge effectively cleared the way for the king's trial in the following month. Fifty Independent MPs, plus 30 others, many of whom resigned in protest, were allowed to retain their seats.

15. A supporter of religious and political radicals, in the late 1630s Bradshaw appeared as counsel for John Lilburne. In January 1649, as president of the court set up to try the king, his was the voice that pronounced the sentence, while his name was among the foremost on the death warrant. In March that same year, he was appointed first President of the Council of State.

16. For an in-depth analysis of this subject, see Bell, 2000.

17. John Owen, "A Sermon preached to the Honourable House of Commons", 1649. John Owen (1616–83), an Independent divine and close friend of Oliver Cromwell, became Vice-Chancellor of Oxford University in 1652. He was also a great influence on the young William Penn.

18. The Council of State was first recommended by Henry Ireton and John Lambert in the Heads of the Army Proposals, 1647. See Chapter 3, page 69.

19. The final version of the Agreement of the People was issued in

May 1649. It called for: the right to vote for all men over the age of 21 (except servants, beggars and Royalists); no Army officer, treasurer or lawyer to be an MP (to prevent conflict of interest); annual elections to Parliament with MPs serving one term only; equality of all before the law; trials to be heard before twelve jurymen, freely chosen by their community; no one to be punished for refusing to testify against themselves in criminal cases; the law to proceed in English with no cases extending beyond six months; the death penalty applied only for murder; the abolition of imprisonment for debt; the abolition of tithes; the right of parishioners to choose their ministers; taxation to be in proportion to real or personal property; the abolition of military conscription, monopolies and excise taxes.

20. The three men were Corporal Perkins, Cornet Thompson and Private Church. Since 1975, they have been remembered each May at the Leveller's Day in Burford, organized by the Oxfordshire branch of the Workers' Educational Association.

21. The Act, 1 Mar. st. 2. cap. 3, punished malicious disturbing of a preacher during his sermon or when celebrating divine service (Braithwaite, *Beginnings*, p. 133, fn. 2).

22. *Short Journal*, pp. 1–2.

23. *Short Journal*, p. 2.

24. I imagine the phenomena to be much the same as that seen in charismatic churches today.

25. *Short Journal*, p. 2.

26. Matthew 10:1–10.

27. Acts 3 – 4.

28. *Short Journal*, pp. 2–3.

29. In his *Journal*, George Fox recalls two very similar healings that he recounts one after the other. One was at Elizabeth Hooton's house at Skegby, and the other, at Mansfield Woodhouse, less than five miles distant. Quite possibly this was the same healing, which many years later was perhaps confused with others and remembered as two.

30. *Short Journal*, p. 2.

31. *Short Journal*, p. 12.

32. Hill, 1991, pp. 189, 191.

33. Hill, 1991, p. 199.

34. Kishlansky, 1997, p. 203.

35. Coppe, *A Fiery Flying Roll*, 1649, p. 5.

36. Braithwaite, *Beginnings*, p. 54.

37. George also states that one of the prisoners was Joseph Salmon, who was widely regarded as a Ranter leader. Almost certainly he must have known about him before his visit to the prison.

38. From this point onwards, all quotations attributed to George Fox, unless otherwise stated, are taken from the Cambridge *Journal* (CUP, 1911).

39. *Short Journal*, p. 4.

40. *Journal*, Bicentenary Edition, i, p. 51.

41. "To redeem them that were under the law, that we might receive the adoption of sons. And because ye are sons, God hath sent forth the Spirit of his Son into your hearts, crying, Abba, Father" (Galatians 4:5–6). "For as many as are led by the Spirit of God, they are the sons of God. For ye have not received the spirit of bondage again to fear; but ye have received the Spirit of adoption, whereby we cry, Abba, Father" (Romans 8:14–15).

42. Matthew 10:8. Also Isaiah 55:1.

43. 2 Timothy 3:5.

44. *Journal*, Bicentenary Edition, i, p. 52.

45. *Journal*, Bicentenary Edition, i, pp. 52–53.

46. *Journal*, Bicentenary Edition, i, p. 54.

47. *Journal*, Bicentenary Edition, i, p. 56.

48. *Journal*, Bicentenary Edition, i, p. 62.

49. Cambridge, i, p. 1.

50. *Journal*, Bicentenary Edition, i, p. 63.

51. Cambridge, i, p. 4. In his *Apology* of 1676, Robert Barclay states that the name came from the trembling of Friends under the powerful working of the Holy Spirit. However, there is no real inconsistency between the two accounts.

52. Babington, 1971, p. 50.

53. James 4:1–2.

54. Although George never used or responded with physical violence, he was very verbally aggressive. Moreover, his physical size probably made him an intimidating opponent.

55. Proverbs 13:24; 22:15; 23:13–14; 29:15.

56. There is no evidence that any massacre of Christians actually took place (Braithwaite, *Beginnings*, p. 56).

57. In the Lichfield Visitors' Centre there is a painting depicting George Fox's dramatic denunciation of the city.

58. For an in-depth study of this subject, see Hill, C., *The World Turned Upside Down*.

59. By the time he wrote his *Journal*, George had clearly forgotten

that one of the spires, since then restored, was smashed. He speaks of espying three.

Chapter 5: A Trumpet in Zion

1. "Brownists" was the name given to the followers of Robert Browne (1550–1633), an English Separatist who in a work of 1582, *A Treatise of Reformation Without Tarying for anie*, argued for a Christian church unsupported by tithes, where each congregation should exist independently. He was one of the precursors of Independency, or Congregationalism.

2. *Gangraena*, Part i, p. 14.

3. For a study of the seventeenth-century Seekers, see McGregor, J. F., "Seekers and Ranters", in McGregor, J. F. & Reay, B., *Radical Religion in the English Revolution*, OUP, 1984.

4. Oliver Cromwell, in writing to his daughter, Bridget, spoke of Seekers: "Happy seeker, happy finder! Who ever tasted that the Lord is gracious, without some sense of self, vanity and badness. Whoever tasted that graciousness of His, and could go less in desire, and less in pressing after full enjoyment." Quoted in Fraser, 2002, p. 507.

5. Anon., *A Publike Conference Betwixt the Six Presbyterian Ministers, And Some Independent Commanders, Held at Oxford*, 1646, p. 3. Quoted in Hill, 1991, p. 192. Also Erbury's quoting of Boehme, see Hill, 1991, p.192.

6. S. Rutherford, *A Survey of the Spirituall Antichrist*, 1648. Quoted in Hill, 1991, p. 80. On the Apostasy, see Hill, 1991, p. 194.

7. Erbury, W., *Nor Truth nor Error*, 1646(–47). Quoted in Hill, 1991, p. 193.

8. Richard Farnsworth, d. 1666.

9. "R. Farnsworth to G. ff. 1652", Swarthmoor Colln, iii, 53 (LSF).

10. "Roundhead". See Note 3 to Chapter 4 above.

11. Braithwaite, *Beginnings*, p. 60.

12. Hill, 1991, p. 77.

13. *Mercurius Politicus*, 23 (7–14 November 1650). Quoted in Hill, 1991, p. 76.

14. James Nayler, 1618–60.

15. Jaffray, 1834, p. 543. Though the writer used the term "Quaker", he wrote his memoir when the word was in more general use.

16. West Ardsley was also known as Woodkirk.

17. "An Examination of James Nayler, upon an Indictment of Blasphemy etc.", Nayler, Works, 1716, pp. 11–16.

18. Pickvance, 1970, p. 19.
19. In the *Journal*, George Fox refers to this officer as Captain Pursloe. However, in *First Publishers of Truth* (1907), in an account submitted in 1704 by the Kelke Monthly Meeting, he is referred to as Richard Purslove.
20. Durant Hotham, 1619–91.
21. Hotham's *Life of Jacob Behmen* was published in 1654.
22. Matthew 10:8.
23. 2 Peter 2:1–10.
24. *Journal*, Bicentenary Edition, i, p. 161.
25. Luke Robinson, of Thornton Riseborough, near Pickering, was elected Member of Parliament for Scarborough in the Long Parliament. He was a leading supporter of the Commonwealth in Yorkshire.
26. Matthew 7:15.
27. Thomas Aldam spent two years as a prisoner in York.
28. Joel 2:1.
29. Either the River Lune, or the Rawthey, a tributary of the Lune. See n. 2, p. 16 of *Short Journal*, p. 279.
30. Revelation 7:9.
31. See *Short Journal*, p. 16.
32. The strike lasted for eight years. The strikers were only defeated when the Rump Parliament of 1659 passed an Act enabling tithe-owners to recover their losses. The Act was endorsed by the newly restored monarchy in the following year (Boulton, 1998, pp. 92–94).
33. Gervase Benson was Mayor of Kendal between 1643 and 1644. Prior to the Civil War, he was Commissary of the Archdeaconry of Richmond, the chief ecclesiastical office under the Bishop of Chester. He was also a Justice of the Peace and a Colonel. As a principal man among the Seekers, and a preacher at their gatherings, he may well have been influential in bringing George Fox into the region.
34. Francis Howgill, 1618–69.
35. John Audland, 1630–64.
36. Howgill, 1656, p. 43.
37. *First Publishers of Truth*, 1907, p. 243.

Chapter 6: Children of Light

1. John Story, c. 1630–1681.
2. Kishlansky, 1997, p. 19.

3. Kunze, 1994, p. 86; Blackwood, 1978, p. 4.

4. In September 1652, after visiting George Fox at Swarthmoor, Thomas Taylor added his name to the Children of Light. See Braithwaite, *Beginnings*, pp. 93–94.

5. *First Publishers of Truth*, 1907, p. 244.

6. Captain Adam Sandys, of Bouth, near Ulverston. Also in Blackwood, 1978, fig. 3, p. 45.

7. Matthew 10:36.

8. Luke 5:11.

9. James Nayler was among many evangelists of the period for whom the call of God was more important than responsibility to family. James Nayler's wife visited him and cared for him during the imprisonment that followed his trial in 1656. Another who left his family was William Dewsbury; for an entirely uncritical account of this see Smith, 1836, p. 143. However, for an example of family conflict resulting from such a decision, see the recollection of Stephen Crisp, another of the first Quaker evangelists, in Jaffray, 1834, pp. 543–44. Although modified to some extent in his second edition, obeying the call of God over responsibility to family was famously justified by John Bunyan in the *Pilgrim's Progress*. See Hill, 1989, p. 227.

10. Thomas Fell, 1598–1658.

11. The first Sequestration Ordinance was passed in March 1643. Land belonging to bishops was ordered to be sold in 1647. The sale of land belonging to the Crown was begun in April 1649. Further Acts for the sale of land belonging to Royalists were passed in July 1651 and November 1652. See Aylmer, 1986, "Table of Events".

12. Blackwood, 1978, pp. 89, 94, 95, 96, 141. There were also allegations of dishonesty. On p. 94, and in n. 178 on p. 107, Blackwood, 1978, refers to documents at the Public Record Office to support the allegation of dishonesty.

13. Although in her testimony regarding George Fox, Margaret Fox (formerly Fell) recounts that he was taken to Swarthmoor by a companion (Bicentenary Edition, ii, p. 512), there is no indication as to who he was, whether he entered the house with George Fox, or whether he left him at that point and went on somewhere else.

14. This was a practice supported by both Royalists and Parliamentarians with regard to ministers who opposed their own views. In 1643, Parliament established a Committee for

Plundered Ministers, whose express purpose was to replace clergy loyal to King Charles. Though the ejected men were described as "scandalous", the term referred mainly to their political and theological views, rather than to their personal morality. The Committee heard evidence, often from local parishioners, of their alleged misdeeds. If the allegations were proved, the minister was removed from his position and his goods and monies were sequestrated. William Lampitt, together with Richard Baxter and many of those who sought refuge in Coventry, were among Puritans who suffered the same situation in reverse.

15. "Margaret Fell to Priest Camelford, 1653". Spence MS, iii, p. 135 (LSF).

16. Although Margaret Fell recorded her birth as occurring in 1614, she gave no indication of either the day or the month.

17. Fell, 1710, *A Brief Relation*, p. 2.

18. "Testimony of Margaret Fox, concerning her late husband". Appendix to the Bicentenary Edition of George Fox's *Journal*.

19. "For he is not a Jew, which is one outwardly; neither *is that* circumcision, which is outward in the flesh: But he *is* a Jew, which is one inwardly; and circumcision *is that* of the heart, in the spirit, *and* not in the letter; whose praise *is* not of men, but of God" (Romans 2:29).

20. "Testimony of Margaret Fox, concerning her late husband". Appendix to the Bicentenary Edition of George Fox's *Journal*.

21. "Testimony of Margaret Fox, concerning her late husband". Appendix to the Bicentenary Edition of George Fox's *Journal*.

22. John Sawrey, of Plumpton Hall, Ulverston. See Blackwood, 1978, pp. 73, 86. In 1653 Sawrey was appointed to the Nominated Parliament.

23. "Testimony of Margaret Fox, concerning her late husband". Appendix to the Bicentenary Edition of George Fox's *Journal*.

24. "Testimony of Margaret Fox, concerning her late husband". Appendix to the Bicentenary Edition of George Fox's *Journal*.

25. "Testimony of Margaret Fox, concerning her late husband". Appendix to the Bicentenary Edition of George Fox's *Journal*, pp. 511–19.

26. "Testimony of Margaret Fox, concerning her late husband". Appendix to the Bicentenary Edition of George Fox's *Journal*.

27. "Testimony of Margaret Fox, concerning her late husband". Appendix to the Bicentenary Edition of George Fox's *Journal*.

28. The Quaker meeting at Swarthmoor Hall was kept until 1690 when George Fox provided a small meeting house nearby to be used in perpetuity.
29. Spence MS, iii, pp. 24–26 (LSF). The letter was signed by Margaret Fell, Thomas Salthouse, Ann Clayton, Mary Askew, Margaret (junior) and Bridget Fell, and William Caton.
30. Spence MS, iii, pp. 24–26 (LSF).
31. Spence MS, iii, pp. 24–26 (LSF). The endorsement is in George Fox's handwriting.
32. The only other reference to Jane Holmes is by Richard Farnsworth. See Braithwaite, *Beginnings*, fn. 5, p. 72.
33. "Thomas Aldam to George Fox, 1652" (no month given), Swarthmore Colln, i, 373 (LSF).
34. For Elizabeth Hooton it was her second sentence; a similar action in 1651 had earned her a sentence at Derby. See Besse, *Sufferings*, i, p. 137.
35. William Dewsbury felt called to leave home and family on behalf of the Children of Light in October 1652.
36. *First Publishers of Truth*, 1907, p. 290.
37. "Richard Farnsworth to Two Friends, 1653" (no month given), *Letters of Early Friends*, 1841, pp. 216–18.
38. *Short Journal*, p. 22.
39. There are many instances of early Quakers being accused of witchcraft. The healing at Elizabeth Hooton's house in 1649 was accompanied by rumours of such. George Fox was accused by his former fellow-prisoner, John Fretwell, of bewitching him at Derby, and by Christopher Marshall, minister of James Nayler's former Independent church at West Ardsley, of carrying bottles which bewitched people into following him (Cambridge, i, p. 38). After George Fox's arrest in 1654 he was accused on his arrival in London of bewitching people with ribbons (Cambridge, i, p. 169). However, it was a common belief at the time, and one to which George Fox himself subscribed. In 1653, as he travelled north to Carlisle, presumably on the basis of what he believed to be his gift of discernment, he accused "some wicked women in a field", and later two other women, of being witches (Cambridge, i, pp. 110, 113).
40. Bugg, *A Finishing Stroke*, 1712, p. 241.
41. Hebrews 2:11; Ephesians 5:30.
42. 1 John 3:2; 1 John 4:17; Ephesians 4:1–13.
43. "The Humble Petition of Several Gentlemen, Justices of the

Peace, Ministers of the Gospel, and People, within the County of Lancashire whose names are subscribed", Besse, *Sufferings*, i, p. 301. (The petition, however, was never sent to London.)

44. "Saul's Errand to Damascus", Besse, *Sufferings*, i, p. 301.

45. *Journal*, Bicentenary Edition, i, pp. 152–53.

46. From the beginning of her involvement with the Quaker movement Margaret Fell took a leading role. Her epistles are a tribute to an extraordinary intellect and a grasp of theology equal, and in many cases, superior to many of her male colleagues. Her journeys throughout England, her long periods of imprisonment, and her later work on behalf of the imprisoned George Fox, are also indications of her courage and perseverance. That she oversaw the long-term organization of the Quaker movement also proves her to have been an unusually capable administrator. However, to dwell to any large extent on Margaret Fell's achievements is outside the scope of this book.

47. See "Thomas Aldam to Friends", Swarthmoor Colln, iii, p. 40 (LSF); and "Richard Farnsworth to Two Friends", 1653, in *Letters of Early Friends*, 1841, pp. 216–18.

48. John 15:14.

Chapter 7: Newes Coming Up Out of the North

1. George Fox, "To Friends, to be faithful, and Valiant in the Lord" (Epistle), 1652.

2. George Fox, "To Friends in the Ministry" (Epistle), 1653.

3. George Fox, "To Whom It May Concern: Friends, concerning the Light, etc." (Epistle), 1653.

4. George Fox, "To Friends, that their Minds go not out from the Spirit of God" (Epistle), 1653.

5. George Fox, "To Friends at Kendal" (Epistle), 1652.

6. George Fox, "Dear Hearts, Brethren and Babes in Christ ..." (Epistle), 1652.

7. George Fox, "To Friends, to stand still in Troubles, and see the Strength of the Lord" (Epistle), 1652.

8. George Fox, "To the Flock of God about Sedburgh" (Epistle), 1652.

9. George Fox, "To Friends, to be faithful and Valiant in the Lord" (Epistle), 1653; "To Friends in the Ministry" (Epistle), 1653.

10. George Fox, "To a Suffering Friend" (Epistle), 1653.

11. Anthony Pearson, 1628–70. His home, Ramshaw Hall, was near St Helen's Auckland, County Durham, known in that period as

Bishoprick. Pearson became secretary to Sir Arthur Haselrig in 1648, and Clerk and Registrar of the Committee for Compounding in March 1649. In February 1652 (new style) he became Sequestration Commissioner for Durham.

12. Arthur Haselrig, 1601–61. Haselrig was heir to extensive estates in the Midlands and served as a Member for Leicestershire in the Short and the Long Parliaments. He was one of the Five Members whom King Charles attempted to arrest in January 1642. A committed republican, he approved the overthrow of the monarchy, and served with distinction during the Civil War, becoming governor of Newcastle in 1647. In 1648 and 1650, he took part in Cromwell's Scottish campaigns.

13. Like Thomas Fell, neither Haselrig nor Pearson were above reproach. Despite accusations of corruption by John Lilburne, Haselrig had added to his already considerable wealth by the acquisition of sequestered Royalist estates. As Clerk and Registrar to the Committee on Compounding, and as Sequestration Commissioner for the county of Durham, Anthony too, used his position to enrich himself (*Dictionary of National Biography*).

14. *The Perfect Pharise under Monkish Holines*, 1654.

15. "Edward Burrough to George Fox, 7 February 1654", Swarthmoor Colln, iii, p. 14 (LSF).

16. Since Nathaniel Stephens was also assisted in 1654 by ministers from elsewhere, it seems reasonable to assume that this was to some extent a common practice among Puritan clergy fearing invasion of their churches by the Children of Light.

17. *Short Journal*, p. 27.

18. *Short Journal*, p. 29.

19. *Short Journal*, p. 31.

20. *Short Journal*, p. 32.

21. *Short Journal*, pp. 32–33.

22. It was also known as the Barebones Parliament after one of its leading members, the London merchant, Praise-God Barbon.

23. As well as providing an income for the clergy, and confirming the property holdings of the church, the rights to many tithes had been bought by laymen or by academic institutions. Some of the tithes from Dentdale, for example, were owned by the University of Oxford. The rights to such tithes could be sold by their lay owners and also bequeathed to children and other relatives.

24. Revelation 20. The Fifth Monarchists based their belief on a

calculation that there had been 1,656 years between the creation and the great flood described in Genesis 6 – 8. Since the same number of years had passed from the birth of Christ to 1656, they were convinced that this would see the advent of the Millennium. See Capp, 1972, p. 105.

25. Journals of the House of Commons VIII, p. 363. Quoted in Fraser, 2002, p. 560.

26. The Instrument of Government of 1653 was England's first written constitution.

27. George Fox, "Concerning Tithes" (Epistle), 1653.

28. George Fox, "Concerning Tithes" (Epistle), 1653.

29. "Again, ye have heard that it hath been said by them of old time, Thou shalt not forswear thyself, but shalt perform unto the Lord thine oaths: But I say unto you, Swear not at all; neither by heaven; for it is God's throne: Nor by the earth; for it is his footstool: neither by Jerusalem; for it is the city of the great King. Neither shalt thou swear by thy head, because thou canst not make one hair white or black. But let your communication be, Yea, yea; Nay, nay: for whatsoever is more than these cometh of evil" (Matthew 5:33–37).

30. *Short Journal*, p. 34.

31. There are no reliable numbers from this period. The enthusiastic letters of the evangelists which speak of huge crowds nevertheless suggest that many individuals joined the movement. Quakerism at this stage was a movement rather than an organized sect.

32. *First Publishers of Truth*, 1907, p. 295.

33. "William Dewsbury to Friends (About 1653)", Swarthmoor Colln, iii, p. 19 (LSF).

34. Braithwaite, *Beginnings*, p. 140.

35. Regarding Cumberland, see *Letters of Early Friends*, p. 312. (NB: Though these are called General Meetings, the inference is that they were meetings for business, rather than worship, and like the Preston Patrick meetings of the Seekers, they were comprised of "delegates", probably the most committed members who were willing to travel in order to meet with colleagues from a particular region. The word "Elder" may or may not have been used at the time.)

36. At this time County Durham was known as Bishoprick.

37. "Gervase Benson to George Fox and James Nayler", London,

29th of 9th month 1653 (November new style), *Letters of Early Friends*, 1841, pp. 2–3.

38. Quoted in Braithwaite, *Beginnings*, p. 156.

39. George Fox, *Newes Coming Up Out of the North*, London, 1654.

40. "Thomas Aldam to George Fox, 1653" (no month given), Swarthmoor Colln, iii, p. 39 (LSF).

41. Cambridge *Journal*, I, p. 141.

42. Luke 10:1–12.

43. George Fox, "To All Friends in the Ministry, 1654", Cambridge *Journal*, i, pp. 142–47.

44. The Kendal Fund was established in June 1654. The records, which are still extant, show that in the first few months the receipts came only from Westmorland and from Margaret Fell herself. Over the next three years, monies came from Westmorland, Cumberland, North Lancashire and the Sedburgh district, as well as from Yorkshire and Durham. During the first three years, approximately £270 was collected and disbursed, a sum roughly equivalent to £21,600 (Bank of England figures, November 2006); see Braithwaite, *Beginnings*, p. 317.

45. John Thurloe, 1616–68. The son of Thomas Thurloe, rector of Abbot's Roding in Essex, rose to high office under the Commonwealth. In 1655, Thurloe was also appointed Postmaster-General, with full powers to intercept correspondence.

46. Morgan Lloyd (or Llwyd), 1619–59. That Morgan shared the Fifth Monarchist view regarding the dating of the Millennium to 1656, see Capp, 1972, p. 105.

47. The two who travelled to Wrexham, in October 1653, were John Lawson of Lancaster, and Richard Hubberthorne. Braithwaite, *Beginnings*, p. 123.

48. The Act of Elizabeth (St. 39 Eliz. Cap. 4) was designed for the punishment of rogues, vagabonds and sturdy beggars (i.e. those deemed able to work but who were regarded as choosing not to) and allowed magistrates to remove them from being a charge in the areas under their control. However, it also encouraged the view that such folk were "workshy" rather than unemployed.

49. Isaiah 20:2–6.

50. James Nayler maintained that those who went naked often did it contrary to their own wills, believing that the command was that of the Spirit. It was also a view endorsed by George Fox, who in 1652 told the people of Ulverston that one who had walked

naked before them had been a figure of their nakedness, a sign that they were naked rather than being covered with the truth.

51. *First Publishers of Truth*, 1907, p. 213.

52. George Fox, *To All Who Would Know the Way to the Kingdom*, London, 1654.

53. Fraser, 2002, p. 717.

54. Fraser, 2002, p. 644.

55. Early in 1655, Royalist conspirators planned a series of coordinated uprisings against the Protectorate. Armed insurrections were to take place at various locations around the country on 8 March. The Earl of Rochester and Sir Joseph Wagstaff crossed to England on 19 February to direct the insurrection, while Charles II moved to Middelburg in the expectation of crossing to England when it gathered force. After details of the conspiracy were discovered by John Thurloe's agents, several of the key conspirators were arrested. Believing that there was still enough support to proceed, Rochester encouraged the rising to go ahead. In the event, only a few isolated groups, one of them in Wiltshire under the leadership of Colonel John Penruddock, attempted to carry out the design, all of which in the end failed. (See Chapter 8.)

56. No firm evidence for a Royalist–Leveller plot was ever produced. Overton was finally released in 1659, but was arrested again in 1660 after the Restoration. He was imprisoned in Chepstow Castle until January 1664, after which he was sent to Jersey, where he remained until December 1671. Wildman was released in June 1656 after agreeing to become a double-agent for John Thurloe. After the Restoration he was imprisoned for six years, accused of involvement in Republican plots. He was imprisoned again in 1683 after being accused of involvement in the Rye House plot to assassinate Charles II and the Duke of York, but was discharged early in 1684. In 1685, after involvement with Monmouth's Rebellion he fled to the Netherlands where he established links with William of Orange and became a propagandist on William's behalf. He returned to England with William and Mary in 1688 and became Postmaster General. He was knighted in 1692.

57. Although Harrison was released after a few days, he was arrested again some months later. Between 1653 and 1658 he was imprisoned four times on suspicion of involvement in various plots and insurrections.

58. George Fox was not the only radical to issue a declaration of peaceful intentions. See Capp, 1972, p. 101.

59. "To Oliver Cromwell, by G.ff.", Cambridge *Journal*, pp. 163–64.

60. "G.F. to Oliver Cromwell", Cambridge *Journal*, pp. 161–62.

61. Romans 13. In the Geneva Bible version of this chapter (i.e. the Bible largely used by Puritans at the time), the text is as follows: "²Whosoever therefore resisteth the power, resisteth the ordinance of God; and they that resist, shall receive to themselves condemnation. ³For Magistrates are not to be feared *for* good works, but *for* evil. Wilt thou then be without fear of the power? Do well, so shalt thou have praise of the same. ⁴For he is the minister of God for thy wealth, but if thou do evil, fear: for he beareth not the sword for nought: for he is the minister of God to take vengeance on him that doeth evil." For the Baptist Confession of 1644, see Lumpkin, 1969, pp. 143–71. The role of magistrates, as set out in Romans, was also emphasized in the Westminster Confession of Faith, adopted briefly in England in 1660.

Chapter 8: Horrid Blasphemy

1. Isabel Buttery seems to have been known to James Nayler, and was possibly a native of Wakefield. Braithwaite, *Beginnings*, p. 157.

2. "Francis Howgill to Robert Widders", London, 23rd of 7th month (9th month new style) 1654, *Letters of Early Friends*, 1841, pp. 18–20.

3. "Edward Burrough and F. Howgill to Margaret Fell", London, 27th of 1st month (3rd month new style) 1655, *Letters of Early Friends*, 1841, pp. 25–27.

4. "Edward Burrough and F. Howgill to Margaret Fell", London, 27th of 1st month (3rd month new style) 1655, *Letters of Early Friends*, 1841, pp. 25–27. "Gathered people" refers to gathered churches – see Chapter 2, p. 48.

5. "Alexander Parker to Margaret Fell", London, 10th of 3rd month (5th month new style) 1655, *Letters of Early Friends*, 1841, pp. 30–32.

6. "Francis Howgill to Margaret Fell", London, 21st of 3rd month 1655, *Letters of Early Friends*, 1841, pp. 32–34.

7. Crouch, William, *Posthuma Christiana*, 1712, p. 26.

8. "Edward Burrough and F. Howgill to Margaret Fell", London,

27th of 1st month (3rd month new style) 1655, *Letters of Early Friends*, 1841, pp. 25–27.

9. For example, see Dewsbury, William, *A True Prophecie of the Mighty Day of the Lord ... which ... shall overspread this Nation, and all Nations of the World*, London, 1655.

10. John Rogers, c. 1627–1670.

11. Christopher Feake, c. 1612–1682.

12. Capp, 1972, pp. 103–104.

13. Capp, 1972, p. 101.

14. Capp, 1972, p. 102.

15. Capp, 1972, p. 102.

16. "Edward Burrough and Francis Howgill to Margaret Fell", London, 29th of 6th month (8th month new style) 1654, *Letters of Early Friends*, 1841, pp. 15–18.

17. "Francis Howgill to Margaret Fell", London (date not given, but a reference in Cambridge *Journal*, ii, p. 329, indicates 14th of 2nd month (April) 1655), *Letters of Early Friends*, 1841, pp. 35–36. Miles Halhead (of Westmorland) and Thomas Salthouse were arrested in Devon in mid 1655 and after being charged with vagrancy served two weeks in Exeter prison. After returning later, and establishing a meeting at Plymouth, they were arrested again, and charged under the Proclamation of February 1655 with disturbing the peace. Insisting on their innocence, the two refused to give bail. They remained in prison at Exeter until May 1656 (Braithwaite, *Beginnings*, pp. 203–204). Thomas Stubbs should not be confused with John Stubbs, who is also mentioned in this chapter.

18. John Camm to George Fox, 1654, probably September. Quoted in Barclay, *Inner Life etc.*, 1876, pp. 308–309.

19. Mary Fisher and Ann Austin were the pioneers of Quaker work on the American continent.

20. The two men eventually left from Newcastle in September 1655. After arriving in Flushing, they preached in English through the streets, and then went on to Middleburg and Rotterdam (see Braithwaite, *Beginnings*, p. 407).

21. In 1654 James Parnell was first arrested in Cambridge and served a sentence of several weeks.

22. Exodus 34:29.

23. The description of James Nayler is taken from the record of his London trial in 1656. See Braithwaite, *Beginnings*, p. 243.

24. "Alexander Parker to Margaret Fell", London, 3rd of 7th month

(9th month new style) 1655, *Letters of Early Friends*, 1841, pp. 36–38.

25. "James Nayler to Margaret Fell", London, 3rd of 9th month (11th month new style); the year is endorsed by George Fox as 1655. *Letters of Early Friends*, 1841, pp. 38–39.

26. "The Western Design": after the ending of the Anglo-Dutch war in April 1654, Cromwell and the Protectorate Council of State turned their attention to England's traditional enemies, France and Spain, who were at war with one another in the Spanish Netherlands. After revising the initial hostility that followed the execution of Charles I, both nations sought an alliance with the increasingly powerful English Protectorate. Though the Council of State was divided over which nation to support, the majority, including Oliver Cromwell, favoured an alliance with France against Spain. Eventually, Cromwell decided to pursue a commercial treaty with France rather than a military alliance against Spain. Although he abandoned the idea of intervening in the current ongoing European military conflict, Cromwell secretly planned an attack on Spanish territories in the West Indies, which was put into operation in 1655. The operation was not a success. Jamaica, however, was seized in 1655 and remained in English hands. Major colonization began after the Restoration.

27. John Disbrowe, who was also brother-in-law to the Protector, was responsible for Cornwall, Devon, Dorset, Gloucestershire, Somerset and Wiltshire. His colleague, Major-General William Goffe, oversaw Berkshire, Hampshire and Sussex.

28. *First Publishers of Truth*, 1907, p. 20.

29. Cambridge *Journal*, i, pp. 206–207.

30. Peter Ceely was a member of a Puritan family from St Ives.

31. Pyott, Edward, *The West Answering to the North*, London, 1657.

32. Manuscripts differ over this figure, being between 400, 4,000 and 40,000. Nickalls, 1997, fn. 1, p. 246.

33. The fine of twenty marks was equivalent to £13.6.8d – somewhere in the region of £1,094 today (Bank of England, November 2006).

34. Braithwaite, *Beginnings*, pp. 237/8.

35. *Journal*, Bicentenary Edition, i, pp. 315–17.

36. Martha Simmonds was wife to Thomas Simmonds, and sister to Giles Calvert, the two chief printers of Quaker books.

37. Farmer, 1657, p. 10.

38. 2 Kings 4:27, 37.

39. "William Farnsworth to Margaret Fell", 5 August 1656, Swarthmoor Colln, iii, p. 56 (LSF).

40. Dorcas Erbury was either the widow or daughter of William Erbury.

41. "Richard Roper to Margaret Fell", 20 October 1656, Swarthmoor Colln, iii, p. 131 (LSF). See also 1 Corinthians 1.

42. James's friend Robert Rich claims that prior to this George Fox demanded that James kiss his hand. When James refused, George proffered his boot. See Rich, 1678, p. 37.

43. Spence MS, iii, p. 38 (LSF). The whole letter is quoted in Ross, 1996, Appendix Nine, pp. 396–98.

44. The letter was dated Swarthmoor, 15 October 1656. James was released at some point between the 18th and the 20th of the same month. Thus it arrived too late for James probably ever to have seen it and was perhaps returned to Margaret Fell. Ross, 1996, p. 106. Whether it would have made any difference to subsequent events, however, is conjecture.

45. On 24 October 1656.

46. "Sabaoth": a Hebrew term used in the New Testament (Romans 9:29; James 5:4), also in various Christian hymns; also in the title of God, translated in the Bible as "Lord of Hosts", as in Isaiah 1:9 and several of the Psalms.

47. Cobbett's *State Trials*, v, cols. 830–31; quoted in Braithwaite, *Beginnings*, p. 248. These phrases were also discussed at length at Westminster and are recorded in the Parliamentary Journal kept by Thomas Burton. See below.

48. "Anthony Pearson and Gervase Benson", 9th month, 18th day (November), Westminster. Swarthmoor Colln, iii, p. 78 (LSF).

49. Davies, 1955, pp. 17–18.

50. The Instrument of Government (published at the end of 1653) defined religious liberty as follows:

> "XXXVII. That such as profess faith in God by Jesus Christ (though differing in judgement from the doctrine, worship, or discipline publicly held forth) shall not be restrained from, but shall be protected in, the profession of the faith and exercise of their religion; so as they abuse not this liberty to the civil injury of others and to the actual disturbance of the public peace on their parts: provided this liberty be not extended

to Popery or Prelacy, nor to such as, under the profession of Christ, hold forth and practice licentiousness.

"XXXVIII. That all laws, statute, and ordinances to the contrary of the aforesaid liberty, shall be esteemed as null and void."

51. Burton, 1828, p. 69.
52. Colonel William Sydenham of Wynford Eagle near Maiden Newton in Dorset, d. 1661.
53. Burton, 1828, p. 62.
54. Henry Lawrence was elected President of the Council of State in December 1653.
55. Burton, 1828, p. 25.
56. Burton, 1828, p. 63.
57. A resolution that James Nayler should hang was defeated by 96 votes to 82.
58. Burton, 1828, p. 155.
59. Nayler, *Works*, George Whitehead's Introduction, p. xvi.
60. Braithwaite, *Beginnings*, p. 268.
61. Nayler, *Works*, George Whitehead's Introduction, p. xii.
62. *Journal*, Bicentenary Edition, i, p. 343.
63. For the meeting at Balby, and its recommendation, see *Letters of Early Friends*, 1841, pp. 276–82. It is pointed out in a footnote to p. 311 of Braithwaite, *Beginnings*, that although the citation given in "Letters etc." states that this document was perhaps issued by a meeting held in 1657 at John Crook's house at Bedfordshire, it was in fact issued at Balby in November 1656.
64. "Thomas Holme to Margaret Fell", 16 April 1657, Swarthmoor Colln, i, p. 196 (LSF).
65. Davies, 1955, p. 223.
66. As well as Captain Davenport, George also mentions a Lieutenant Foster, a Lieutenant Dove and a Captain Watkinson, as well as referring to several other officers and soldiers whom he does not name.
67. There seems to be some difference on this issue. While some historians have alleged that there was a general purge of Quakers at this time, Godfrey Davies, in his *Restoration*, 1955, p. 223, maintains that in the autumn of 1657, Monck simply supported the actions of senior officers. In this respect I have followed Davies.

68. Henry Vane, 1613–62. Vane was widely admired among radicals, and George Fox perhaps does him a disservice.

69. Thomas Ellwood, in his more polished version of the *Journal* (see Note 1 to Chapter 1 above), described the Bedfordshire meeting as "a general Yearly Meeting for the whole nation". By this time, the Quaker system of yearly meetings, involving delegates from a wide area, had been established. Looking back at the huge meeting in Bedfordshire, it probably seemed appropriate to label it as such. However, whether it involved representatives from various local meetings is unknown. In the *Journal* dictated to Thomas Lower (the Spence MS), George Fox's only comment regarding the meeting's structure is that he spoke there to friends who were in the ministry. Whether this included the whole gathering, or was simply a part of it, is not clear.

70. John Crook lived at Beckerings Park, near Ampthill in Bedfordshire.

71. *Journal*, Bicentenary Edition, i, pp. 418–21.

72. George Fox, *The Law of God, the Rule for Law-makers*, London, 1658.

73. Charles Harvey was a groom of the bedchamber.

Chapter 9: The Good Old Cause

1. Davies, 1955, p. 8.

2. "From the Armies in England, Scotland and Ireland", quoted in Davies, 1955, p. 8.

3. *First Publishers of Truth*, 1907, p. 351 (the date "November 1657" should be corrected to 27 November 1658 – Braithwaite, *Beginnings*, p. 453).

4. The Second Protectorate Parliament had been dissolved by Oliver Cromwell in February 1658.

5. This is a very brief outline of an extremely complex situation. For a detailed account of the events leading to the Restoration of the English monarchy, see Davies, 1955.

6. Richard Cromwell inherited Army pay arrears amounting to some £900,000, as well as a national budget deficit of £500,000.

7. The crisis had brought hundreds of junior officers to London. See Davies, 1955.

8. "Humble Representation and Petition of the General Council of the Officers of the Armies of England, Scotland and Ireland", quoted in Davies, 1955, pp. 76–77. The petition seems not to have been published separately, but was printed in the official

newspapers (in the *Publick Intelligencer* for 11/18 April) and also reprinted in the old *Parliamentary History*, XXI, pp. 340–45. See Davies, 1955, p. 77, fn. 32.

9. "Humble Representation and Petition of the General Council of the Officers of the Armies of England, Scotland and Ireland", quoted in Davies, 1955, p. 77.

10. The large meetings were at the Bull and Mouth, and at Horslydown, south of the Thames.

11. Braithwaite, *Beginnings*, pp. 454–55.

12. "A true Copie of a paper delivered to Lt. G. Fleetwood … to be communicated to the General Council of Officers", London, 1659.

13. Davies, 1955, p. 87.

14. There were 42 surviving members including the Speaker, William Lenthall.

15. Davies, 1955, p. 92.

16. George Fox, *To the Parliament of the Comon-Wealth of England; Fifty nine Particulars laid down for the Regulating things, and the taking away of Oppressing Laws and Oppressors, and to ease the Oppressed*, London, 1659.

17. Davies, 1955, p. 115. The Militia Act applied to London at the beginning of July, and all other counties in England and Wales at the end of the month.

18. Reay, 1985, p. 87.

19. At the conclusion of the discussion on toleration, Parliament resolved that all who believed in the Trinity and in the Scriptures as the revealed word of God should be encouraged and protected, provided they did not disturb the worship of others, or practise licentiousness in the name of religion.

20. Davies, 1955, p. 120; Reay, 1985, p. 83.

21. Davies, 1955, p. 121; William Prynne never relinquished his opposition to Catholicism. For a conversation he had on the issue with Samuel Pepys, see Pepys' Diary under the date 26 May 1662.

22. Davies, 1955, p. 96; the debarment included all those who had refused to take an oath of allegiance to the Commonwealth, as well as those shut out for various other reasons since 1648.

23. Georger Fox, *The Lambs Officer Etc.*, London, 1659, p. 13.

24. Parker to Fox, 7 August 1659, Swarthmoor Colln, iii, p. 143 (LSF).

25. Reay, 1985, p. 88.

26. "Mr Mordaunt to the Lord Chancellor Hyde", Clarendon, pp. 489–90; "Mr Mordaunt to the King", Clarendon, pp. 488–89.

27. *Mercurius Politicus*, 21–28 July 1659.

28. Davies, 1955, pp. 125/6.

29. "A Letter from Sir George Booth to a Friend", quoted in Davies, 1955, p. 136.

30. *A Phanatique League and Covenant Solemnly enter'd into by the Assertors of the Good Old Cause*, London, 1659 (British Library). Among the 41 supposed signatories to this satirical document were: Luke Robinson, John Lambert, Hugh Peter, Christopher Feake, William Lilly, William Kiffin, Barbon (*sic*), Thomas Harrison, Robert Tichborne, Charles Fleetwood, Henry Vane, Isaac Penington, Arthur Haselrig, Vasavor Powell, John (George) Fox, Bulstrode Whitlock, John Disbrowe, and James Nayler.

31. "A Declaration of the Maids of the City of London, &c.", London, 1659 (British Library).

32. "The Derby House Petition", Davies, 1955, p. 147.

33. The earlier petition was drawn up in May 1659. See Davies, 1955, p. 97.

34. Rich, *Hidden Things Brought to Light*, 1678, pp. 29–30. In this particular accusation, Richard Rich referred to accusations made previously by John Harwood.

35. Rich, *Hidden Things*, 1678, p. 29.

36. Although George Fox denied the allegations relating to the magistracy, Harwood maintained that even if his name was not attached to relevant documents, he was more than aware of them.

37. "James Nayler to Margaret Fell" (no date but endorsed by George Fox as 1658; the date is clearly wrong, as James was released in September 1659, during which time George himself was at Reading), *Letters of Early Friends*, 1841, pp. 58–59.

38. For details of this purge, see Davies, 1955, Chapter 10.

39. Davies, 1955, p. 170.

40. Davies, 1955, p. 171.

41. Davies, 1955, p. 157.

42. Reay, 1985, p. 96. In the Cambridge *Journal*, i, p. 341, George Fox refers to "wilde-fire". Presumably it was a form of home-made incendiary or explosive.

43. The village went on to give its name to Monck's army, who became known as Coldstreamers.

44. Reay, 1985, p. 98.

45. Burrough, Edward, *To the Whole English Army*, London, 1659.

46. Pepys' *Diary*, ed. Latham, 2003, p. 16.

47. "Henry Fell to Margaret Fell", London, 7th of 12th month 1659 (new style 2nd month 1660), *Letters of Early Friends*, 1841, pp. 73–74.

48. This was alleged by Robert Rich. See Rich, 1678, p. 37.

49. Braithwaite, W. C., "The Penal Laws affecting Early Friends etc.", in *First Publishers of Truth*, 1907, p. 353.

50. Or if they were, their names are unknown.

51. "Richard Hubberthorne to George Fox", London, 29th of 3rd month (new style 5th month) 1660, *Letters of Early Friends*, 1841, pp. 80–82.

52. *First Publishers of Truth*, 1907, p. 13.

53. Besse, *Sufferings*, i, pp. 488–89.

54. The meeting at Skipton was described by George Fox as "a general meeting". Although it is not entirely clear what was meant, after this meeting the general or Yearly Meeting was moved to London as being a more convenient place. See Braithwaite, *Beginnings*, pp. 335, 337.

55. Henry Porter, 1613–66, Mayor of Lancaster in 1659 and 1661. In 1660 he was appointed Constable of Lancaster Castle. He was also an MP for the borough for a few years from 1654.

56. *Mittimus*: an ancient term meaning a writ committing someone to prison.

57. "The Sum of such Particulars as Charged against George Fox at Lancaster Castle", 1660, quoted in Cambridge, i, pp. 375–80.

58. *Journal*, Bicentenary Edition, i, pp. 482–83.

59. "Margaret Fell to the King", Spence MS, iii, p. 105 (LSF).

60. Ann Curtis had also visited George earlier at Lancaster. See Cambridge, i, p. 243.

61. Hubberthorne, Richard, "Something that lately passed in discourse between the King and R.H.", in Hubberthorne, *A Collection etc.*, London, 1665.

62. All but 100 persons and estates received pardons. Together with the regicides, those who did not were Sir Henry Vane, tried in 1662 for high treason and beheaded on Tower Hill on 16 June; Sir Arthur Haselrig, who died in the Tower in January 1661 before he could be brought to trial for treason; and John Lambert, imprisoned for life and who died in February 1684 at the age of 64, having spent the last 24 years of his life in prison. Francis Hacker, who arrested George Fox in Leicestershire in 1655, who

had earlier supervised the guard on Charles I's scaffold, was hanged at Tyburn on 19 October 1660. He was not drawn, perhaps because his brother had remained loyal to the monarchy.

63. The conclusions were issued as the Worcester House Declaration.

64. "Something that passed betwixt the King and me, Thomas Moore of Hartswood, in the County of Surrey", 14th of 10th month (new style 12th month) 1660, *Letters of Early Friends*, 1841, pp. 92–95.

65. "Richard Ellsworth to Secretary Nicholas, Bristoll", 21 November 1660, *Extracts from State Papers*, 1913, p. 122.

66. "Something that passed betwixt the King and me, Thomas Moore of Hartswood, in the County of Surrey", 14th of 10th month (new style 12th month) 1660, *Letters of Early Friends*, 1841, pp. 92–95.

Chapter 10: War on Terror

1. Pepys' *Diary*, ed. Latham, 2003, p. 109.

2. Richard Browne, b. before 1616 – 24 September 1669. In October 1645 and in December 1648, Browne was elected Member of Parliament for High Wycombe, Buckinghamshire. He was Sheriff of London between 1648 and 1649, Alderman of London between June 1648 and December 1649, and Member of Parliament for London between 1656 and 1660. He was Lord Mayor of London between 1660 and 1661. Invested as a Knight on 29 May 1660, he was appointed Major-General in 1661 in the service of the City of London. He was again an Alderman between November 1663 and March 1663/64. Between 1661 and 1669 Sir Richard was MP for Ludgershall.

3. Braithwaite, *The Second Period of Quakerism*, 1961, p. 9.

4. Isaac Penington, 1616–79, became a Quaker in 1658, and was the eldest son of Sir Isaac Penington, zealous Puritan and merchant of London. John Whitehead was originally convinced by William Dewsbury in the early 1650s.

5. Spence MS, iii, p. 85 (LSF).

6. Margaret Fell returned to Swarthmoor in September.

7. According to the Julian Calendar then in use, the Declaration was produced in January 1660, i.e. the eleventh month of the year. Thus, although according to present calculations, it was produced in January 1661, it is known as the Declaration of 1660.

8. There is a document to be found in Margaret Fell, *A Brief Collection*, 1710, that has never, or rarely, been reproduced in full elsewhere. It is entitled "A Declaration and an Information from us the People of God called Quakers, to the present Governors, the King and both Houses of Parliament, and all whom it may concern. (This was delivered into the King's Hand, the 22nd Day of the Fourth Month, 1660, by M.F.)" Although there is no way of knowing, it could be that this document of June 1660 provided the basis for the famous "Peace Testimony" produced some months later.

9. *Journal*, Bicentenary Edition, vol. i, pp. 494–99.

10. Oliver Cromwell's head was placed on a spike at Westminster Hall. During a gale in the 1680s it blew down, and was picked up by a soldier who sold it later to a Cambridgeshire family. After a long and adventurous journey, it was finally installed in 1960 at the Lord Protector's old college, Sidney Sussex, Cambridge.

11. *Journal*, Bicentenary Edition, i, p. 494.

12. "George Fox to Friends of Passage", Swarthmoor Colln, vii, p. 111 (LSF).

13. John Perrot was convinced by Edward Burrough during the latter's earlier missionary work in Ireland.

14. It was as a member of this party that Mary Fisher of Selby made her famous visit to the Ottoman Sultan.

15. Quoted in Braithwaite, *Second Period*, pp. 232–33.

16. "Isaac Penington on John Perrott", Crosse Colln, p. 6 (LSF).

17. John 3:8.

18. See Chapter 3 of this work, p. 74.

19. Isaac Penington at this time lived at the Grange, Chalfont St Peter in Buckinghamshire.

20. *Journal*, Bicentenary Edition, i, pp. 519–20.

21. "A Proclamation of Grace, for the Inlargement of the People Called Quakers", *Extracts from State Papers*, 1913, pp. 132–33.

22. The Cavalier Parliament sat from May 1661 until January 1679.

23. Kishlansky, 1997, p. 229.

24. The Quaker Act. See Besse, *Sufferings*, i, pp. xi–xiii.

25. "A Brief Account of the Proceedings of Parliament Concerning the People Called Quakers", *Letters of Early Friends*, 1841, pp. 99–114.

26. Braithwaite, W. C., "The Penal Laws affecting early Friends in England", in *First Publishers of Truth*, 1907.

27. Babington, 1971, p. 55.

28. For the paper see *Journal*, Bicentenary Edition, i, p. 521.

29. Besse, *Sufferings*, i, p. 389.
30. *Short Journal*, pp. 61–62.
31. *Short Journal*, p. 62.
32. Thomas, third Viscount Beaumont of Swords in the peerage of Ireland. Died 1702.
33. *Short Journal*, p. 63.
34. *Short Journal*, p. 63.
35. The larger number is found in the *Short Journal*, an account written in Lancaster Prison between 1663 and 1664.
36. Ellwood, 1714, pp. 161–62.
37. "Ellis Hookes to Margaret Fell", London, 28th of 8th month (10th month new style) 1662, *Letters of Early Friends*, 1841, pp. 114–17.
38. After leaving London at the end of 1661, John Perrot travelled via Bristol to his home at Waterford before returning again to London in the spring of 1662. In June he was arrested under the Quaker Act and committed to Newgate. He accepted liberty on the condition of going into voluntary exile and sailed for Barbados in the autumn of the same year. He died in Jamaica in 1665.
39. "Edward Burrough to George Fox", ARB Colln, No. 171 (LSF).
40. *Journal*, Bicentenary Edition, i, p. 536.
41. *Short Journal*, p.66.
42. *Short Journal*, p. 67.
43. Sir Daniel Fleming, 1633–1701, of Rydal Hall. In his *Journal* George Fox says Fleming was a justice whose area of operation covered Westmorland and Lancashire (Cambridge, ii, p. 42).
44. "Daniel Fleming to Williamson", Kendall, Nov. 14. 63, *Extracts from State Papers*, 1913, p. 177.

Chapter 11: Prisoner of Conscience

1. A copy of the paper may be found in *Journal* Bicentenary, i, pp. 450–51; see also note 1 to p. 35, in Cambridge, ii, p. 388.
2. "Mary Fell to her Mother Margaret Fell, Mile-end Green, near London", 27th of 4th month, (6th month new style) 1664, *Letters of Early Friends*, 1841, pp. 129–31.
3. For persons who had been involved with the Friends earlier, see Braithwaite, *Second Period*, p. 30.
4. Richard Kirkby, c. 1625–1681, of Kirkby Hall in Furness. Justice of the County of Lancaster. During the Civil War the Kirkbys had lost land to sequestration. Blackwood, 1978, pp. 114, 141–42, and note 20 on p. 149.

5. The reference to Romans 13 was presumably one with which his hearers would all have been familiar.

6. Sir George Middleton, c. 1600–1673/74, of Leighton Hall, and lord of the manor of Yealand. Middleton was widely regarded as a harsh and unjust landlord. As well as losing land to sequestration, as a Catholic family, the Middletons had been fined heavily during the Commonwealth. Blackwood, 1978, pp. 20, 114, 141, and note 20 on p. 149.

7. *Short Journal*, p. 70.

8. *Short Journal*, p. 70.

9. *Short Journal*, p. 70.

10. *Short Journal*, p. 71. At this point the *Short Journal* reaches an end, concluding very nearly with the words, "And so I was sent to prison where now I am with 8 more." See also n. 1 to p. 71 in *Short Journal*, p. 293.

11. "Daniel Fleming to Joseph Williamson, Whitehall. Kendall, Jan. 16 63/64", *Extracts from State Papers*, 1913, p. 186. Sir Joseph Williamson was assistant to Sir Henry Bennet, Secretary of State, 1662–74. Bennet had succeeded Edward Nicholas, Secretary of State to Charles II between 1660 and 1662, and who had held the same office under Charles I, from 1641.

12. Kishlansky, 1997, pp. 234–35.

13. There were two judges on the bench, Thomas Twisden, and Christopher Turner. Although George mentions Turner at the beginning of the session, it is not clear from his account which judge was speaking. Francis Howgill appeared before Turner in August at Appleby.

14. Braithwaite, *Second Period*, p. 42.

15. Pepys' *Diary*, ed. Latham, 2003, pp. 413–14.

16. Baxter, ed. Keeble, 1974, p. 179.

17. Baxter, ed. Keeble, 1974, p. 189.

18. Baxter, ed. Keeble, 1974, p. 189.

19. Braithwaite, *Second Period*, pp. 41–42.

20. "Thomas Curtis to George Fox. Reading", 15th of 11th month 1664 (1st month 1665 new style), *Letters of Early Friends*, 1841, pp. 240–41.

21. Baxter, ed. Keeble, 1974, p. 190.

22. Journal, Bicentenary Edition, ii, p. 58.

23. Defoe, Daniel, ed. Wall, 2003, p. 118.

24. "Ellis Hookes to Margaret Fell. London", 7th of 9th month (11th month new style) 1665, Letters of Early Friends, 1841, pp. 153–54.

25. Baxter, ed. Keeble, 1974, pp. 195–96.
26. The Five Mile Act was the final piece of legislation in what is known as the Clarendon Code: four legal statutes passed between 1661 and 1665 which effectively re-established the supremacy of the Anglican Church after the interlude of Cromwell's Commonwealth, and which finally ended toleration for dissenting religions. The Code was named for Edward Hyde, 1st Earl of Clarendon, who was Charles II's Lord Chancellor. Clarendon enforced the laws despite his personal opposition to many of the provisions of the Code.

   (1) The Corporation Act (1661): required all municipal officials to take Anglican communion and to formally reject the Solemn League and Covenant of 1643. The effect was to exclude Nonconformists from public office.
   (2) The Act of Uniformity (1662): made use of the Book of Common Prayer compulsory in religious services. Upwards of 2,000 clergy refused to comply with this act, and were forced to resign their livings.
   (3) The Coventicle Act (1664): forbade unauthorized meetings for worship of more than five people who were not members of the same household. The purpose was to prevent dissenting religious groups from meeting.
   (4) The Five-Mile Act (1665): aimed at Nonconformist ministers, who were forbidden from coming within five miles of incorporated towns or the place of their former livings. They were also forbidden to teach in schools. This act was not rescinded until 1812.

27. Kishlansky, 1996, p. 235.
28. See note 8 to Chapter 4.
29. Fernando Fairfax, 1584–1648, father to Sir Thomas.
30. This Dr Cradock is not to be confused with the Dr Cradock of Coventry. See Cambridge, ii, p. 400, n. 2 to p. 97.
31. In 1653 the Commonwealth had made civil marriage legal. In 1661, at least some Quaker marriages were deemed legally acceptable (Sharman, 1991, p. 164). However, the whole issue of what did or did not constitute a "true" marriage continued to provoke anxiety.
32. John Audland died on 22 March 1664; Richard Farnsworth died in London in June 1666.

33. Pepys' *Diary*, ed. Latham, 2003, p. 662.
34. Christopher Fox died sometime before 1664.

Chapter 12: Gospel Order

1. The first hackney carriages appeared in 1634. The term derives from the French haquenée, an ambling horse or a hack. The first licences were issued in 1662.
2. George Fox refers to this practice in his *Journal*; see Cambridge, ii, p. 117.
3. Baxter, ed. Keeble, 1974, p. 197.
4. Before the Industrial Revolution these were small market towns. In the mid-1600s, for example, the population of Birmingham was about 7,000. Though the Population Census of 2001 numbered 977,087 people resident in Birmingham, this was later considered to be an underestimate. A revised estimate for mid-2001 gave the city's population as 984,600.
5. Gabriel Camelford, for example, who was ejected in 1662 from his living at Staveley, had become by 1669 the first pastor of the Baptist meeting house at Tottlebank, five miles from Ulverstone (Boulton, 1998, p. 175).
6. Baxter, ed. Keeble, 1974, p. 197.
7. "A Testimony from the Brethren, who were met together at London in the Third Month, 1666, to be Communicated to Faithful Friends and Elders in the Counties, by them to be Read in their Several Meetings, and Kept as a Testimony Among Them", *Letters of Early Friends*, 1841, pp. 318–24.
8. Reay, 1985, p. 10, estimates Quaker numbers within a decade of the mid-1650s as being somewhere between 35,000 and 60,000.
9. William Dewsbury was imprisoned on suspicion of involvement in the Fifth Monarchy uprising, and then in the northern plot. Arrested again late in 1663, he was imprisoned at Warwick.
10. "A Testimony from the Brethren", as note 7 above.
11. The five new meetings were Devonshire House, Horslydown or Southwark, Peel, Ratcliff and Westminster. A Two Week Meeting dating from 1656 became responsible for issues within London's city walls. This particular meeting eventually became the Gracechurch Street Monthly Meeting which then continued for nearly 120 years as a meeting with special responsibility for London's Quaker marriages.
12. "Another Letter from Stephen Crisp to the Mayor of Colchester", in Crisp, *Works*, London, 1694, p. 112.

13. Fell, Margaret, "A Letter sent to the King, from M.F.", *Works*, pp. 325–30.

14. Fell, Margaret, "An Epistle to the Flock of God", *Works*, pp. 293–98.

15. Fell, Margaret, "Women's speaking justified, proved, and allowed of by the Scripture, all such as speak by the spirit and power of the Lord Jesus, 1666", in *Works*.

16. 1 Corinithians 14:34.

17. Harwood, 1663, p. 7. On p. 336 of Cambridge, ii, George Fox states that Harwood was an "apostate from the Truth".

18. The school at Waltham Abbey was for young children, while that at Shacklewell was for girls. Eleven years after its founding the Waltham school was moved to Edmonton, then a village north of London.

19. Ross, 1996, pp. 77–78.

20. Kishlansky, 1997, p. 200.

21. Braithwaite, *Second Period*, p. 260.

22. 1 Kings 18.

23. Margaret Fell, *Works*, p. 8.

24. Ross, 1996, p. 219. In a footnote to this page, Ross states that "being disliked by large numbers of Friends", most copies of the Epistle were later destroyed. She quotes from a rare copy found in "Yearly Meeting Minutes, etc., 1668–1741", held at the Friends' Meeting House in Lancaster. However, it was also reprinted by Francis Bugg. See Braithwaite, *Second Period*, p. 263.

25. Margaret Fell also lost 50 acres of land left to her by Thomas Fell. She did, however, retain a one-third portion of the nearby estate of Marsh Grange left to her by her father. See Ross, 1998, p. 215.

26. William Penn, General-at-Sea, c. 1621–1670. The youngest son of Giles Penn, a merchant of Bristol whose family owned estates in Buckinghamshire and Gloucestershire, Penn went to sea, and was a ship's captain by 1642. He served in the Parliamentary navy during the First and Second Civil Wars and took part in Cromwell's campaigns in Ireland. Following the Restoration, Penn served Charles Stuart and later became a key advisor to James, Duke of York, in the administration of the Restoration navy. One of Penn's junior colleagues at the Navy Office was Samuel Pepys, who refers to him frequently in the diary. Although Penn took part in the Second Anglo-Dutch War (1664–67), after quarrelling with George Monck, now Duke of

Albemarle, he was obliged to resign his commission after being brought before Parliament to answer charges of seizing prizes illegally. He withdrew from public life and died in September 1670.

27. William Penn, 1644–1718, was the eldest son of the Admiral.
28. MS in Portfolio 10:53 (LSF); see also Revelation 21:11.

Chapter 13: Resist in the Power of God

1. *Journal*, Bicentenary Edition, ii, pp. 122–23.
2. Kishlansky, 1997, p. 245.
3. Braithwaite, *Second Period*, p. 7.
4. Staley, 1913, pp. 127–31.
5. Murray 1999, p. 160.
6. *Journal*, Bicentenary Edition, ii, p. 123.
7. *Journal*, Bicentenary Edition, ii, p. 122.
8. Sir William Starling was Lord Mayor of London 1669–70.
9. "For where two or three are gathered together in my name, there am I in the midst of them" (Matthew 18:20).
10. Walter Newton, possibly a member of the Newton family of Atherstone. See Cambridge *Journal*, n. 4 to p. 154 on p. 416.
11. See Revelation 19.
12. For more on George Fell see Ross, 1996, chapters 9 and 13.
13. Fell, Margaret, *Works*, p. 9.
14. Cadbury, Henry J., "Intercepted Correspondence of William Penn, 1670", *Pennsylvania Magazine*, Vol. LXX, January 1946.
15. Bugg, *A Finishing Stroke*, 1712, p. 241.
16. This was the fate of the Horslydown Meeting House in Southwark. Overseeing the demolition was the King's Surveyor, Christopher Wren.
17. "John Rous to Sarah Fell, Wansworth [*sic*]", 15th of 6th month (8th month new style) 1670, *Letters of Early Friends*, 1841, pp. 177–78.
18. "John Rous to Sarah Fell, Wansworth [*sic*]", 15th of 6th month (8th month new style) 1670, *Letters of Early Friends*, 1841, pp. 177–78.
19. In 1681, William Mead married Margaret Fox's daughter, Sarah Fell.
20. For a transcript of the Penn trial see Besse, I, pp. 416–26.
21. Braithwaite, *Second Period*, p. 294.
22. Calendar of State Papers, 1671, 171; Ext. 329, quoted in Kunze, 1994, p. 52.

23. Braithwaite, *Second Period*, pp. 77–78.
24. George Fox did not leave any record of his voyage, and thus the details are taken from a log kept by John Hull, which was later also used in part by Thomas Ellwood as if they had in fact been written by George Fox himself. In the Cambridge *Journal*, 1911, the Hull Log, together with various letters written from the Caribbean, is to be found between pp. 176 and 202 of the Second Volume.
25. Since the Treaty of Dover such rumour had been rife. So too were rumours of Louis' preparations for war on Holland. See Pennington, 1989, p. 508.
26. Possibly *Grampus griseus* (Risso's dolphin), although the term might also have referred to any large sea mammal that was not identifiable as a dolphin.
27. This point marks the end of John Hull's log.
28. The letter, dated "Barbadoes ye 1st of ye 10th mo. 71", is a copy and should read "9th mo." Quoted in Cambridge, ii, pp. 187–88. See also note 1 to this page on p. 429 of the volume.
29. John Hull's letter is quoted in Cambridge, ii, pp. 192–95.
30. Thomas, 1998, p. 202.
31. Thomas, 1998, p. 185.
32. Braithwaite, *Second Period*, p. 618.
33. The document is printed in Cambridge, ii, pp. 197–202.
34. Joshua 24:15.
35. John Hull's letter, Cambridge, ii, pp. 192–95.
36. "Barbados, 1st of 10th month, 1671". See note 29 above.
37. John Hull's letter, Cambridge, ii, pp. 192–95.
38. "John Stubbs to Margaret Fox. Barbados, 2nd of 10th month, (12th mo.) 1671", Cambridge, ii, pp. 189–91.
39. MS. Portfolio 10:41 (LSF).

Chapter 14: The Wild Woods of America

1. On reaching Barbados, the original travelling party split, travelling on as individuals or small groups to various destinations in the Caribbean and on the American mainland. Between October 1671, when George Fox and part of the original party left Barbados, and 11 April, 1673, when Cliffs, Maryland was reached for the last time, part of the journey was recorded in two small note-books, the handwriting being that of James Lancaster and Robert Widders. The style is that of George Fox, and that part of the narrative is in the first person indicates that it was

dictated by him. The account is reproduced, with slight revisions, in Cambridge, ii, pp. 202–55. The pages also include various letters. Unless otherwise stated, words attributed to George Fox are taken from this narrative.

2. "George Fox to Margaret Fox. Jamaica, 23rd 12th mo. 1671/2" (February 1672), *Journal*, Bicentenary Edition, ii, p. 160.

3. A local word for a Native American chief or headman.

4. *Journal*, Bicentenary Edition, ii, p. 169.

5. *Journal of the Travels of John Burnyeat*, pp. 145–46, in Evans and Evans, eds, Vol. 11, Philadelphia, 1847.

6. *Journal of the Travels of John Burnyeat*, pp. 145–46, in Evans and Evans, eds, Vol. 11, Philadelphia, 1847.

7. A number of Quakers suffered in Puritan Massachusetts. Among them was Mary Fisher, accused of witchcraft and then banished, and William Robinson and Marmaduke Stephenson, who were hung in October 1659.

8. The wedding was that of Joseph Bryar and Mary Gould.

9. *Journal*, Bicentenary Edition, ii, p. 169.

10. In Cambridge, ii, p. 224, this person is named as Joseph Silvester – possibly a mistake.

11. "William Edmondson to Margaret Fox. Dublin ye 7 of ye 9 mon. 1672 (11th month)", Cambridge, ii, pp. 220–21.

12. Tred Avon – now Third Haven, near the town of Easton, Talbot County, Maryland.

13. *Journal*, Bicentenary Edition, ii, p. 184.

14. Cone-oak Bay – now Edenton Bay, North Carolina.

15. Although Charles II had many lovers, Nell Gwynne was the people's favourite. She was born in 1650, traditionally in the city of Hereford, although possibly in the Coal Yard off Drury Lane, London. Originally an orange-seller in the precincts of the Drury Lane Theatre, through the influence of her first lover, the actor Charles Hart, she became an actress at the age of fifteen. In 1670, she became the mistress of the king, and continued so to his death. She also bore him two sons. She died in London in November 1687, and was buried in the church of St Martin-in-the-Fields, her funeral sermon being preached by the vicar, Thomas Tenison, afterwards Archbishop of Canterbury.

16. A memorial plaque to the steadfastness of the jury in "Bushell's Case" hangs in the Old Bailey. The jury's power of a verdict according to conscience is enshrined as a bulwark against oppressive measures by the state.

17. Kishlansky, 1997, p. 246. The declaration, which nevertheless also defended the rights and privileges of the Anglican Church, was issued on 15 March 1672.

18. John Bunyan published two books attacking Quaker beliefs, *Some Gospel Truths Opened*, in 1656, to which Edward Burrough responded with *The True Faith of the Gospel of Peace*. When Bunyan replied in 1657 with *A Vindication of Some Gospel Truths Opened*, Burrough answered him with *Truth (the Strongest of All) Witnessed Forth*. Later George Fox attacked Bunyan in *The Great Mystery of the Great Whore Unfolded*.

19. *The Spirit of the Hat*, 1673, pp. 18–20.

20. "Let the woman learn in silence with all subjection. But I suffer not a woman to teach, nor to usurp authority over the man, but to be in silenced" (1 Timothy 2:11–12).

21. Braithwaite, *Second Period*, p. 273, quotes from originals in Kendal, *Early Record Book*, and Marsh, *Early Friends in Surrey and Sussex*, p. 40, from the *Guildford Minute Book*.

22. Joel 2:28; Acts 2:17–21.

23. Acts 9:36.

24. Journal of the Friends Historical Society (JFHS), VII, p. 79.

25. JFHS, VII, p. 79.

26. JFHS, XI, pp. 157–58.

27. JFHS, XI, pp. 157–58.

28. JFHS, XI, p. 100.

29. *Journal*, Bicentenary Edition, ii, p. 227.

30. *Journal*, Bicentenary Edition, ii, p. 227.

31. "Thomas Lower to Margaret Fox, 11 Feb. 1675", Spence MS, iii, p. 165 (LSF).

Chapter 15: My Holy Element

1. "Sarah Fell to Margaret Fell", Spence MS, iii, p. 174 (LSF).

2. Robert Barclay, 1648–90. Although the Barclay family were Scottish Calvinists of long standing, Robert's mother was distantly related to the Stuart monarchs. His father, Colonel David Barclay, after serving with distinction in the Army of the Covenant, subsequently sat in two of Oliver Cromwell's Protectorate Parliaments. Colonel David was also a free-thinker and eventually abandoned the Calvinist Kirk for the Friends. Robert Barclay was also an ancestor of the Quaker prison reformer, Elizabeth Fry.

3. The tract in question was "A Dialogue between a Quaker and a stable Christian" (Braithwaite, *Second Period*, p. 339).
4. Two years later Barclay's original Latin text was translated and published in English as *An Apology for the True Christian Divinity*.
5. See Cambridge, i, p. 311. The project was abandoned after representations from the Universities of Oxford and Cambridge. A University at Durham was finally established in 1837.
6. Mucklow, *The Spirit of the Hat*, 1673, pp. 20–21.
7. The allegations were made by Rogers in his book, *The Christian Quaker*, London, 1680 (Part V, pp. 55–59). A number of books were produced in response. The charges are refuted in Pearson et al, *Anti-christian Treachery Discovered, and its Way Block'd up ... Etc.*, c. 1686. Thomas Ellwood also defended George Fox against William Rogers with *An Antidote Against the Infection of William Rogers' Book, Miscalled the Christian Quaker Distinguished from the Apostate and Innovator, etc.*, 1682.
8. See Chapter 10, p. 213.
9. Spence MS, iii, pp. 24–26 (LSF). See note 29 to Chapter 6.
10. Cambridge, ii, note 2 to p. 325 on p. 466.
11. *Household Account Book*, ed. Penney, 1920, p. 371.
12. Quoted in Braithwaite, *Second Period*, p. 429.
13. Charles II acknowledged fourteen illegitimate children.
14. Sir Thomas Osborne, 1631–1712.
15. Braithwaite, *Second Period*, p. 310.
16. George Fox, "To Friends in Holland" (Epistle), 1676.
17. The *Haistwell Diary*. Unless otherwise stated, the quotations are taken from the volume published in 1925 by Cambridge University Press, which contains the *Short Journal*, the *Haistwell Diary* and the *Itinerary Journal*. I am indebted to them for their permission to quote extensively.
18. The *Haistwell Diary*, note 3 to p. 238 on p. 364 of the 1925 edition.
19. John Lodge. See *Haistwell Diary*, note 4 to p. 238 on p. 364.
20. Princess Elizabeth of Bohemia was born in Heidelberg, Germany, on 26 December 1618. She was the eldest daughter of Elector Palatine Frederick V and Elizabeth Stuart, daughter of King James I of England. A student of theology, physics and philosophy, in 1640 Edward Reynolds, Bishop of Norwich, dedicated his *Treatise of the Passions and Faculties of the Soule of Man* to her. In 1643, she began a correspondence with Descartes, who in 1644 dedicated the first edition of the *Principia philosophiae*

to her. Their continuing correspondence resulted in the publication of *The Passions of the Soul* in 1649. She became Abbess of Herford in 1667 and worked and studied there until her death in 1680.

21. Braithwaite, *Second Period*, p. 281, and note to p. 284 on p. 676.

Chapter 16: All Stand Steadfast

1. "Friends, Know what the Lord doth require... Etc.", 1678 (Epistle 351).

2. Thomas bought the estate from Sarah Fell in 1676. Sarah herself had bought out George Fell's widow, Hannah, in 1671. Hannah and her son, Charles, meanwhile, now lived at another of the Fell properties, the Manor of Osmotherley, near Ulverston. (Ross, 1997, p. 227; also JFHS, XI, pp. 161–62.

3. "Joseph Bowden to Curtis and Arthur Estmead, 20 November 1678", Portfolio MS XXIII, p. 156 (LSF).

4. George Fox, "To Live in Truth, which admits of no Evil" (Epistle), 1679.

5. George Fox, "An Epistle to Friends, for them to read" (Epistle), 1679.

6. George Fox, "Be a Fool for Christ's Sake" (Epistle), 1678.

7. George Fox, "To all the Men and Women's Meetings Every where" (Epistle), 1679.

8. "Testimony of Margaret Fox, concerning her late husband", Appendix to *Journal*, Bicentenary Edition.

9. Titus Oates was the son of the General Baptist preacher, Samuel Oates (1610–83). George Fox met Samuel in 1649 in Leicestershire and recounts the encounter in the *Journal*.

10. Kishlansky, 1996, p. 258; The Green Ribbon Club of the Whigs was named for the Levellers' green ribbons.

11. Algernon Sidney, c. 1620–1683; also see Braithwaite, *Second Period*, p. 95.

12. Penn, William, *England's Great Interest in the Choice of the New Parliament*, in Penn, Works, 1726, pp. 678–82.

13. Devonshire House. See note 4 to p. 75 of the *Itinerary Journal* on p. 293 of the volume.

14. Braithwaite, *Second Period*, p. 280.

15. Braithwaite, *Second Period*, pp. 281–86.

16. "From the Meeting for Sufferings to Friends, London, 21st of 11th mo. 1680 (1st mo. 1681)", *Letters of Early Friends*, 1841, pp. 203–94.

17. The *Itinerary Journal*. Unless otherwise stated, the quotations are taken from the volume published in 1925 by Cambridge University Press, which contains the *Short Journal*, the *Haistwell Diary* and the *Itinerary Journal*. I am indebted to them for their permission to quote extensively and to transcribe into modern English.

18. George Fox, "To Suffering Friends at Horsham in Sussex" (Epistle), 1681.

19. George Fox, "An Epistle to Friends, for them to read" (Epistle), 1678.

20. Braithwaite, *Second Period*, p. 106.

21. Shaftesbury died in Holland in 1683.

22. For the Savoy Meeting House and colony see note 2 to p. 79 of the *Itinerary Journal* on p. 297 of the volume.

23. For the meeting at the Peel, see note 1 to p. 79 of the *Itinerary Journal* on p. 297 of the volume.

24. Kishlansky, 1996, p. 260.

25. Cadbury, 1948, p. 124.

26. Docwra, 1699, pp. 45–47.

27. Kishlansky, 1996, p. 260.

28. Hicks Hall, St John Street, Clerkenwell. See note 1 to p. 92 of the *Itinerary Journal* on p. 307 of the volume.

29. Francis Bugg, 1640–1724, of Mildenhall in Suffolk, was also nephew to Ann Docwra. Earlier, Bugg had been accused of being an informer against the Quaker movement (*Dictionary of National Biography*).

30. Bugg, 1683, Preface.

31. Bugg made the allegations regarding sexual impropriety in *A Finishing Stroke*, 1712. See note 40 to Chapter 6. For Bugg's clearly exaggerated accusations of George Fox's illiteracy, see *Battering Rams against New Rome*, 1691, p. 16. (Quoted in Brayshaw, 1933, p. 181.)

32. Bugg, 1683, Preface.

33. Spence MS, iii, p. i (LSF).

34. Braithwaite, *Second Period*, p. 119.

35. George Fox, *A Distinction Between True Liberty and False*, London, 1685.

36. Braithwaite, *Second Period*, note to p. 222 on p. 670 of the volume. For the Quakers released, see Kishlansky, 1996, p. 274.

37. Pennsylvania was established 1681/82.

38. "The Humble and Grateful Acknowledgements of his peaceable

subjects called Quakers, in this kingdom", in Sewel, 1844, pp. 307–308.

39. Kishlansky, 1996, p. 275.
40. Kishlansky, 1996, p. 277.
41. John Churchill was later created Duke of Marlborough and was the ancestor of Winston Churchill.
42. For the chamber, see *Itinerary Journal*, note 2 to p. 190 on p. 347 of the volume.
43. Sir Robert Napier, 1642–1700. MP for Weymouth and Melcombe Regis in 1689–90.
44. "To Henry Coward, Thomas Green, Thomas Dockrey, Richard Barrow, William Higginson, and Thomas Widders. London, the 15th of 11th mo. 1690. (first month 1691)", *Letters of Early Friends*, 1841, pp. 205–206.
45. William Penn, Preface.

Epilogue

1. Reay, 1985, p. 27; Punshon, 1984, p. 103; also see Chapter 12, p. 244.
2. See note 1 to Chapter 1.
3. Cadbury, Henry J., ed., *George Fox's Book of Miracles*, CUP, 1948.
4. George Fox, "To Friends, to stand still in Troubles, and see the Strength of the Lord" (Epistle), 1652.
5. *Journal*, Bicentenary Edition, i, pp. 315–17.

Select Bibliography

Abbott, W. C., *The Writings and Speeches of Oliver Cromwell* (4 vols), Harvard University Press, Cambridge, Massachusetts, 1937–47

Anon. (A People who through Grace have been hitherto kept from the Great Apostacie of this day), "A true Copie of a paper delivered to Lt. G. Fleetwood ... to be communicated to the General Council of Officers", London, 1659

Anon., "A Phanatique League and Covenant Solemnly enter'd into by the Assertors of the Good Old Cause", London, 1659 (Broadside)

Anon., "A Declaration of the Maids of the City of London, &c.", London, 1659 (Broadside)

Anon. (Mad-Tom), "Twenty Quaking Queries ... Having been Clowded and now Brought forth to Light", London, 1659

Aylmer, G. E., *Rebellion or Revolution*, OUP, Oxford, 1986

Babington, Anthony, *The English Bastille: A History of Newgate Gaol and Prison Conditions in Britain 1188–1902*, Macdonald and Co., London, 1971

Barclay, A. R., ed., *Letters of Early Friends*, Harvey & Darton, Gracechurch Street, London 1841

Barclay, Robert, *The Inner Life of the Religious Societies of the Commonwealth*, Hodder & Stoughton, London, 1876

Baxter, Richard, *The Autobiography of Richard Baxter*, ed. N. H. Keeble, J. M. Dent & Sons, London, 1974

Bell, Dr Mark R., *Apocalypse How? Baptist Movements During the English Revolution*, Mercer University Press, Georgia, 2000

Besse, Joseph, *A Collection of the Sufferings of the People called Quakers* (2 vols), Luke Hinde, London, 1753

Blackwood, B. G., *The Lancashire Gentry and the Great Rebellion 1640–1660*, The Chetham Society, Manchester, 1978

Boulton, David and Anthea, *In Fox's Footsteps*, Dales Historical Monographs, Dent, Cumbria, 1998

Braithwaite, William C., *The Beginnings of Quakerism to 1660*, Cambridge University Press, 1955

Braithwaite, William C. *The Second Period of Quakerism*, Cambridge University Press, 1961

Brayshaw, A. Neave, *The Personality of George Fox*, Allensen & Co., London, 1933

Bridge, Revd William, "Babylons Downfall: A Sermon Lately Preached at Westminster Before sundry of the Honourable House of Commons", London, 1641

Burton, Revd Henry, *The Sounding of the Last Two Trumpets*, London, 1641

Burton, Thomas, *The Diary of Thomas Burton Esq.*, ed. John Towill Rutt, Henry Colburn, London, 1828

Bugg, Francis, *The Painted Harlot, Both Stript and Whipt*, London, 1683

Bugg, Francis, *A Finishing Stroke*, London, 1712

Burrough, Edward, "To the Whole English Army", London, 1659 (Broadside)

Cadbury, Henry J., ed., *George Fox's Book of Miracles*, Cambridge University Press, 1948

Calamy, Revd Edmund, "Englands Looking-Glasse: Presented in a Sermon Preached for the Honorable House of Commons", London, 1641

Camm, J. and Audland, J., *The Memory of the Righteous Revived*, London, 1689

Capp, B. S., *The Fifth Monarchy Men: A Study in Seventeenth-Century English Millenarianism*, Faber and Faber, London 1972

Clarke, Celia B., Lancaster, Joan C., Rose, R. B. & Tomlinson, Margaret, "Protestant Nonconformity" in *The Victoria History of the County of Warwick*, Oxford University Press, London, 1969

Claxton, Laurence, *The Quakers Downfall*, London, 1659

Collier, Thomas, *A Looking-Glasse for the Quakers*, London, 1657

Coppe, Abiezer, *A Fiery Roll: A Word from the Lord to all the Great Ones of the Earth ... at the Dreadful Day of Judgement*, London, 1649

Coppe, Abiezer, *A Second Fiery Flying Roule: To All the Inhabitants of the Earth, specially to the rich ones*, London, 1649

Crisp, Stephen, *A Memorable Account ... of that Ancient Servant of Christ, Stephen Crisp*, London, 1694

Croese, G., *The General History of the Quakers*, London, 1696

Crouch, William, *Posthuma Christiana*, J. Sowle, London, 1712

Davies, Godfrey, *The Restoration of Charles II: 1658–1660*, Oxford University Press, London, 1955

Defoe, Daniel, *A Journal of the Plague Year*, ed. Cynthia Wall, Penguin Books, London, 2003

Dewsbury, William, *A True Prophecie of the Mighty Day of the Lord ... which ... shall overspread this Nation, and all Nations of the World*, London, 1655

Docwra, Ann, *An Apostate Conscience Exposed*, London, 1699

Edward, Earl of Clarendon, *State Papers*, Vol. III, ed. T. Monkhouse, Oxford, 1786

Edwards, Thomas, *Gangraena: or a Catalogue and Discovery of many of the Errours, Heresies, Blasphemies and pernicious Practices of the Sectaries of this time, vented and acted in England in these four last years*, London, 1646

The Rota and the University of Exeter, 1977

Ellwood, Thomas, *The History of the Life of Thomas Ellwood*, London, 1714

Ehrenreich, Barbara, and English, Deirdre, *Complaints and Disorders: The Sexual Politics of Sickness*, The Feminist Press at The City University of New York, New York, 1973

Farmer, R. *Sathan Inthron'd in his Chair of Pestilence*, London, 1657

Fell, Margaret, *A Brief Collection of Remarkable Passages ... of that Ancient, Eminent, and Faithful Servant of the Lord, Margaret Fell. But by her Second Marriage, Margaret Fox*, T. Sowle, London, 1710

Fox, George, *The Works of George Fox* (8 vols), T. H. S. Wallace, Gen. Ed., New Foundation Publications, George Fox Fund Inc., State College, Pennsylvania, 1831

Fox, George, *The Journal* (2 vols), Friends' Tract Association, London, 1891 (Eighth and Bicentenary Edition)

Fox, George, *The Journal* (2 vols), ed. Norman Penney, Cambridge University Press, 1911

Fox, George, *The Journal*, ed. John L. Nickalls, Religious Society of Friends, London and Philadelphia, 1997

Fox, George, *The Short Journal*, *The Itinerary Journal* and *The Haistwell Diary* (in one vol.), ed. Norman Penney, Cambridge University Press, Cambridge, 1925

Fox, George, selected Epistles (titles are provided when given, otherwise the Epistle is indicated by the opening words of the document):

- "To Friends, to stand still in Trouble, and see the Strength of the Lord", 1652
- "Dear Hearts, Brethren and Babes in Christ", 1652
- "To the Flock of God about Sedburgh", 1652
- "To Friends at Kendal", 1652
- "O Friends keep close to the Light in you", 1652
- "To Friends, to be faithful and Valiant in the Lord", 1652
- "Concerning Marriages", 1653
- "Concerning Tithes", 1653
- "To a Suffering Friend", 1653
- "To Friends, that their Minds go not out from the Spirit of God", 1653
- "To Friends in the Ministry", 1653
- "To Friends, Concerning the Light, in which they may see their Saviour, and the Deceivers", 1653
- "To Friends, Concerning Judging", 1653
- "This is to be sent among Friends, who be in the Light", 1653
- "The Spiritual Warfare", 1653
- "An Exhortation to Friends, not to make Flesh their Arm", 1654
- "To Friends, Concerning Marriages", 1654

- "Concerning Tithes", 1654
- "To all Friends, to abide in their Callings", 1654
- "To Seek the Kingdom of God First", 1654
- "The Friends should have a sense of one anothers Sufferings", 1655
- "An Exhortation to Patience in the tiume of Suffering", 1655
- "Concerning the Light, (to be read among Friends)", 1655
- "To Friends, to take Care of such, who suffer for owning the Truth", 1656
- "Men in the Fall are in the Wars and Strife, but Truth restores, and brings unto Peace", 1656
- "An Epistle to Friends, for all to keep in the Light, and to watch over one another", 1656
- "To Friends, to gather up their Sufferings and lay them before the Judges", 1657
- "To Friends, to keep their Meetings", 1658
- "To all Friends, Prisoners", 1661
- "Concerning keeping on the hat in time of Prayer", 1661
- "The Saints' Weapons are spiritual that the Blessing of God may come upon all Men", 1665
- "A Warning to all to keep out of the vain Fashions of the World", 1667
- "Not to be over thoughtful of the things of this World", 1669
- "To Friends at Bristol in time of Suffering", 1670
- "To all the Elect and Chosen of God in Christ Jesus, before the Foundation of the World", 1675
- "To Friends in Holland", 1676
- "Epistle to Friends", 1677
- "Concerning Subjection of the Spirits of the Apostles", 1677
- "The Lord Requireth but in Proportion to what he giveth", 1678
- "An Epistle to Friends, to Keep in the Power of God", 1678
- "Be a Fool for Christ's Sake", 1678

- "To Friends in America Concerning their Negroes and Indians", 1679
- "To Live in Truth, which admits no Evil", 1679
- "An Epistle to be Read amongst Friends", 1679
- "To all Men and Womens Meetings Everywhere", 1679
- "An Epistle to Friends, for them to read", 1679
- "To Suffering Friends in Horsham in Sussex", 1681
- "To Suffering Friends in Leicester", 1681
- "To Friends that are Prisoners in York", 1682
- "To Suffering Friends in Prison at Bristol", 1683
- "To the Household of Faith, which is the Church of Christ", 1683 or 1684
- "An Epistle to All the Prisoners and Sufferers for the Name of the Lord Jesus Christ", 1684

Fox, George, selected other works:

- *News Coming up out of the North, Sounding towards the South*, London, 1654
- *To All Who Would Know the Way to the Kingdom*, London, 1653
- *The Vials of the Wrath of God poured forth upon the Man of Sin*, 1654
- *A Word from the Lord to all the World*, 1654
- *To all the Rulers of the Earth*, 1655
- *To the High and Lofty Ones*, 1655
- *A Visitation to the Jews*, 1656
- *A Visitation to all you that have long had the Scriptures*, 1656
- *A Declaration of the Difference of the Ministers of the Word, from the Ministers of the World, who call the Writings the Word*, 1656
- *A Cry for Repentance unto the Inhabitants of London Chiefly*, 1656
- *The Woman Learning in Silence, or the Mystery of the Womans Subjugation to her Husband*, 1656
- *A Declaration Concerning Fasting, and the Prayer that God Accepts*, 1656

- *The Promise of God Proclaimed*, 1656
- *An Epistle to all People on the Earth*, 1657
- *To all Magistrates in London*, 1657
- *The Fashions of the World Made Manifest; also a Few Words to the City of London*, 1657
- *A Warning to all the Merchants in London, and such as Buy and Sell*, 1658
- *The Law of God, The Rule for Law Makers*, London, 1658
- *The Pearl Found in England*, 1658
- *The Wrath of the Lamb*, 1658
- *To the Parliament of the Comon-Wealth of England: Fifty-nine Particulars laid down for the Regulating things and the taking away of Oppressing Laws and Oppressors, and to Ease the Oppressed*, 1659
- *The Lamb's Officer is Gone Forth with the Lamb's Message*, 1659
- *The Serious People's Reasoning and Speech, with the World's Teachers and Professors*, 1659
- *The Great Mistery ... of the great Whore Unfolded ... and Antichrists Kingdom Revealed Unto Destruction etc.*, 1659
- *A Word In the Behalf of the King*, 1660
- *To the Turk and all that are under his Authority, to Read this over, which concerns their Salvation*, 1660
- *To the Pope*, 1660
- *To all the Nations Under the Whole Heaven*, 1660
- *To Both Houses of Parliament*, 1660
- *A Declaration to the Jews*, 1661
- *To all that Profess Christianity*, 1661
- *A Measuring Rule Concerning Liberty and Persecution*, 1662
- *To all Rulers of Families*, 1662
- *Concerning the Act That Prohibits, that not above Four or Five may Meet*, 1668
- *Gospel Liberty and the Royal Law of Love*, 1668
- *A Warning to England, And to all that profess themselves Christians*, 1674
- *For all the Bishops and Priests in Christendom*, 1674
- *A Small Treatise Concerning Swearing*, 1675

- *To all Magistrates and People in Christendom… To turn from the Persecuting Mind*, 1676
- *The People of God, In Scorn Called Quakers, their Love to all Mankind Asserted*, 1676
- *The Beginning of Tythes In the Law, and Ending of Tythes in the Gospel*, 1676
- *Election and Reprobation Clearly Discovered*, 1679
- *A Distinction Between the New Covenant and the Old*, 1679
- *Concerning the Living God of Truth, and the World's God*, 1680
- *The Devil was and is The Old Informer Against the Righteous*, 1682
- *Concerning Persecution in all Ages to this Day*, 1682
- *The Saints, (or they that are born of the Spirit,) their Heavenly and Spiritual Worship, Unity and Communion*, 1684
- *A Word of admonition to such as Wander from the Anointing and Teaching within*, 1684
- *To the Chief Magistrates, Rulers, Ministers, Justices of the Peace, and other Officers*, 1684
- *To all Kings, Princes, Rulers, Governors, Bishops and clergy, that Profess Christianity in Christendom*, 1685
- *A Distinction Between True Liberty, and False*, 1685
- *To all Magistrates in Christendom, that do Profess Christianity – Concerning Christian Gospel-Liberty, against Persecution*, 1686
- *Concerning the Antiquity of the People of God called Quakers*, 1688
- *The Inward and spiritual Warfare, and the False Pretence of it*, 1689

Fraser, Antonia, *Cromwell: Our Chief of Men*, Phoenix, London, 2002

Goodwin, Revd Thomas, *A Glimpse of Sions Glory*, London, 1641

Haller, William, *Foxe's Book of Martyrs and the Elect Nation*, Jonathan Cape, London, 1963

Harwood, John, *To all People that Profess the Eternal Truth of the Living God*, London, 1663

Hill, C., ed., *Winstanley, Gerrard, The Law of Freedom and Other Writings*, Pelican Books, Middlesex, 1973

Hill, C., *A Turbulent, Seditious, and Factious People: John Bunyan and his Church*, Oxford University Press, Oxford, 1989

Hill, Christopher, *The World Turned Upside Down*, Penguin, 1991

Howe, David, *Willingly to School? The story of nine hundred years of education in Warwickshire*, Warwickshire Publications, Warwick, 2003

Howgill, Francis, *The Inheritance of Jacob Discovered after his Return from Egypt*, London, 1656

Hubberthorne, Richard, *A Collection of the Several Books and Writings etc.*, London, 1665

Hughes, Ann, *"Gangraena" and the Struggle for the English Revolution*, OUP, Oxford & New York, 2004

Ingle, H. Larry, *First Among Friends: George Fox and the Creation of Quakerism*, OUP, Oxford & New York, 1994

Jaffray, Alexander, *Diary of Alexander Jaffray*, ed. John Barclay, Darton & Harvey, London, 1834

James, William, *The Varieties of Religious Experience*, Penguin, Middlesex, England, 1985

Jones, Rufus M. and Sharpless, Isaac, *The Quakers in the American Colonies*, Macmillan & Co, London, 1923

Kishlansky, Mark, *A Monarchy Transformed: Britain 1603–1714*, Penguin, London, 1997

Knight, Rachel, *The Founder of Quakerism: A Psychological Study*, Swarthmoor Press, London, 1922

Koenigsberger, H. G., Mosse, George L., Bowler, G. Q., *Europe in the Sixteenth Century*, Longman, Harlow, Essex, 1989

Kunze, Bonnelyn Young, *Margaret Fell and the Rise of Quakerism*, Stanford University Press, California, 1994

Latham, Robert, ed., Pepys, Samuel, *The Diary of Samuel Pepys: A Selection*, Penguin Books, 2003

Lindley, Keith, *The English Civil War and Revolution*, Routledge, London, 1998

Lloyd-Jones, Dr Martyn, *Joy Unspeakable: The Baptism and Gifts of the Holy Spirit*, Kingsway Publications, East Sussex, 1995

Lumpkin, William L., *Baptist Confessions of Faith*, Judson Press, Valley Forge, 1969 (orig. 1959)

McFarlane, K. B., *John Wycliffe and the Beginnings of English Nonconformity*, English Universities Press, London, 1952

McGregor, J. F. & Reay, B., eds, *Radical Religion in the English Revolution*, OUP, Oxford, 1986

Mucklow, William, *The Spirit of the Hat*, London, 1673

Murray, Nicholas, *World Enough and Time: The Life of Andrew Marvell*, Little, Brown & Co., London, 1999

Nayler, James, *A Collection of Sundry Books, Epistles and Papers written by James Nayler*, London, 1716

Nigg, Walter, *The Heretics*, Dorset Press, New York, 1990 (abridged version of the original English, 1962, Alfred A. Knopf, Inc., New York, and translated from German, *Der Buch der Ketzer*, Artemis Verlag AG, Zurich, 1949)

Owen, John, "A Discourse About Toleration And the Duty of the Civill Magistrate about Religion. A Sermon Preached to the Honourable House of Commons in Parliament Assembled... on January 31. A Day of Solemn Humiliation", London, 1649

Pearson et al., *Anti-Christian Treachery Discovered and its Way Blocked Up*, London, c. 1686

Penn, William, *A Collection of the Works of William Penn* (2 vols), J. Sowle, London, 1726

Penn, William, *The Penn Papers* (5 vols), Dunn & Dunn, eds, University of Pennsylvania Press, 1981

Penney, Norman, ed., *The First Publishers of Truth: Being Early*

Records of the Introduction of Quakerism into the Counties of England and Wales, Headley Brothers, 14 Bishopsgate Without, London, 1907

Penney, Norman, ed., *Extracts from State Papers Relating to Friends 1654–1672*, Headley Bros, London, 1913

Penney, Norman, ed., *The Household Account Book of Sarah Fell*, Cambridge University Press, 1920

Pennington, D. H., *Europe in the Seventeenth Century*, Longman Group UK, 1989

Pennington, Isaac, *Works*, London, 1761

Pickvance, T. Joseph, *George Fox and the Purefeys: A Study of the Puritan Background in Fenny Drayton in the 16th and 17th Centuries*, Friends Historical Society, London, 1970

Punshon, John, *Portrait in Grey: A Short History of the Quakers*, Quaker Books, London, 2001

Pyott, Edward. *The West Answering to the North, in the fierce and Cruell Persecution of the Manifestation of the Son of God ... Etc.* London, 1657.

Reay, Barry, *The Quakers and the English Revolution*, Maurice Temple Smith, Middlesex, 1985

Rich, Robert, *Hidden Things Brought to Light or the Discord of the Grand Quakers among Themselves*, 1678

Rogers, William, *The Christian Quaker, Distinguished from the Apostate and Innovator (In Five Parts)*, London, 1680

Ross, Isabel, *Margaret Fell, Mother of Quakerism*, Longman Green and Co., 1996

Sewel, William, *The History of the Rise, Increase and Progress of the Christian People Called Quakers* (2 vols), Baker & Crane, New York and Philadelphia, 1844

Sharman, Cecil W., *George Fox and the Quakers*, Quaker Home Service, London, UK and Friends United Press, Richmond, USA, 1991

Sheppard, Gerald T., ed., *The Geneva Bible: The Annotated New Testament, 1662 Edition*, Pilgrim Press, New York, 1989

Smith, Edward, *The Life of William Dewsbury*, Darton & Harvey, London, 1836

Stayer, James M., *Anabaptists and the Sword*, Coronado Press, Kansas, 1976

Staley, Vernon, *The Life and Times of Gilbert Sheldon*, Wells Gardner, Darton & Co., London, 1913

Stephen, Sir Leslie & Lee, Sir Sidney, *The Dictionary of National Biography*, Oxford University Press, Oxford

Taylor, Christopher, *The Whirl-wind of the Lord gone forth as a Fiery Flying Roule ... to the persecuting Rulers, Priests and People in the county of Westmorland*, London, 1655

Thomas, Hugh, *The Slave Trade, 1440–1870*, Papermac (Macmillan), London, 1998

Tichborne, Colonel Robert, *The Rest of Faith*, London, 1649

Tolmie, Murray, *The Triumph of the Saints: The separate churches of London 1616–1649*, Cambridge University Press, Cambridge, 1977

Underhill, Thomas, *Hell broke Loose, or an History of the Quakers Both Old and New*, London, 1660

Veith, Ilza, *Hysteria: The History of a Disease*, Jason Aronson Inc., Northvale, New Jersey, 1993; originally published by University of Chicago Press, Chicago, 1965

Vipont, Elfrida, *George Fox and the Valiant Sixty*, Hamish Hamilton, London, 1975

Weld, Thomas, et al., *The Perfect Pharise Under Monkish Holines*, London, 1654

Manuscript collections

ARB Collection (LSF)

Crosse Collection (LSF)

Swarthmoor Collection, 8 vols (LSF)

Spence MS, 3 vols (LSF)

Portfolio 10 (LSF)

Newspapers

Mercurius Politicus (under the year 1659) (British Library)

The Publick Intelligencer (under the year 1659) (British Library)

Periodicals

Journal of the Friends Historical Society, Vols VII and XI

The Friends Library, Evans & Evans, eds, Philadelphia, 1847, Vol. 11

The Pennsylvania Magazine of History and Biography, Vol. LXX, January 1946, No. 1

Transactions of the Baptist Historical Society, Vol. 1: 1908–1909; Vol. 5: 1916–1917

Internet resources

www.british-civil-wars.co.uk

Index of Subjects